Drafting & Design

James H. Earle
TEXAS A&M UNIVERSITY

Second Printing, January 1974 (10Y)
First Printing, January 1973 (10.5Y)

ORDER FROM:
Creative Publishers, phone 713-846-7128
Box 9292, College Station, Texas 77840

TO THE STUDENT

DRAFTING & DESIGN is designed to introduce the fundamentals of drafting to a student whether he is a high school student or a student in a beginning college course. Many examples have been taken from industry to give applications of basic principles. The drawing fundamentals presented are in agreement with the major standards agency, the American National Standards Institute (ANSI).

The problems in this book are sufficient for a nine-month high school course or a one-semester college course. The student will be able to cover more material when using these problems than when working on blank paper where each problem must be laid out. This rapid coverage of material will permit you to learn more of the field of drafting and will give you additional time for the application of these principles to comprehensive design problems.

Creativity is very important to the engineer, technologist and member of the industrial team since all products and processes must be developed by them. Many problems in this book are structured to have more than one solution to exercise your imagination. Some problems require that you design and present a solution that is entirely original and based on your thinking and analysis. It is impossible to develop an original design without a thorough understanding of drafting principles and graphical methods. Many freehand sketches and pictorials must be drawn to stimulate the creative process of developing a solution to a technical problem.

Each problem sheet should be removed carefully from the book one at a time as assigned by your instructor. When instruments must be used to solve a problem, the problem sheet should be taped to your table. If desired, you may draw a border around the edge of the sheet beginning with the title strip and drawing upward to the corner marks at the upper edge of the sheet. Most industrial drawings have printed borders and title strips to save drafting time.

Graded problems that have been returned to you should be maintained in a three-ring notebook for permanent reference. All grades should be listed on page iv to assit you in keeping a course average as the course progresses.

January 1973

James H. Earle
College Station, Texas

TABLE OF CONTENTS AND REFERENCES BY CHAPTER

Page	Topic	1	2	3	4	5	6
		Reference books (see below)					
1-6	Lettering	3	5	3	4	3	4
7	Instruments	4	5	4	3	2	9
8-9	Scales	4	5	6	3	2	7
10-13	Geometric Constr.	5	5	5	5	4	13
14-16	Tangencies	5	5	5	5	4	13
17	Spiral & Helix	5			14	4,12	
18-19	Conic Sections	5	5,11		5	4	
20-32	Orthographic Proj.	7	5	8	6	5,7	8
33-35	Sketching	8	5	2,8	6,2	6	3,6
36-38	Design Sketching	6,8	2,5	2,8	2,6	6	3
39-42	Isometrics	9	17	2	16	14	20
43-45	Obliques	9	17		16	14	20
46-48	Perspectives	18	17	2	16	14	20
49-52	Auxiliary Views	10,	5,8	9	12	9	8
53	Revolution	10	10		13	9	
54,62	Sections	11	5	10	11	10	14
63-66	Threaded Fasten.	12	19		14	12	17
67-78	Dimensioning	13	19	11	9	11	10
79-82	Graphs	16	15	12	18	24	21
83-86	Intersections	17	11		17	20	12
87-90	Developments	17	12	1	17	20	12
91-92	Design Problems	6,14	19,20	Appen.			
93-98	Working Drawings	14	19	Appen.	10,15	11,13	15,16
99-106	Tests						

REFERENCES

1. DESIGN DRAFTING by James H. Earle, Addison-Wesley Publishing Company, Reading, Mass.
2. ENGINEERING DESIGN GRAPHICS BY James H. Earle, Addison-Wesley Publishing Company, Reading, Mass.
3. TECHNICAL GRAPHICS--A FIRST COURSE by Jack Sinewitz, Addison-Wesley Publishing Company, Reading, Mass.
4. BASIC TECHNICAL DRAWING by Henry C. Spencer and John T. Dygdon, The Macmillan Company, New York.
5. MECHANICAL DRAWING by Thomas E. French and Carl L. Svensen, McGraw-Hill Book Company, New York.
6. DRAWING AND BLUEPRINT READING by Shriver L. Coover, McGraw-Hill Book Company, New York.

GRADE SHEET

Problems	Grade	Problems	Grade	Problems	Grade	Problems	Grade

Test #1 ____

Test #2 ____

Test #3 ____

Test #4 ____

Test #5 ____

Test #6 ____

Test #7 ____

Test #8 ____

USE 2H-4H PENCIL WITH SHARP POINT FOR LIGHT GUIDELINES.

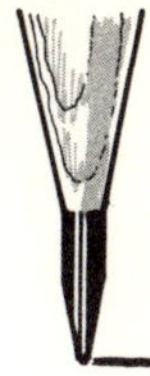

USE F OR HB PENCIL WITH A SLIGHTLY ROUNDED POINT FOR LETTERING.

1. LOWER CASE LETTERS ARE 2/3RDS AS TALL AS CAPITAL LETTERS. GUIDELINES CAN BE SPACED USING A SCALE OR BRADDOCK-ROWE TRIANGLE. VERTICAL GUIDELINES SHOULD BE DRAWN AS VISUAL GUIDES. CONSTRUCT VERTICAL GUIDELINES AND LETTER THE TWO LINES OF TEXT.

2H
H
2H

Place vertical guide lines randomly

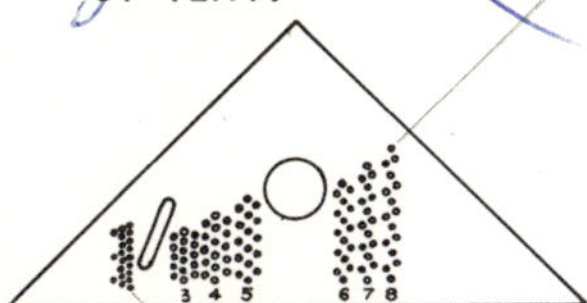

BRADDOCK ROWE-TRIANGLE: NUMBERS REPRESENT THIRTY-SECONDS. 4=4/32 or 1/8".

$21'\text{-}0\frac{1}{2}$ X $7'\text{-}5\frac{1}{4}$ X $0'\text{-}8\frac{1}{16}$

2. CONSTRUCT VERTICAL GUIDE LINES AND REPEAT THE DIMENSIONS GIVEN.

SCALE: 1/4" = 1'-0"

NAME: EDWARDS, E.T. FILE NO: 14 SEC: 21 DATE: 2-1-73	grade 12

3. CONSTRUCT GUIDELINES ON THE TITLE STRIP, SIMILAR TO THE SAMPLE, AND LETTER IT USING YOUR NAME.

NAME FILE NO SEC DATE	grade	

$\frac{1}{8}$ LETTERING

$\frac{3}{8}$ SPACING

GEOMETRIC CONSTRUCTION	
BY: EDWARDS, E.T.	SECT. 102
DATE: JAN. 2, 74	SHEET 1
SCALE: $1\frac{1}{2}$ = 1'-0	OF 1 SHEET

5

4. REPEAT THE TITLE BLOCK BELOW USING THE FULL SIZE DIMENSIONS SHOWN. USE 1/8" LETTERS.

Drafting & Design
© James H. Earle

NAME
FILE NO SEC DATE

grade

THE AMES LETTERING GUIDE CAN BE USED FOR CONSTRUCTING GUIDELINES FOR VERTICAL AND INCLINED LETTERING. HOLES ARE PROVIDED FOR LOWER-CASE LETTERS THAT ARE TWO-THIRDS AND THREE-FIFTHS AS TALL AS CAPITALS. THE DIAL CAN BE SET AT ANY OF THE NUMBERS THAT REPRESENT 32NDS OF AN INCH. EXAMPLE: 4 = 1/8".

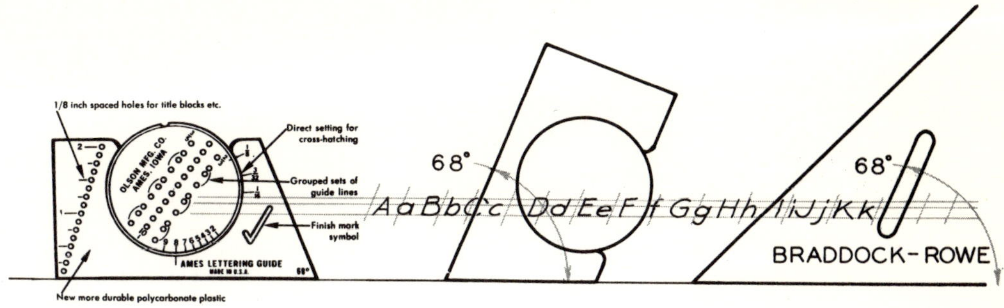

1. CONSTRUCT INCLINED GUIDELINES AND LETTER THE FOLLOWING USING CAPITALS AND LOWER-CASE LETTERS: "LOWER-CASE LETTERS ARE TWO-THIRDS AS TALL AS CAPITAL LETTERS. USE AN AMES LETTERING GUIDE."

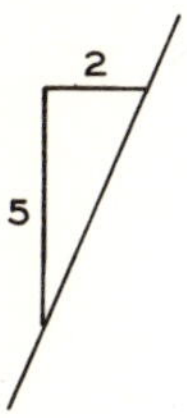

2. CONSTRUCT INCLINED GUIDELINES AND LETTER THE FOLLOWING USING INCLINED CAPITAL LETTERS: "THE DESIGN PROCESS IS A SYSTEMATIC APPROACH TO THE SOLUTION OF A DESIGN PROBLEM. MANY PEOPLE HAVE THE MISCONCEPTION THAT DESIGNS COME IN AN INSPIRATIONAL FLASH. IN FACT, MOST DESIGNS RESULT FROM A DISCIPLINED ATTACK ON A PROBLEM IN A SYSTEMATIC MANNER."

3. REPEAT THE NOTE GIVEN BELOW IN THE SPACE AT THE RIGHT USING 1/8" TALL INCLINED, CAPITAL LETTERS. SPACE THE LINES 1/8" APART. USE GUIDE-LINES.

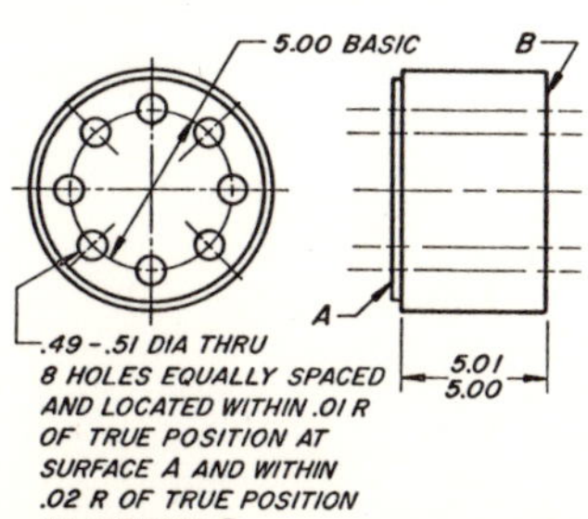

NAME
FILE NO SEC DATE
grade

Drafting & Design

NAME
FILE NO. SEC. DATE
grade

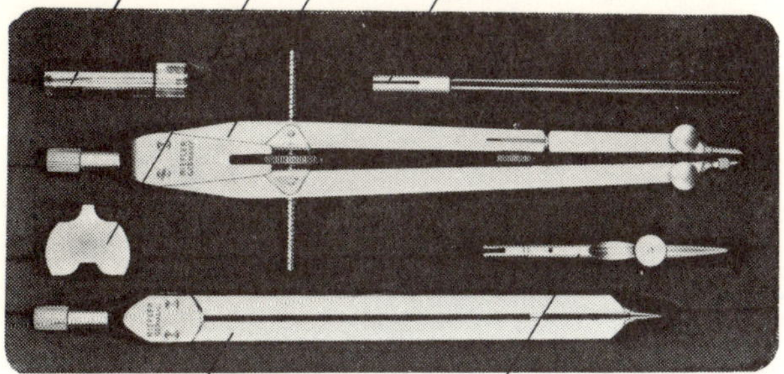

INSTRUMENT SET

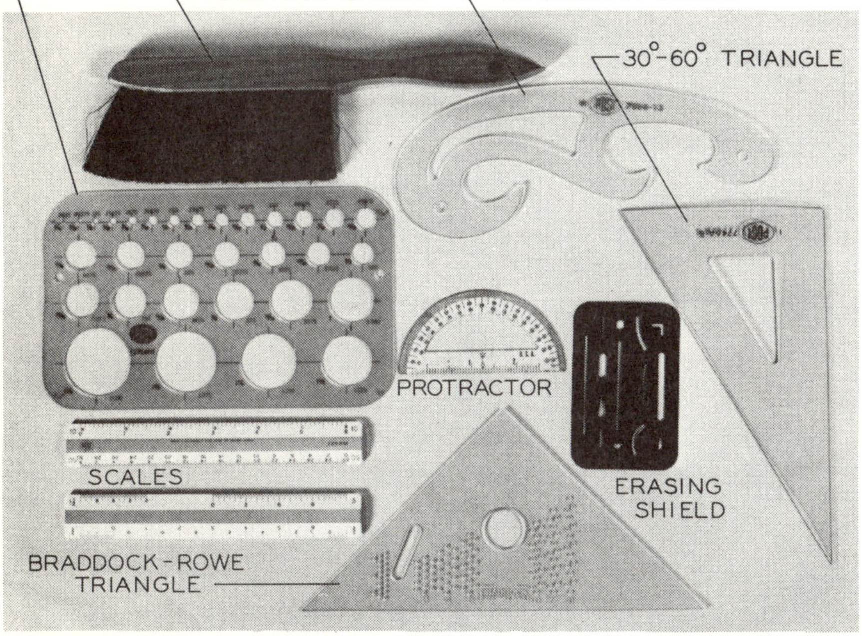

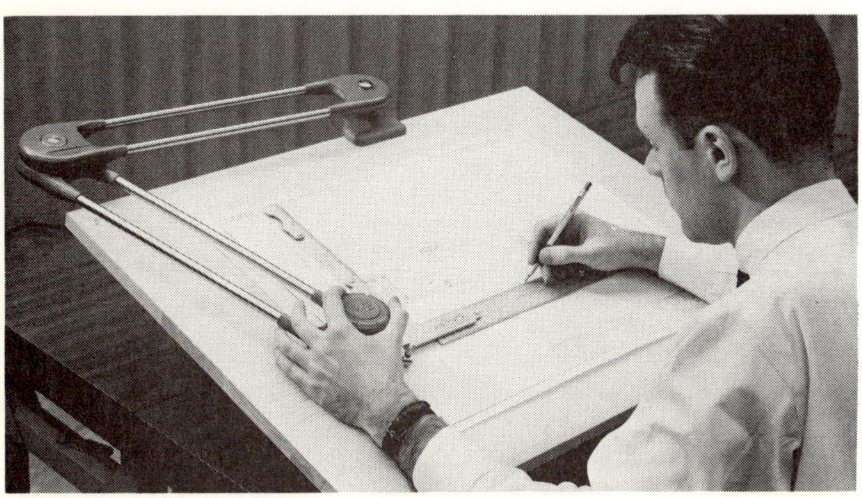

DRAFTING MACHINE

DRAFTING INSTRUMENTS

THE INSTRUMENTS SHOWN HERE ON THIS SHEET ARE THE MORE STANDARD ONES USED BY THE AVERAGE STUDENT. YOU SHOULD BECOME FAMILIAR WITH THESE AND THEIR USES AS EARLY IN THE COURSE AS POSSIBLE.

BELOW ARE LISTED THE NAMES OF THE INSTRUMENTS SHOWN IN THE PHOTOGRAPHS WITH BLANKS AT THE LEFT OF EACH NAME. PLACE THE CORRECT LETTER FROM THE LIST OF USES (THE SECOND LIST) THAT DESCRIBES THE APPLICATION OF EACH.

_____ 1. SCREWDRIVER
_____ 2. LEADS
_____ 3. BOW COMPASS
_____ 4. PEN HOLDER
_____ 5. DIVIDERS
_____ 6. PEN POINT
_____ 7. CIRCLE TEMPLATE
_____ 8. DUSTING BRUSH
_____ 9. IRREGULAR CURVE
_____ 10. 30°- 60° TRIANGLE
_____ 11. PROTRACTOR
_____ 12. ERASING SHIELD
_____ 13. SCALES
_____ 14. BRADDOCK-ROWE TRIANGLE
_____ 15. DRAFTING MACHINE

A. FOR DRAWING SMALLER CIRCLES
B. FOR DRAWING LARGER CIRCLES
C. FOR TIGHTENING AND ADJUSTING INSTRUMENTS
D. FOR MEASURING ANGLES
E. FOR MEASURING A DRAWING AT A REDUCED BUT PROPORTIONAL SCALE
F. FOR DRAWING 45° ANGLES AND FOR THE CONSTRUCTION OF GUIDELINES FOR LETTERING
G. FOR ERASING PORTIONS OF LINES
H. FOR DRAWING COMPLIMENTARY ANGLES
I. FOR CONNECTING POINTS WITH A SMOOTH CURVE
J. FOR SWEEPING ERASURES FROM YOUR DRAWING
K. FOR DRAWING INK LINES WITH A COMPASS
L. FOR HOLDING A PEN POINT FOR RULING LINES
M. FOR TRANSFERRING MEASUREMENTS FROM ONE PART OF THE DRAWING TO ANOTHER
N. POINTS FOR DRAWING PENCIL CIRCLES WITH A COMPASS
O. A MULTIPLE-PURPOSE DEVICE THAT REPLACES THE T-SQUARE AND TRIANGLE

Courtesy of Gramercy Guild and Keuffel & Esser Co.

NAME
FILE NO. SEC. DATE
grade

Drafting & Design

©James H. Earle

NAME

FILE NO SEC DATE

grade

ARCHITECTS' SCALE

THE ARCHITECTS' SCALE IS USED TO DIMENSION PLANS OF AN ARCHITECTURAL NATURE. THIS GENERALLY APPLIES TO ANY INDOOR FEATURES SUCH AS CABINETS, FLOOR PLANS, FURNITURE AND MECHANICAL EQUIPMENT. THESE MEASUREMENTS ARE USUALLY MADE IN FEET AND INCHES USING A STANDARD TAPE MEASURE OR YARDSTICK. CONSEQUENTLY, THE ARCHITECTS' SCALE IS CALIBRATED IN FEET AND INCHES SO THAT DRAWINGS CAN BE MADE USING THE SAME UNITS THAT WILL BE USED IN MAKING THE MEASUREMENTS.

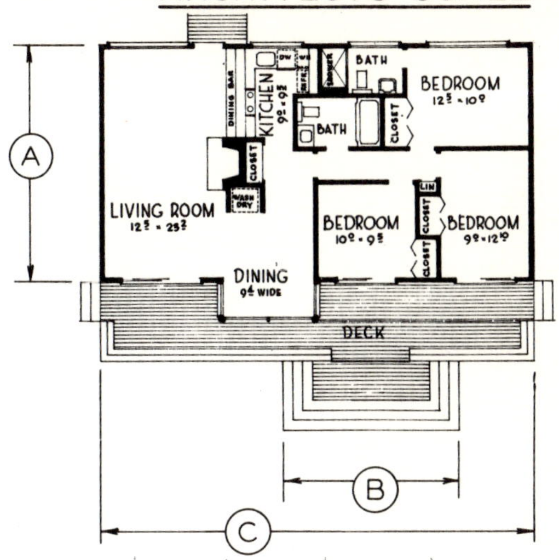

REQUIRED

USING THE SCALES GIVEN BELOW, MEASURE THE LINES ON THE PLAN AND LETTER THEIR MEASUREMENTS USING THE GUIDELINES PROVIDED.

	A	B	C
EX. SCALE: 1 = 1'-0	1'-1$\frac{1}{2}$	0'-10	2'-0$\frac{1}{2}$
1. SCALE: $\frac{3}{4}$ = 1'-0			
2. SCALE: $\frac{1}{2}$ = 1'-0			
3. SCALE: $\frac{1}{8}$ = 1'-0			
4. SCALE: 1$\frac{1}{2}$ = 1'-0			
5. SCALE: $\frac{1}{4}$ = 1'-0			
6. SCALE: $\frac{3}{8}$ = 1'-0			
7. SCALE: $\frac{3}{16}$ = 1'-0			
8. SCALE: 3 = 1'-0			
9. SCALE: $\frac{3}{32}$ = 1'-0			

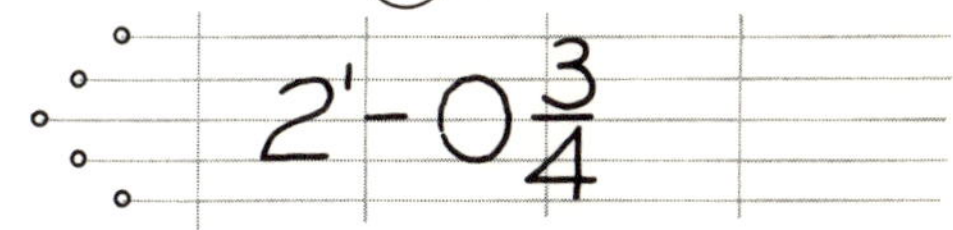

FRACTIONS ARE TWICE AS TALL AS WHOLE NUMBERS.

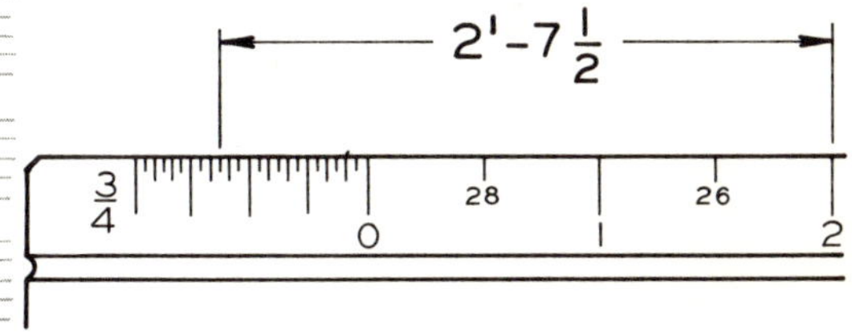

THE CALIBRATIONS AT THE END OF EACH SCALE REPRESENT 12 INCHES.

USING THE SCALES GIVEN BELOW, DRAW DIMENSION LINES OF THE LENGTHS INDICATED. CONSTRUCT THESE LINES IN THE SAME MANNER AS THE EXAMPLE.

EX. 3'-6 SCALE: 1 = 1'-0 |←——— 3'-6 ———→|

10. 5'-3 SCALE: $\frac{1}{2}$ = 1'-0 |——

11. 1'-2$\frac{3}{8}$ SCALE: 3 = 1'-0 |——

12. 12'-3 SCALE: $\frac{1}{4}$ = 1'-0 |——

13. 0'-7$\frac{7}{8}$ SCALE: 6 = 1'-0 |——

14. 5'-3 SCALE: $\frac{3}{4}$ = 1'-0 |——

15. 3'-2$\frac{1}{4}$ SCALE: 1 = 1'-0 |——

Drafting & Design	NAME	grade	8
© James H. Earle	FILE NO. SEC. DATE		

Drafting & Design © James H. Earle	NAME FILE NO SEC DATE	grade	

ENGINEERS' SCALE

THE ENGINEERS' SCALE IS USED PRIMARILY FOR DIMENSIONING PLOTS AND INSTALLATIONS LOCATED OUT-OF-DOORS. STREETS, LOTS, BRIDGES, AND OTHER LARGE STRUCTURES ARE USUALLY DIMENSIONED WITH THE ENGINEERS' SCALE IN CONTRAST TO THE ARCHITECTS' SCALE. SINCE THE DIMENSIONS ARE IN DECIMAL FORM, IT IS EASIER TO MULTIPLY AND DIVIDE VARIOUS MEASUREMENTS THAN WHEN USING FEET AND INCHES ON THE ARCHITECTS' SCALE.

REQUIRED
SCALE THE MEASUREMENTS A, B AND C ON THE DRAWING AT THE RIGHT USING THE SCALE INDICATED IN PROBLEMS 1 THROUGH 6. LETTER THE MEASUREMENTS IN THE SPACES PROVIDED.

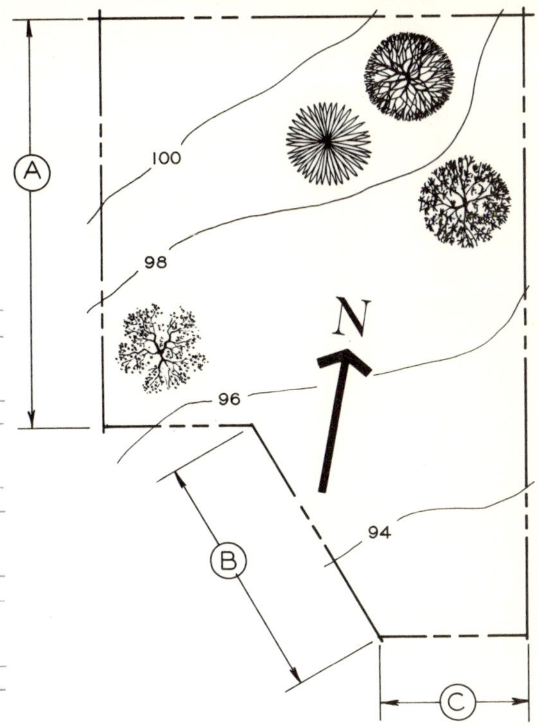

	A	B	C
EX. SCALE: 1 = 2.0'	4.27'	2.55'	1.52'
1. SCALE: 1 = 10'			
2. SCALE: 1 = 20'			
3. SCALE: 1 = 3.0'			
4. SCALE: 1 = 400'			
5. SCALE: 1 = 5.0'			
6. SCALE: 1 = 600'			

DRAW DIMENSION LINES TO THE LENGTH SPECIFIED IN PROBLEMS 7 THROUGH 14 USING THE SCALE SPECIFIED. SHOW ARROWHEADS AND THE LENGTH OF THE DIMENSION LINES AS SHOWN IN THE EXAMPLE.

EX. 700' SCALE: 1 = 200' |←——— 700' ———→|

7. 132.0' SCALE: 1 = 40' |—

8. 2.1' SCALE: 1 = 5.0' |—

9. 87.0' SCALE: 1 = 30' |—

10. 3.25" SCALE: 1 = 1.0" |—

11. 4000' SCALE: 1 = 1000' |—

12. 1525' SCALE: 1 = 600' |—

13. 0.68" SCALE: 1 = 0.2" |—

14. 0.102' SCALE: 1 = 0.03' |—

NAME
FILE NO. SEC. DATE

grade	9

Drafting & Design

NAME

FILE NO SEC DATE

grade

PERPENDICULAR BISECTOR

COMPASS METHOD

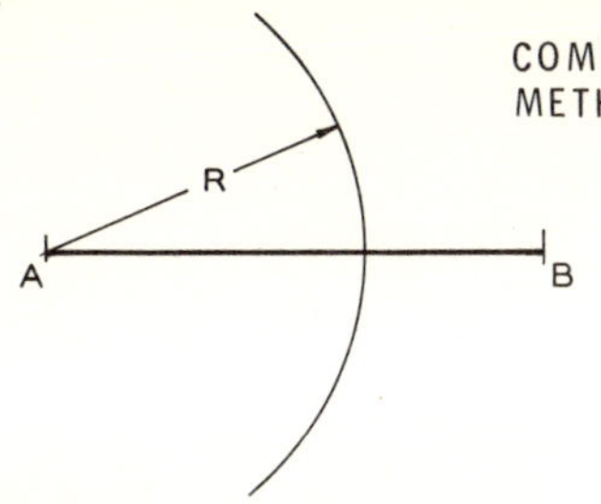

STEP 1: TO BISECT AB, CONSTRUCT AN ARC, R, USING A AS THE CENTER.

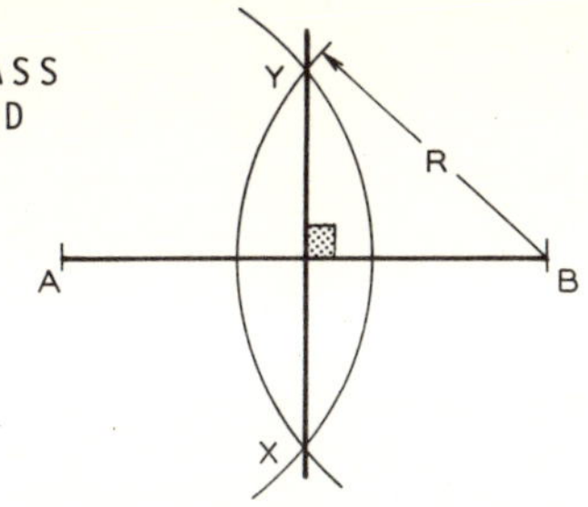

STEP 2: USING THE SAME RADIUS, CONSTRUCT AN ARC FROM B. LINE XY IS THE PERPENDICULAR BISECTOR OF LINE AB.

TRIANGLE METHOD

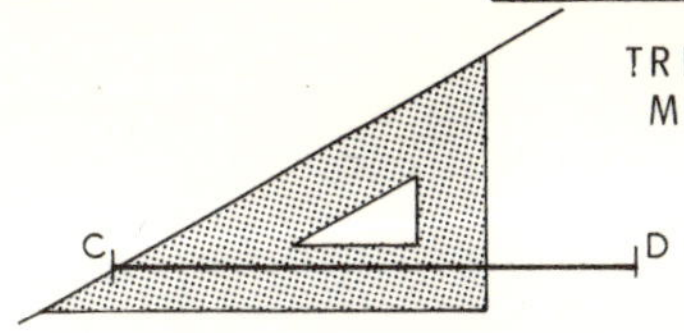

STEP 1: CONSTRUCT A LINE THROUGH POINT C WITH YOUR TRIANGLE AS SHOWN. A 45° TRIANGLE COULD HAVE BEEN USED.

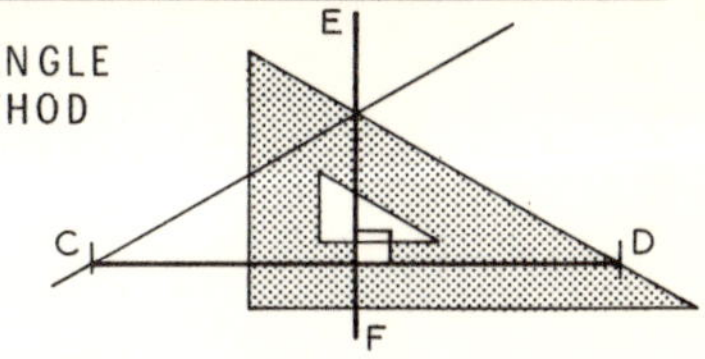

STEP 2: REVERSE THE TRIANGLE & DRAW A LINE THROUGH D. USING YOUR TRIANGLE, DRAW THE PERPENDICULAR BISECTOR OF CD.

1 USING THE COMPASS METHOD, LOCATE THE CENTER OF THE CIRCLE BY CONSTRUCTING PERPENDICULAR BISECTORS OF CHORDS 1-2 AND 3-4. COMPLETE THE CIRCLE AND SHOW CONSTRUCTION.

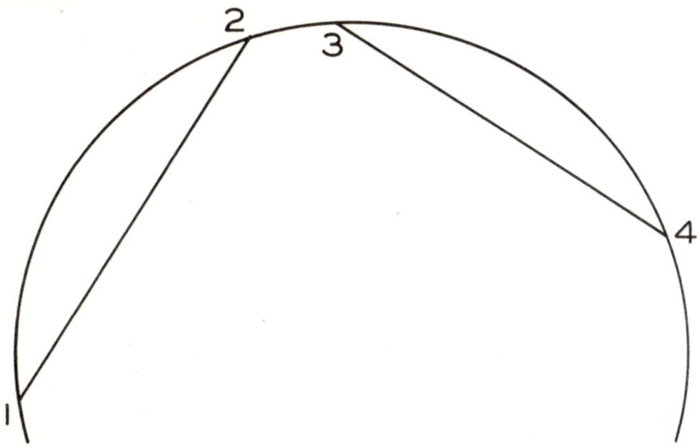

2 USING THE TRIANGLE METHOD, FIND THE INTERSECTION BETWEEN THE PERPENDICULAR BISECTORS OF LINES AB AND CD. SHOW CONSTRUCTION.

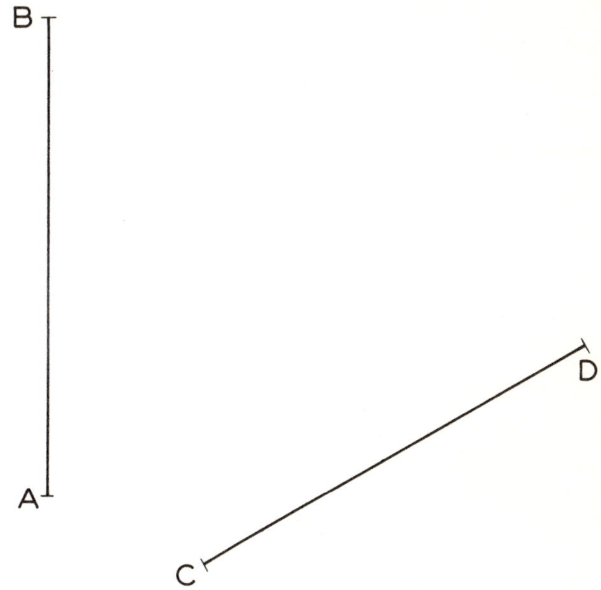

3 COMPLETE THE PARTIAL VIEW OF THE STRUCTURAL SECTION BY CONSTRUCTING THE CENTERLINE PERPENDICULAR TO EF. USE THE DIMENSIONS SHOWN IN THE SKETCH AND SHOW CONSTRUCTION.

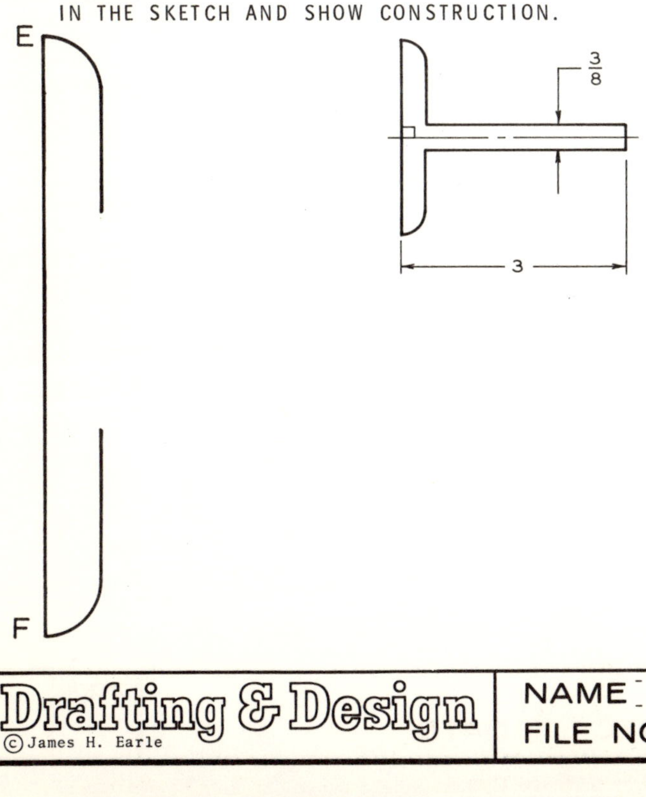

4 LINE CT IS THE RADIUS OF AN ARC. CONSTRUCT A TANGENT TO THE ARC THROUGH POINT T THAT IS 1-1/2" LONG ON EACH SIDE OF POINT T. HINT: THE TANGENT MUST BE PERPENDICULAR TO CT. SHOW CONSTRUCTION.

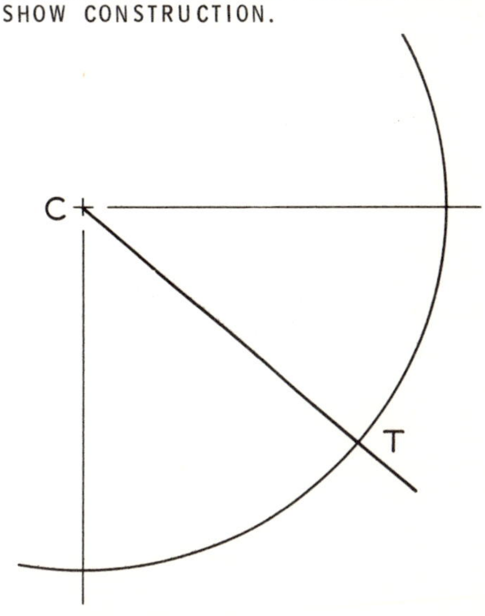

Drafting & Design ©James H. Earle	NAME FILE NO SEC DATE	grade	11

Drafting & Design

NAME

FILE NO SEC DATE

grade

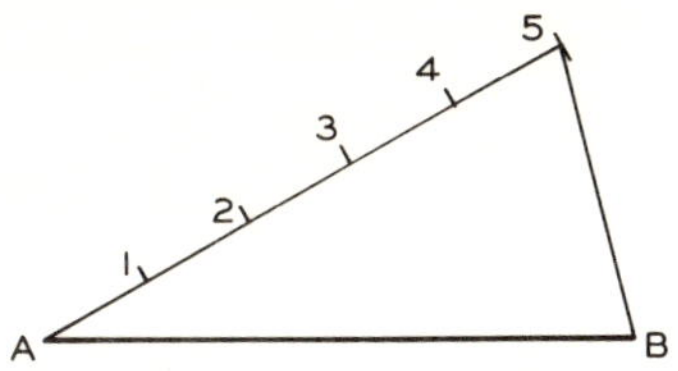

STEP 1: TO DIVIDE AB INTO 5 DIVISIONS, DRAW A LINE THRU A AT ANY ANGLE AND MEASURE 5 DIVISIONS ALONG IT.

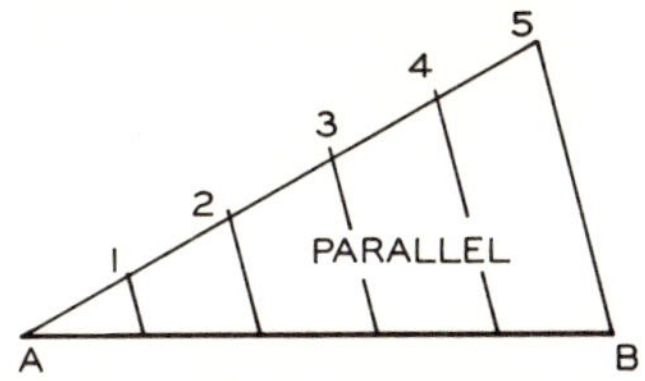

STEP 2: CONNECT DIVISION 5 WITH POINT B AND DRAW OTHER CONSTRUCTION LINES PARALLEL TO IT TO DIVIDE THE LINE AB.

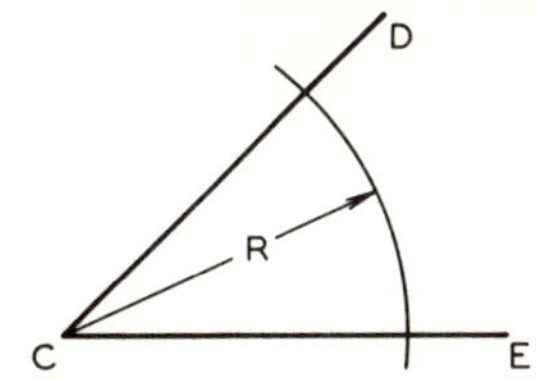

STEP 1: TO BISECT DCE, DRAW AN ARC WITH ANY RADIUS R.

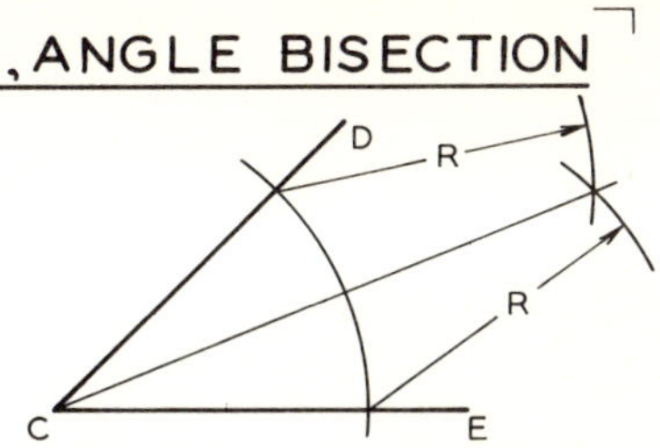

STEP 2: USING ANY RADIUS R, DRAW TWO ARCS TO LOCATE THE BISECTOR.

1 DIVIDE AB INTO FOUR DIVISIONS AND BC INTO THREE DIVISIONS. SHOW CONSTRUCTION.

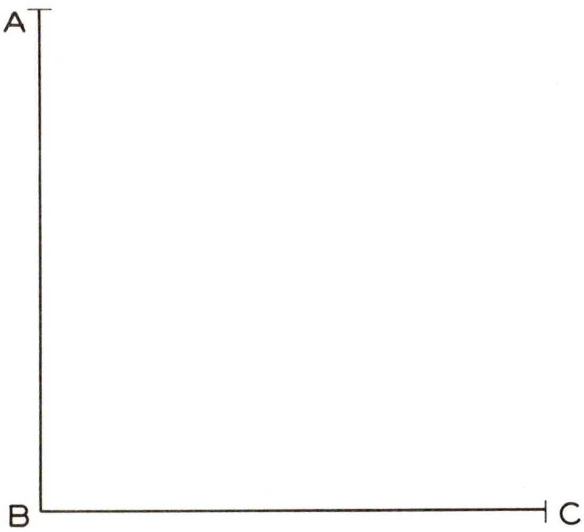

2 THE PLAN VIEW OF AN OVERHEAD PIPE IS SHOWN. DIVIDE BOTH DE AND FG INTO THREE EQUAL DIVISIONS TO LOCATE PIPE HANGERS THAT WILL SUPPORT THE PIPE. SHOW CONSTRUCTION.

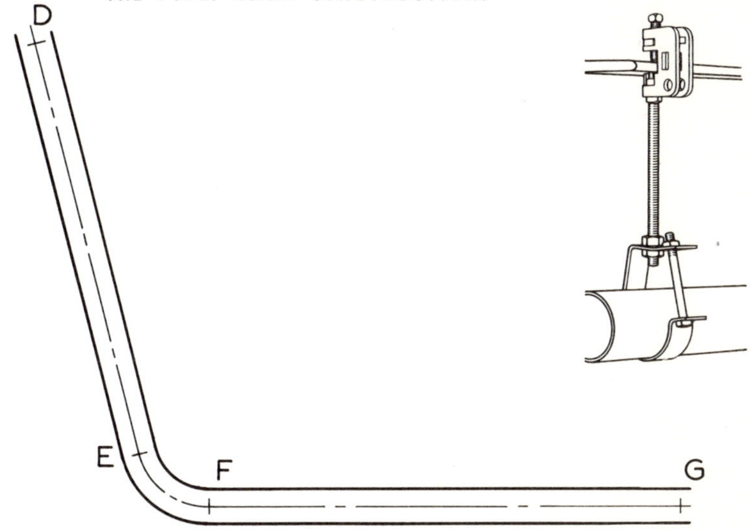

3 CONSTRUCT BISECTORS OF THE THREE ANGLES OF THE TRIANGLE. SHOW CONSTRUCTION.

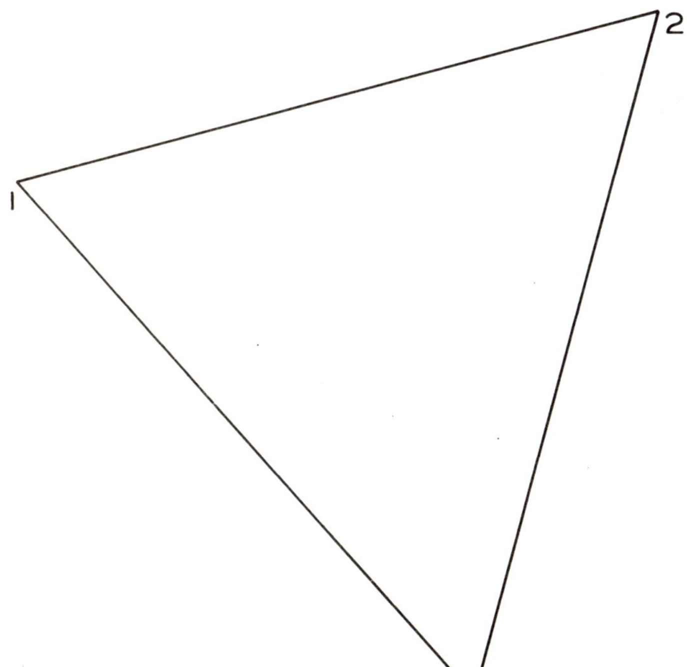

4 THE EXTERIOR CORNER WALL OF A CONTROL TOWER IS SHOWN IN PLAN. BISECT THE ANGLE AT P AND LOCATE A STRUCTURAL MEMBER THAT EXTENDS 2 FT FROM THE INSIDE WALL ALONG THE BISECTOR.

SCALE: $\frac{1}{2}$ = 1'-0

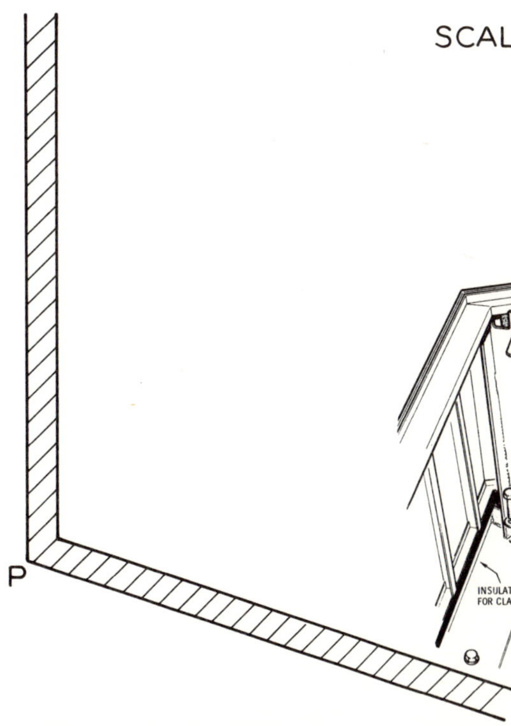

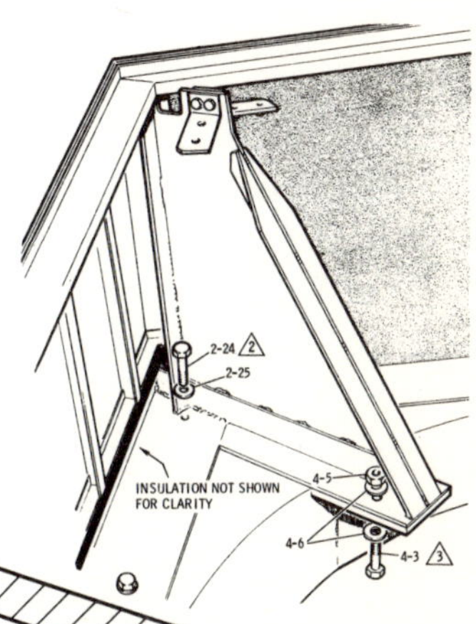

Drafting & Design

NAME
FILE NO SEC DATE
grade

POLYGONS

PENTAGON

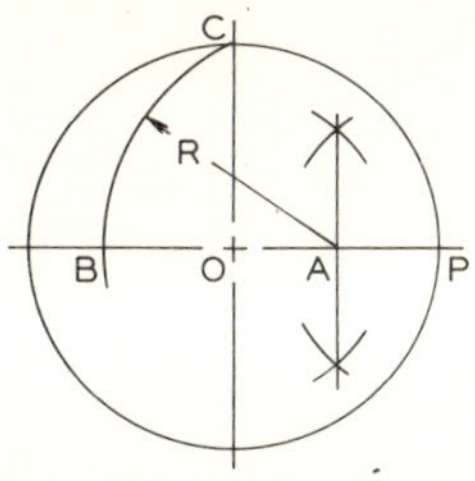

STEP 1: TO INSCRIBE A PENTAGON IN A CIRCLE, BISECT RADIUS OP. DRAW AN ARC FROM A TO C TO LOCATE B.

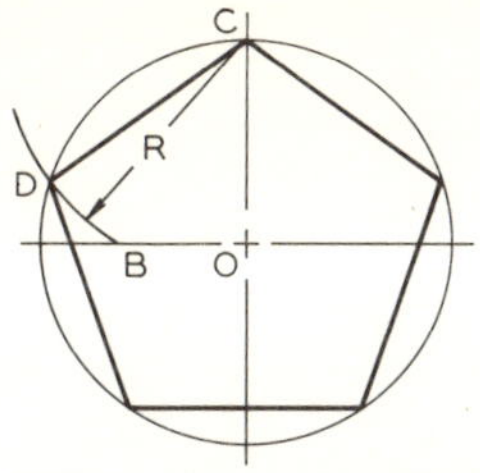

STEP 2: USING RADIUS BC, LOCATE THE FIVE CORNERS OF THE PENTAGON. CONNECT THESE POINTS TO COMPLETE THE PENTAGON.

HEXAGON

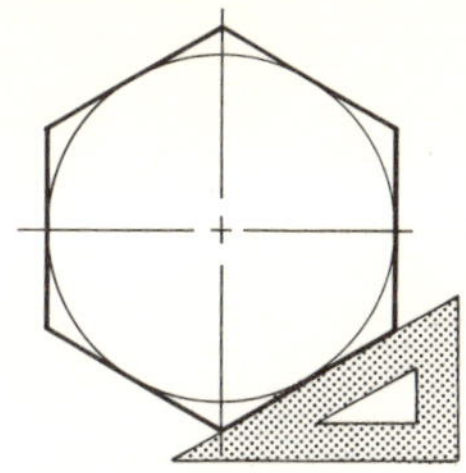

A HEXAGON CIRCUMSCRIBED ABOUT A CIRCLE.

OCTAGON

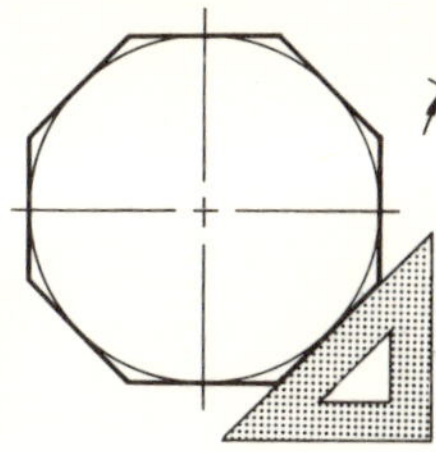

AN OCTAGON CIRCUMSCRIBED ABOUT A CIRCLE.

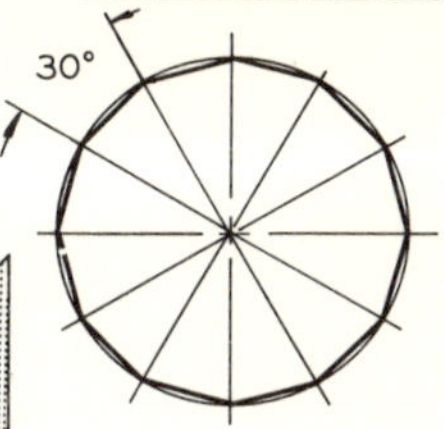

A TWELVE-SIDED POLYGON INSCRIBED IN A CIRCLE.

1 CONSTRUCT A 3" DIAMETER CIRCLE AND INSCRIBE A PENTAGON TO REPRESENT THE FLOOR PLAN OF A CONTROL TOWER.

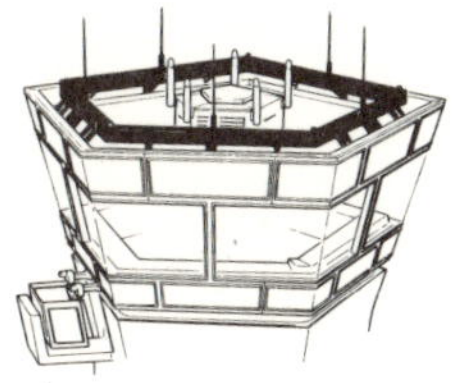

2 CONSTRUCT A 3" DIAMETER CIRCLE AND CIRCUMSCRIBE A HEXAGONAL NUT ABOUT IT.

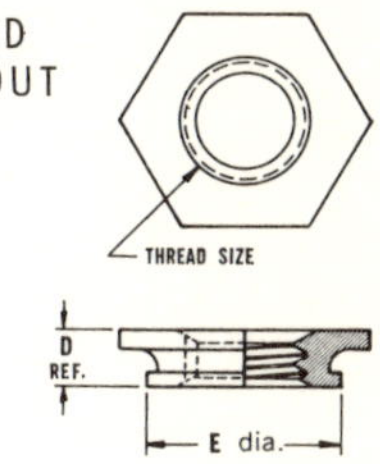

3 CIRCUMSCRIBE AN OCTAGON ABOUT THE CIRCLE BELOW.

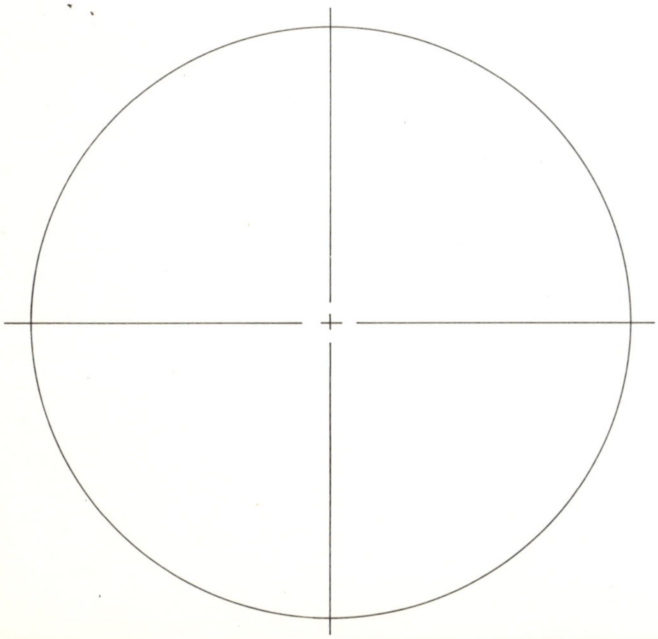

4 CIRCUMSCRIBE A TEN-SIDED FLOOR PLAN OF A SCHOOL ABOUT THE CIRCLE BELOW.

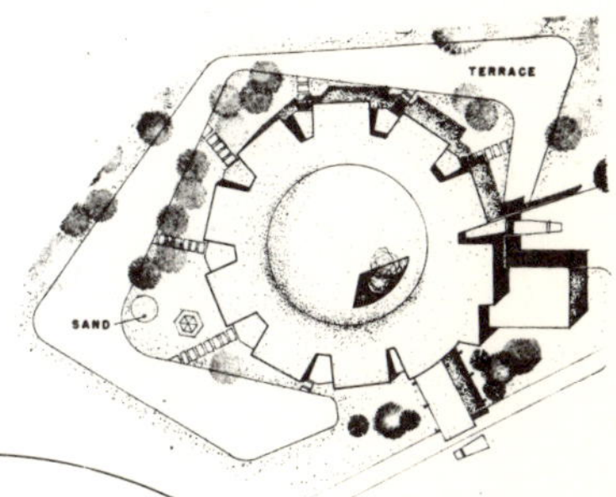

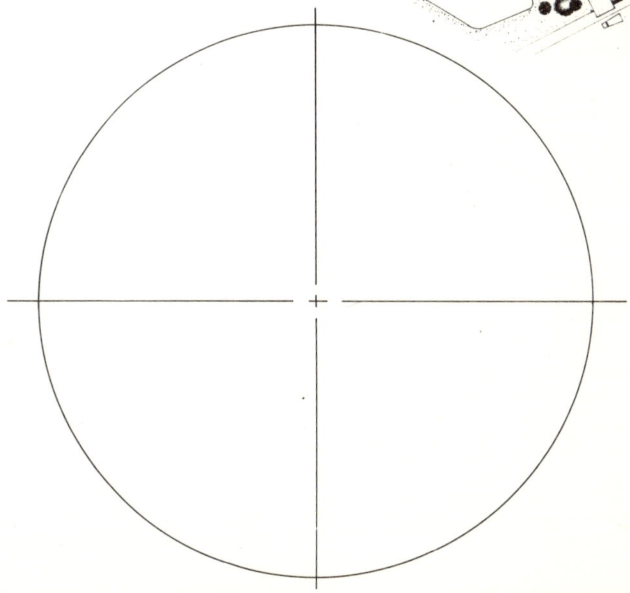

Drafting & Design

NAME

FILE NO SEC DATE

grade

TANGENCIES

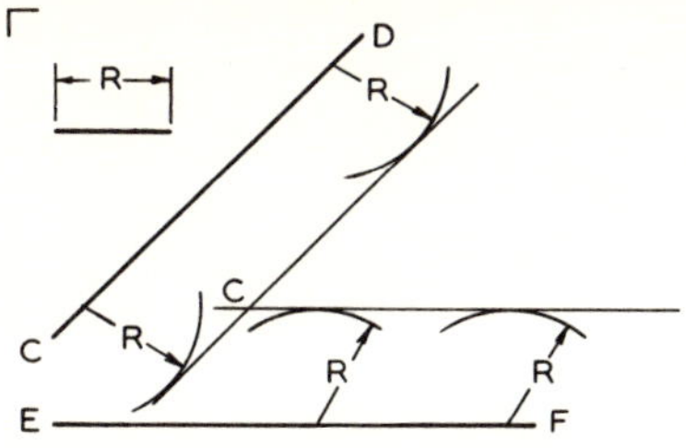

STEP 1: DRAW ARCS WITH RADIUS R TO LOCATE TWO LINES R-DISTANT FROM CD AND EF. THEY INTERSECT AT C.

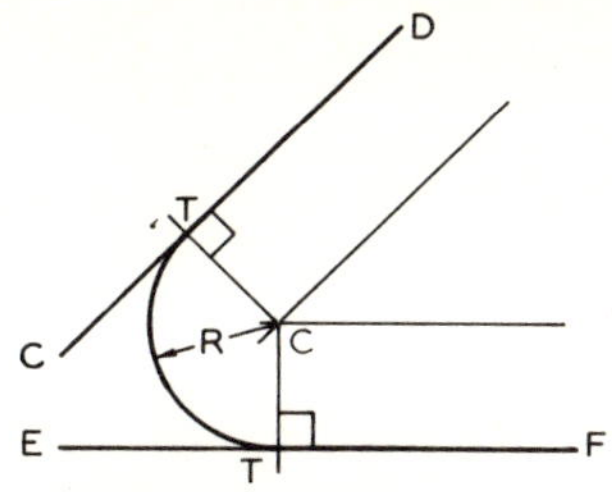

STEP 2: AN ARC WITH RADIUS R IS DRAWN TANGENT TO THE LINES USING C AS THE CENTER. THE TANGENT POINTS ARE LOCATED.

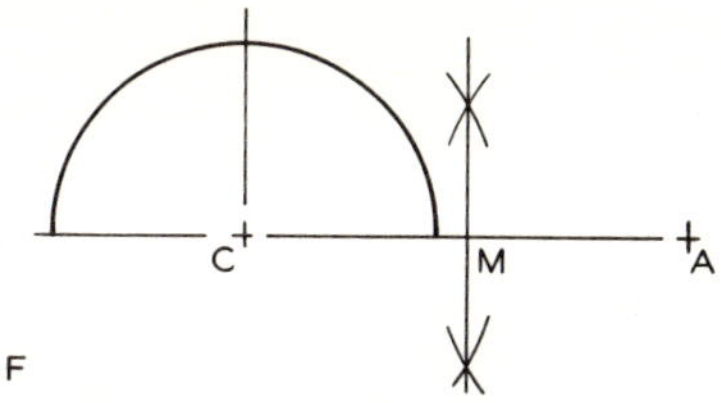

STEP 1: POINT A AND CENTER C ARE CONNECTED AND THE MIDPOINT OF AC IS FOUND.

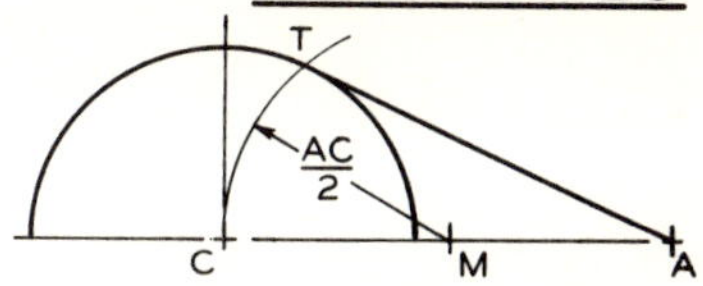

STEP 2: THE POINT OF TANGENCY IS FOUND BY CONSTRUCTING AN ARC FROM MIDPOINT C USING RADIUS MC.

1 CONSTRUCT A 1-1/2" RADIUS ARC TANGENT TO AB AND BC. LOCATE POINTS OF TANGENCY AND SHOW CONSTRUCTION.

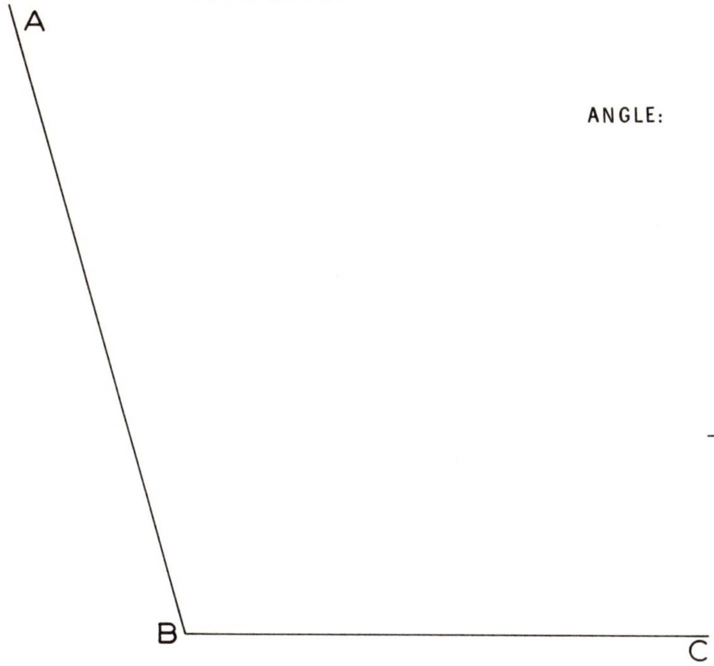

2 CONSTRUCT TWO LINES FROM POINT P TANGENT TO THE CIRCLE. LOCATE POINTS OF TANGENCY AND SHOW CONSTRUCTION. THE ANGLE BETWEEN THESE TWO LINES IS:

+P

ANGLE:

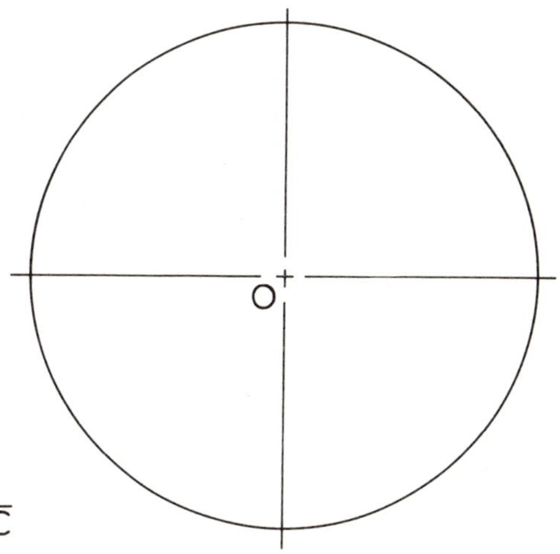

3 YOU ARE TO COMPLETE THE DESIGN FOR THE PIPE HANGER BAND USED TO SUPPORT OVERHEAD UTILITY PIPES. IT MUST HOLD A 3-1/4" OUTSIDE DIAMETER PIPE. EXTEND THE GIVEN LINES AS NECESSARY TO COMPLETE THE DRAWING. LOCATE THE CIRCULAR PORTION AND POINTS OF TANGENCY. SHOW CONSTRUCTION.

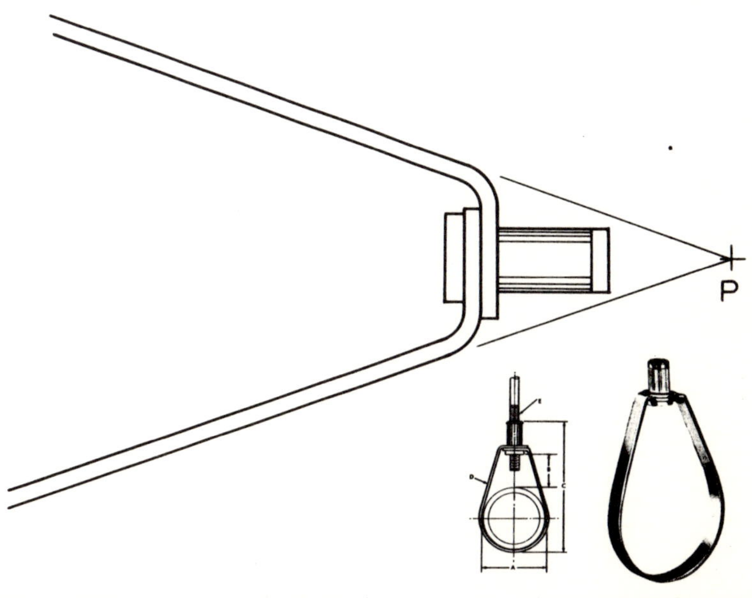

Drafting & Design

NAME
FILE NO SEC DATE
grade

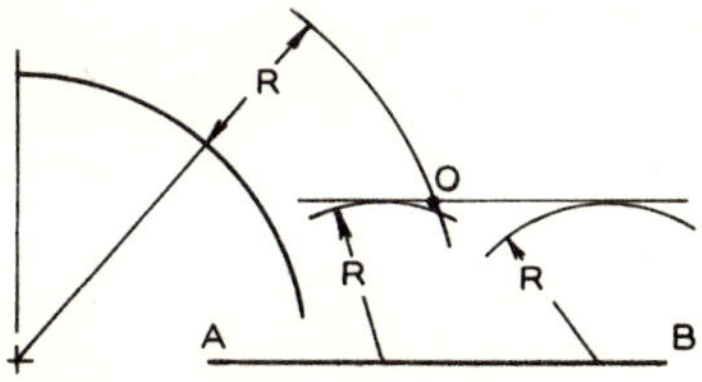

STEP 1: DRAW A CONCENTRIC ARC THAT IS R-DISTANT FROM THE GIVEN ARC. DRAW A LINE R-DISTANT FROM AB TO LOCATE O.

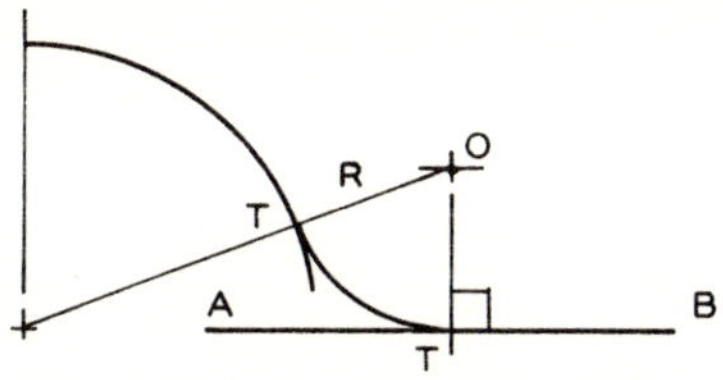

STEP 2: DRAW AN ARC WITH RADIUS R AND CENTER O. LOCATE POINTS OF TANGENCY.

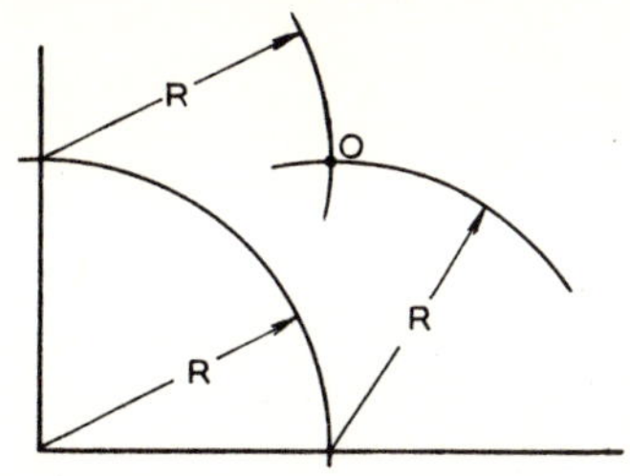

STEP 1: DRAW AN ARC FROM THE INTERSECTION OF TWO PERPENDICULARS TO LOCATE POINTS ON EACH. SWING ARCS FROM THESE POINTS TO LOCATE POINT O.

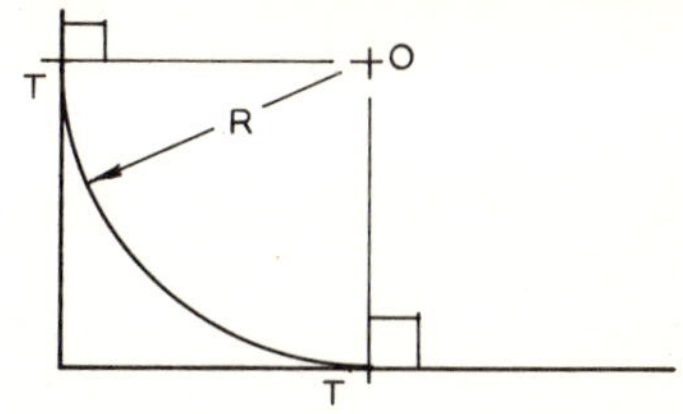

STEP 2: USING CENTER O AND RADIUS R, DRAW AN ARC WITH RADIUS R TANGENT TO THE GIVEN LINES. LOCATE TANGENT POINTS.

1 AN END VIEW OF A SPRING STOP THAT IS USED WITH JIGS AND FIXTURES IS SHOWN BELOW. CONSTRUCT A 1" RADIUS ARC TANGENT TO THE ARC AND LINE. SHOW CONSTRUCTION AND LOCATE TANGENT POINTS.

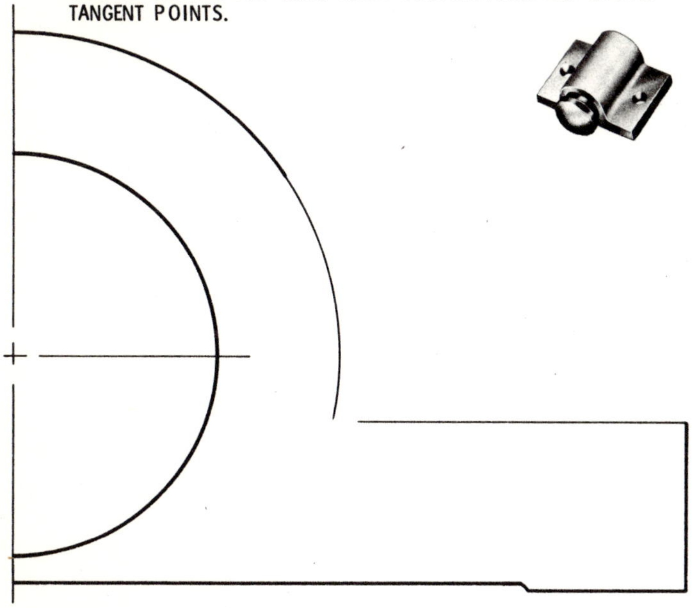

2 CONSTRUCT A 2" RADIUS ARC TANGENT TO THE PERPENDIULAR LINES BELOW. SHOW CONSTRUCTION AND LOCATE POINTS OF TANGENCY.

3 CONSTRUCT A 1" RADIUS ARC TANGENT TO THE LINES AT D AND E. SHOW CONSTRUCTION AND LOCATE POINTS OF TANGENCY.

BEAM CLAMP with SWING CONNECTOR

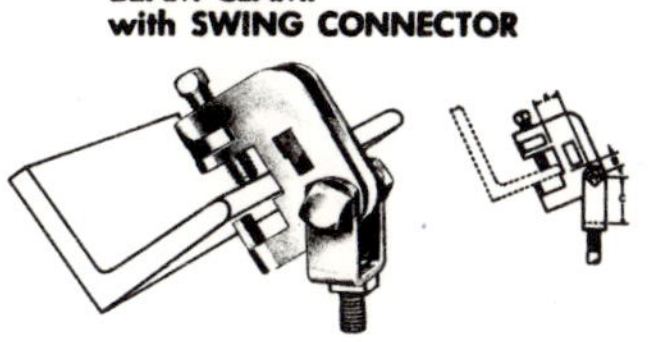

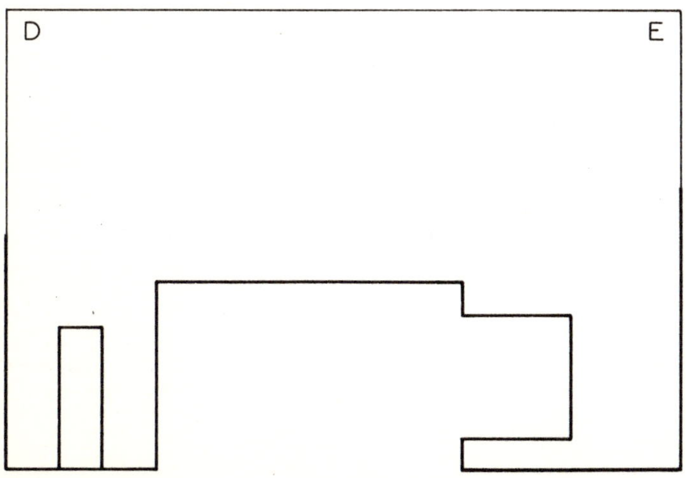

4 THE CENTERLINES OF 20 FT WIDE DRIVEWAY ARE GIVEN. CONSTRUCT A PORTION OF THE DRIVEWAY THAT HAS A 50 FT RADIUS AND IS TANGENT TO THE GIVEN CENTERLINES. DRAW THE WIDTH OF DRIVEWAY ABOUT THE CENTERLINES AND LOCATE POINTS OF TANGENCY.

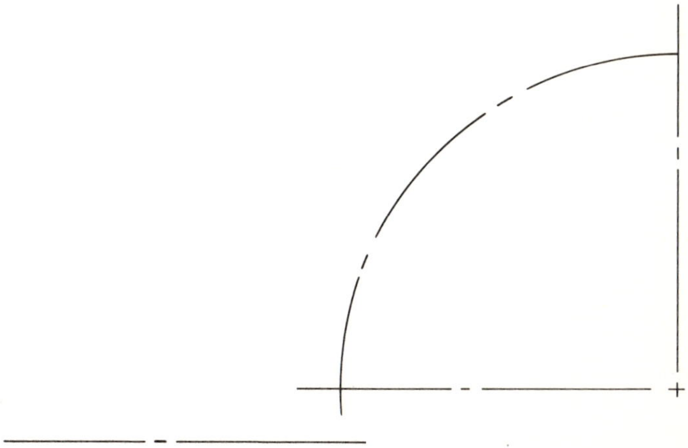

SCALE: 1 = 40'

Drafting & Design © James H. Earle	NAME: FILE NO: SEC: DATE:	grade	

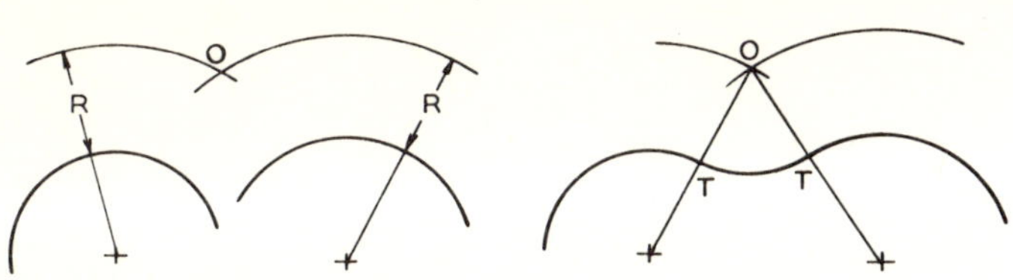

STEP 1: ADD RADIUS R TO THE RADII OF THE TWO ARCS. SWING THE TOTAL RADII DISTANCES FROM THE CENTERS TO LOCATE POINT O.

STEP 2: USING RADIUS R AND CENTER O, SWING AN ARC TANGENT TO THE GIVEN ARCS. TANGENT POINTS ARE LOCATED ON LINES DRAWN BETWEEN O AND THE CENTERS.

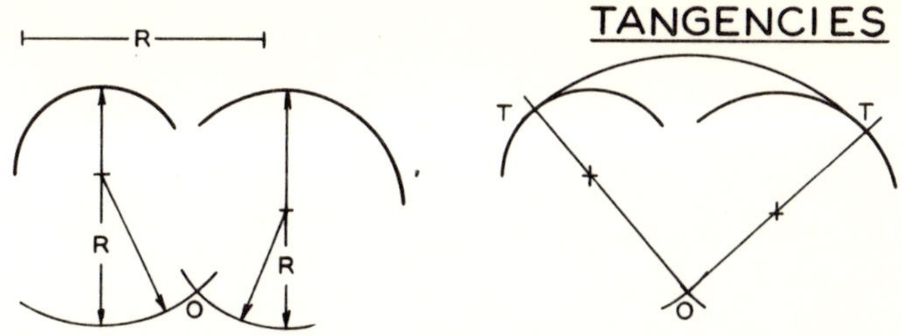

STEP 1: LAY OFF RADIUS R FROM EACH ARC ALONG A LINE DRAWN THROUGH EACH CENTER. SWING ARCS FROM EACH TO LOCATE O.

STEP 2: USING RADIUS R AND CENTER O, CONSTRUCT AN ARC TANGENT TO THE GIVEN ARCS. LOCATE TANGENT POINTS BY DRAWING LINES CONNECTING THE CENTERS.

1 CONSTRUCT A 1" RADIUS ARC TANGENT TO THE GIVEN ARCS ON BOTH THE LOWER AND UPPER SIDES. SHOW CONSTRUCTION AND TANGENT POINTS.

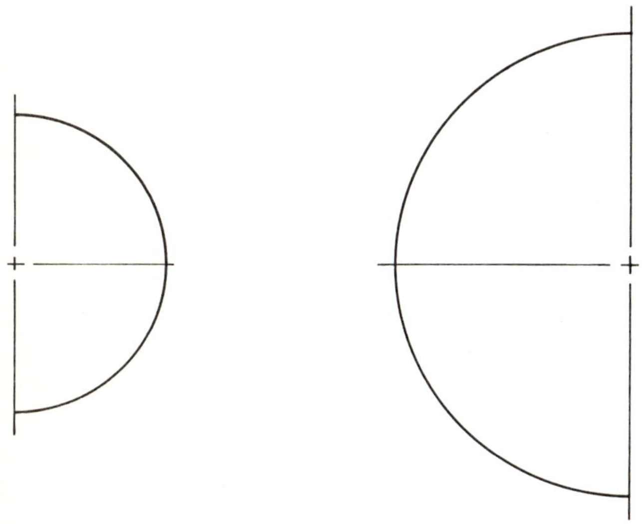

2 CONSTRUCT A 2-1/8" RADIUS TANGENT TO THE GIVEN ARCS WITH THE CENTER LOCATED AT THE RIGHT. SHOW CONSTRUCTION AND TANGENT POINTS.

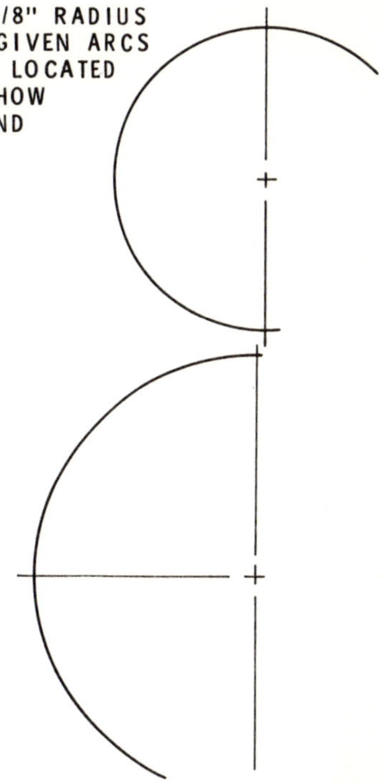

3 CONSTRUCT A 1" RADIUS ARC TANGENT TO THE GIVEN ARCS TO COMPLETE THE VIEW OF THE WING STUD. SHOW CONSTRUCTION AND TANGENT POINTS.

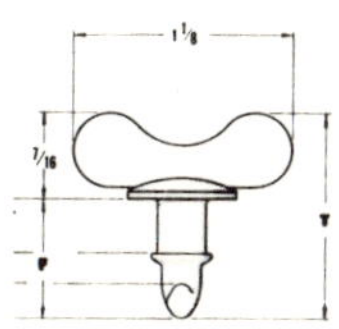

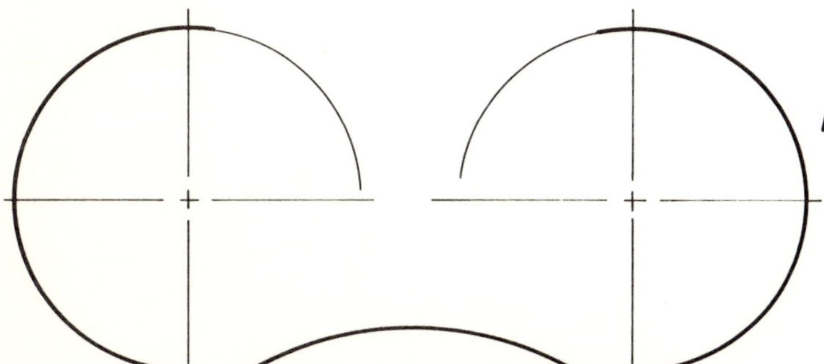

4 CONSTRUCT A 2-5/8" RADIUS ARC TANGENT TO THE ARCS WITH CENTERS AT A & B TO COMPLETE THE PARTIAL VIEW OF THE LATCHING DEVICE. SHOW CONSTRUCTION AND TANGENT POINTS.

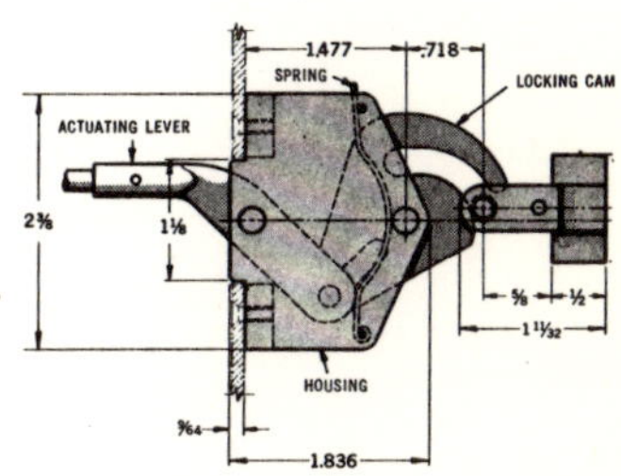

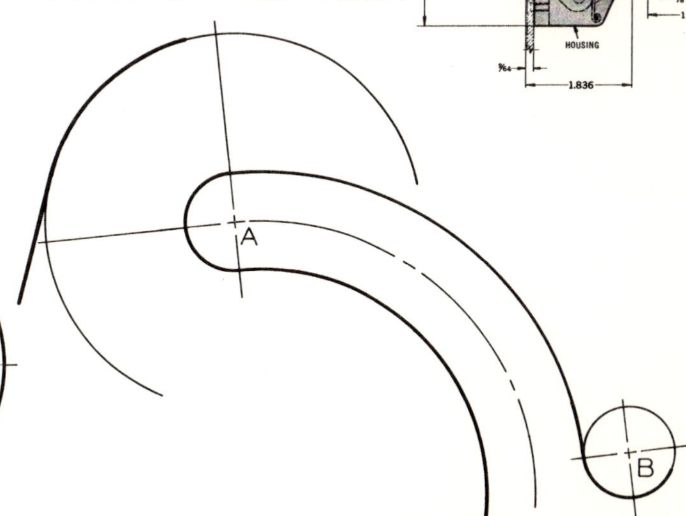

Drafting & Design © James H. Earle	NAME FILE NO SEC DATE	grade	16

Drafting & Design ©James H. Earle	NAME FILE NO SEC DATE	grade	

HELIX

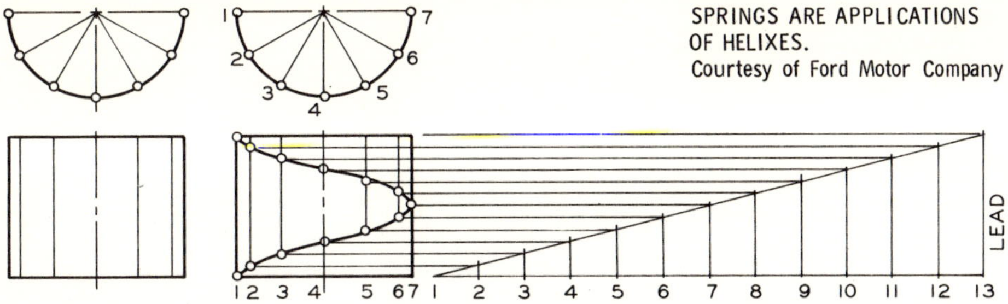

STEP 1: DIVIDE THE CIRCULAR VIEW INTO EQUAL DIVISIONS & PROJECT TO THE FRONT VIEW TO LOCATE ELEMENTS ON THE CYLINDER.

STEP 2: TRANSFER THE CHORDAL DISTANCES BETWEEN THE POINTS IN THE CIRCULAR VIEW TO A HORIZONTAL LINE. CONSTRUCT A RIGHT TRIANGLE USING THE HORIZONTAL LINE AND THE LEAD OF THE HELIX. THE POINTS ARE PROJECTED FROM THE HYPOTENUSE TO THEIR RESPECTIVE ELEMENTS TO LOCATE POINTS ON THE HELIX.

SPRINGS ARE APPLICATIONS OF HELIXES.
Courtesy of Ford Motor Company

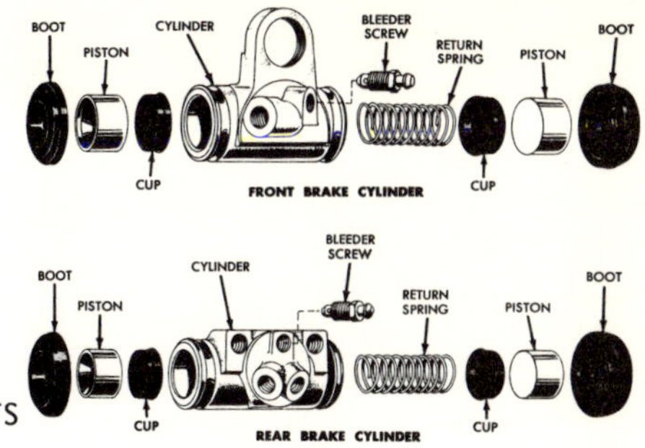

Front and Rear Wheel Cylinders

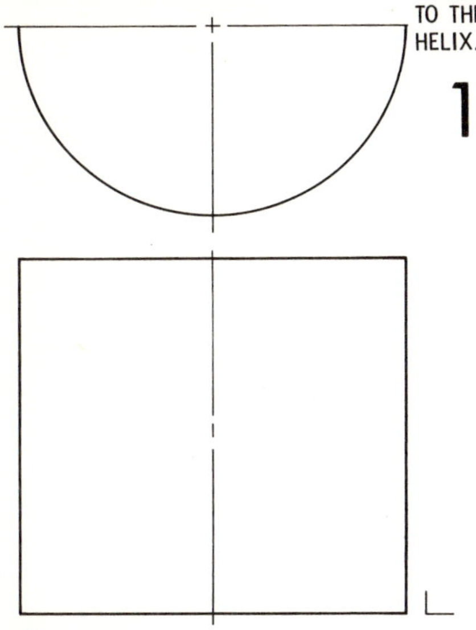

1 CONSTRUCT A HELIX ABOUT THE CYLINDER. DIVIDE THE CIRCULAR VIEW INTO 15° INTERVALS. SHOW CONSTRUCTION OF THE FULL HELIX EVEN THOUGH THE TOP VIEW IS A HALF VIEW.

2 CONSTRUCT A SPIRAL BY DIVIDING THE GIVEN CIRCLE INTO 30° INTERVALS. SHOW CONSTRUCTION.

SPIRAL

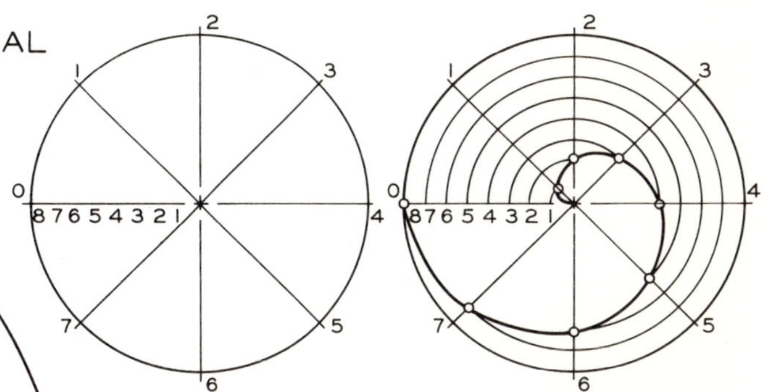

STEP 1: DIVIDE THE CIRCLE INTO EQUAL DIVISIONS. DIVIDE THE RADIUS INTO THE SAME NUMBER OF DIVISIONS.

STEP 2: CONSTRUCT ARCS FROM THE CENTER TO EACH UNIT ON THE RADIUS TO THEIR RESPECTIVE RADII TO LOCATE POINTS ON THE SPIRAL.

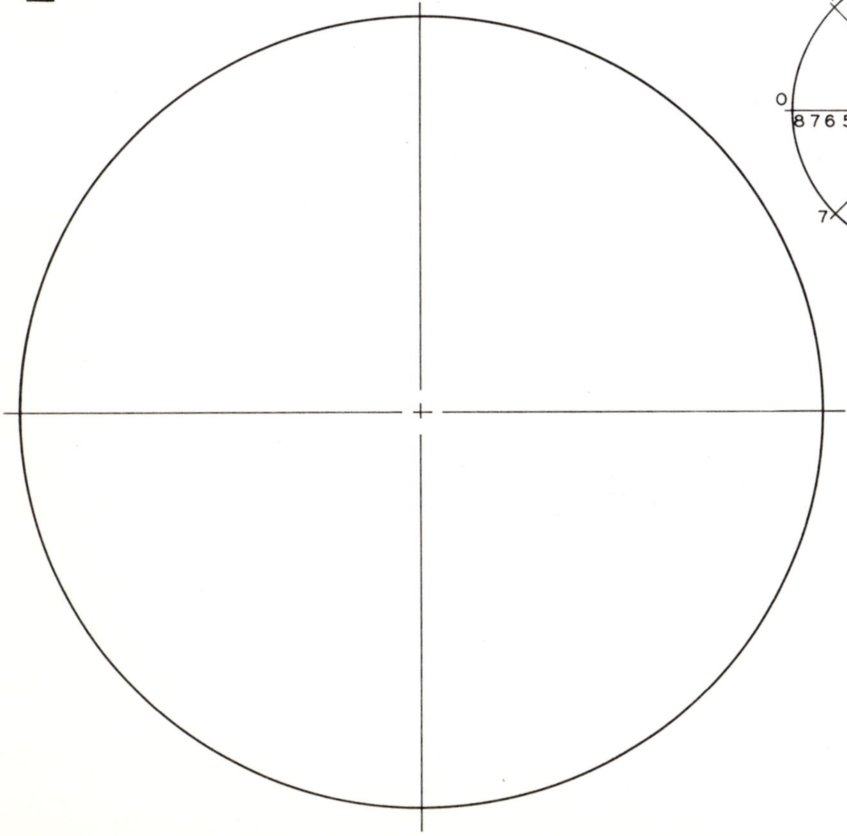

NAME

FILE NO SEC DATE

grade

Drafting & Design © James H. Earle	NAME FILE NO SEC DATE	grade	

GRAPHICAL SOLUTION

PARABOLA

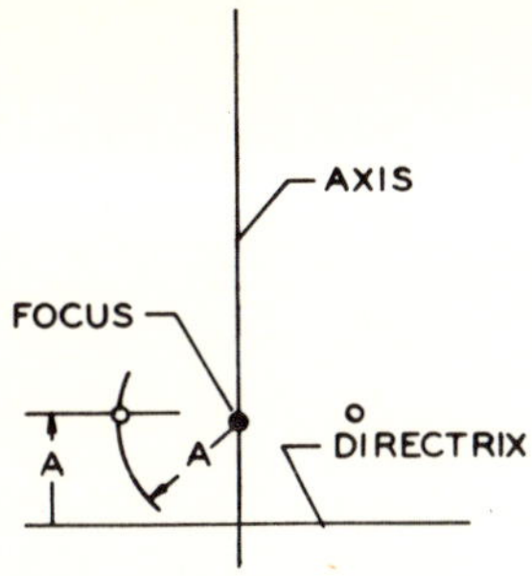

STEP 1: TO PLOT A PARABOLA, LOCATE POINTS A-DISTANCE FROM THE DIRECTRIX AND THE FOCUS.

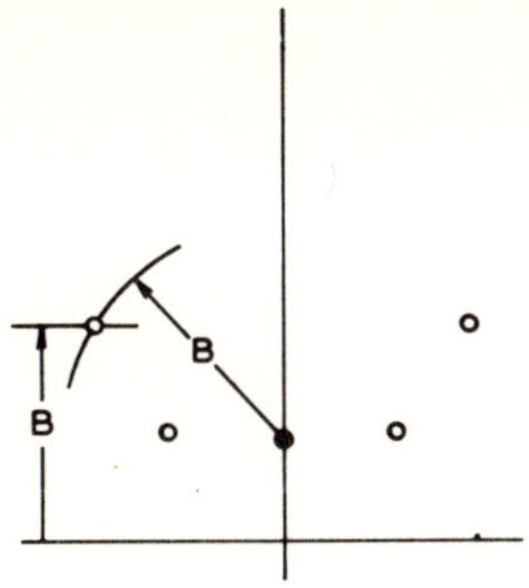

STEP 2: ADDITIONAL POINTS ARE PLOTTED EQUIDISTANT FROM THE DIRECTRIX AND THE FOCUS.

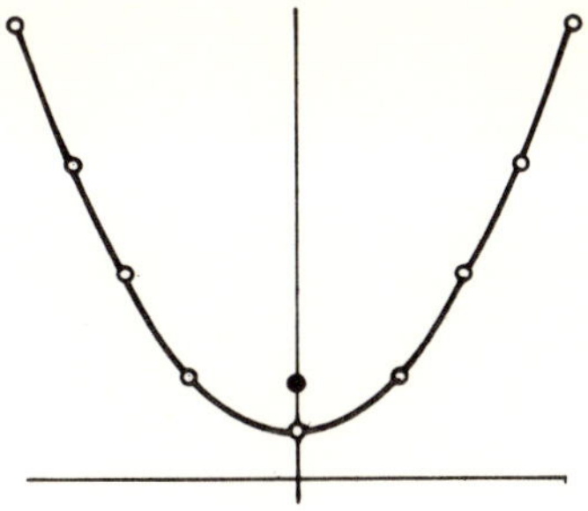

STEP 3: OTHER POINTS ARE PLOTTED IN THIS MANNER AND ARE CONNECTED WITH A SMOOTH CURVE.

$X^2 = 2Y + 1$

X	Y
0	−1
± 1	0
± 1.7	1
± 2.2	2
± 2.6	3
± 3.0	4
± 3.3	5
± 3.6	6
± 3.9	7
± 4.1	8
± 4.4	9

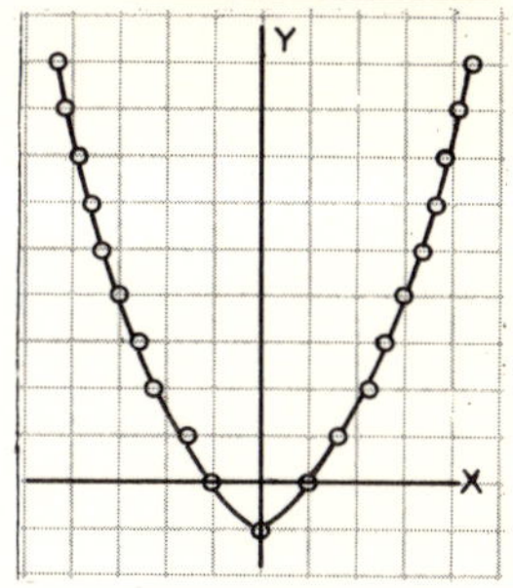

MATHEMATICAL SOLUTION: COORDINATES OF POINTS ARE FOUND BY SUBSTITUTING VALUES OF X INTO THE EQUATION. THESE COORDINATES ARE PLOTTED ON THE X-Y AXES

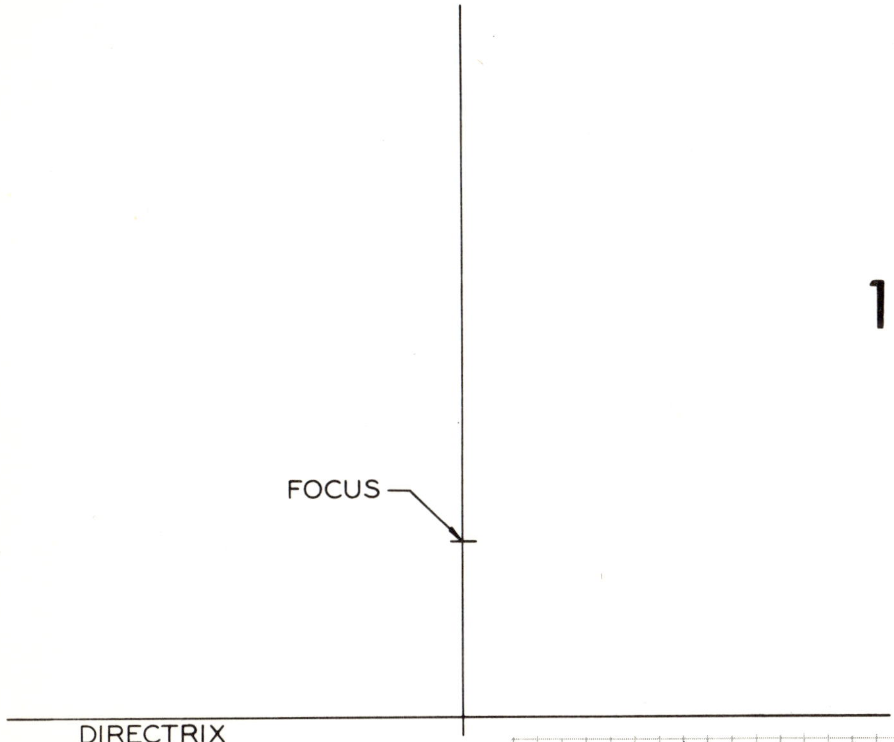

1 THE CROSS SECTION OF AN AUTOMOBILE HEADLIGHT IS PARABOLIC SINCE IT WILL PROJECT PARALLEL RAYS OF LIGHT WHEN THE LIGHT IS LOCATED AT THE FOCUS. PLOT THE PARABOLA AT THE LEFT USING THE FOCUS AND DIRECTRIX GIVEN. USE THE GRAPHICAL METHOD.

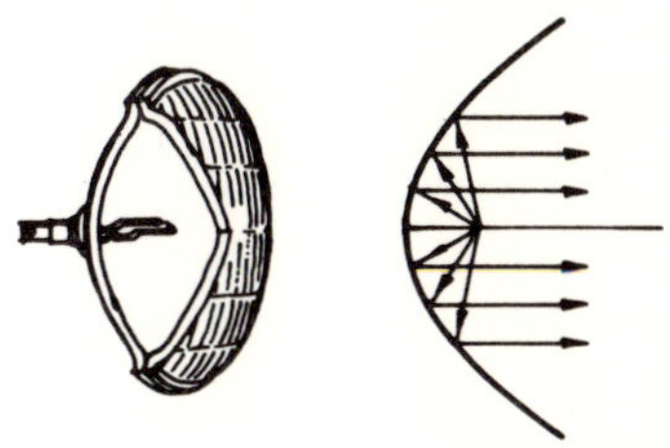

2

THE VALUES OF X AND Y HAVE BEEN DETERMINED FOR THE EQUATION BELOW AND ARE GIVEN IN THE TABLE. USING THESE VALUES, PLOT THE COORDINATES OF THE PARABOLA AND CONNECT THEM WITH A SMOOTH CURVE.

$Y^2 = 3X + 3$

X	Y
−1	± 0
0	± 1.73
1	±2.45
2	±3.00
3	±3.46
4	±4.12
5	±4.24
6	±4.58
7	±4.90
8	±5.19
9	±5.48
10	±5.74
11	±6.00

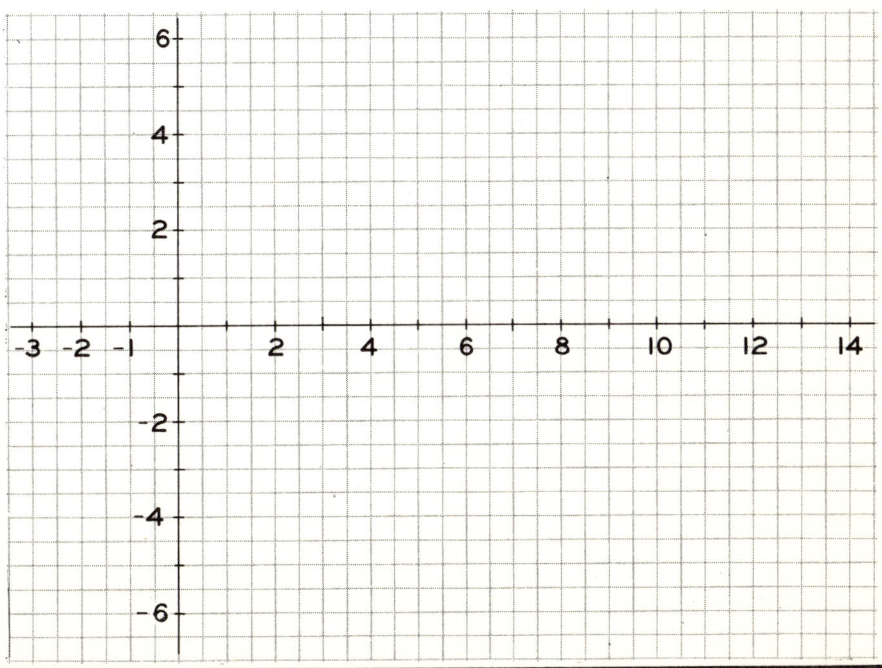

Drafting & Design © James H. Earle	NAME: FILE NO: SEC: DATE:	grade	

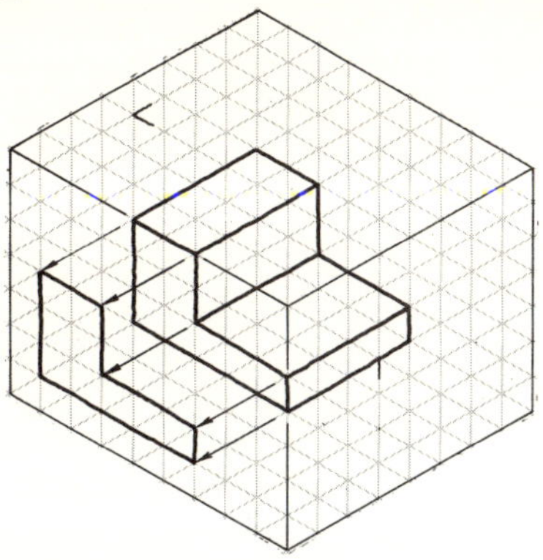

STEP 1: THE FRONT VIEW OF THE OBJECT IS PROJECTED ONTO THE FRONTAL PLANE WITH PARALLEL PROJECTORS.

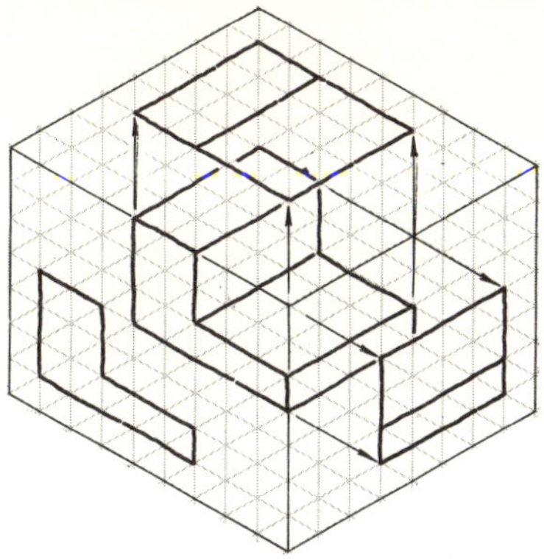

STEP 2: THE TOP VIEW IS PROJECTED ONTO THE HORIZONTAL PLANE AND THE SIDE VIEW ONTO THE PROFILE PLANE.

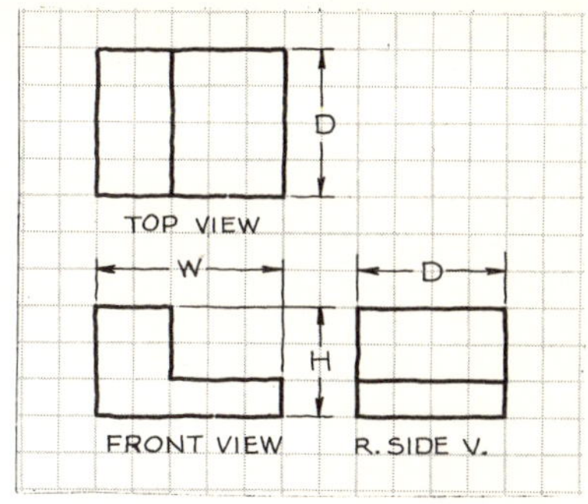

STEP 3: THE THREE VIEWS ARE SHOWN AS ORTHOGRAPHIC VIEWS IN THEIR CONVENTIONAL ARRANGEMENT.

REQUIRED: SKETCHING FREEHAND, PROJECT THE THREE VIEWS OF THE OBJECTS ONTO THE PICTORIAL PLANES. SKETCH THE THREE VIEWS IN THEIR CONVENTIONAL ORTHOGRAPHIC ARRANGEMENT AS SHOWN IN STEP 3 USING THE SPACE PROVIDED.

1

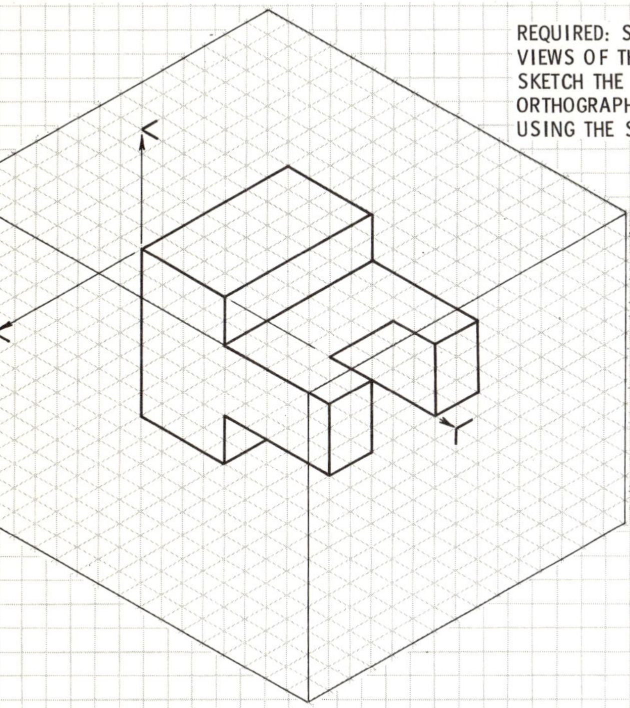

2

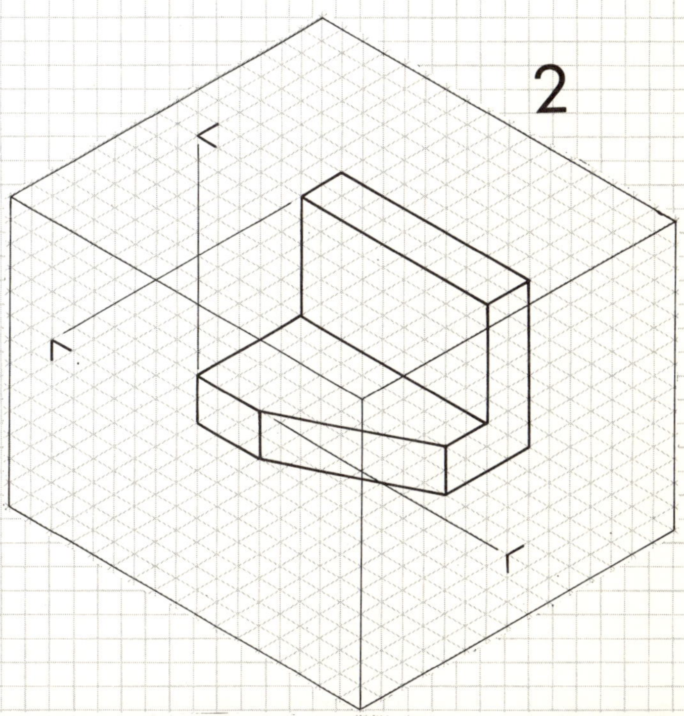

Drafting & Design © James H. Earle	NAME FILE NO SEC DATE	grade	

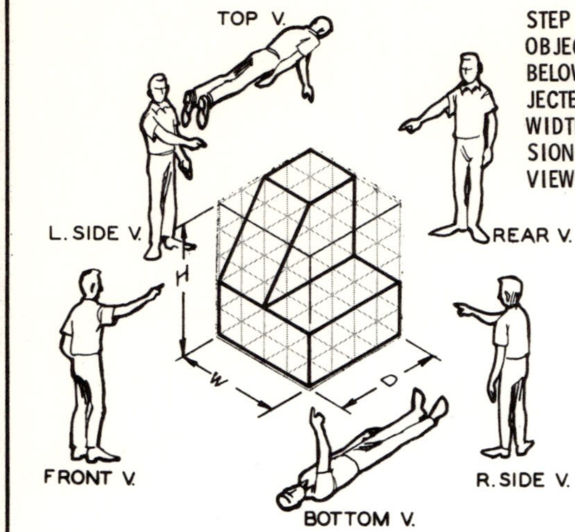

STEP 1: TO LAY OUT SIX VIEWS OF AN OBJECT, USE THE ARRANGEMENT SHOWN BELOW. THE HEIGHT DIMENSION IS PROJECTED TO APPLY TO FOUR VIEWS AND WIDTH APPLIES TO THREE. THESE DIMENSIONS ARE USED TO BLOCK IN THE VIEWS.

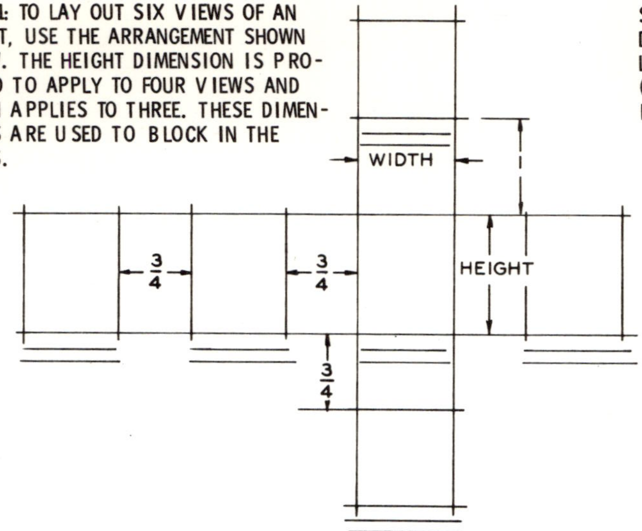

STEP 2: THE VIEWS ARE COMPLETED IN DETAIL, LINES ARE STRENGTHENED, AND LABELS ARE ADDED. DIMENSIONS DEPTH (D), WIDTH (W) AND HEIGHT (H) ARE ADDED IN THE ARRANGEMENT SHOWN.

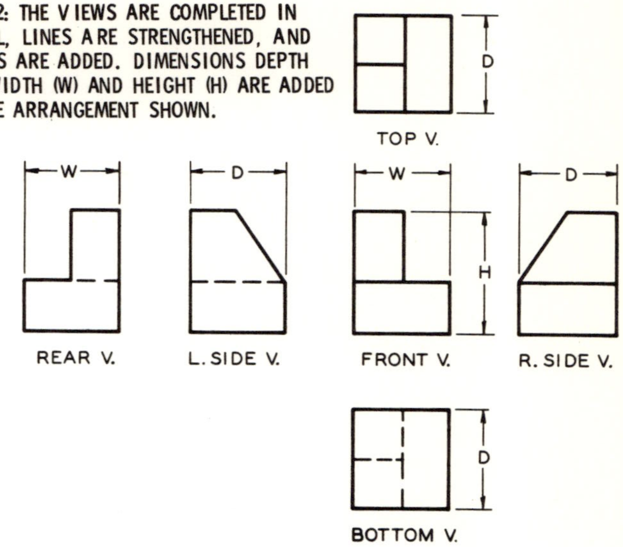

REQUIRED: DRAW SIX VIEWS OF THE PART ASSIGNED USING INSTRUMENTS BEGINNING WITH THE FRONT VIEW AT POINT O. EACH DIVISION ON THE PICTORIAL GRID REPRESENTS 1/8". LABEL THE VIEWS AND SHOW DIMENSIONS W, D AND H.

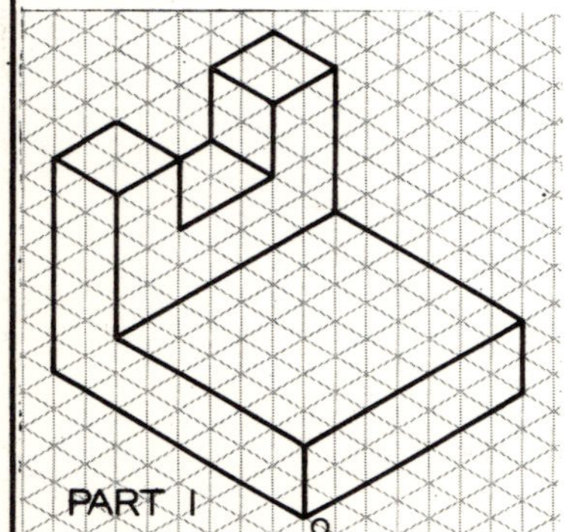

PART 1

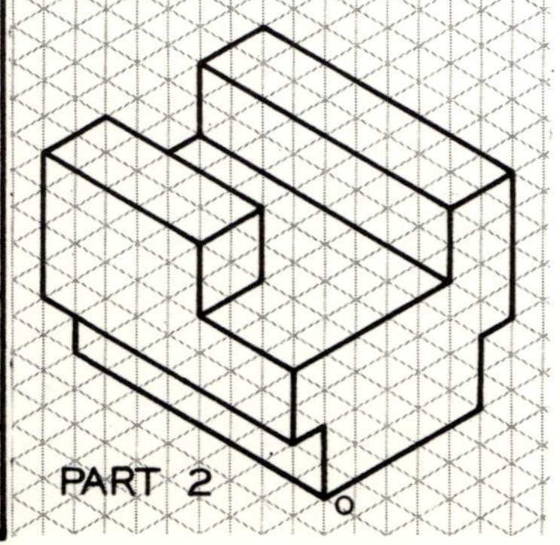

PART 2

O

Drafting & Design

NAME

FILE NO. SEC. DATE

grade

Drafting & Design

NAME

FILE NO SEC DATE

grade

ORTHOGRAPHIC VIEWS

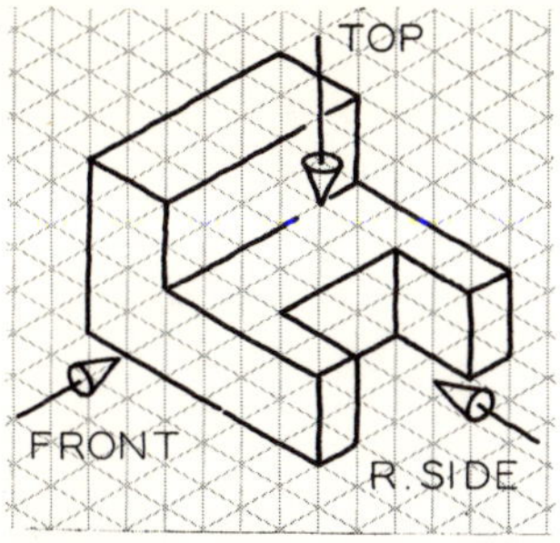

REQUIRED: DRAW THE TOP, FRONT AND RIGHT SIDE VIEWS OF THE PARTS GIVEN IN THE SPACE PROVIDED WITH INSTRUMENTS. TAKE THE DIMENSIONS FROM THE PICTORIALS WHERE EACH GRID DIVISION REPRESENTS 1/4". LABEL THE VIEWS AND SHOW DIMENSIONS W, D AND H.

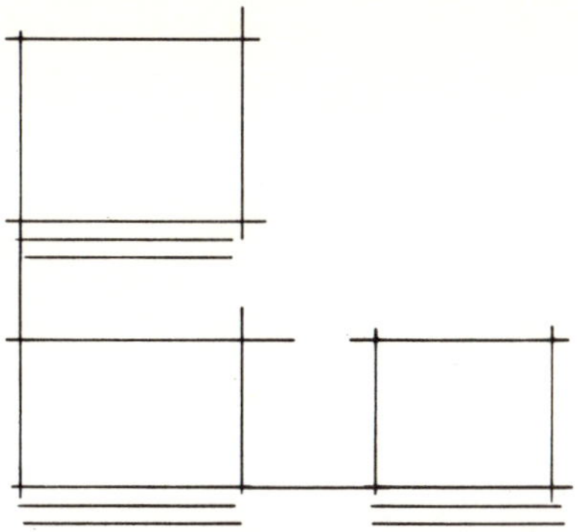

STEP 1: TO DRAW THREE VIEWS OF AN OBJECT SHOWN IN PICTORIAL, BEGIN BY BLOCKING IN THE OVERALL DIMENSIONS. LEAVE SPACE FOR DIMENSIONS AND LABELS BETWEEN THE VIEWS.

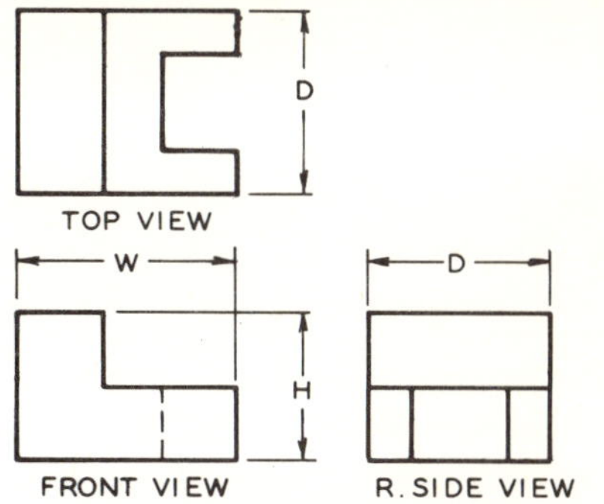

STEP 2: COMPLETE THE VIEWS AND STRENGTHEN THE LINES TO THE PROPER LINE WEIGHT. ADD LABELS AND DIMENSIONS W, D AND H. THESE VIEWS FULLY DESCRIBE THE OBJECT.

1

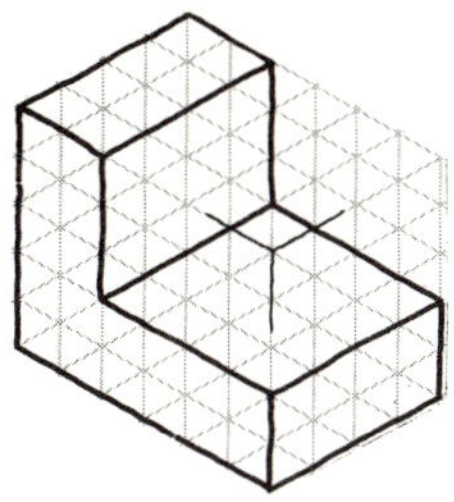

2

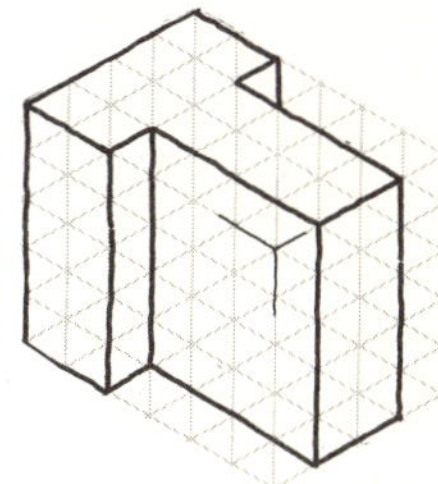

3

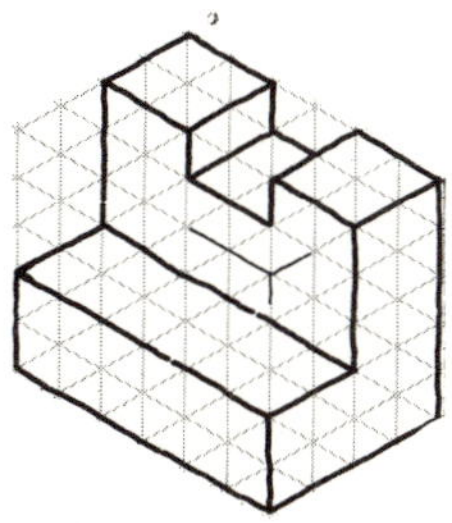

4

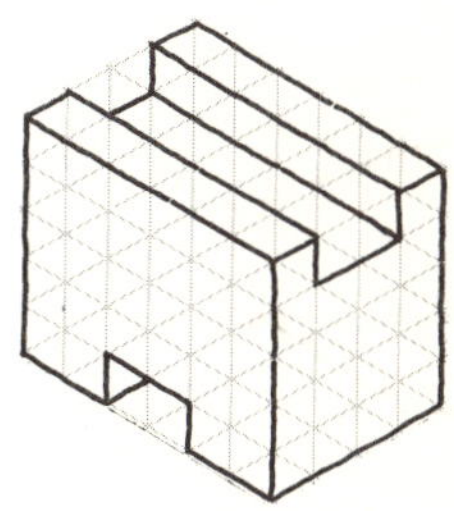

Drafting & Design

Drafting & Design © James H. Earle	NAME FILE NO SEC DATE	grade	

ORTHOGRAPHIC VIEWS

REQUIRED: DRAW THE TOP, FRONT AND RIGHT SIDE VIEWS OF THE PARTS IN THE SPACE PROVIDED USING INSTRUMENTS. TAKE THE DIMENSIONS FROM THE PICTORIALS WHERE EACH GRID DIVISION REPRESENTS 1/4". LABEL THE VIEWS AND SHOW THE OVERALL DIMENSIONS USING NUMERALS INSTEAD OF W, D AND H. FOR EXAMPLE, IF THE PART IS FIVE DIVISIONS WIDE IT IS 1-1/4" WIDE. OMIT INCH MARKS.

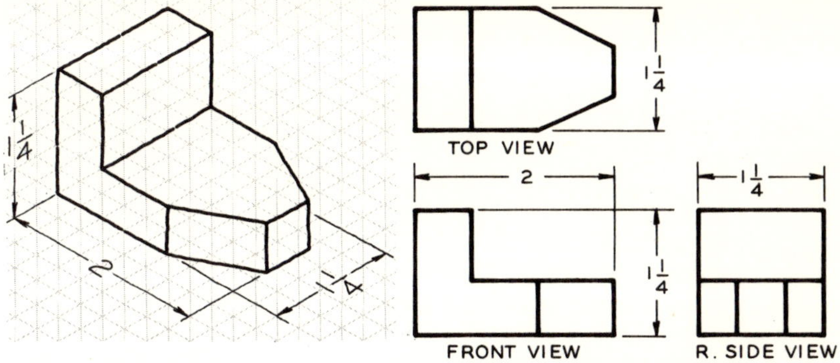

THREE ORTHOGRAPHIC VIEWS OF AN OBJECT CAN BE DRAWN FROM A PICTORIAL IF A PICTORIAL GRID IS USED TO REPRESENT DIMENSIONS. IN THIS CASE, THE GRID DIVISIONS REPRESENT 1/4" AND THESE UNITS ARE USED TO SIZE THE OBJECT AND TO DETERMINE THE OVERALL DIMENSIONS. EACH VIEW IS LABELED.

1

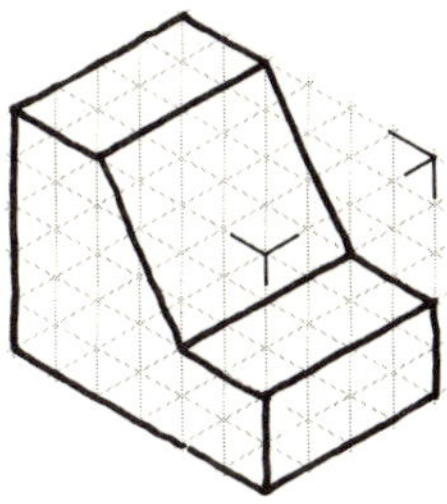

2

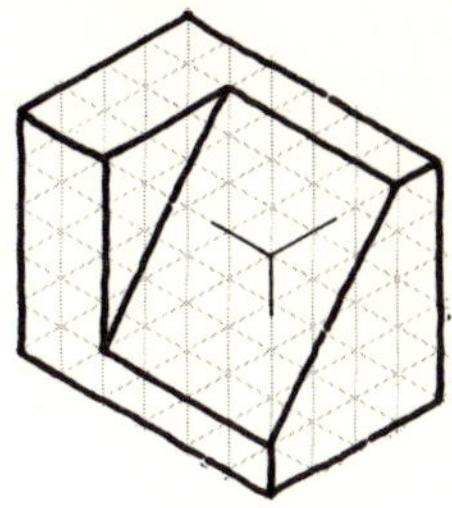

3

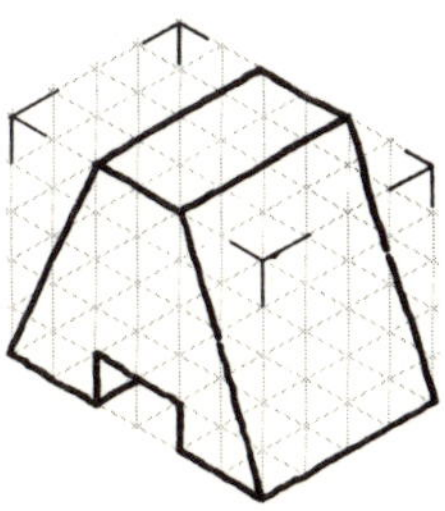

4

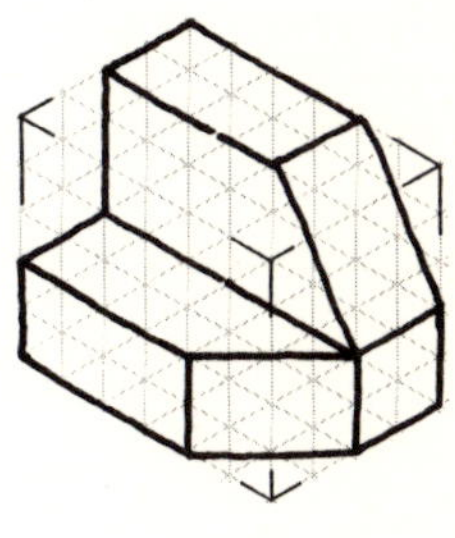

Drafting & Design

NAME

FILE NO SEC DATE

grade

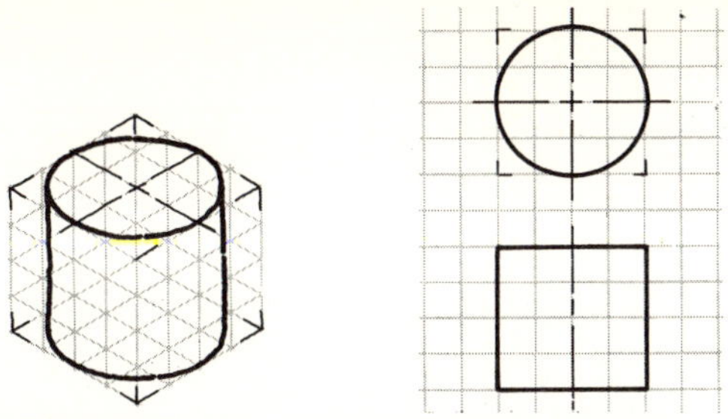

ORTHOGRAPHIC VIEWS

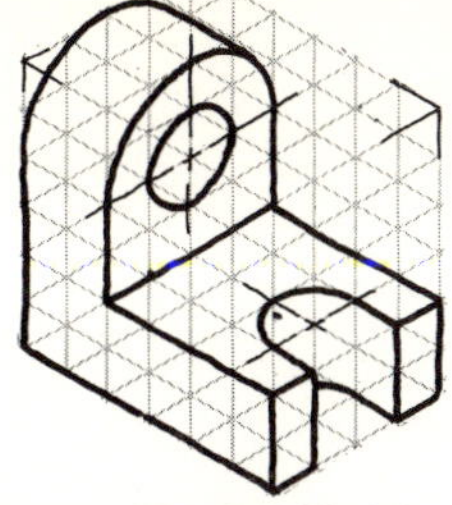

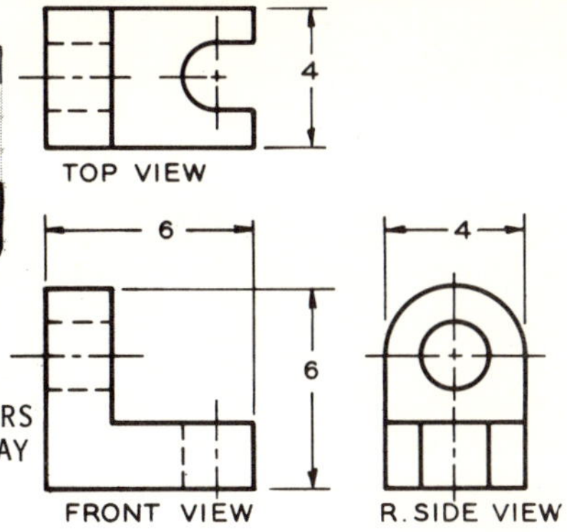

CENTERLINES ARE USED IN BOTH CIRCULAR AND RECTANGULAR VIEWS OF CYLINDERS. CROSSING CENTERLINES LOCATE THE CENTER IN THE CIRCULAR VIEW AND A SINGLE CENTERLINE LOCATES THE AXIS OF CYLINDERS IN THE RECTANGULAR VIEW.

CENTERLINES ARE HELPFUL IN ORTHOGRAPHIC PROJECTION TO REPRESENT CYLINDRICAL FEATURES. THESE ARE USED WHETHER THE CYLINDERS ARE HOLES OR SOLID SHAPES. CENTERLINES MAY BE OMITTED IF THEY CONFUSE A DRAWING.

REQUIRED: DRAW THE TOP, FRONT AND RIGHT SIDE VIEWS OF THE PARTS IN THE SPACE PROVIDED USING INSTRUMENTS. TAKE THE DIMENSIONS FROM THE PICTORIALS WHERE EACH GRID REPRESENTS 1/4". LABEL THE VIEWS AND SHOW THE OVERALL DIMENSIONS USING NUMERALS INSTEAD OF W, D AND H. FOR EXAMPLE, IF THE PART IS FIVE DIVISIONS WIDE IT IS 1-1/4" WIDE.

1

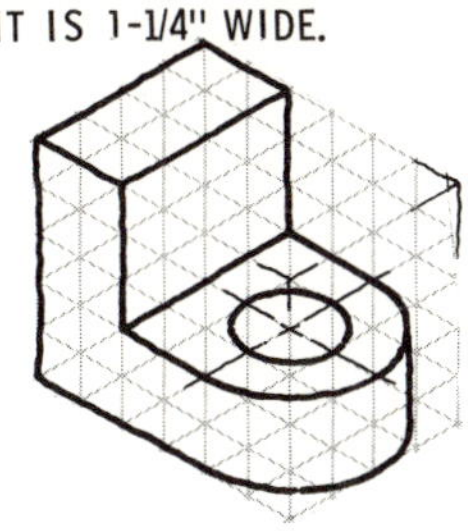

2

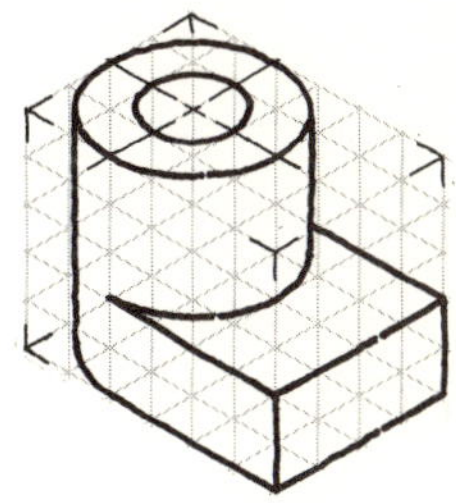

3

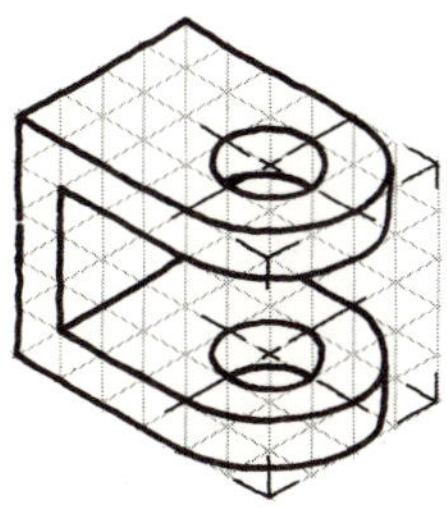

4

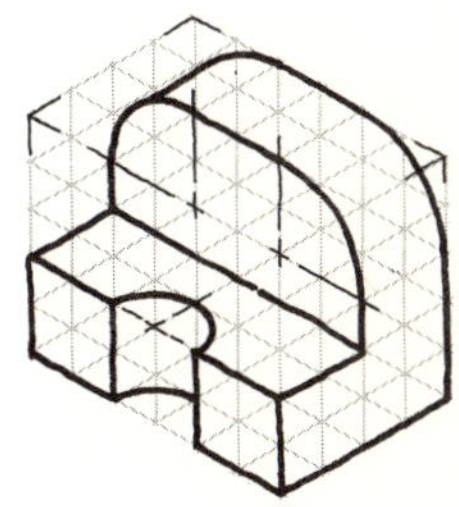

Drafting & Design

NAME

FILE NO SEC DATE

grade

TECHNIQUES OF HANDLING INTERSECTING LINES ARE SHOWN AT THE RIGHT AND IN THE ENLARGED EXAMPLES AT THE FAR RIGHT. THESE EXAMPLES ARE SUGGESTED BY DRAFTING STANDARDS.

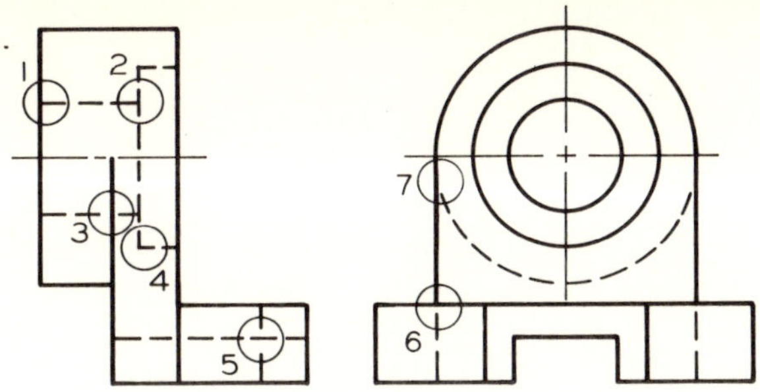

LINE INTERSECTIONS

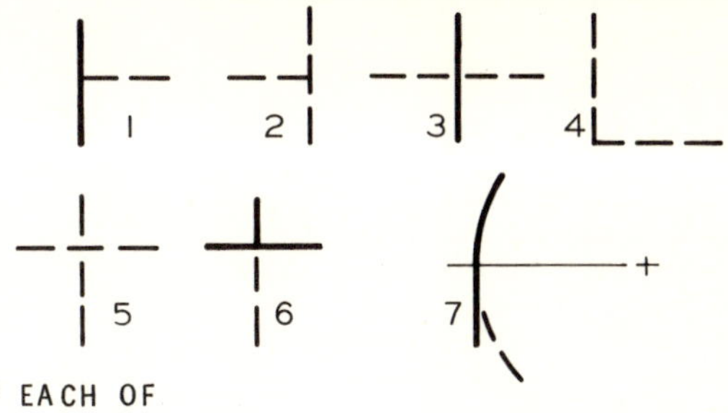

REQUIRED: COMPLETE THE THREE VIEWS OF EACH OF THE OBJECTS SHOWN BELOW AND APPLY THE TECHNIQUES OF LINE INTERSECTIONS.

1 YOKE

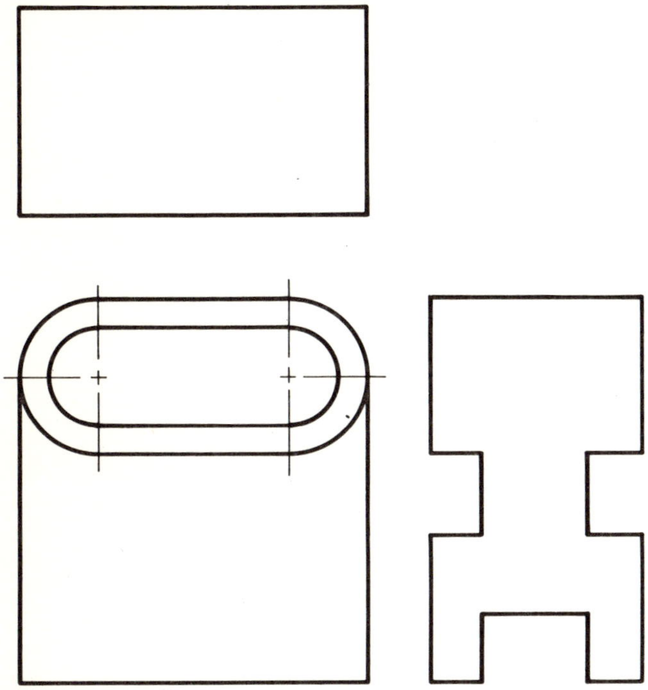

2 SIDE ANGLE

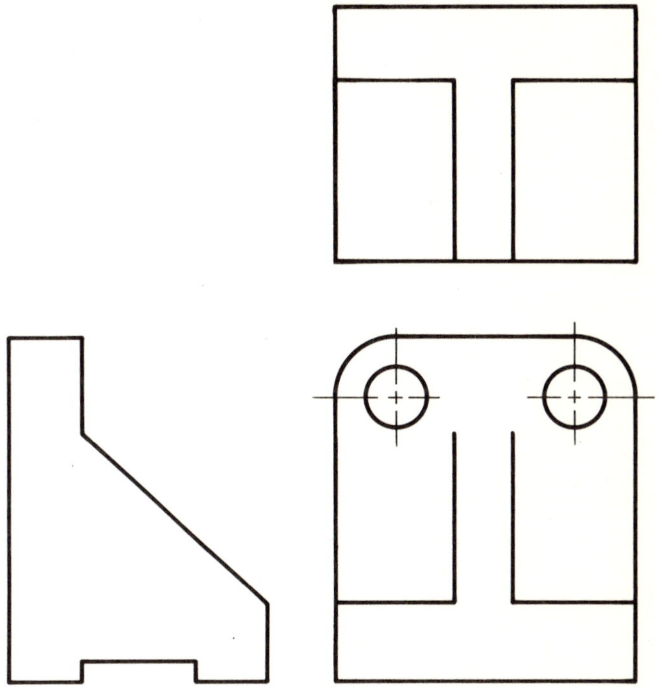

3 CLEVIS

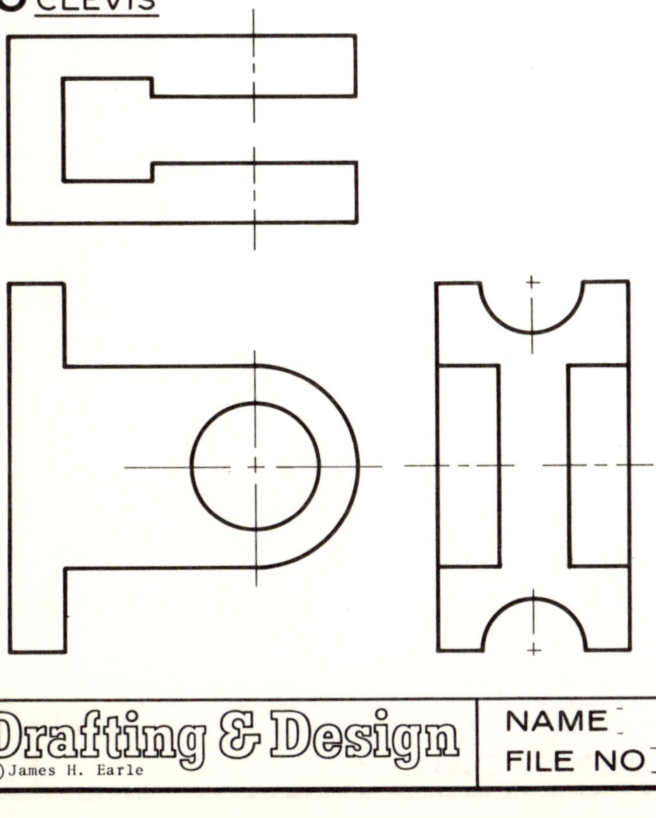

4 BEARING

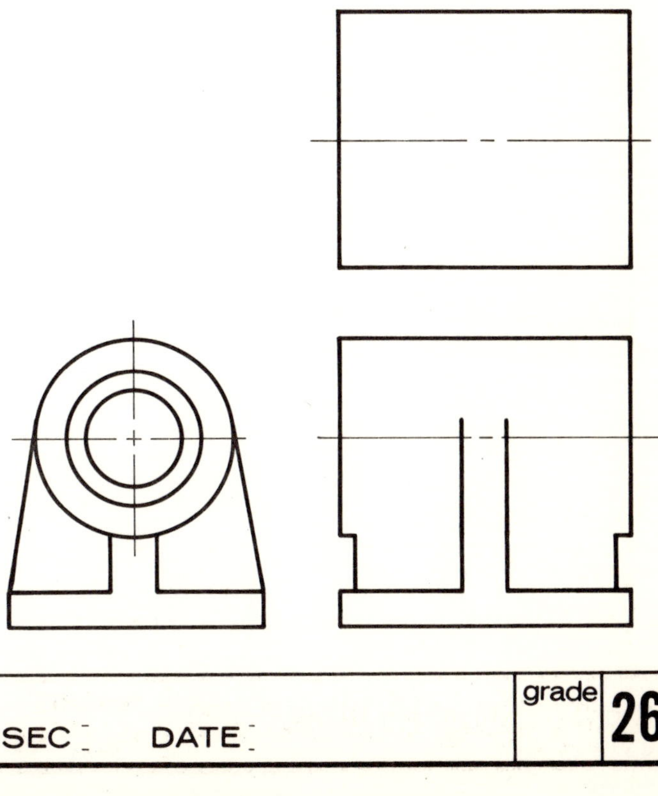

Drafting & Design

NAME

FILE NO SEC DATE

grade

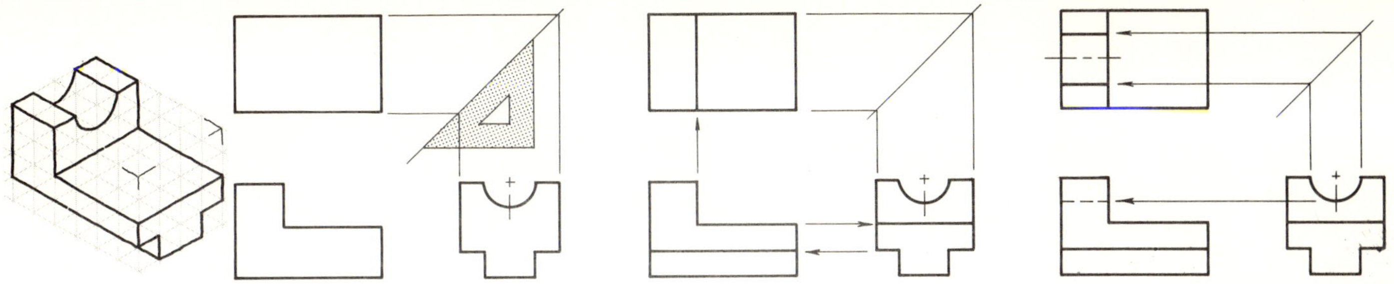

STEP 1: THREE VIEWS OF AN OBJECT SHOULD BE DEVELOPED TOGETHER TO ADD MISSING LINES.

STEP 2: LINES IN EACH VIEW ARE FOUND BY PROJECTING FROM ADJACENT VIEWS.

STEP 3: THE TOP AND FRONT VIEWS ARE COMPLETED TO FINISH THE THREE-VIEW DRAWING.

REQUIRED: COMPLETE THE VIEWS OF THE OBJECTS. LINES MAY BE MISSING IN EACH OF THE VIEWS. NOTICE THAT PROBLEMS 2 AND 4 HAVE LEFT SIDE VIEWS INSTEAD OF RIGHT SIDE VIEWS.

SLIDER

1

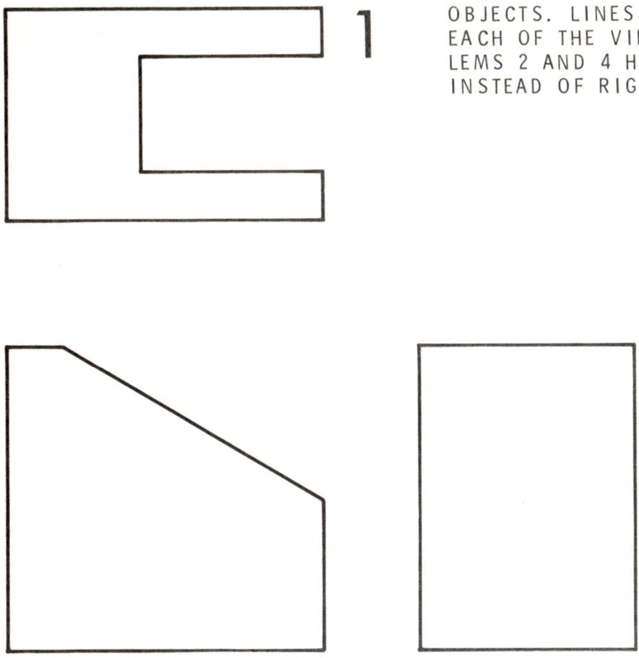

SEPARATOR

2

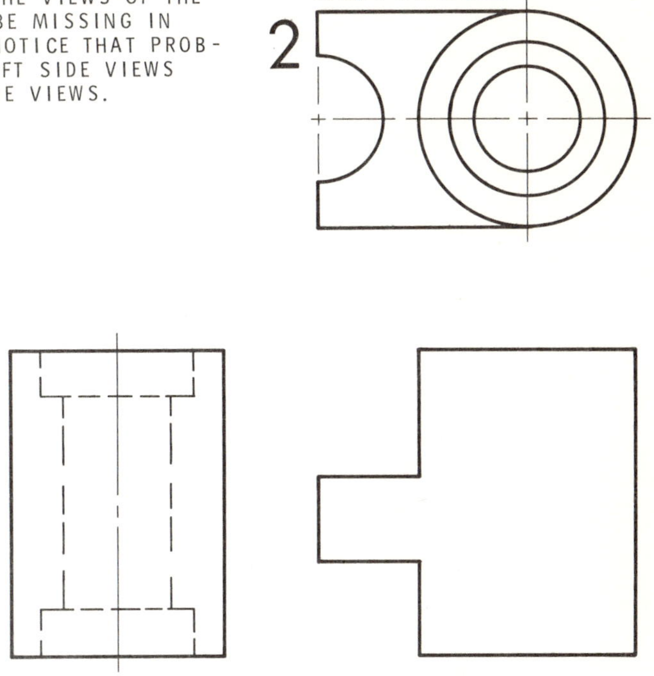

LIFT BLOCK

3

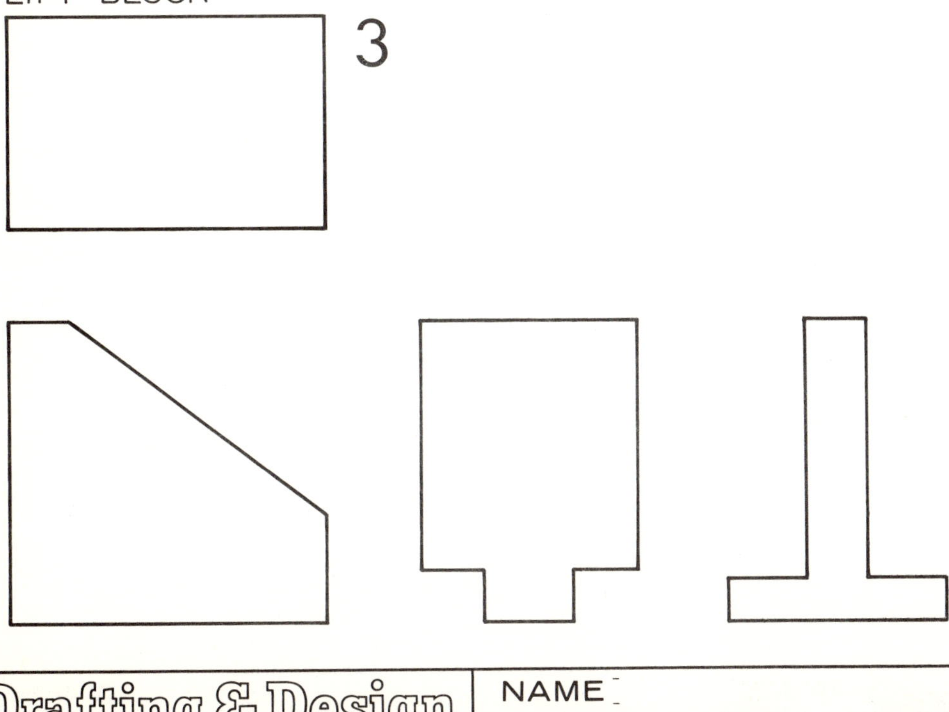

HASP PIECE

4

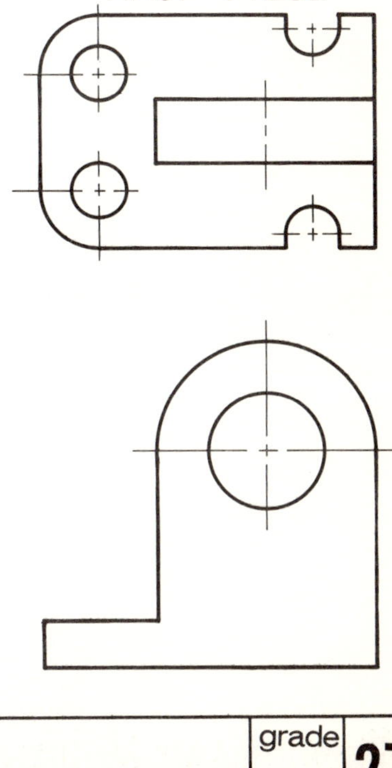

Drafting & Design
© James H. Earle

NAME
FILE NO SEC DATE
grade

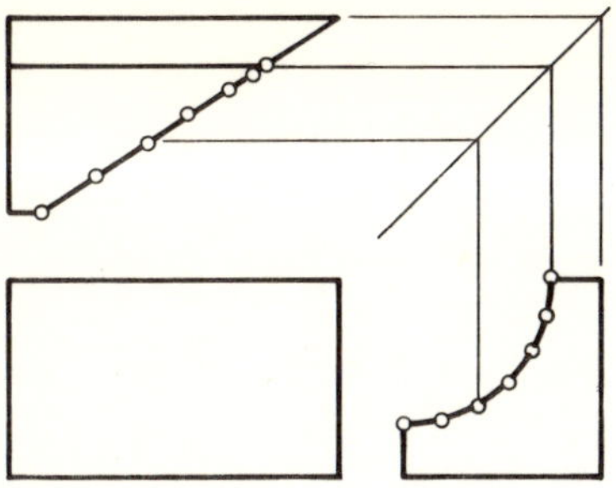

STEP 1: TO COMPLETE THE FRONT VIEWS OF THE CURVE, POINTS ARE PROJECTED FROM THE SIDE VIEW TO THE TOP VIEW.

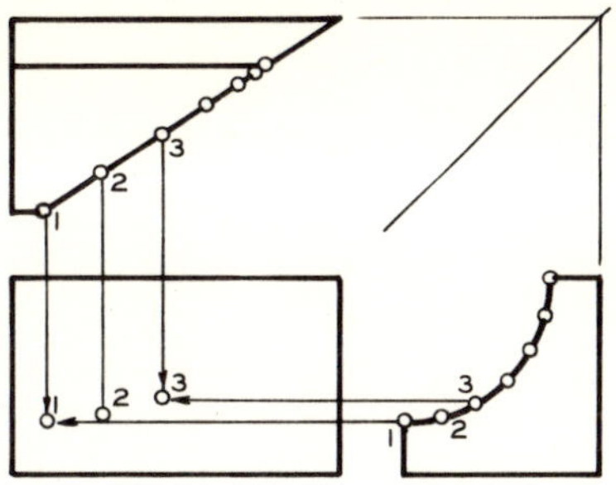

STEP 2: THE TOP AND SIDE VIEWS OF THESE POINTS ARE LOCATED IN THE FRONT VIEW BY PROJECTION.

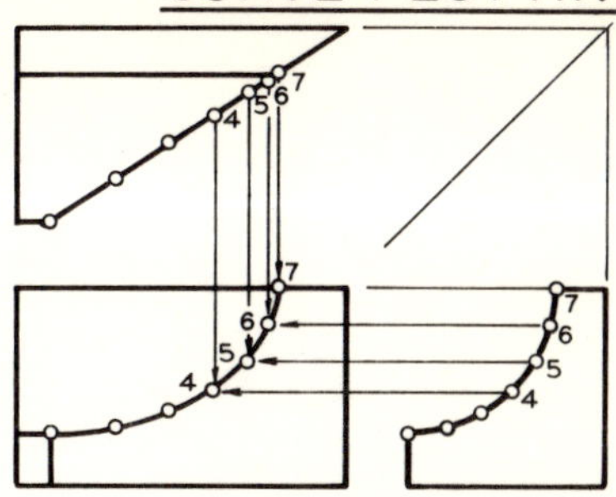

STEP 3: THE REMAINING POINTS ARE LOCATED IN THE SAME MANNER AND ARE CONNECTED TO COMPLETE THE VIEWS.

REQUIRED: COMPLETE THE TOP VIEW OF THE PART BY PROJECTING FROM THE FRONT AND RIGHT SIDE VIEWS.

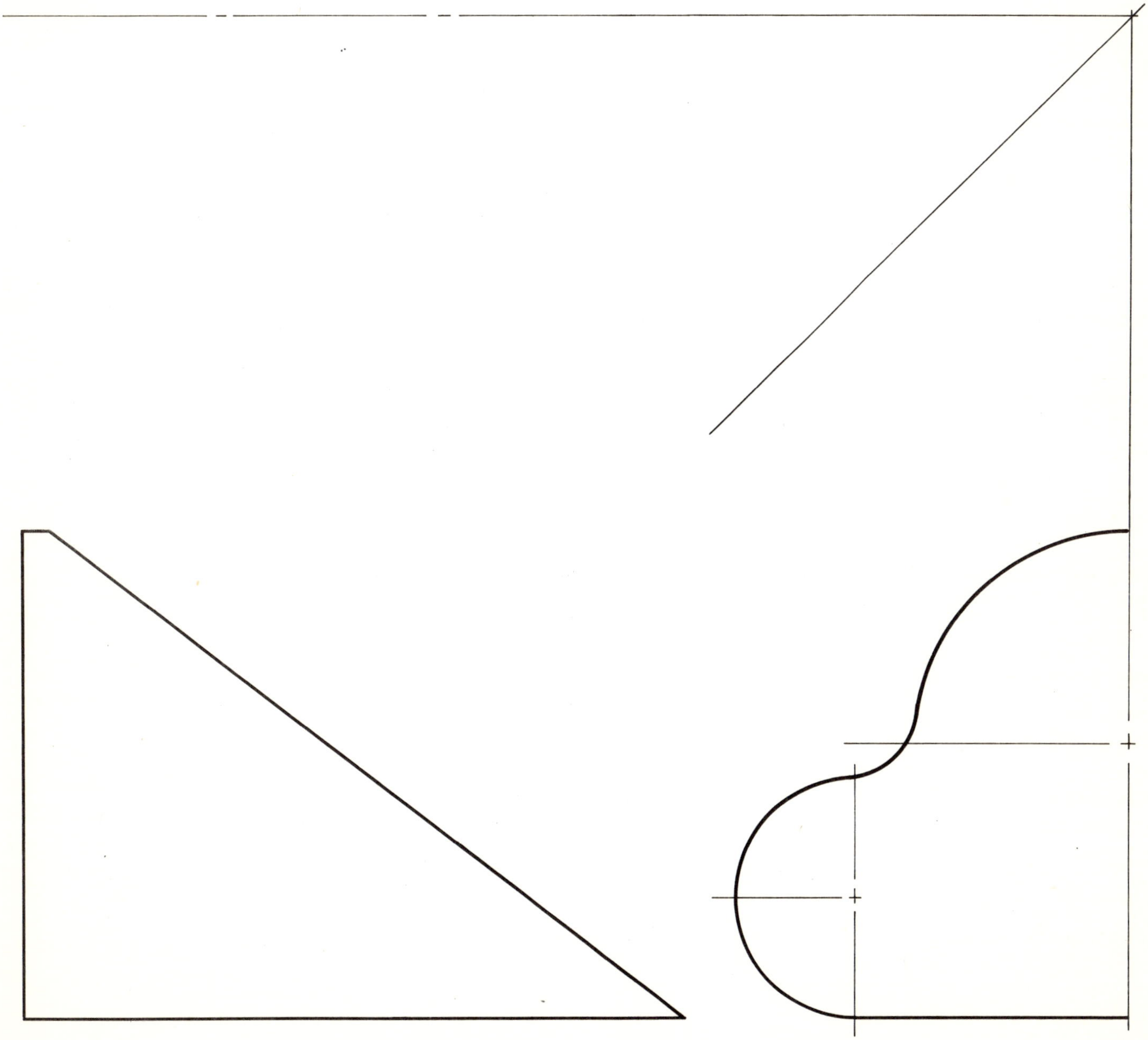

Drafting & Design

NAME

FILE NO SEC DATE

grade

FILLETS & ROUNDS

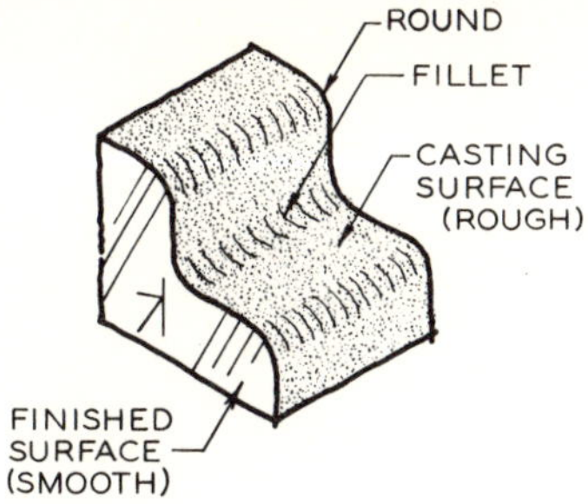

MOST CASTINGS HAVE FILLETS AND ROUNDS INSTEAD OF SHARP CORNERS.

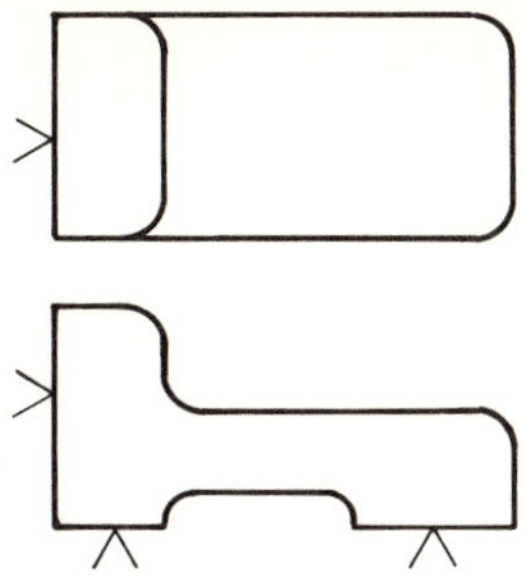

REPRESENTATION OF FILLETS AND ROUNDS IN ORTHOGRAPHIC VIEWS.

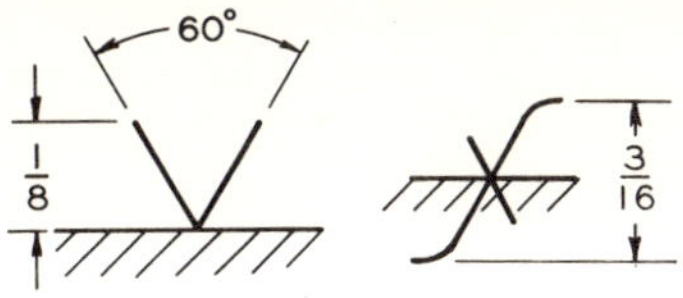

TWO TYPES OF FINISH MARKS THAT ARE PLACED ON THE EDGE VIEWS OF SURFACES THAT ARE TO BE MACHINED. THESE ARE REPEATED ON EACH VIEW OF THE EDGE WHETHER THE EDGE IS VISIBLE OR HIDDEN.

Courtesy of Lear Siegler, Inc.

REQUIRED: COMPLETE THE GIVEN VIEWS AND THE TOP VIEWS USING THE FRONT AND SIDE VIEWS THAT ARE GIVEN.

1

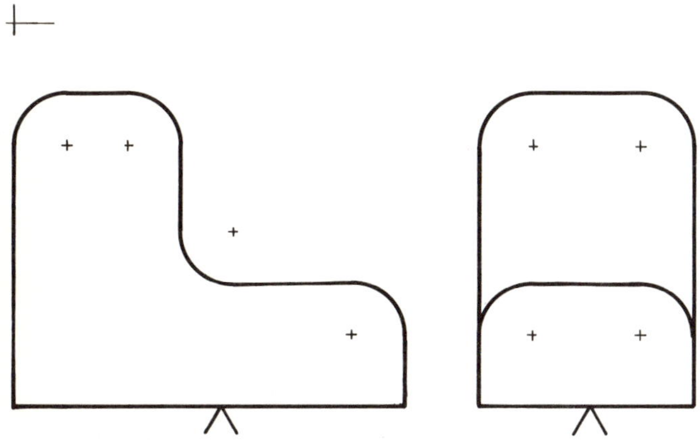

2

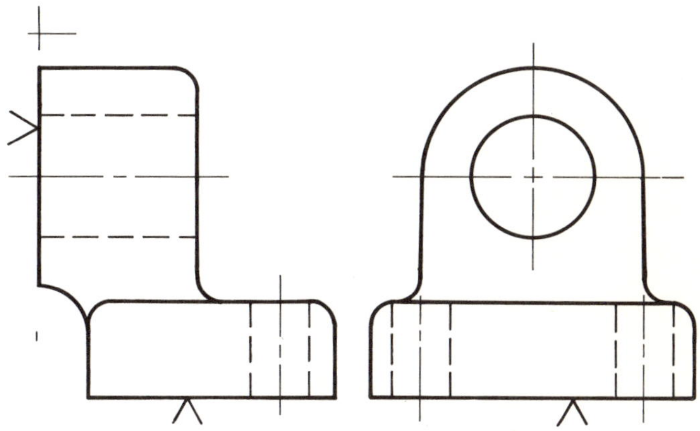

3

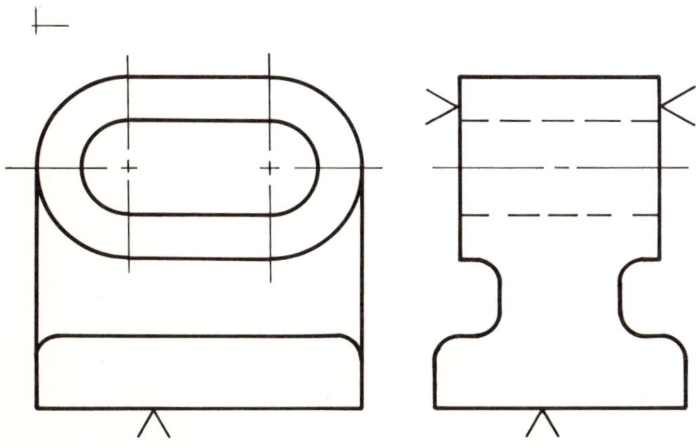

4

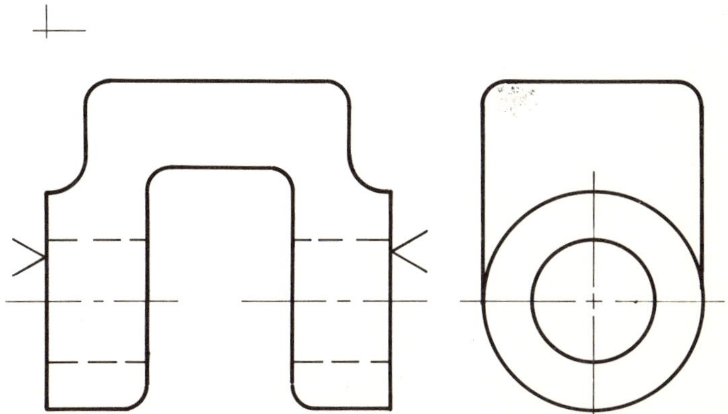

Drafting & Design © James H. Earle	NAME FILE NO SEC DATE	grade	

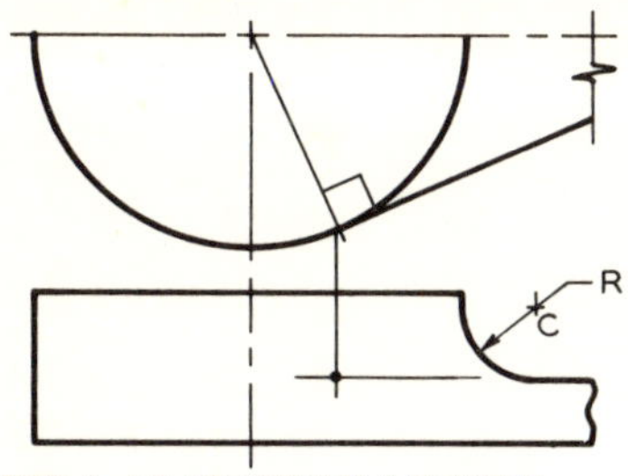

STEP 1: TO CONSTRUCT A RUNOUT WHERE A FILLET INTERSECTS A CYLINDER, THE POINT OF TANGENCY IS PROJECTED TO THE FRONT VIEW.

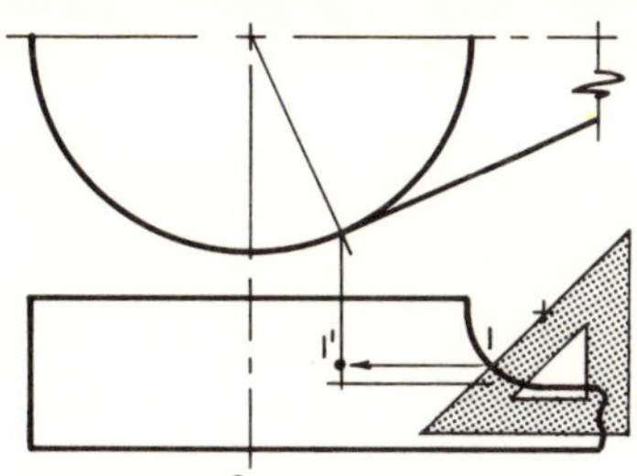

STEP 2: A 45° LINE IS DRAWN THROUGH THE FILLET'S CENTER TO LOCATE POINT 1 AND THEN POINT 1'.

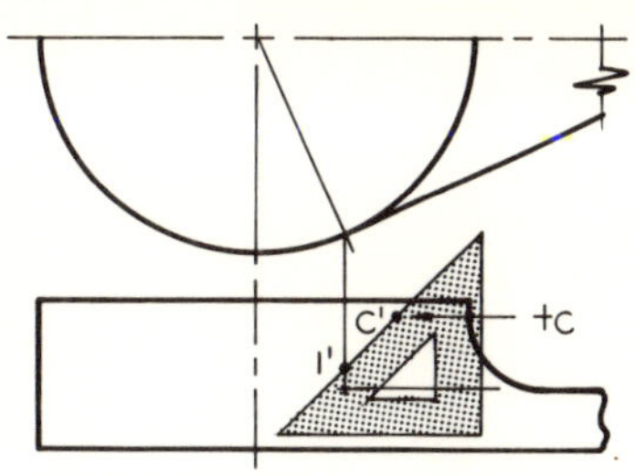

STEP 3: THE CENTER, C, OF THE RUNOUT IS FOUND BY PROJECTING FROM 1' AT 45° TO THE HORIZONTAL PROJECTOR THROUGH C.

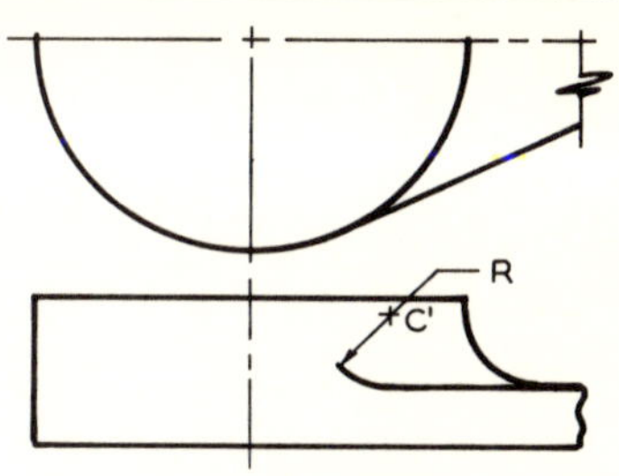

STEP 4: THE GIVEN RADIUS, R, IS USED TO CONSTRUCT THE RUNOUT FROM 1' USING CENTER C'.

1

REQUIRED: CONSTRUCT THE FOUR RUNOUTS IN THE FRONT VIEW OF THE CONNECTOR ARM.

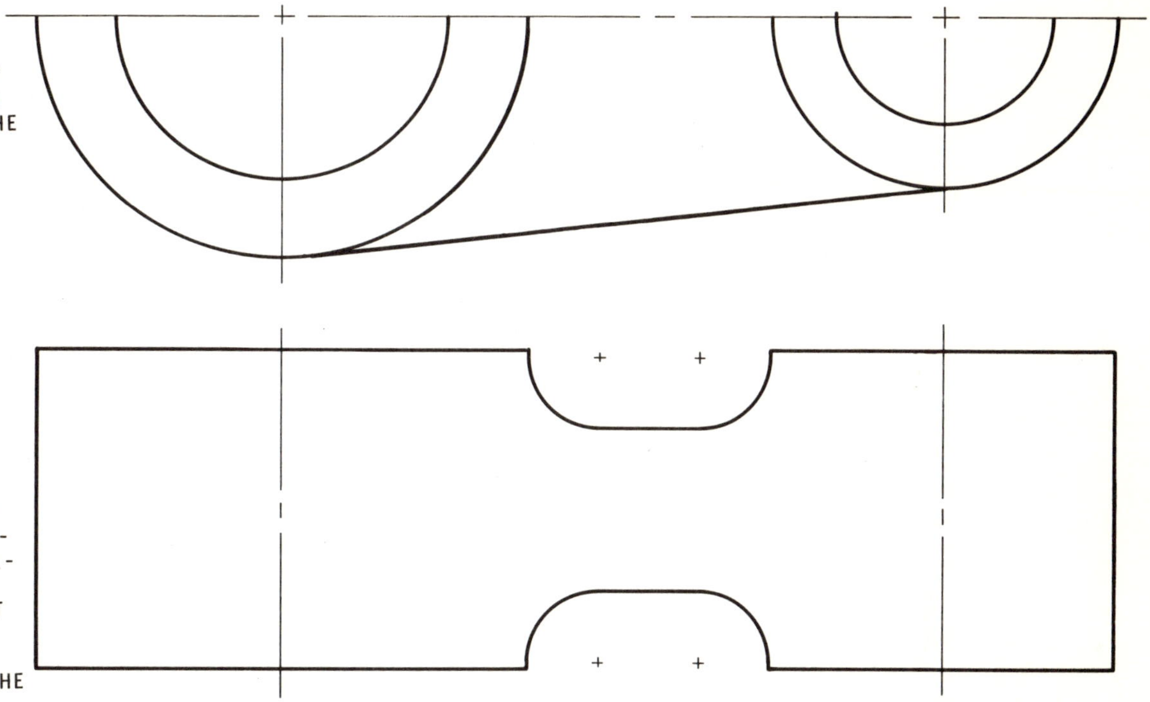

2

REQUIRED: CONSTRUCT THE FOUR RUNOUTS RESULTING FROM THE FILLETS AT THE LOWER SURFACE IN THE FRONT VIEW. THE RADIUS OF THE FILLET FOR THE LOWER SURFACE HAS THE SAME RADIUS AS THE UPPER SURFACE.

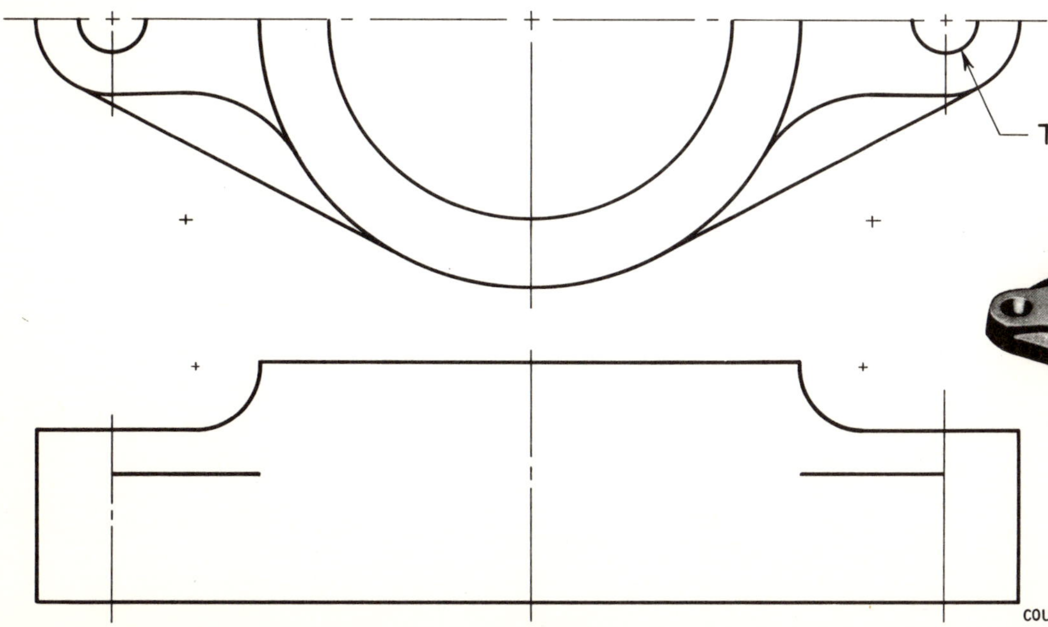

courtesy of Stephens-Adamson Mfg. Co.

Drafting & Design © James H. Earle	NAME FILE NO SEC DATE	grade	

CONVENTIONAL INTERSECTIONS

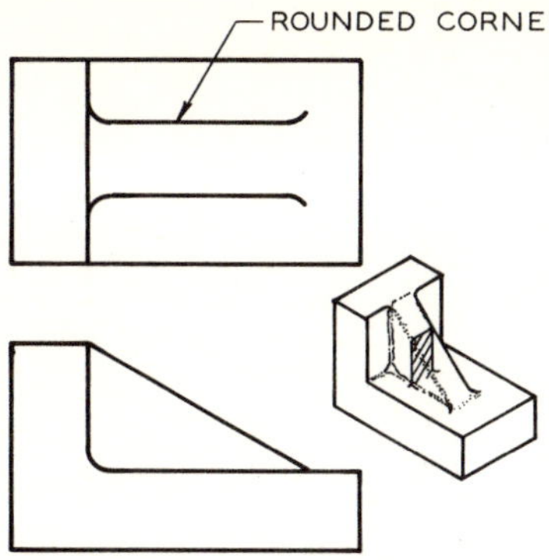

A RIB WITH ROUNDED CORNERS.

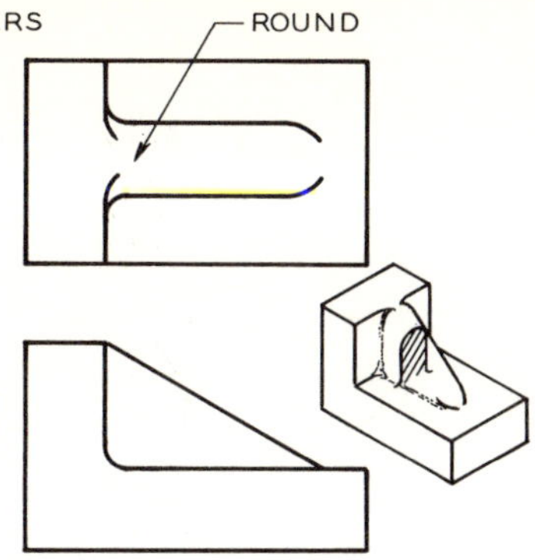

A RIB THAT IS COMPLETELY ROUND.

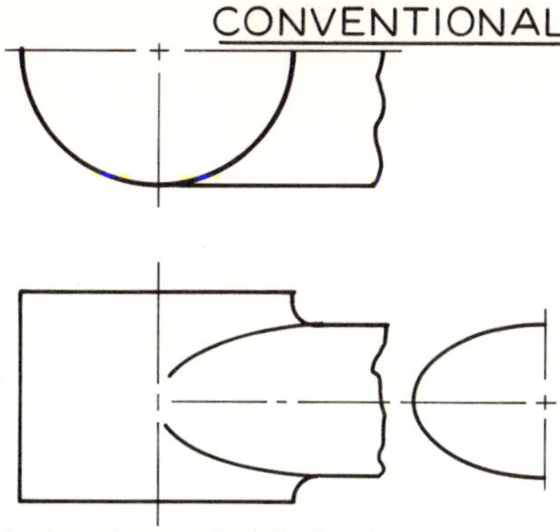

INTERSECTION BETWEEN A CY- LINDER AND AN ELLLPTICAL PART.

Courtesy of Stephens-Adamson Mfg. Co.

REQUIRED: COMPLETE THE VIEWS OF THE OBJECTS APPLYING THE PRINCIPLES COVERED ABOVE.

BASE

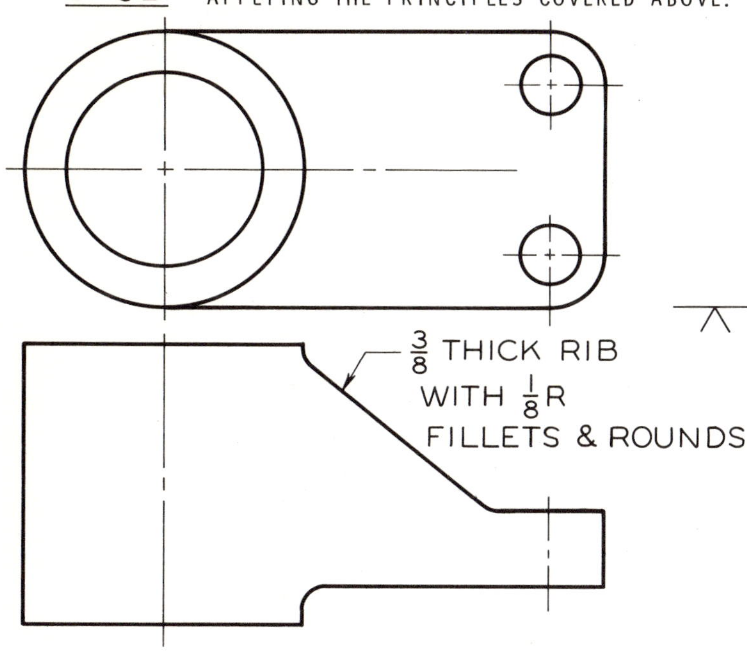

END BRACKET

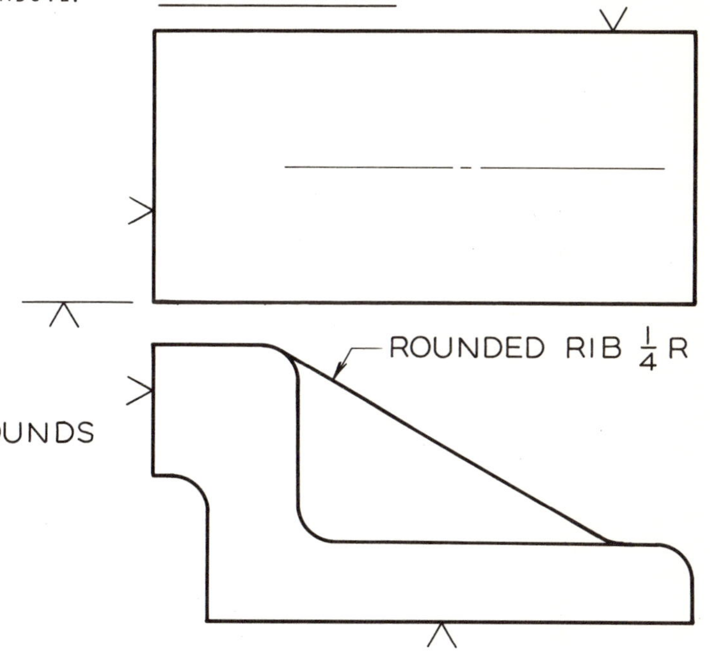

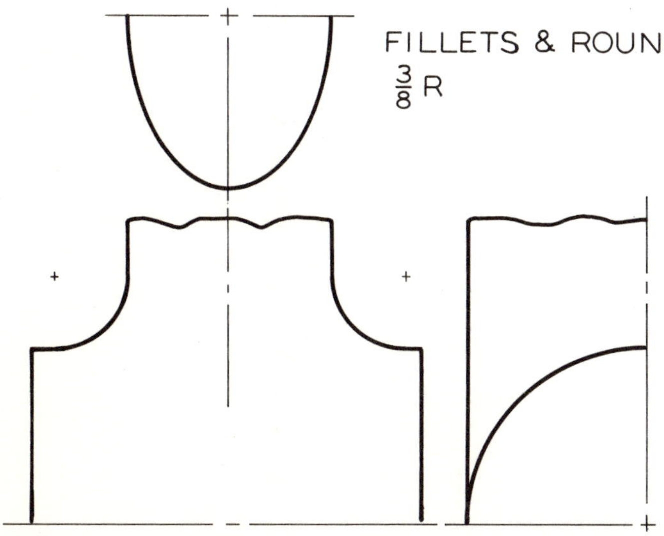

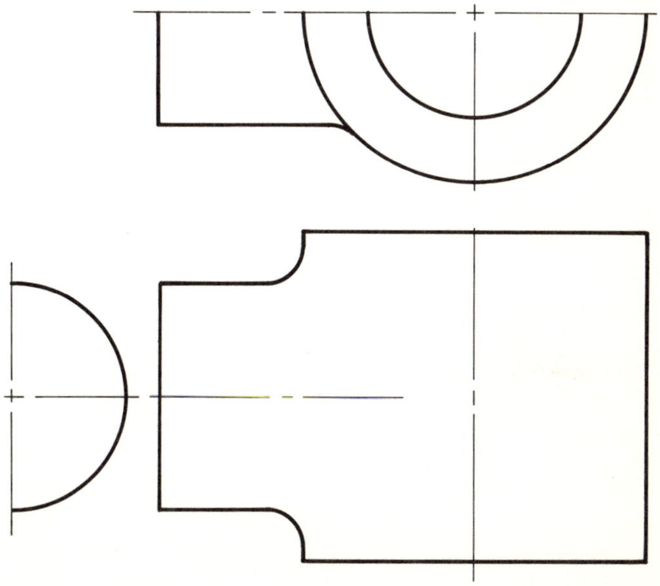

Drafting & Design
© James H. Earle

NAME
FILE NO SEC DATE
grade

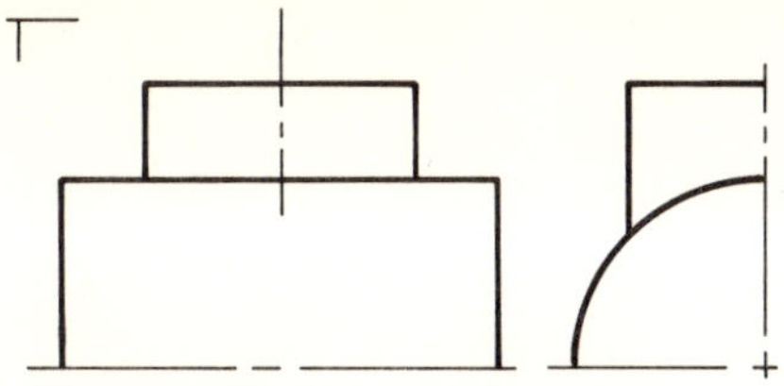

INTERSECTION OF A SMALL CYLINDER WITH A LARGER CYLINDER.

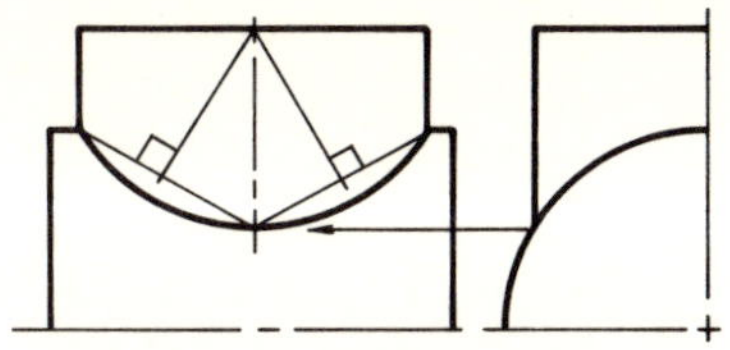

INTERSECTION BETWEEN A MEDIUM-SIZED CYLINDER AND A LARGER ONE.

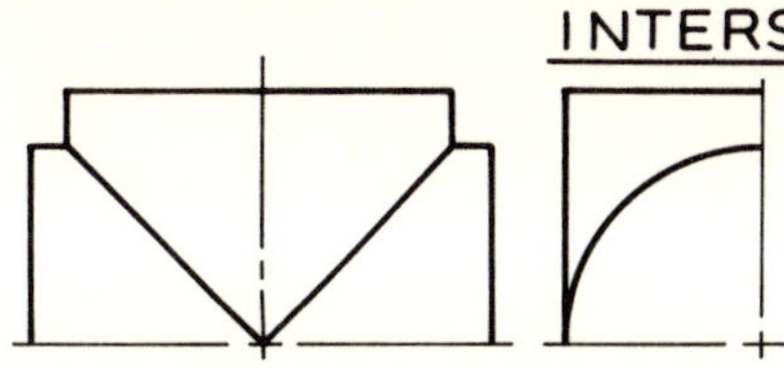

INTERSECTION BETWEEN EQUAL-SIZED CYLINDERS.

REQUIRED: COMPLETE THE VIEWS USING CONVENTIONAL INTERSECTIONS.

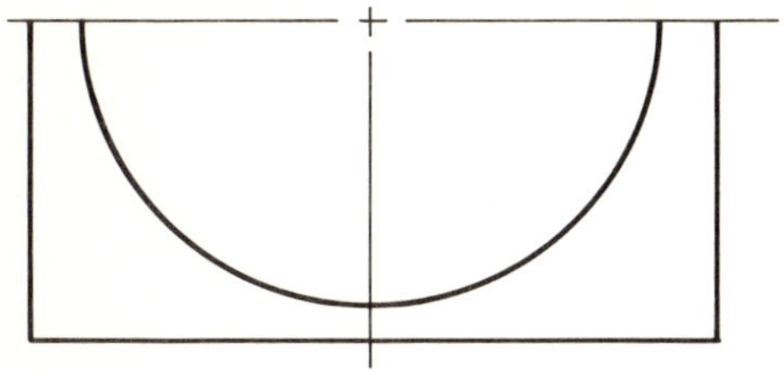

1

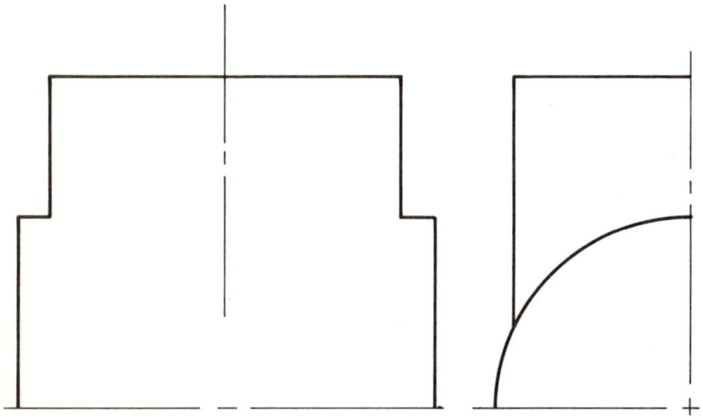

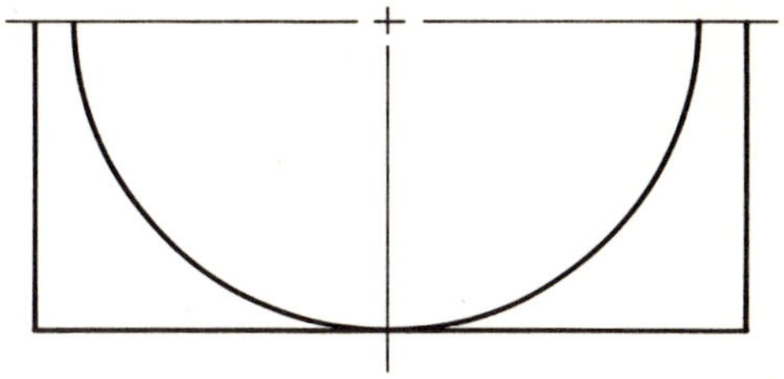

2

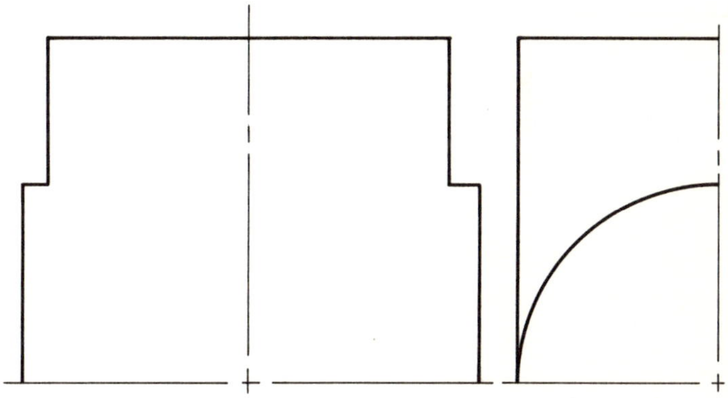

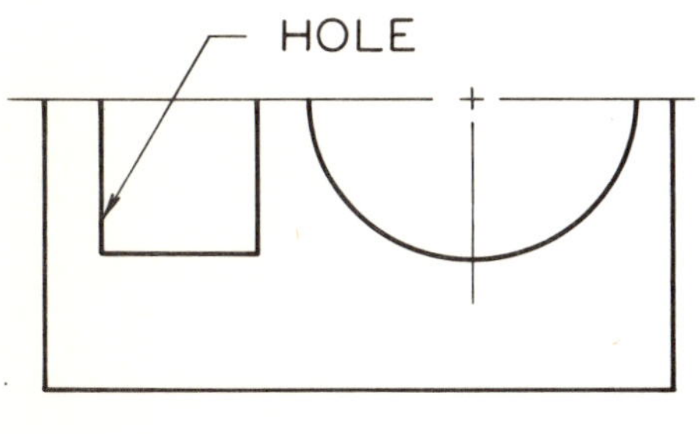

3

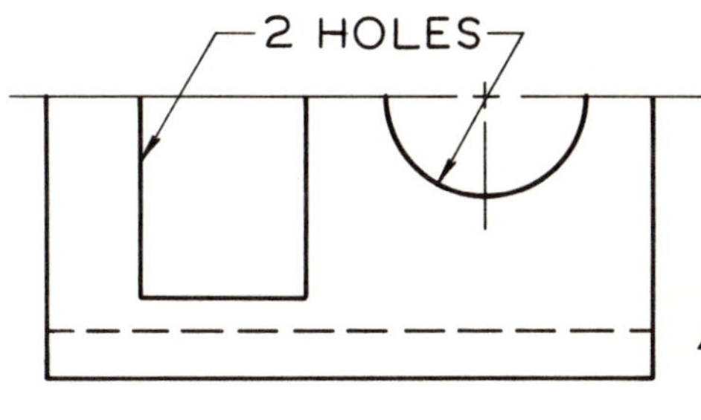

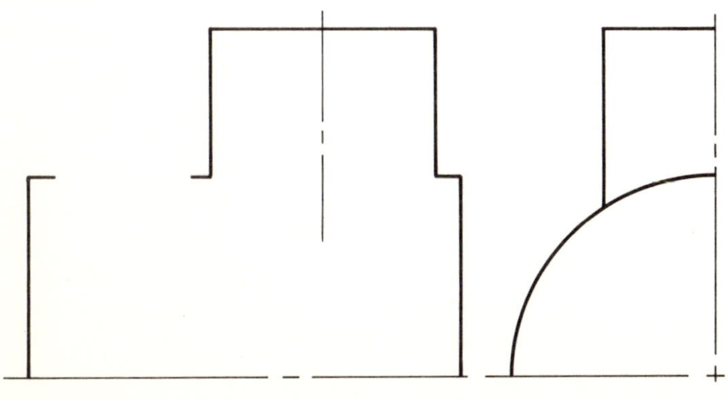

4

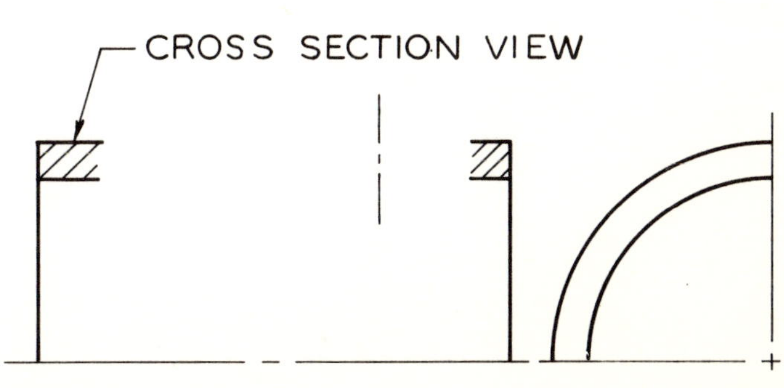

NAME
FILE NO. SEC. DATE.
grade

Drafting & Design © James H. Earle	NAME FILE NO SEC DATE	grade	

THE ENGINEER AND TECHNICIAN MUST DEVELOP AN ABILITY TO SKETCH IDEAS TO IMPROVE COMMUNICATION. SKETCHES OF THE THREE PARTS ARE GIVEN AS EXAMPLES. USING AN F OR HB PENCIL, SKETCH EACH OF THESE TWICE -- ONCE ON THE GRID AND ONCE AT THE RIGHT WITHOUT THE GRID. STRIVE TO KEEP THE SAME PROPORTIONS AND LINE WEIGHTS AS GIVEN IN THE EXAMPLES.

1 ANGLE

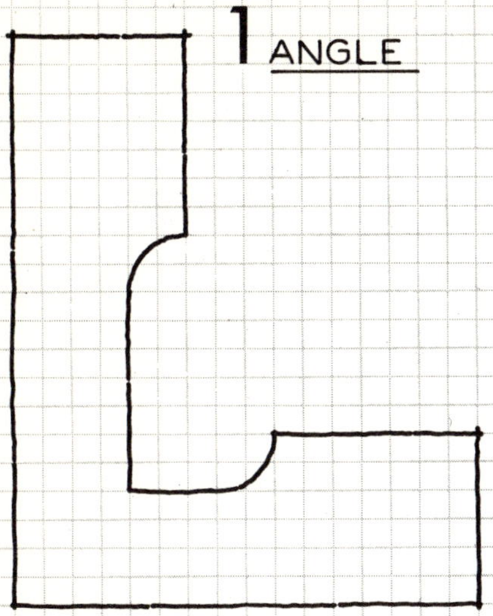

2 BEARING

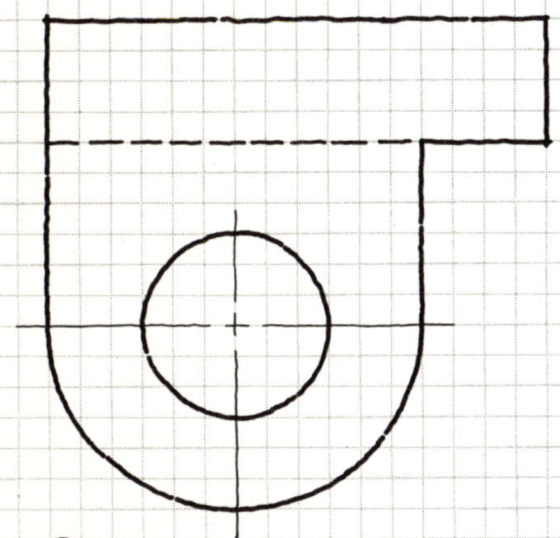

3 LEVER

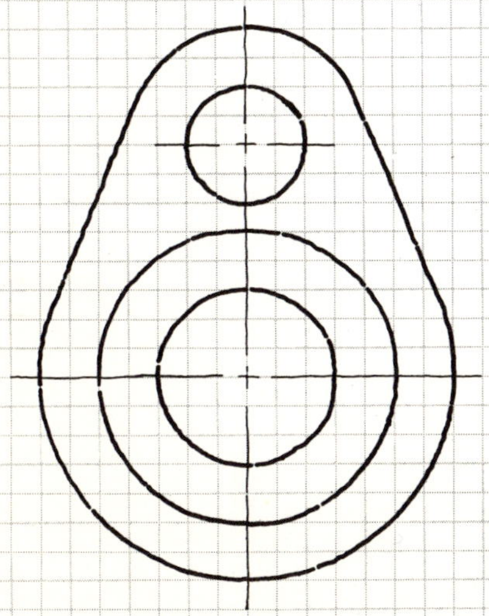

NAME

FILE NO SEC DATE

grade

Drafting & Design

NAME

FILE NO SEC DATE

grade

PICTORIAL SKETCHING IS AN EFFECTIVE MEANS OF HELPING YOU VISUALIZE AN OBJECT THAT YOU ARE DRAWING OR DESIGNING. THE EXAMPLE AT THE RIGHT IS EASIER TO UNDERSTAND IN PICTORIAL FORM AND CONSEQUENTLY, IT IS EASIER FOR YOU TO COMPLETE THE ORTHOGRAPHIC VIEWS OF THE OBJECT.

REQUIRED: USING THE GIVEN, PARTIAL VIEWS, CONSTRUCT ISOMETRIC PICTORIALS AND SKETCH THE MISSING ORTHOGRAPHIC VIEWS.

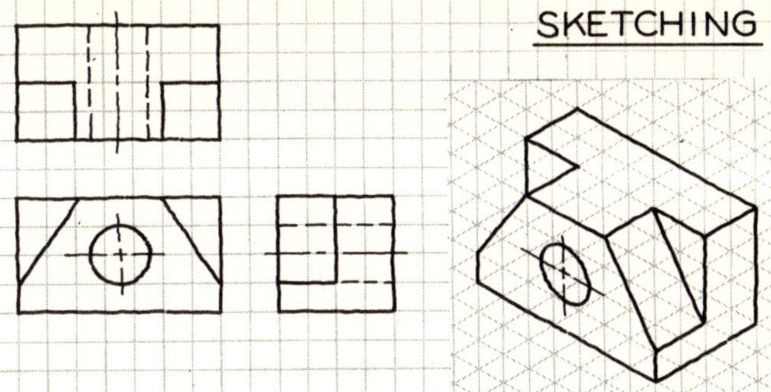

1

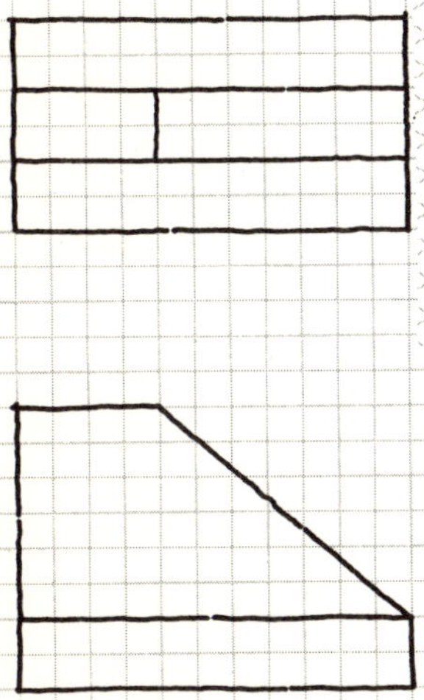

2

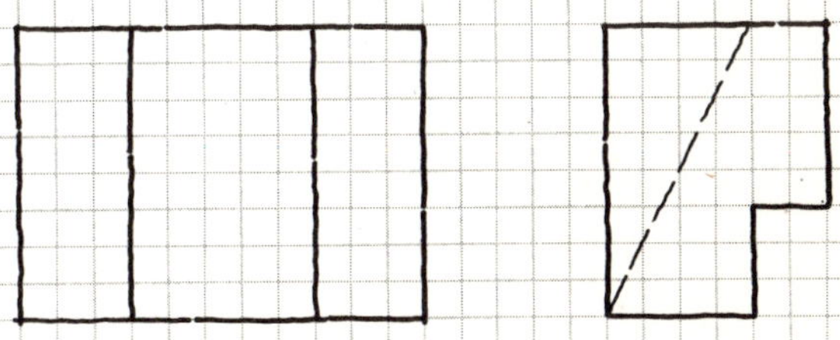

3

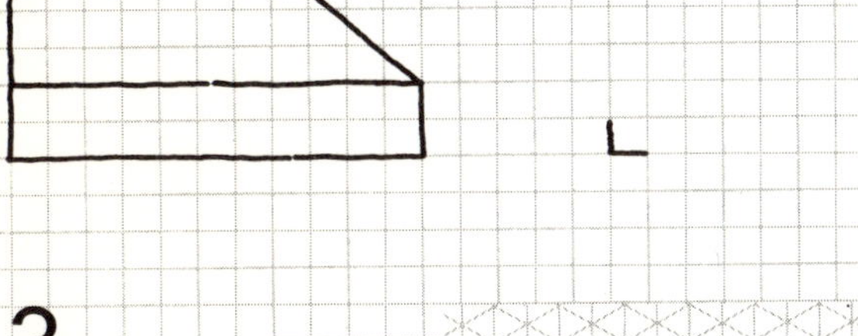

4

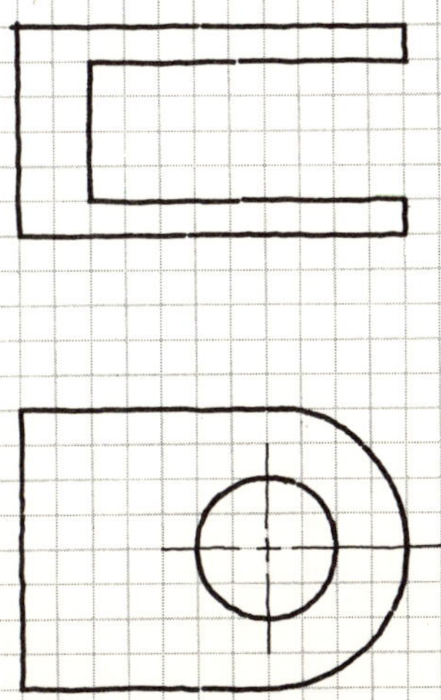

Drafting & Design

NAME

FILE NO SEC DATE

grade

Drafting & Design © James H. Earle	NAME FILE NO SEC DATE	grade	

THE TECHNICIAN AND ENGINEER MUST BE ABLE TO DESCRIBE HIS IDEAS TO HIS ASSOCIATES AND THOSE WHO WILL ASSIST HIM IN DEVELOPING THESE IDEAS. FREEHAND SKETCHING IS A MAJOR METHOD USED IN COMMUNICATION. ORTHOGRAPHIC VIEWS ARE USED TO ILLUSTRATE A PART IN TERMS FAMILIAR TO THOSE ACCUSTOMED TO USING WORKING DRAWINGS.

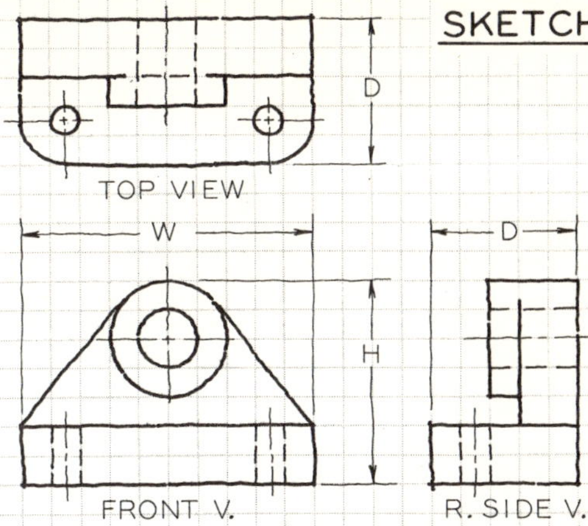

REQUIRED:
SKETCH THREE VIEWS OF THE PARTS BELOW. APPROXIMATE THEIR PROPORTIONS BY EYE. LABEL THE VIEWS AND SHOW OVERALL DIMENSIONS H, W & D.

1 STRAP

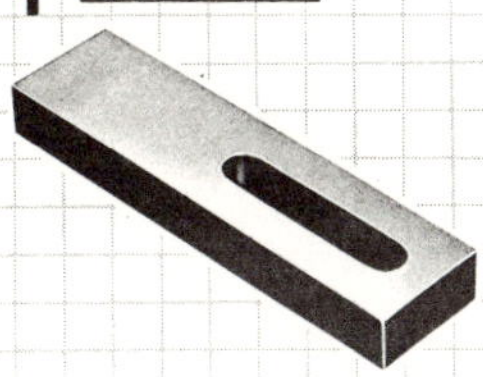

2 REST PAD

3 FIXTURE BASE

4 ANGLE PLATE

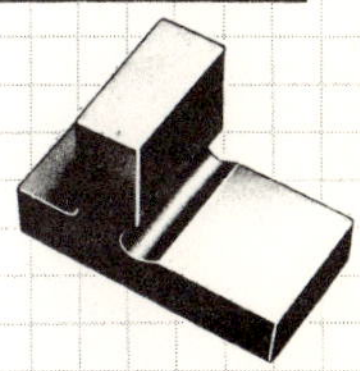

Drafting & Design ©James H. Earle	NAME FILE NO SEC DATE	grade	35

Drafting & Design
©James H. Earle

NAME	grade	
FILE NO SEC DATE		

THE DESIGNER MUST MAKE MANY FREEHAND SKETCHES OF HIS IDEAS -- BOTH ORTHOGRAPHIC AND PICTORIAL SKETCHES. MOST PROBLEMS HAVE AN UNLIMITED NUMBER OF SOLUTIONS, BUT MOST SOLUTIONS HAVE MANY FEATURES IN COMMON SINCE THE FINAL DESIGN MUST SATISFY THE SAME REQUIREMENTS. THE DESIGNER FIRST SKETCHES TO COMMUNICATE WITH HIMSELF AND THEN WITH OTHERS.

REQUIRED:
ON SEPARATE SHEETS, MAKE A NUMBER OF SKETCHES OF YOUR IDEAS FOR A TABLE TOP ASH TRAY. IT MUST BE USABLE FOR CIGARETTES, CIGARS AND PIPES. MAKE A LIST OF THE CRITERIA THAT MUST BE INCLUDED IN YOUR SOLUTION TO ASSIST YOU IN EVALUATING YOUR PRELIMINARY IDEAS. SHOW YOUR COMPLETED DESIGN WITH THE NECESSARY FREEHAND ORTHOGRAPHIC SKETCHES ON THIS SHEET. ATTACH THE SHEETS ON WHICH YOUR PRELIMINARY IDEAS ARE SKETCHED TO THIS SHEET WHEN IT IS TURNED IN. USE THE NECESSARY NOTES TO SUPPLEMENT YOUR SKETCHES. SHOW OVERALL DIMENSIONS AND INDICATE THE MATERIALS THAT YOU RECOMMEND.

NAME
FILE NO SEC DATE
grade

Drafting & Design

© James H. Earle

NAME

FILE NO SEC DATE

grade

A SKETCH OF A BRACKET THAT SUPPORTS A MEASURING DIAL IS SHOWN AT THE RIGHT. THE DIAL MEASURES DISTANCES ON LATHES, DRILL PRESSES AND OTHER MACHINES. SKETCH THE NECESSARY ORTHOGRAPHIC VIEWS OF THIS DESIGN OR AN ORIGINAL DESIGN OF YOUR OWN. NOTICE THAT THE BASE OF THE BRACKET MUST ALLOW A CLEARANCE OF 3" TO RECEIVE THE DIAL INSTRUMENT. NOTICE THAT THE INSTRUMENT IS HELD BY A SINGLE CAP SCREW: THE TWO SET SCREWS DO NOT SCREW INTO THE BRACKET. TWO 3/16" DIA CAP SCREWS ATTACH THE BRACKET TO THE LATHE.

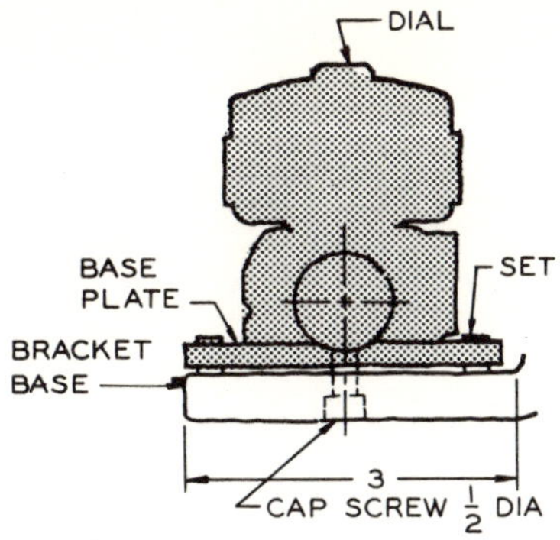

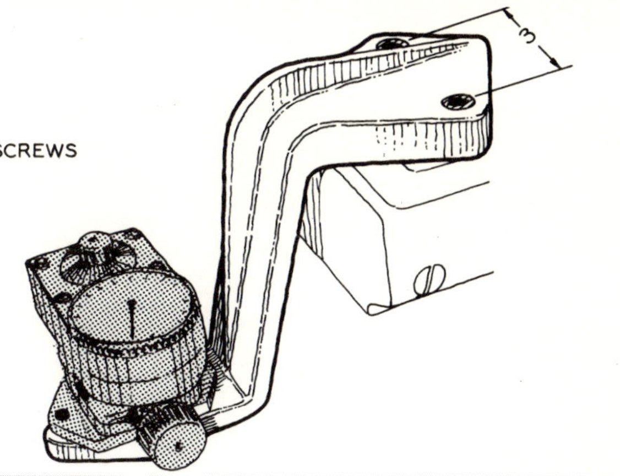

Drafting & Design

NAME

FILE NO SEC DATE

grade

STRING CUTTER FOR ELECTRONIC WIRE BUNDLES

MANY HAND TOOLS WERE DEVELOPED FOR SPECIAL APPLICATIONS BY THE NATIONAL AERONAUTICS AND SPACE ADMINISTRATION TO ASSIST WITH THE SPACE PROGRAM. THIS CUTTER IS ONE OF THOSE.

SPOT TIES ON CABLE BUNDLES MUST SOMETIMES BE REMOVED WHEN REROUTING OR ADDING WIRES. IN THE PAST, KNIVES, HEM RIPPERS, END CUTTERS AND BANDAGE SCISSORS HAVE BEEN USED FOR THIS PURPOSE, BUT CARELESS HANDLING HAS RESULTED IN DAMAGE TO INDIVIDUAL WIRES.

A SIMPLE, HAND-HELD CUTTER ACCOMPLISHES THE TASK QUICKLY AND EASILY WITHOUT THE DANGER OF WIRE DAMAGE. THE CUTTER HAS A FINGER HOLE TO ANCHOR IT IN THE HAND WHILE A SPRING-LOADED CUTTING BLADE IS MOVED BY THE THUMB TO CUT THE CABLE TIE. THE TIE IS CAPTURED IN A HOOK-AND-EYE TYPE APERTURE IN THE FORWARD END OF THE TOOL. THE APERTURE IS WIDE ENOUGH TO RECEIVE A SPOT TIE STRING BUT NARROW ENOUGH TO EXCLUDE RECEIVING A WIRE AT THE SAME TIME. THE SKETCH SHOWS THE CUTTER BEING USED AND ITS GENERAL APPEARANCE.

THE BASIC DESIGN CONSISTS OF TWO MATING PARTS THAT COMPRISE THE BODY: THESE ARE HELD TOGETHER BY SCREWS.

REQUIRED: PREPARE FREEHAND SKETCHES TO DESCRIBE THE PARTS THAT MAKE UP THIS DESIGN. GIVE CONSIDERATION TO ITS PROBABLE SIZE SINCE IT MUST FIT THE HUMAN HAND. SHOW EACH PART INDIVIDUALLY WITH THE NECESSARY NOTES. CAN YOU THINK OF A BETTER DESIGN THAT WILL SERVE THIS PURPOSE?

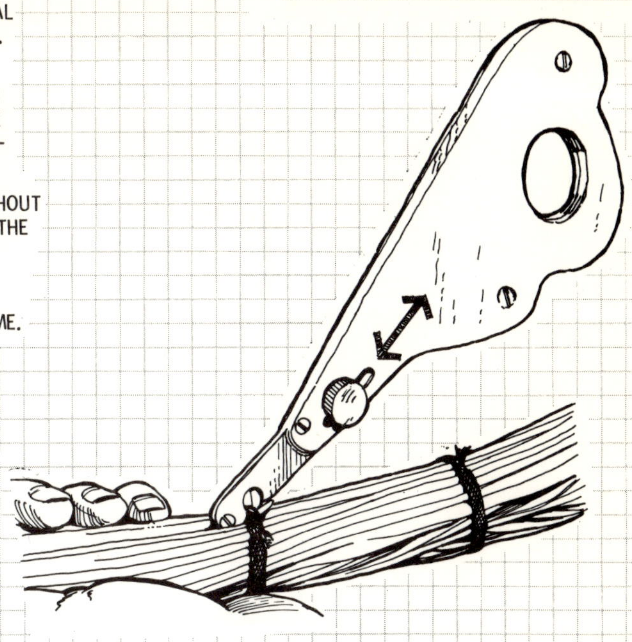

Drafting & Design

NAME

FILE NO SEC DATE

grade

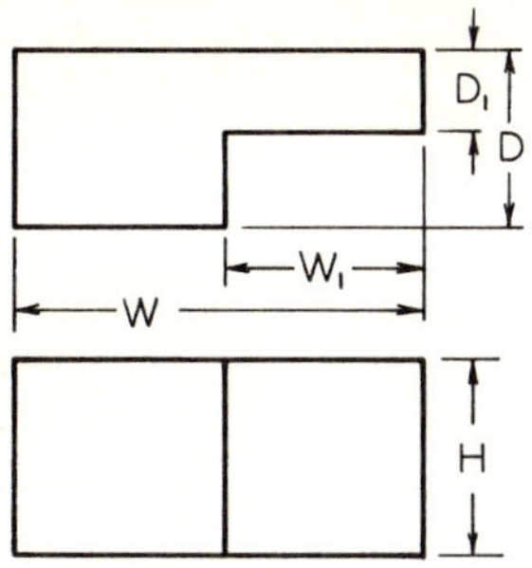

REQUIRED: CONSTRUCT AN ISOMETRIC DRAWING OF THE OBJECT ABOVE.

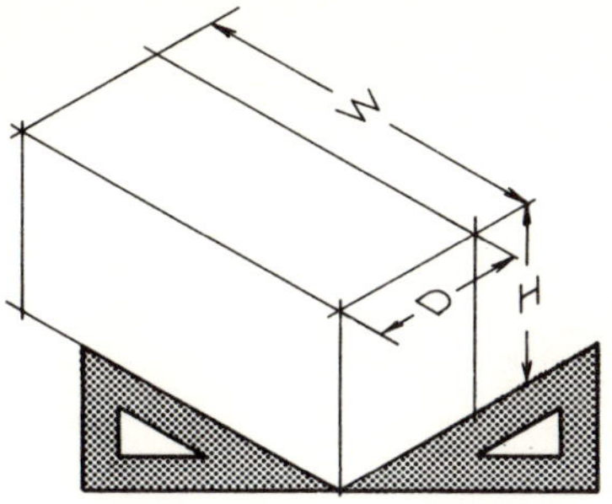

STEP 1: BEGIN THE ISOMETRIC BY BLOCKING IN THE OBJECT USING OVERALL DIMENSIONS OF W, D & H.

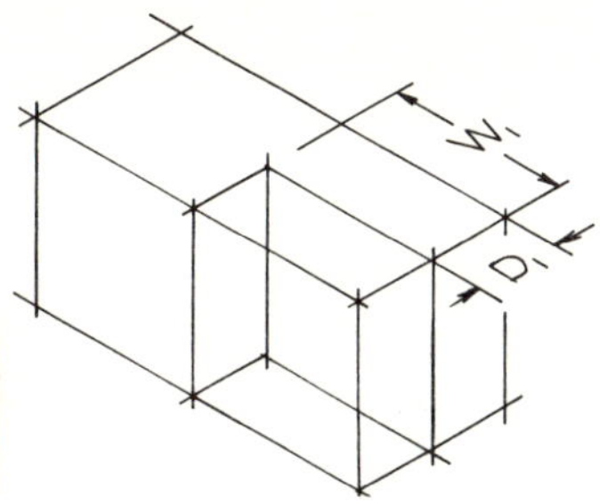

STEP 2: THE NOTCH IS REMOVED BY MEASURING W_1 AND D_1 ALONG THE ISOMETRIC AXES.

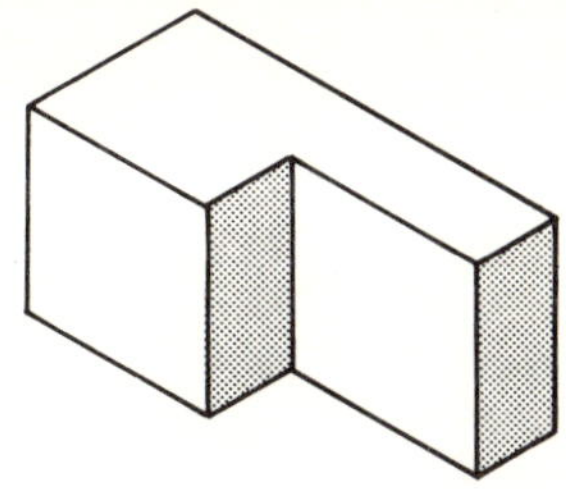

STEP 3: DARKEN THE FINISHED ISOMETRIC DRAWING TO COMPLETE THE PICTORIAL.

REQUIRED: USING YOUR DIVIDERS AND DOUBLING THE DIMENSIONS OF THE ORTHOGRAPHIC VIEWS, CONSTRUCT ISOMETRICS OF THE OBJECTS IN THE SPACES PROVIDED.

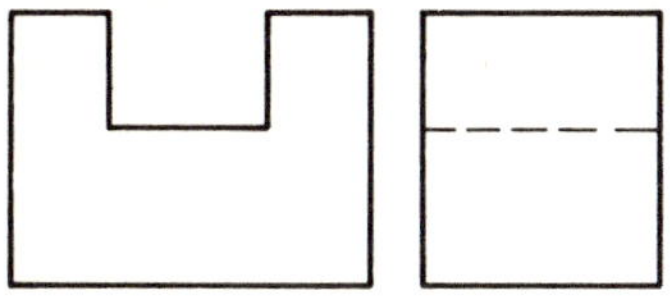

1

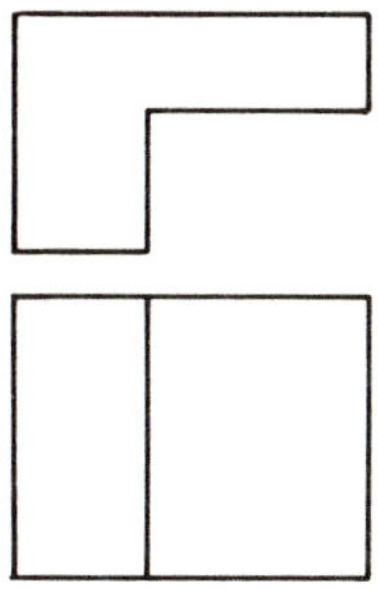

2

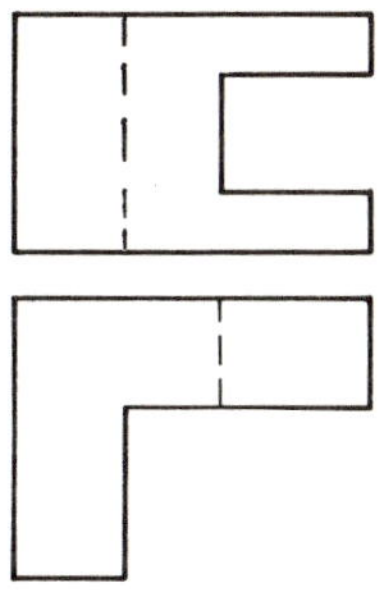

3

4

1

2

3

4

NAME
FILE NO   SEC   DATE

grade

Drafting & Design © James H. Earle	NAME FILE NO SEC DATE	grade	

ISOMETRIC DRAWING

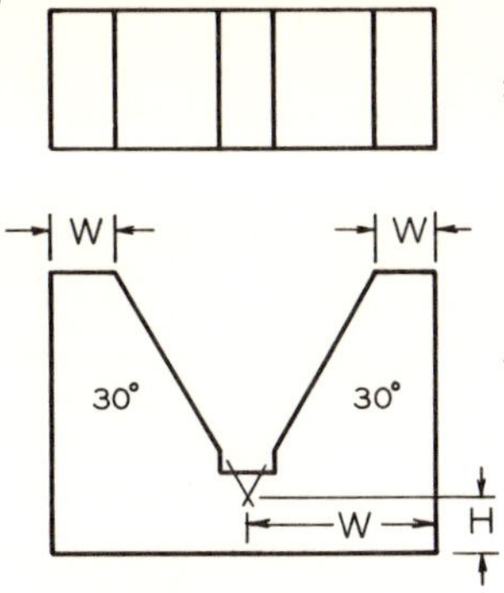

REQUIRED: CONSTRUCT AN ISOMETRIC DRAWING OF THE OBJECT ABOVE.

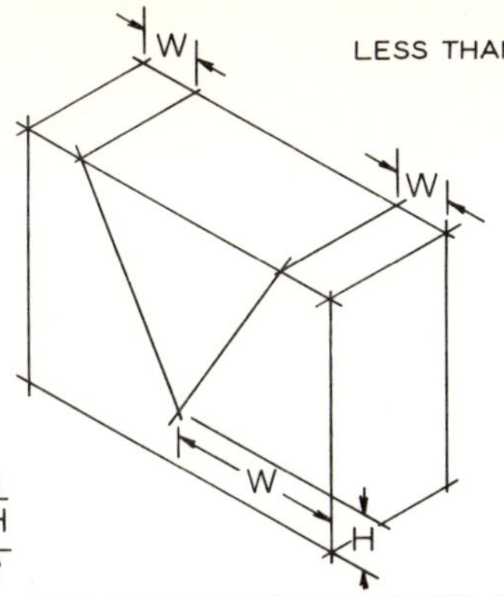

STEP 1: THE OBJECT IS BLOCKED IN WITH THE OVERALL DIMENSIONS. THE ANGLES ARE LOCATED BY MEASURING COORDINATES PARALLEL TO THE ISOMETRIC AXES.

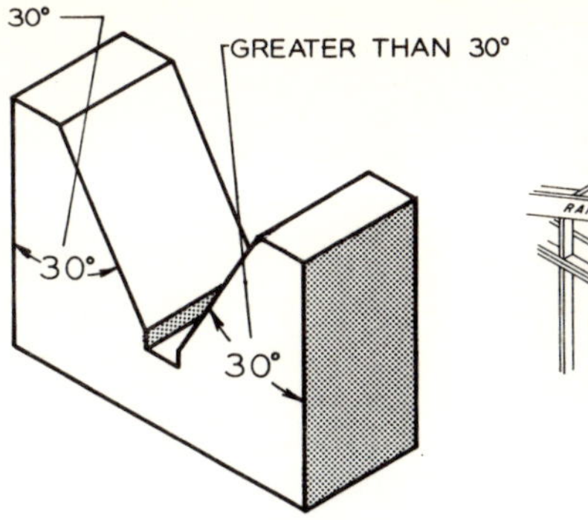

STEP 2: THE DETAILS OF THE OBJECT ARE COMPLETED AND THE LINES STRENGTHENED TO COMPLETE THE ISOMETRIC DRAWING.

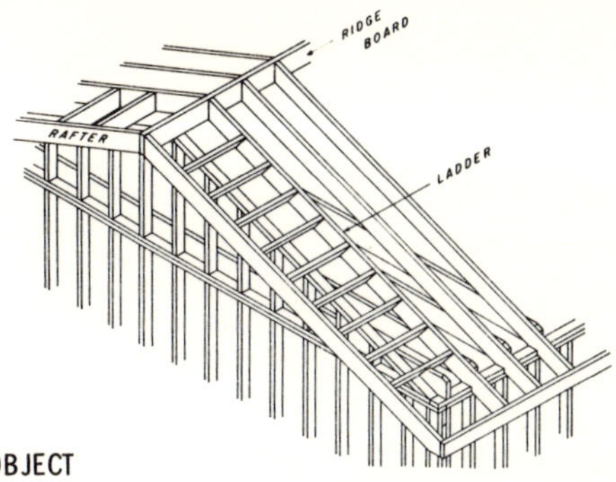

REQUIRED: DRAW ISOMETRIC PICTORIALS OF THE OBJECTS IN THE SPACES BELOW. DOUBLE THE DIMENSIONS OF THE ORTHOGRAPHIC VIEWS WITH YOUR DIVIDERS; BEGIN EACH WITH POINT O.

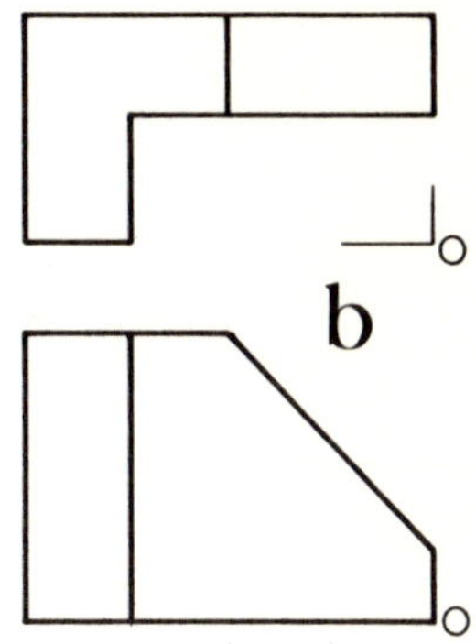

b

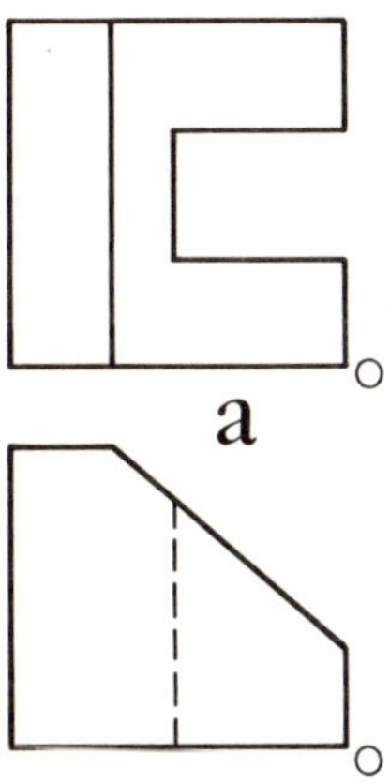

a

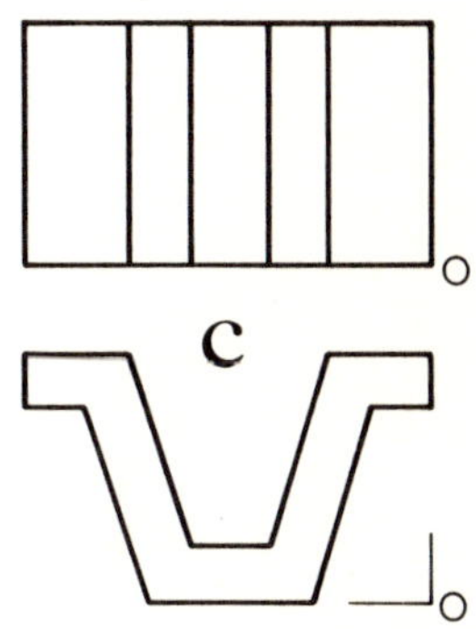

c

A 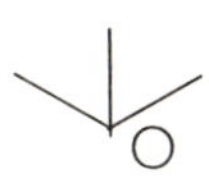

B 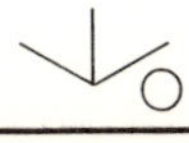

C 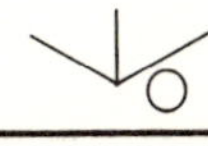

NAME

FILE NO   SEC   DATE

grade

Drafting & Design

NAME

FILE NO SEC DATE

grade

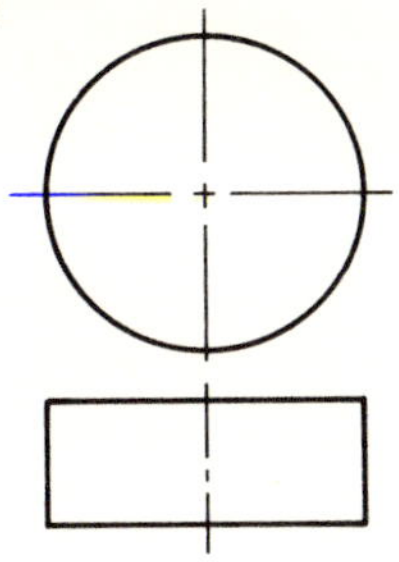

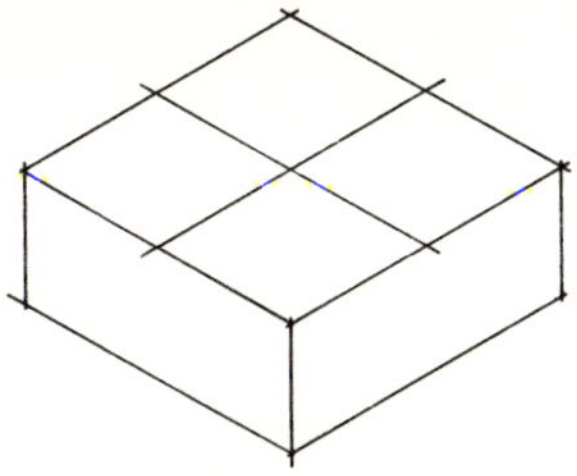

STEP 1: DRAW AN ISOMETRIC BOX USING THE DIAMETER OF THE CYLINDER AS THE SIDES. LOCATE THE MIDPOINTS.

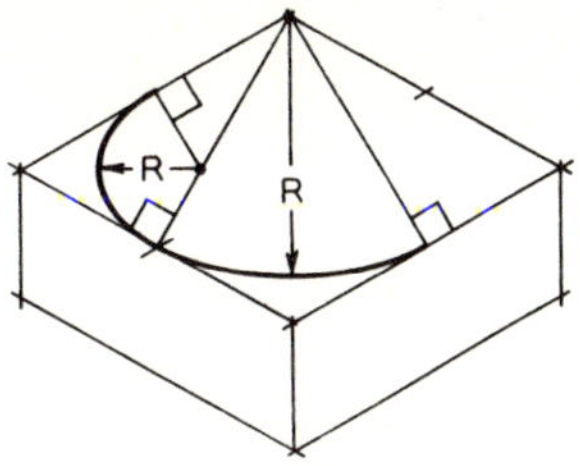

STEP 2: DRAW PERPENDICULARS TO EACH SIDE AT THE MIDPOINTS AND DRAW ARCS FROM THE FOUR CENTERS THAT ARE FOUND.

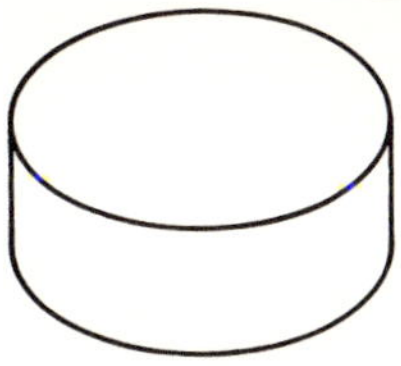

STEP 3: REPEAT THIS CONSTRUCTION FOR THE LOWER ELLIPSE OF THE CYLINDER AND STRENGTHEN THE FINAL LINES.

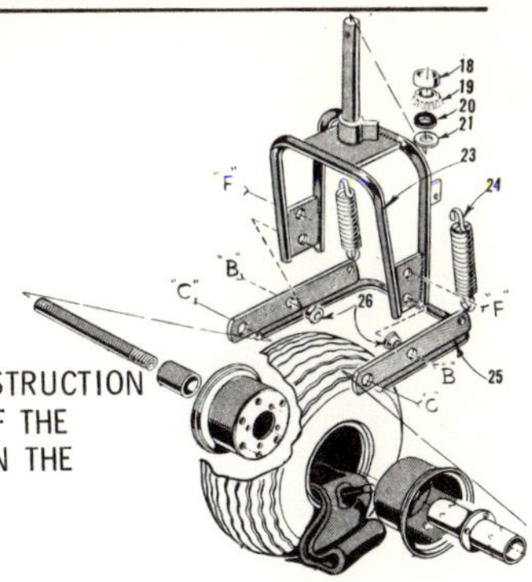

1 REQUIRED: CONSTRUCT A FOUR-CENTER ELLIPSE WITH A 3-1/2" DIA USING THE CENTERLINES GIVEN. SHOW CONSTRUCTION.

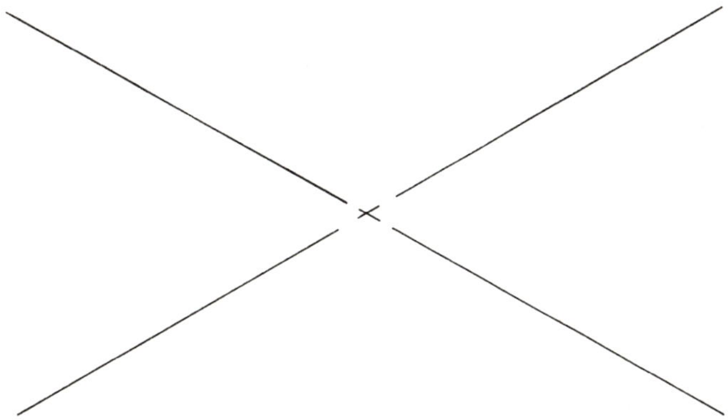

2

COMPLETE THE ISOMETRIC DRAWING SO IT WILL HAVE THE CIRCULAR FEATURES SHOWN IN THE EXAMPLE DRAWING.

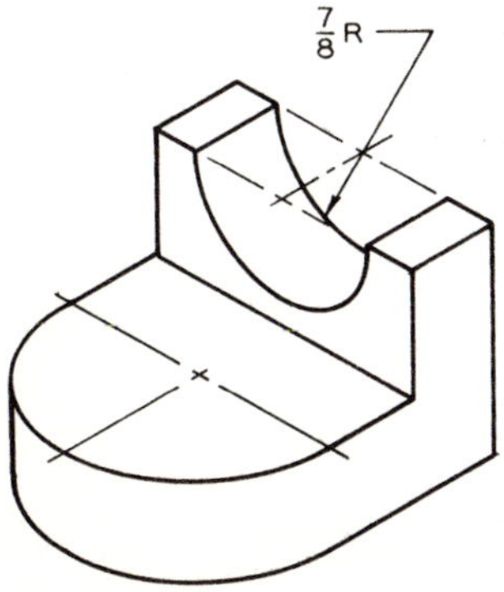

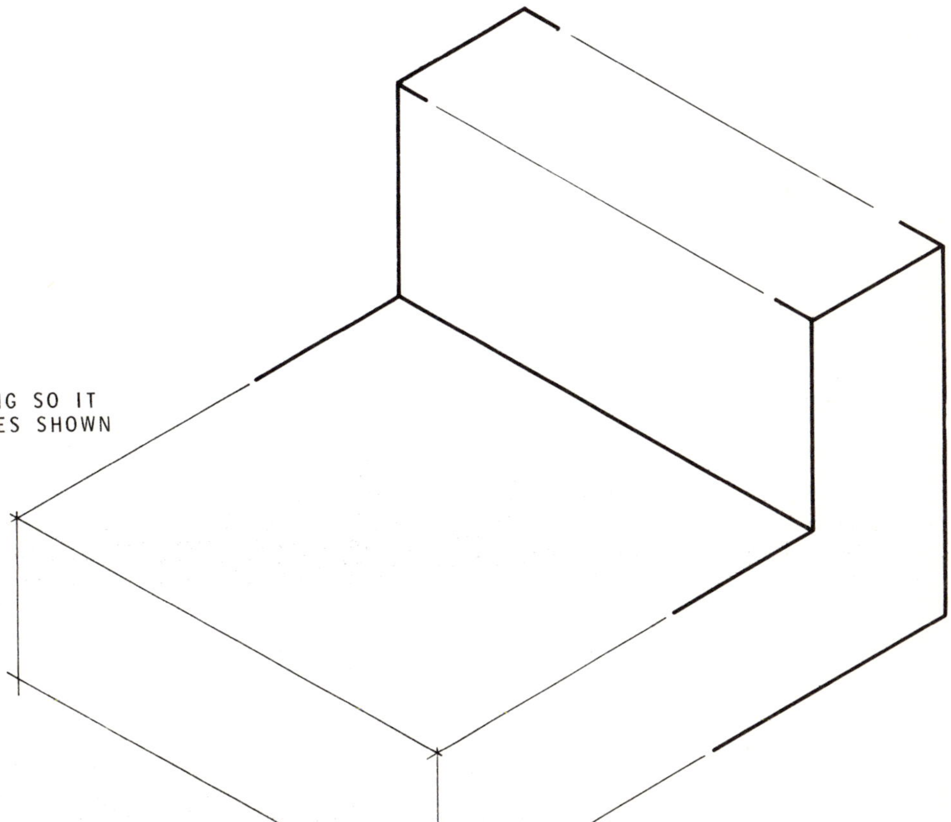

Drafting & Design © James H. Earle	NAME FILE NO SEC DATE	grade	

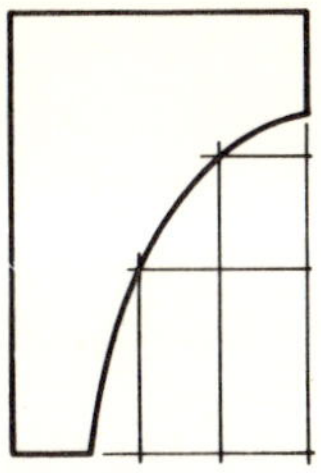

STEP 1: TO CONSTRUCT AN ISOMETRIC OF AN IRREGULAR CURVE, COORDINATES MUST BE LOCATED IN THE ORTHOGRAPHIC VIEW.

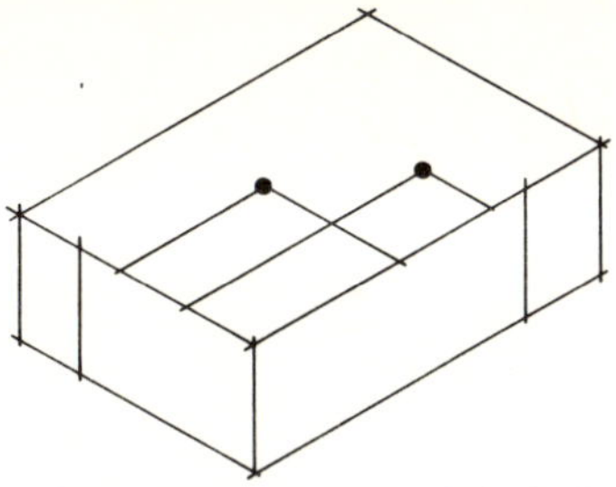

STEP 2: THE COORDINATES ARE LAID OFF PARALLEL TO THE ISOMETRIC AXES.

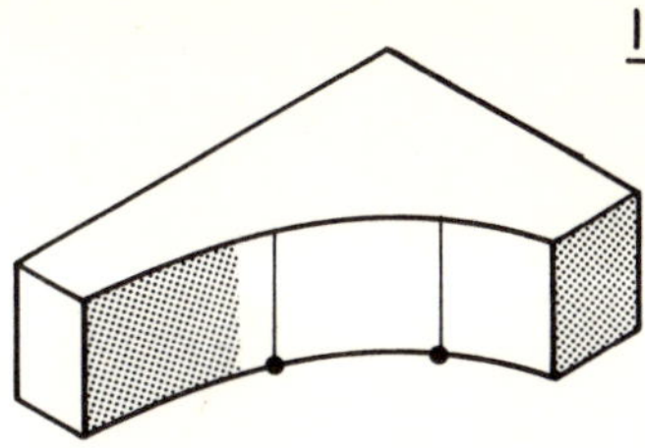

STEP 3: THE LOWER CURVE IS FOUND BY PROJECTING EACH POINT DOWNWARD A DISTANCE EQUAL TO THE PART'S THICKNESS.

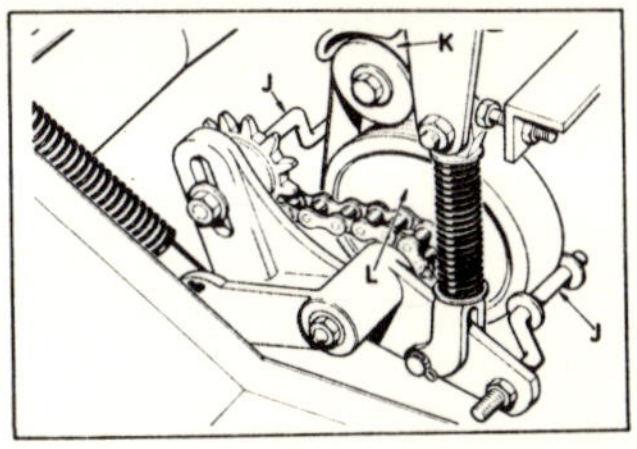

courtesy of Planaprint International

1 REQUIRED: CONSTRUCT AN ISOMETRIC DRAWING OF THE PART BEGINNING WITH POINT O.

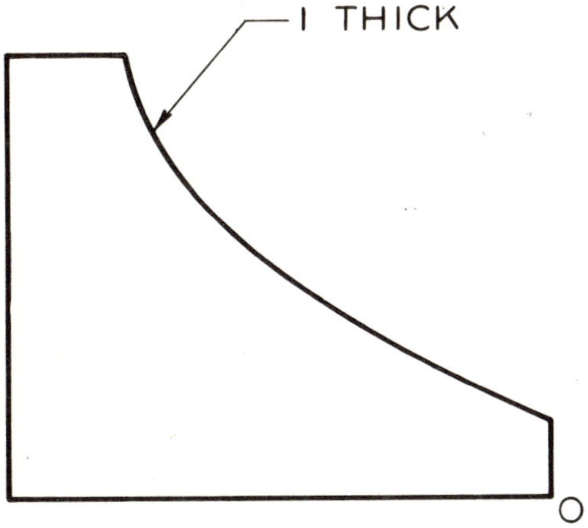

2 REQUIRED: COMPLETE THE ISOMETRIC DRAWING OF THE BEAM CLAMP.

BEAM CLAMP

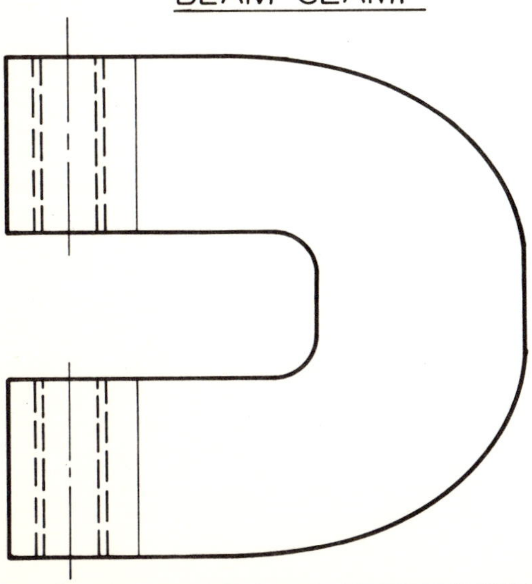

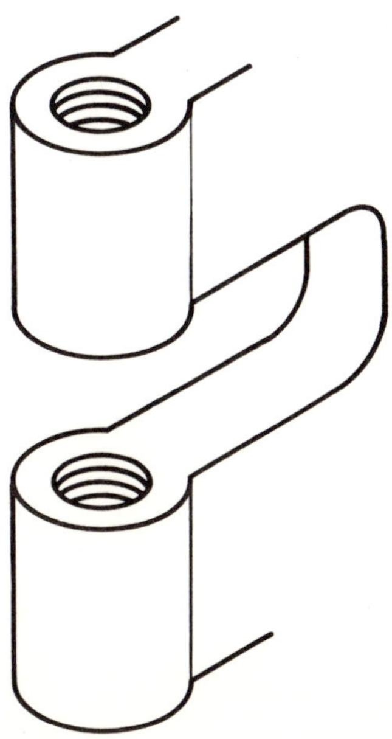

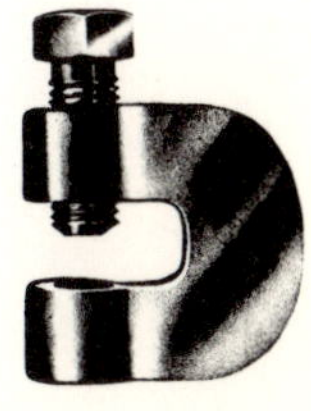

OBLIQUE DRAWING

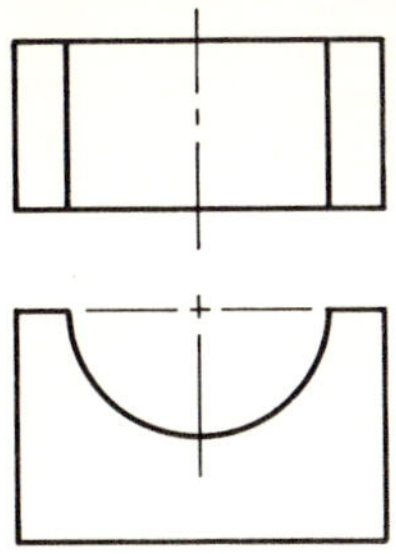

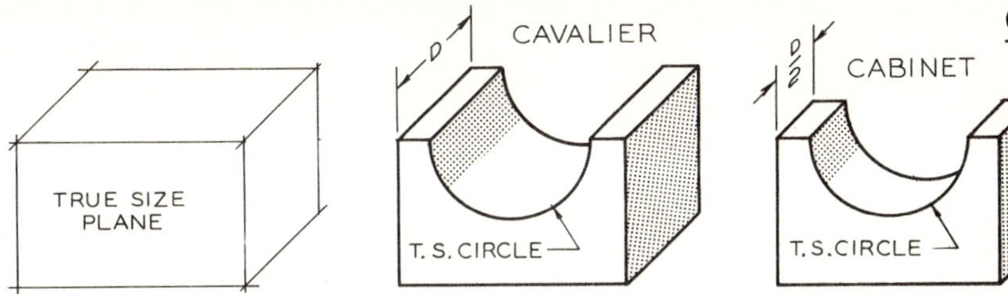

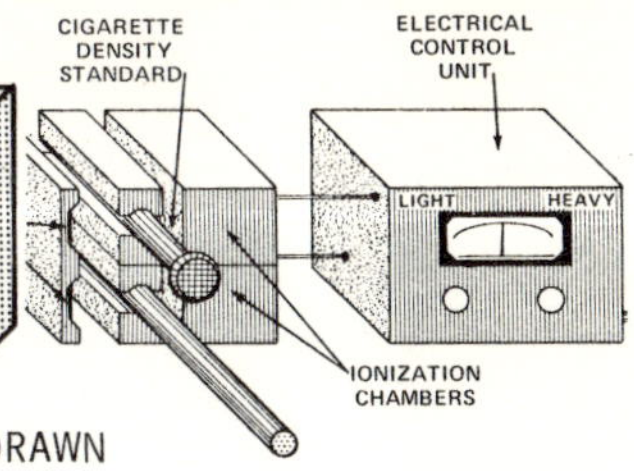

STEP 1: TO DRAW A CAVALIER OBLIQUE, BLOCK IN THE OBJECT WITH THE OVERALL DIMENSIONS.

STEP 2: THE SEMICIRCLE IS DRAWN TRUE SIZE AND THE LINES ARE STRENGTHENED.

A CABINET OBLIQUE IS DRAWN IN THE SAME MANNER EXCEPT THE DIMENSION ALONG THE RECEDING AXIS IS HALF LENGTH.

REQUIRED: DOUBLE THE DIMENSIONS OF THE OBJECTS AND CONSTRUCT CAVALIER OBLIQUES OF PROBLEMS 1 AND 3.

REQUIRED: DOUBLE THE DIMENSIONS OF THE OBJECTS AND CONSTRUCT CABINET OBLIQUES OF PROBLEMS 2 AND 4.

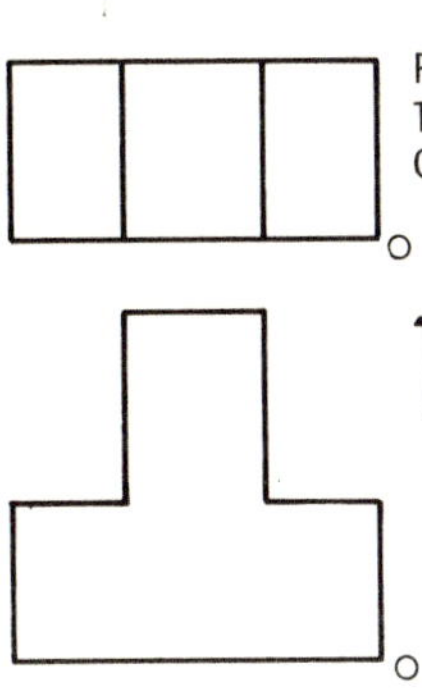

1

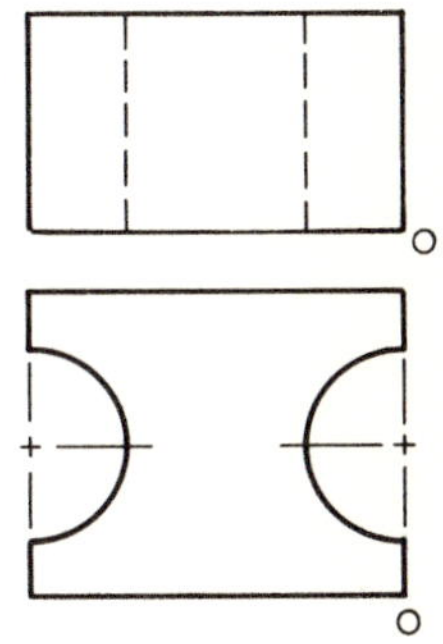

2

3

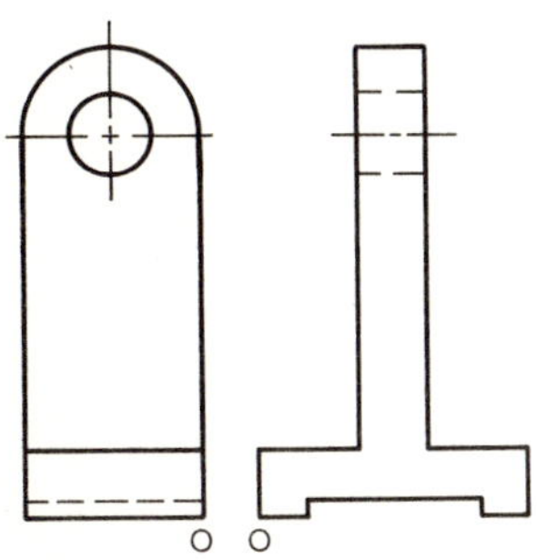

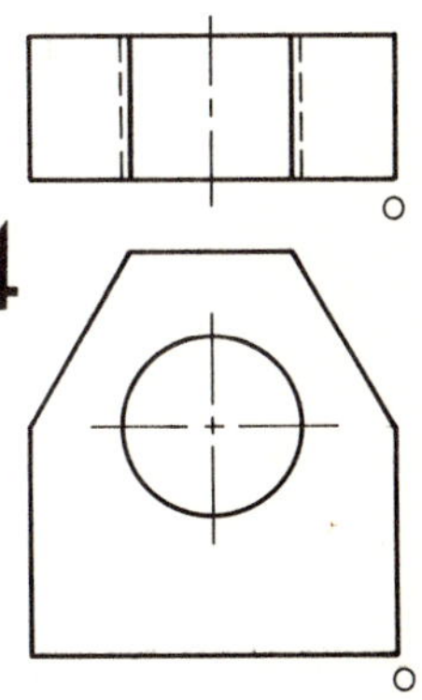

4

Drafting & Design ©James H. Earle	NAME FILE NO SEC DATE	grade	43

Drafting & Design

NAME

FILE NO SEC DATE

grade

OBLIQUE DRAWING

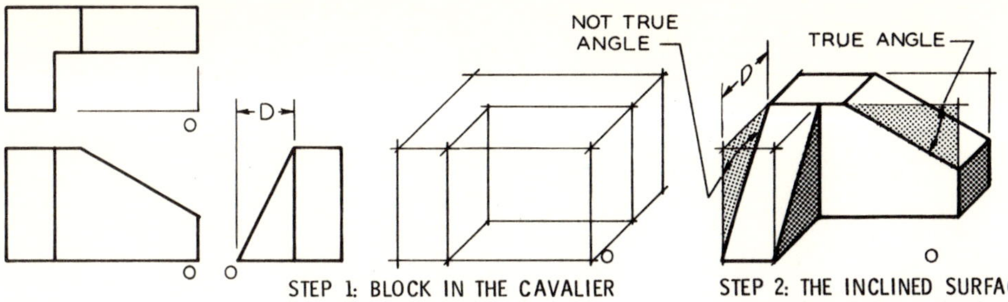

STEP 1: BLOCK IN THE CAVALIER OBLIQUE WITH THE OVERALL DIMENSIONS AND LOCATE THE NOTCH.

STEP 2: THE INCLINED SURFACE ALONG THE RECEDING AXIS IS LOCATED WITH COORDINATE D. THE OTHER ANGLE IS TRUE SIZE.

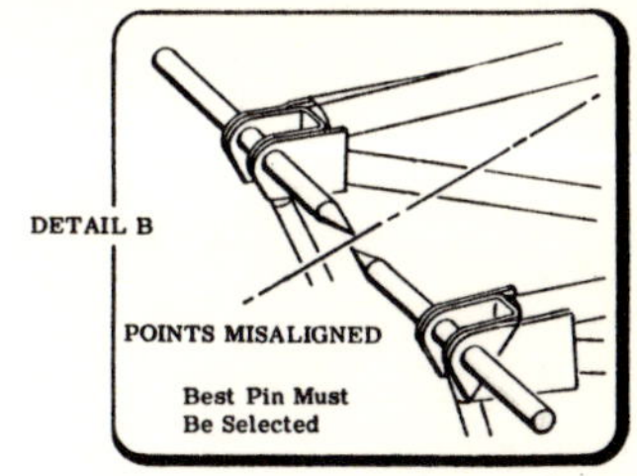

Courtesy of Bell Helicopter Corp.

REQUIRD: CONSTRUCT CAVALIER OBLIQUES OF PROBLEMS 1 AND 3 AND A CABINET OBLIQUE OF PROBLEM 2. DOUBLE ALL MEASUREMENTS.

1

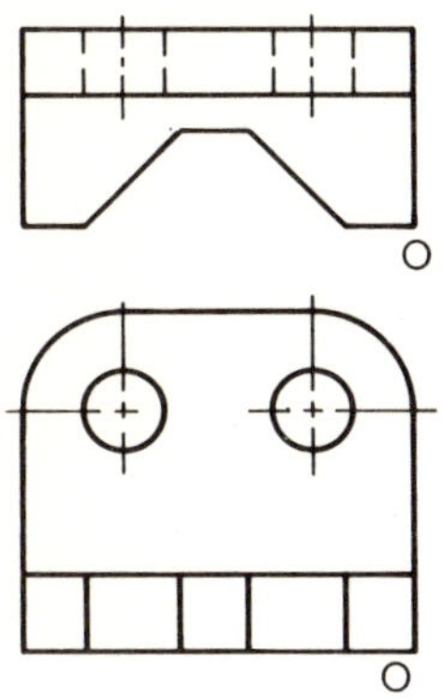

2

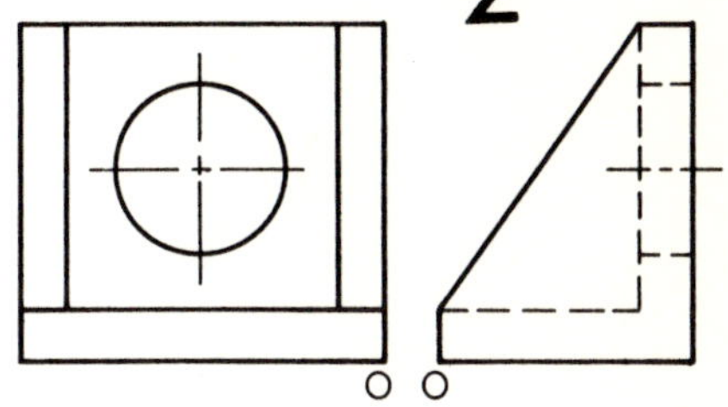

3

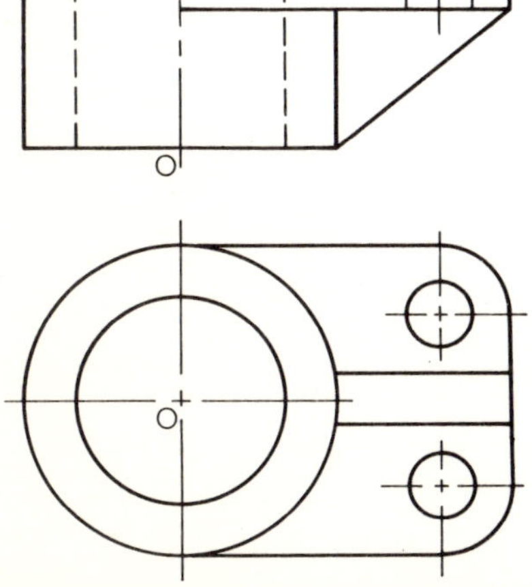

Drafting & Design

NAME
FILE NO
SEC
DATE
grade

Drafting & Design © James H. Earle	NAME FILE NO SEC DATE	grade	

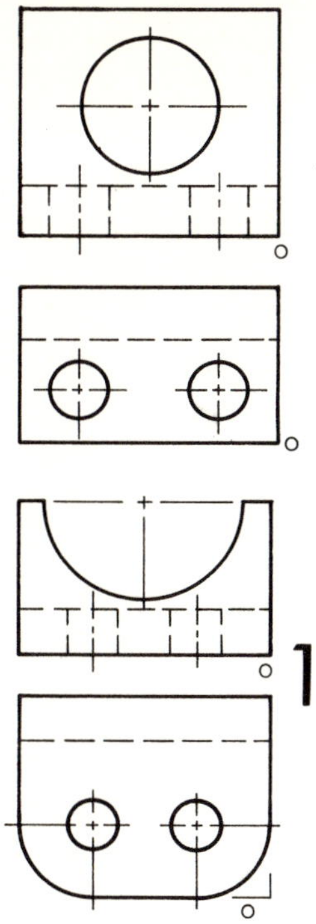

1

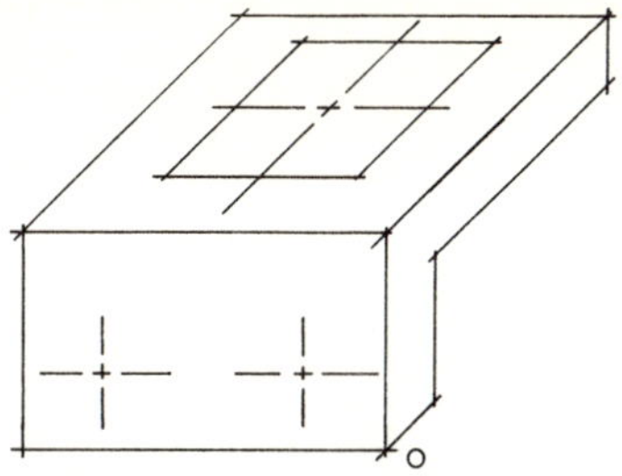

STEP 1: BLOCK IN THE OBJECT AND THE CIRCULAR HOLE ON THE TOP SURFACE.

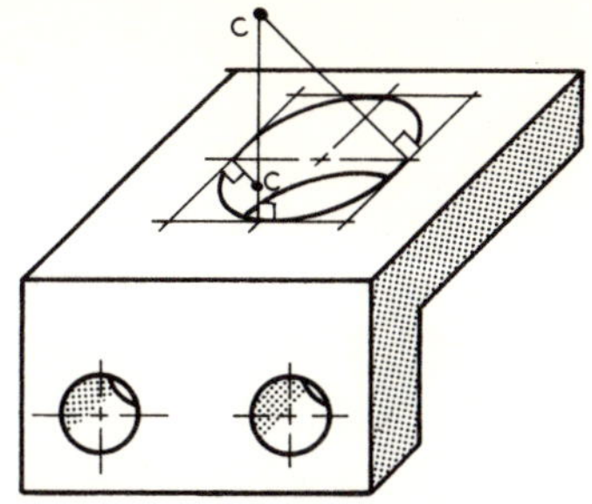

STEP 2: DRAW PERPENDICULARS FROM THE MIDPOINTS OF THE BLOCKED-IN CIRCLE TO FIND FOUR CENTERS (TWO ARE SHOWN).

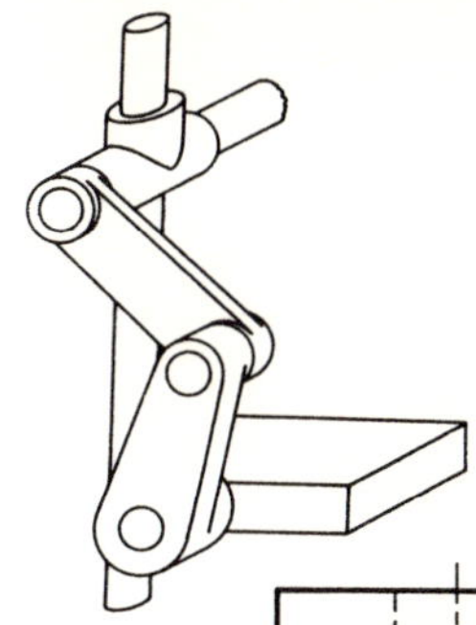

REQUIRED: CONSTRUCT CAVALIER OBLIQUES OF EACH OF THE OBJECTS BEGINNING WITH POINT O AND BY DOUBLING ALL DIMENSIONS.

2

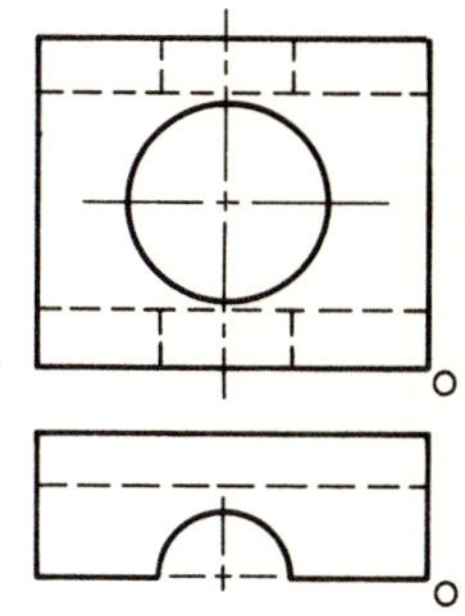

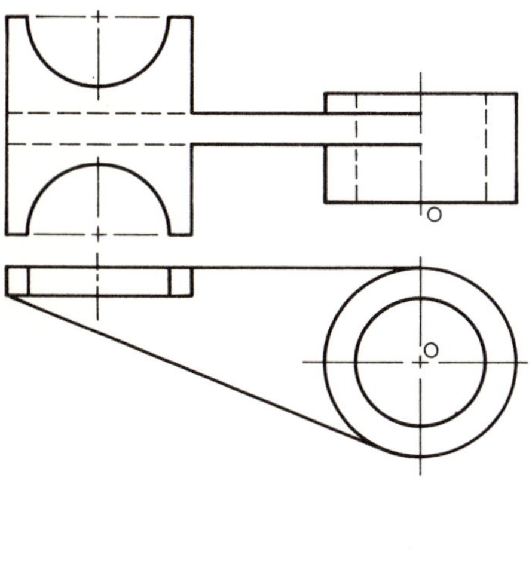

3

Drafting & Design ©James H. Earle	NAME FILE NO SEC DATE	grade	45

Drafting & Design

NAME

FILE NO SEC DATE

grade

CONSTRUCT A TWO-POINT PERSPECTIVE OF THE BUILDING AND THE FENCES USING THE PLAN AND SIDE VIEWS GIVEN.

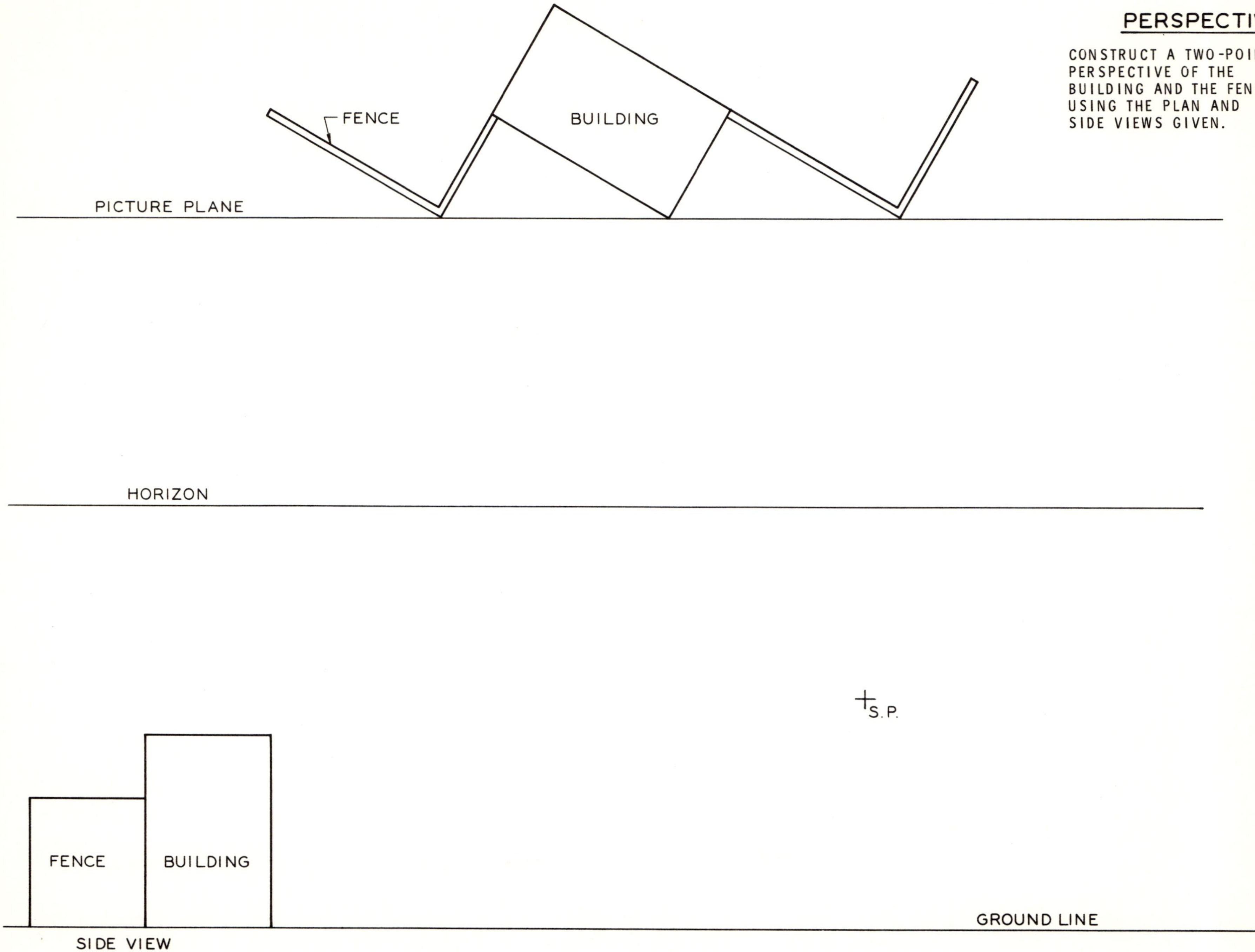

Drafting & Design

NAME
FILE NO. SEC. DATE.
grade

Drafting & Design

NAME

FILE NO SEC DATE

grade

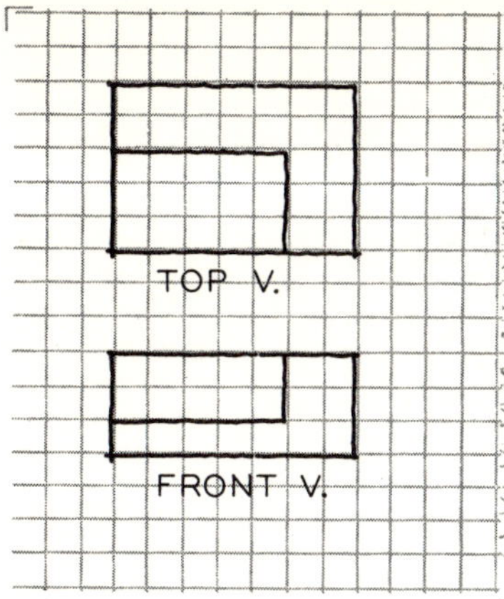

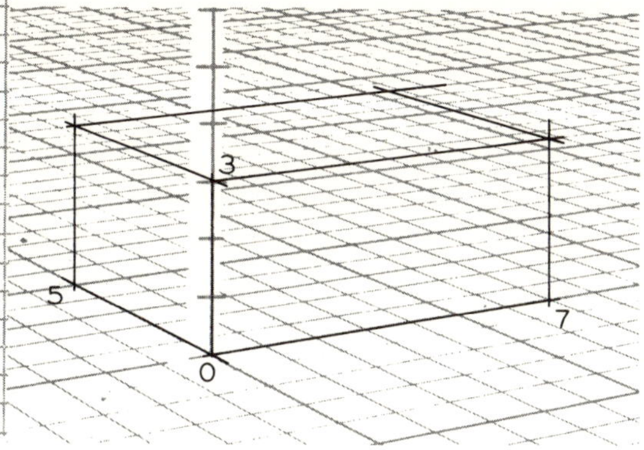

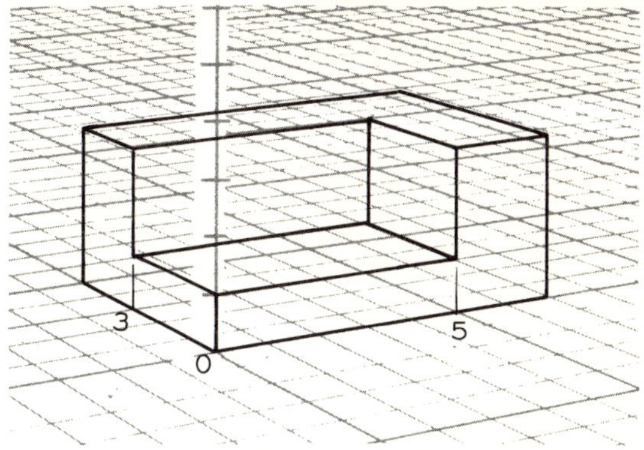

STEP 1: THE OBJECT AT THE LEFT CAN BE DRAWN AS A PERSPECTIVE BY USING ITS OVERALL DIMENSIONS TO BLOCK IT IN ON THE PERSPECTIVE GRID.

STEP 2: THE NOTCH CAN BE REMOVED BY COUNTING FROM POINT O ALONG THE TWO BASE LINES ON THE GRID AND PROJECTING UPWARD. DARKEN THE LINES TO COMPLETE THE PERSPECTIVE.

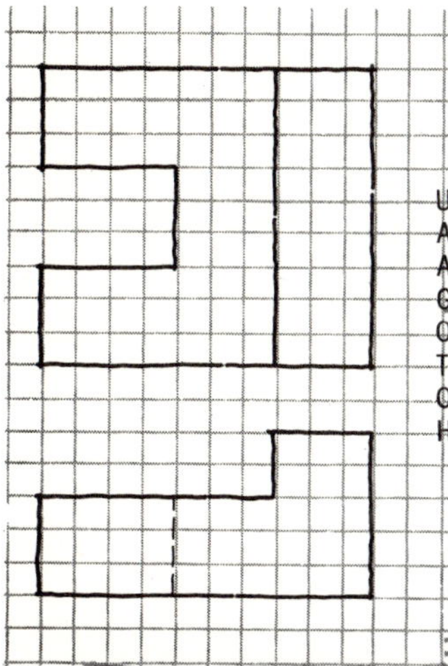

USING THE GRID BELOW, CONSTRUCT A PERSPECTIVE OF THE OBJECT SHOWN AT THE LEFT. EACH GRID ON THE ORTHOGRAPHIC VIEWS IS EQUAL TO THREE ON THE PERSPECTIVE GRID. NOTICE THE RELATIONSHIP BETWEEN THE UNITS ON THE VERTICAL SCALE AND THE TWO HORIZONTAL SCALES THROUGH POINT O.

HORIZON

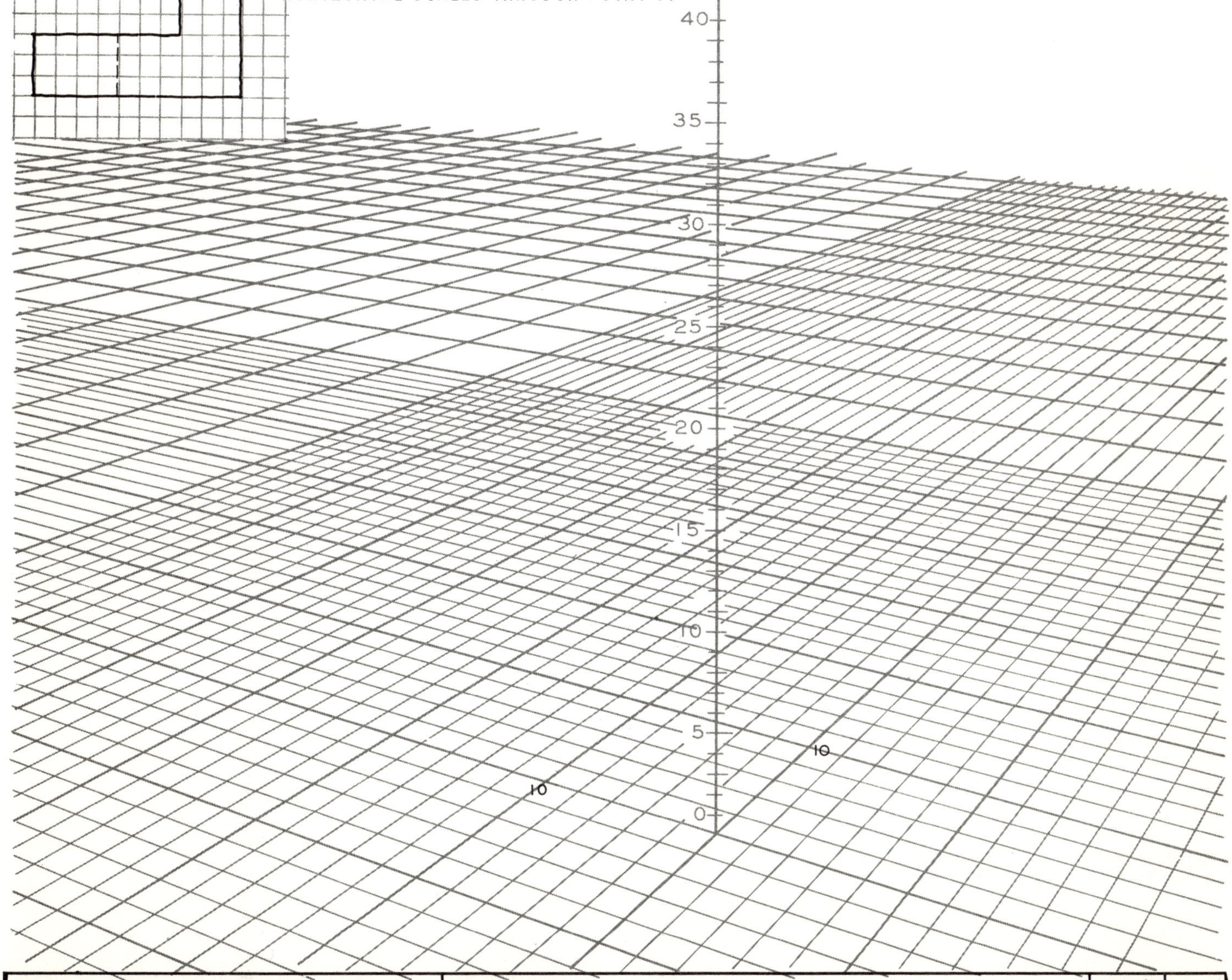

Drafting & Design © James H. Earle	NAME FILE NO SEC DATE	grade	47

Drafting & Design © James H. Earle	NAME: FILE NO: SEC: DATE:	grade	

PERSPECTIVE CHART

THIS PERSPECTIVE CHART CAN BE USED OVER AND OVER AGAIN IF IT IS OVERLAYED WITH TRACING PAPER AND THE DRAWINGS MADE ON THE OVERLAY SHEET. NOTE: A set of charts called Lawson Perspective Charts (21"x24") similar to this one can be purchased from Reinhold Publishing Co., 430 Park Ave., NYC.

Drafting & Design	NAME	grade	48
	FILE NO SEC DATE		

Drafting & Design © James H. Earle	NAME FILE NO SEC DATE	grade	

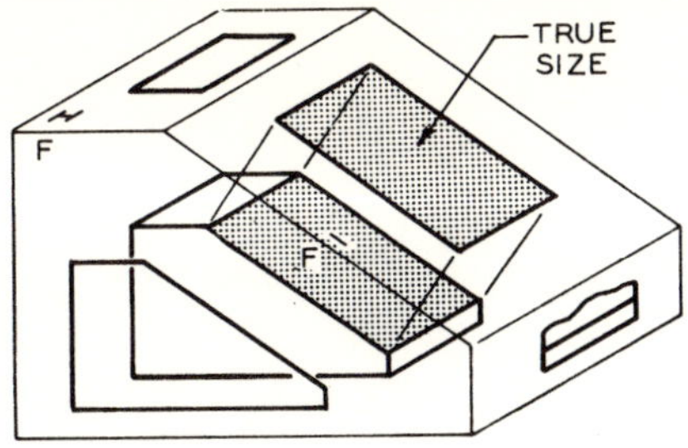

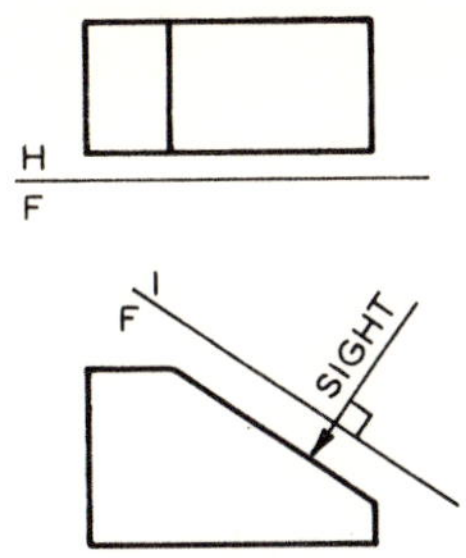

STEP 1: DRAW FOLD LINE H-F BETWEEN THE VIEWS. LINE F-1 IS DRAWN PARALLEL TO THE INCLINED PLANE; THE LINE OF SIGHT IS PERPENDICULAR TO THE PLANE AND F-1.

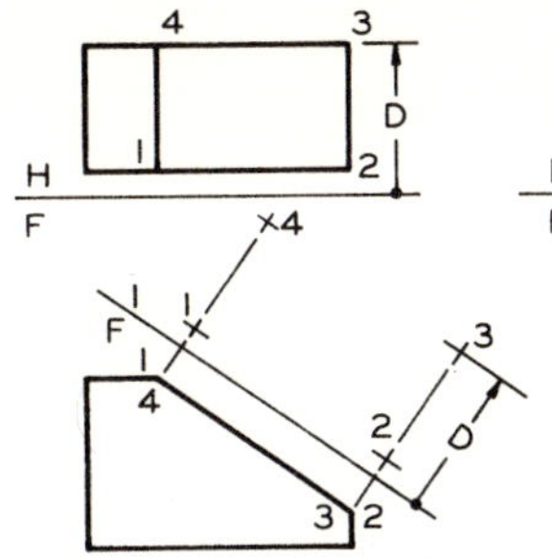

STEP 2: POINTS ARE PROJECTED PERPENDICULAR TO F-1 AND ARE LOCATED BY MEASURING FROM THE H-F AND F-1 LINES.

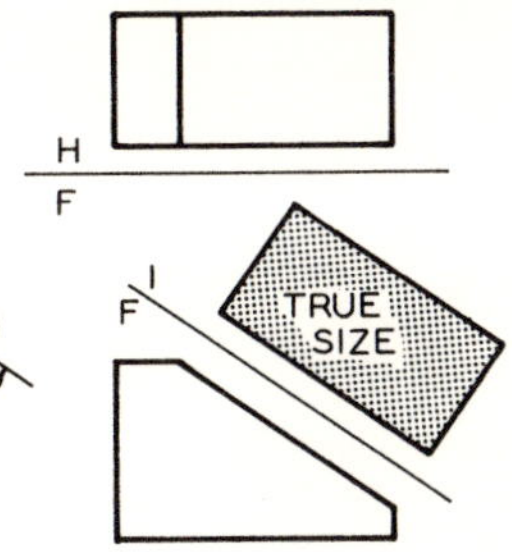

STEP 3: THESE POINTS ARE CONNECTED TO COMPLETE THE TRUE SIZE VIEW OF THE INCLINED PLANE.

1 PROJECT THE INCLINED PLANE ONTO THE PARALLEL AUXILIARY PLANE IN THE PICTORIAL. POINT 1 IS PROJECTED AS AN EXAMPLE.

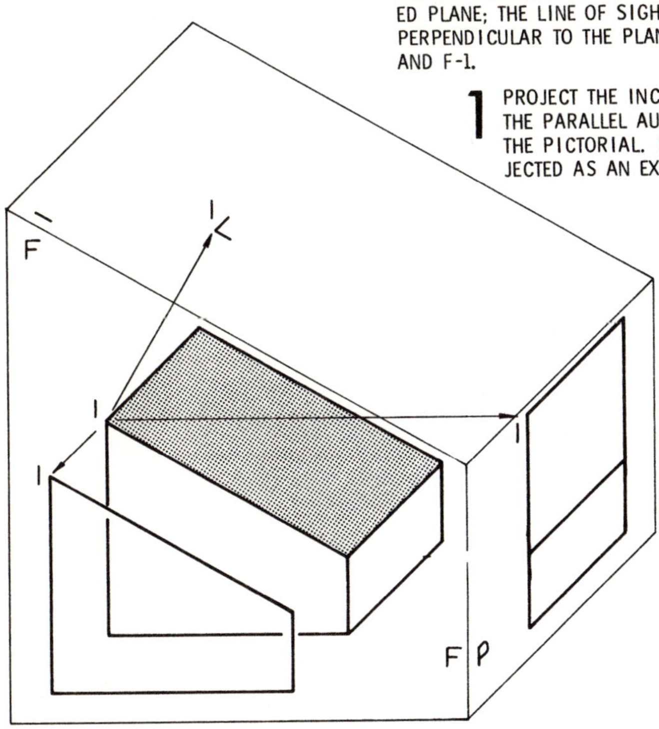

2 FIND THE TRUE SIZE VIEW OF THE INCLINED SURFACE BY AN AUXILIARY VIEW. REFER TO THE PICTORIAL.

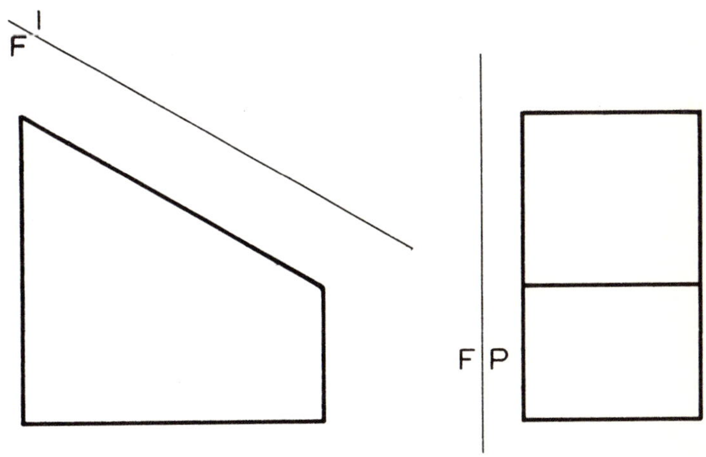

FIND THE TRUE SIZE VIEWS OF THE INCLINED SURFACES BY AN AUXILIARY VIEW.

3

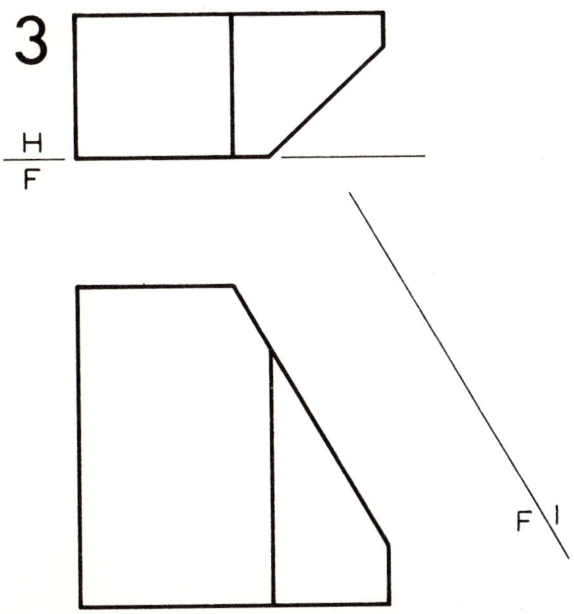

4

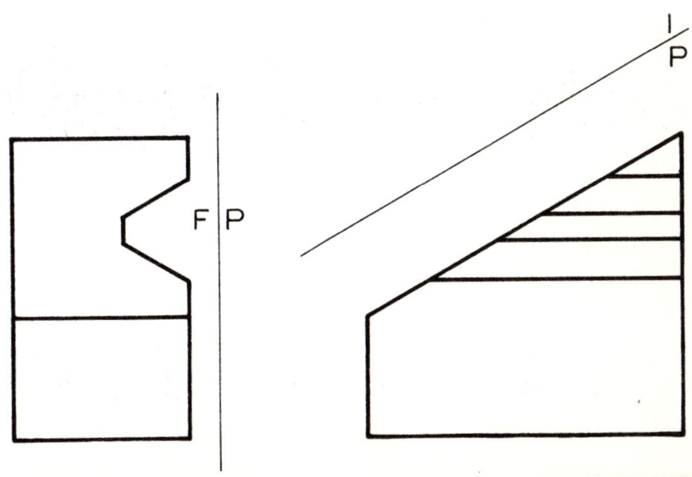

Drafting & Design © James H. Earle	NAME FILE NO SEC DATE	grade	

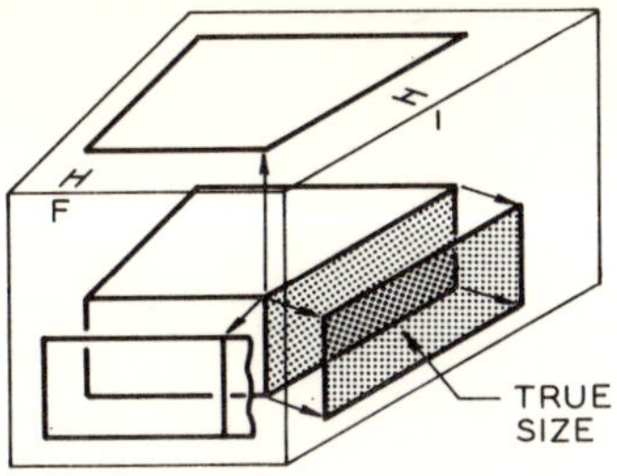

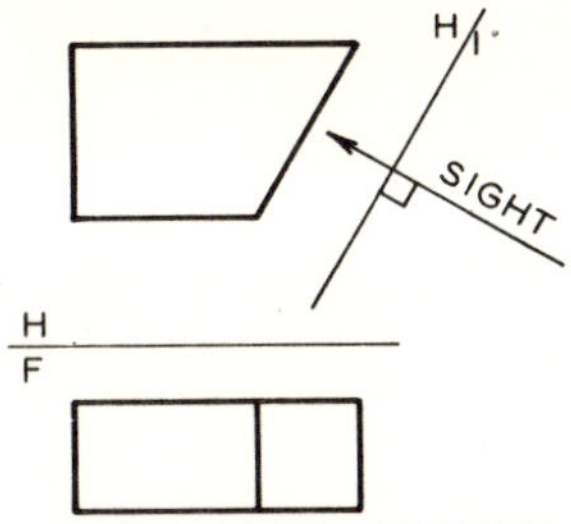

STEP 1: DRAW HF BETWEEN THE VIEWS AND H-1 PARALLEL TO THE INCLINED SURFACE. THE LINE OF SIGHT IS PERPENDICULAR TO THE SURFACE AND H-1.

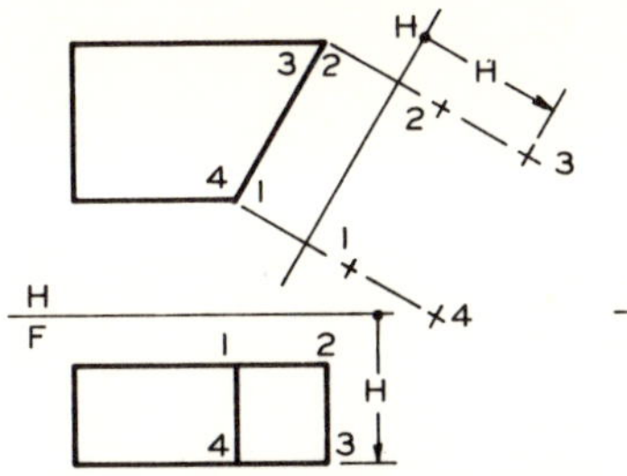

STEP 2: LOCATE POINTS BY TRANSFERRING H-DIMENSIONS FROM THE FRONT VIEW TO THE AUXILIARY VIEW.

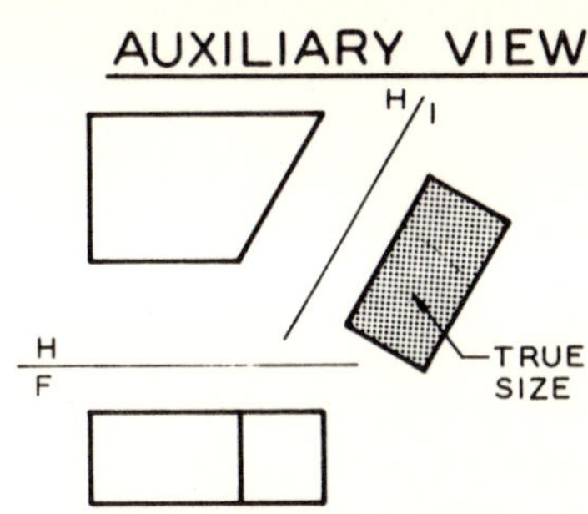

STEP 3: CONNECT THE POINTS TO GIVE THE TRUE SIZE VIEW OF THE INCLINED PLANE.

1 REQUIRED: FIND THE TRUE SIZE VIEW OF THE INCLINED SURFACE BY PROJECTING ONTO THE AUXILIARY PLANE IN THE PICTORIAL. POINT 1 IS AN EXAMPLE POINT.

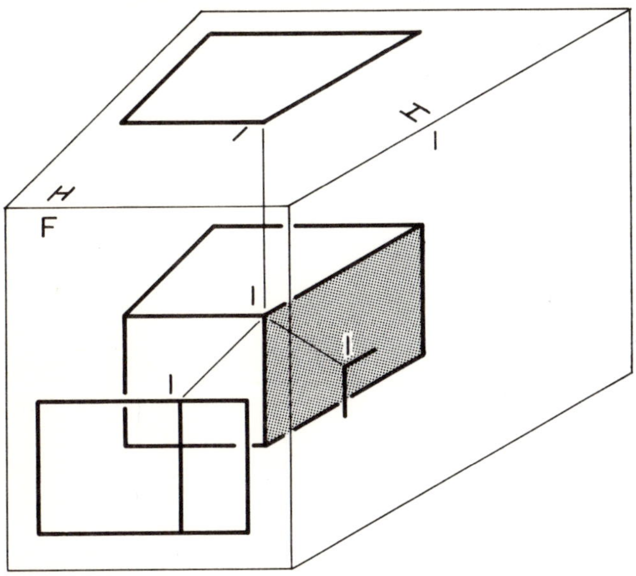

2 REQUIRED: FIND THE TRUE SIZE VIEWS OF PROBLEMS 2, 3 and 4 BY AUXILIARY VIEWS.

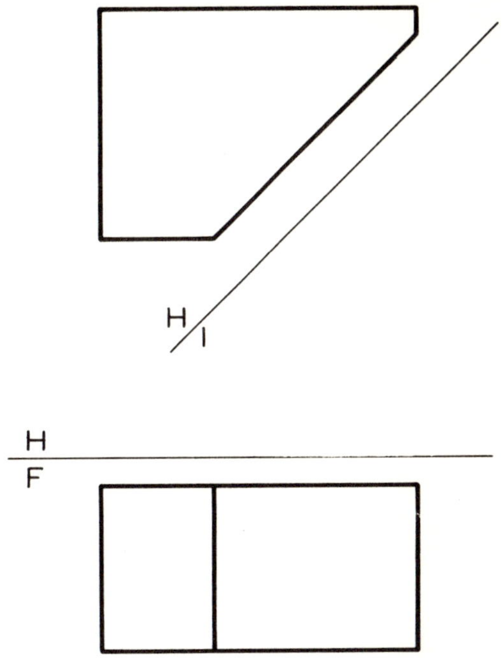

3

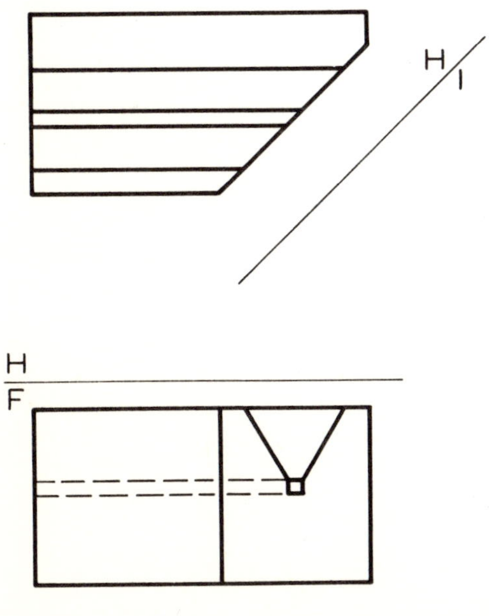

4

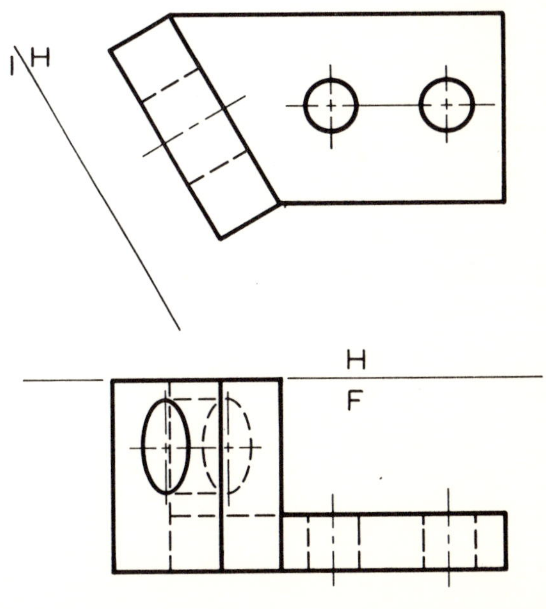

Drafting & Design

NAME
FILE NO SEC DATE
grade

A FRONT VIEW AND A PARTIAL SIDE VIEW OF A PART ARE GIVEN BELOW. CONSTRUCT A FULL AUXILIARY VIEW OF THE ENTIRE PART BY PROJECTING FROM THE FRONT VIEW AS SHOWN BY THE LINE OF SIGHT. EVEN THOUGH A HALF SIDE VIEW IS GIVEN, CONSTRUCT THE AUXILIARY VIEW AS A COMPLETE VIEW SHOWING THE OBJECT ON BOTH SIDES OF THE CENTER LINE. ALSO, COMPLETE A PARTIAL HALF VIEW AS THE TOP VIEW.

PARTIAL
TOP VIEW

FULL
AUXILIARY
VIEW

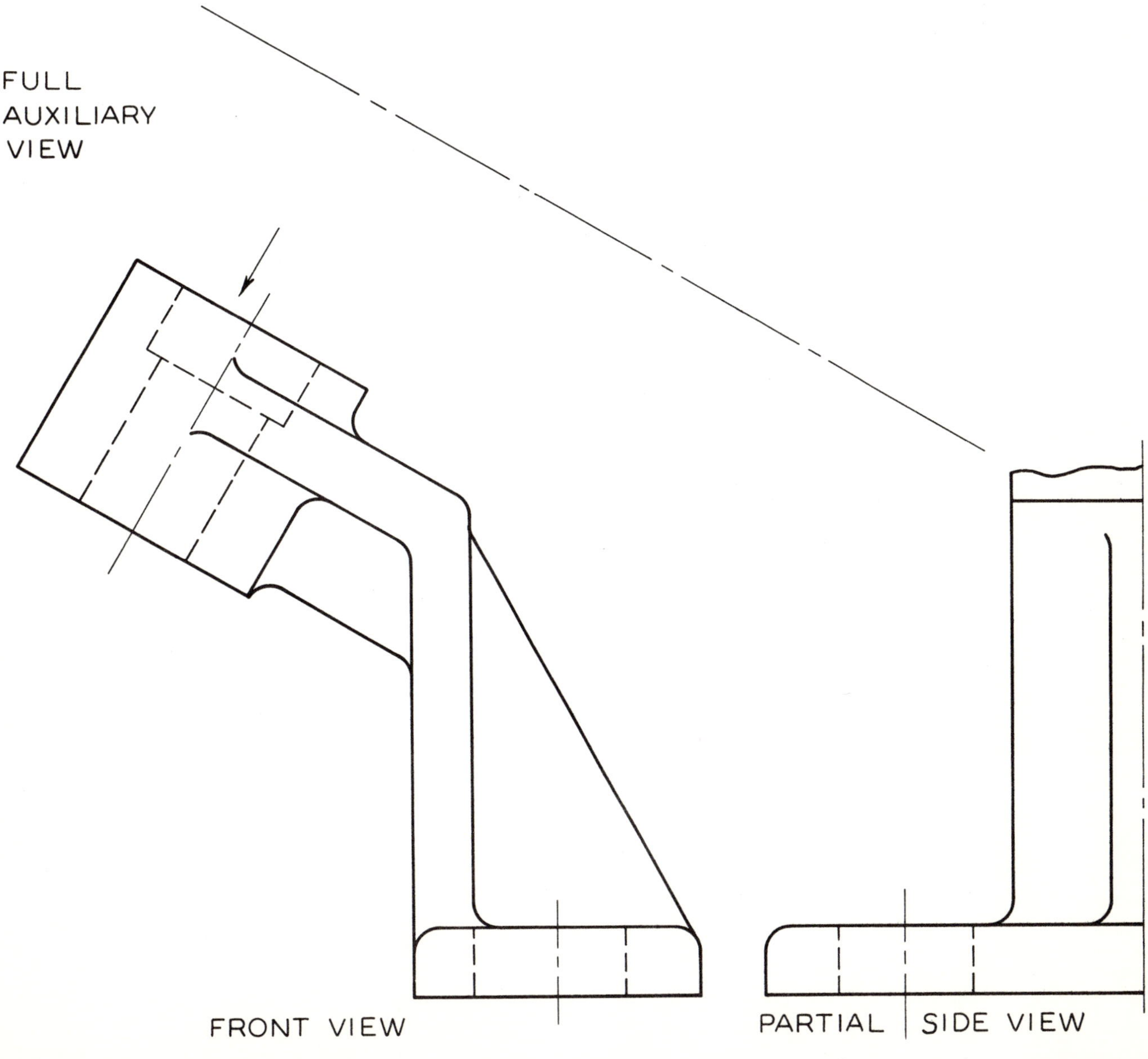

FRONT VIEW

PARTIAL SIDE VIEW

Drafting & Design © James H. Earle	NAME FILE NO SEC DATE	grade	

CONSTRUCT AUXILIARY VIEWS OF THE INCLINED SURFACES OF THE PART BELOW AS INDICATED BY THE LINES OF SIGHT. USE A REFERENCE PLANE THROUGH THE CENTER OF THE TOP VIEW.

1

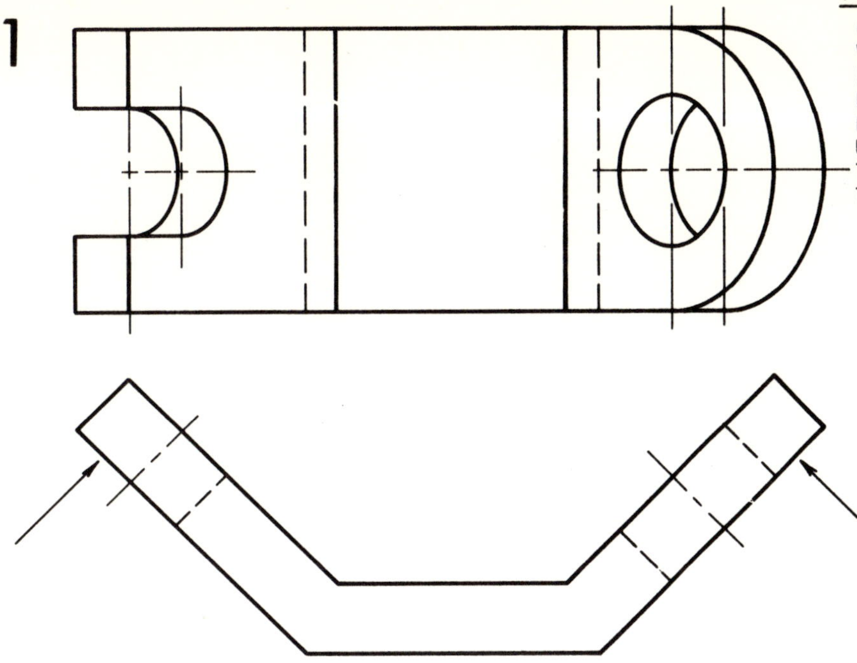

2

THE HYPERBOLA AND PARABOLA ARE CONIC SECTIONS. CUTTING PLANES HAVE BEEN PASSED THROUGH THE FRONT VIEW TO GIVE CURVES IN THE TOP VIEW. PROJECT AUXILIARY VIEWS FROM THE FRONT VIEW TO FIND TRUE SIZE VIEWS OF A HYPERBOLA AND A PARABOLA. NOTICE THAT HALF OF THE POINTS IN THE FRONT VIEW HAVE NOT BEEN LABELED. LABEL THESE AND ALL POINTS IN THE AUXILIARY VIEWS.

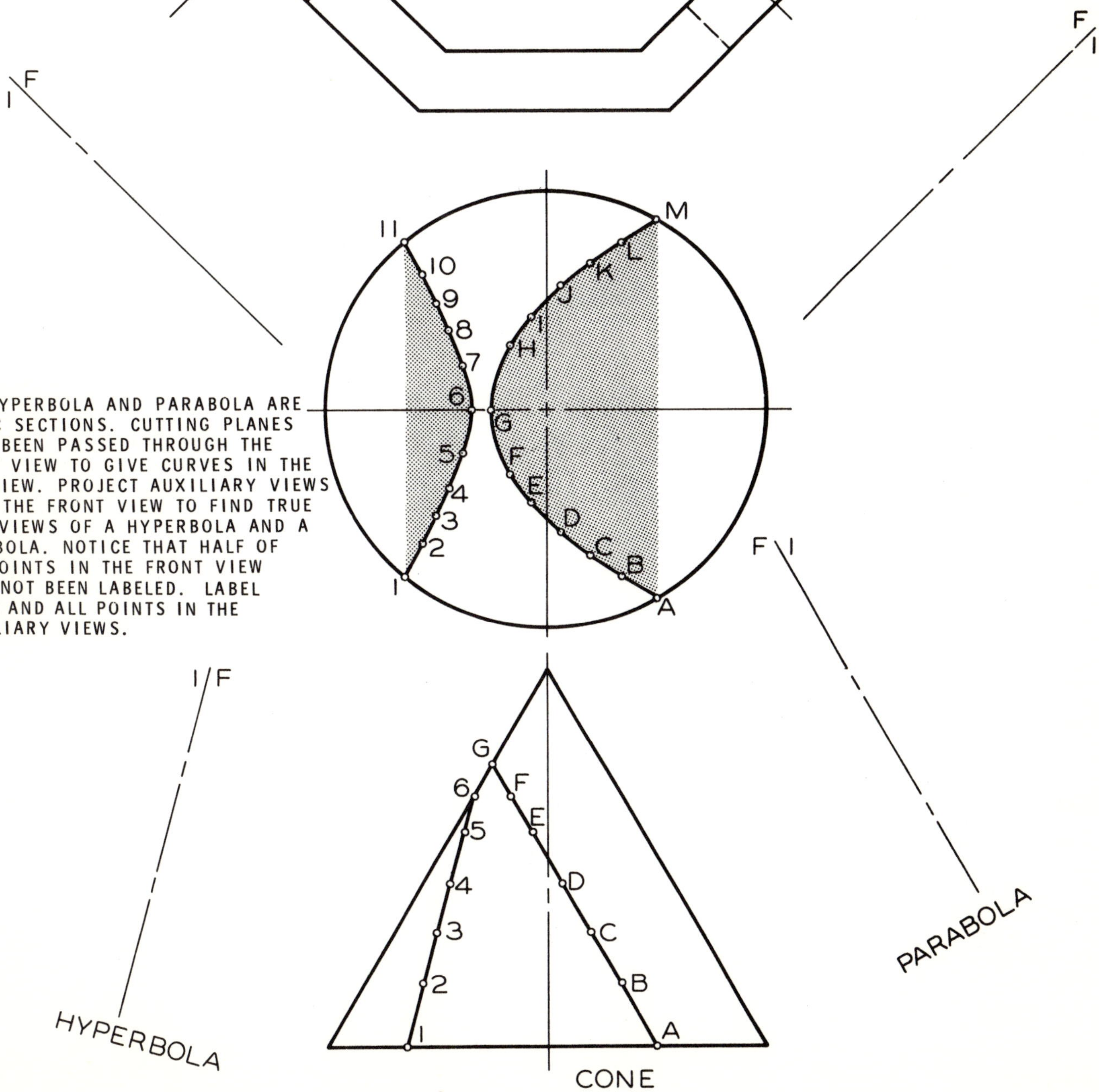

Drafting & Design

NAME
FILE NO SEC DATE
grade

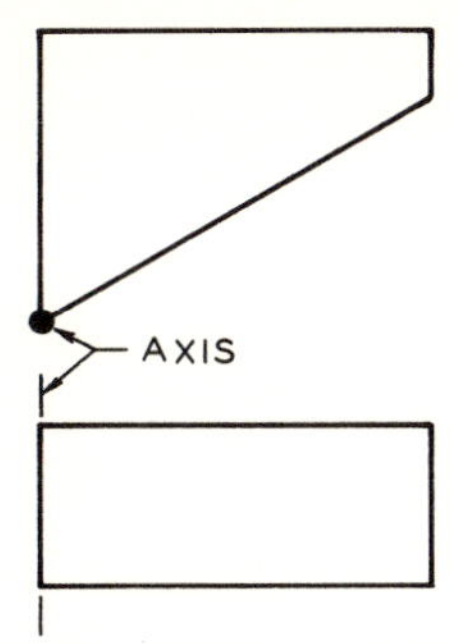

STEP 1: TO FIND THE TRUE SIZE VIEW OF THE INCLINED PLANE, LOCATE AN AXIS AS A POINT IN THE VIEW WHERE THE PLANE IS AN EDGE.

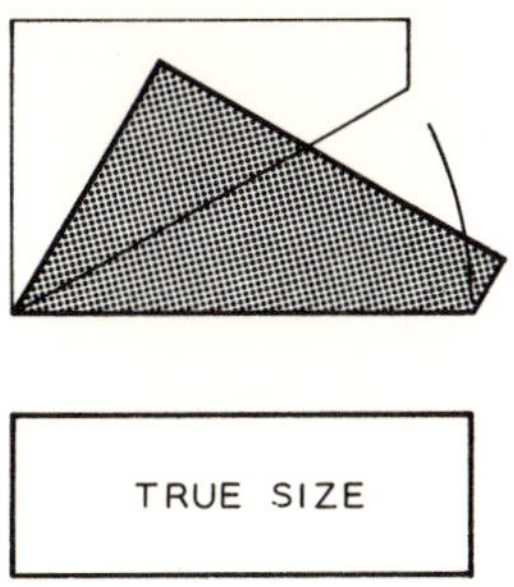

STEP 2: REVOLVE THE OBJECT ABOUT THE AXIS UNTIL THE INCLINED PLANE IS A FRONTAL PLANE. THE NEW FRONT VIEW IS TRUE SIZE.

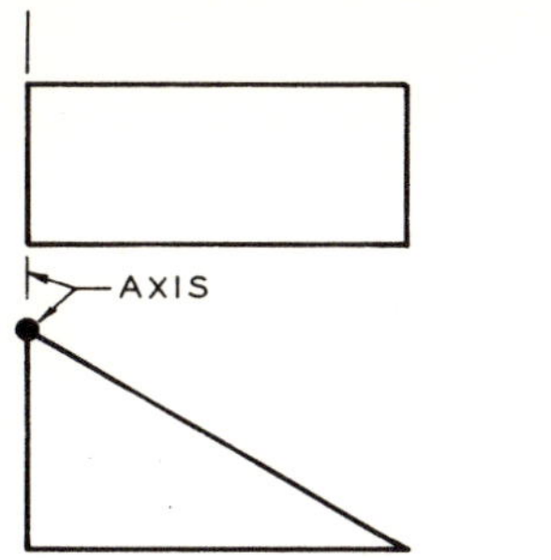

STEP 1: LOCATE THE POINT VIEW OF THE AXIS IN THE VIEW WHERE THE INCLINED PLANE APPEARS AS AN EDGE.

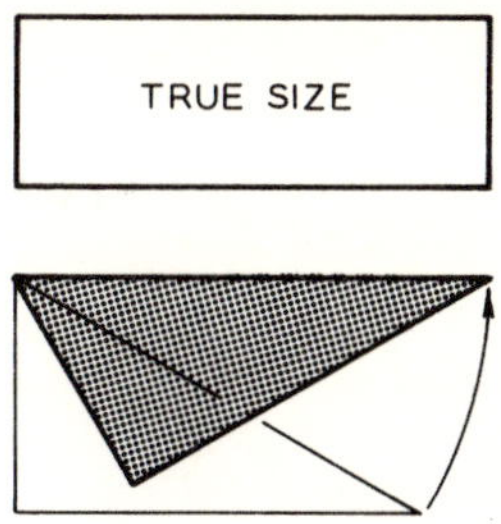

STEP 2: REVOLVE THE OBJECT ABOUT THE AXIS UNTIL THE PLANE IS HORIZONTAL. THE NEW TOP VIEW WILL BE TRUE SIZE.

REQUIRED: REVOLVE THE VIEWS IN PROBLEMS 1 AND 2 TO FIND THE INCLINED PLANES TRUE SIZE. SHOW THE REVOLUTION IN ALL VIEWS.

1

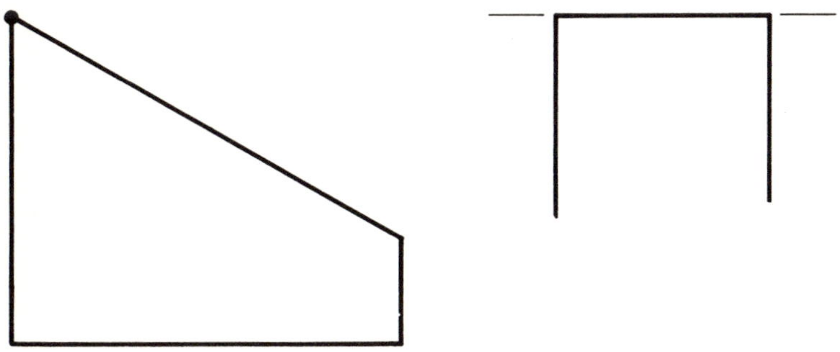

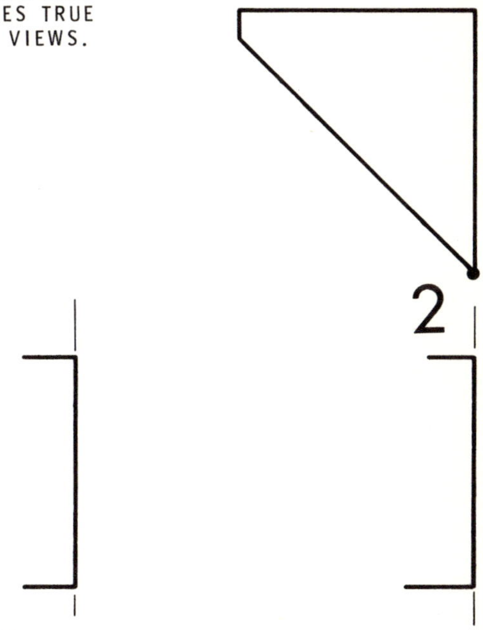

2

REQUIRED: COMPLETE THE TOP VIEWS AS CONVENTIONAL REVOLUTIONS. PROVIDE ALL MISSING LINES IN THE GIVEN VIEWS.

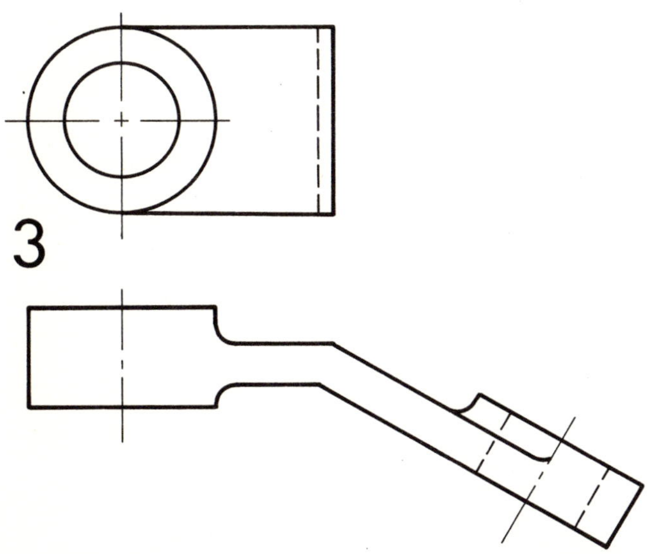

3

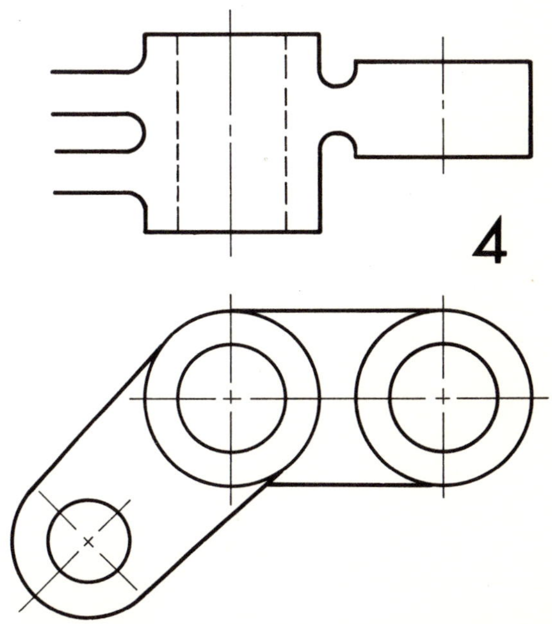

4

NAME
FILE NO SEC DATE
grade

Drafting & Design ©James H. Earle	NAME FILE NO SEC DATE	grade	

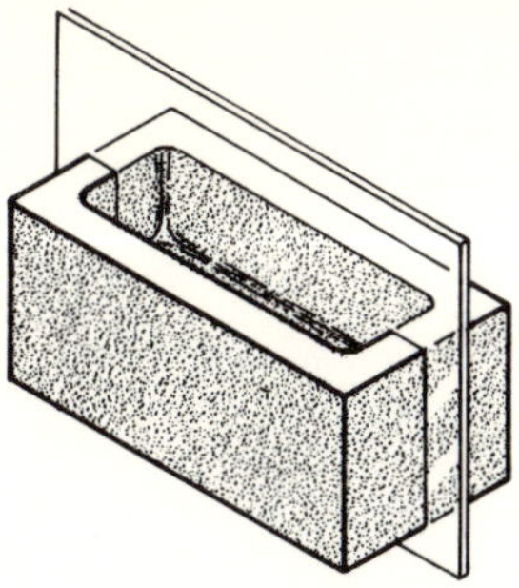

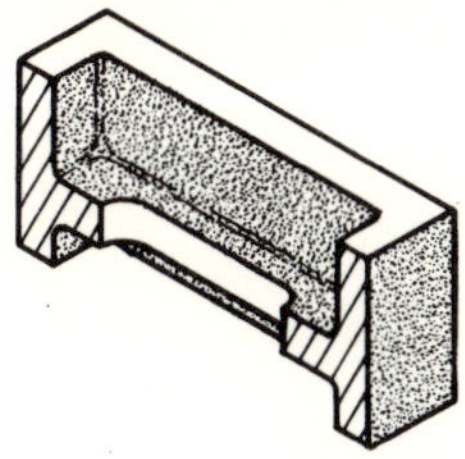

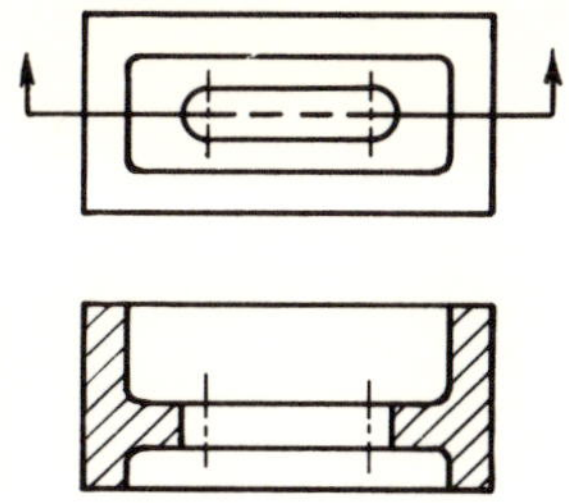

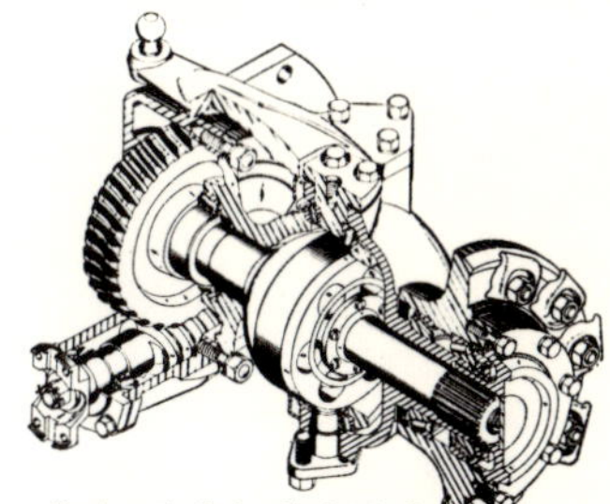

Drawing courtesy Goodman Manufacturing Co.

A FULL SECTION IS FOUND BY PASSING A CUTTING PLANE FULLY THROUGH AN OBJECT AND BY REMOVING HALF OF IT.

A FULL SECTION SHOWN AS AN ORTHOGRAPHIC PROJECTION. THE CUTTING PLANE IS SHOWN AS AN EDGE IN THE TOP VIEW.

COMPLETE THE FRONT VIEW AS A FULL SECTION.

1 FIXTURE BLOCK

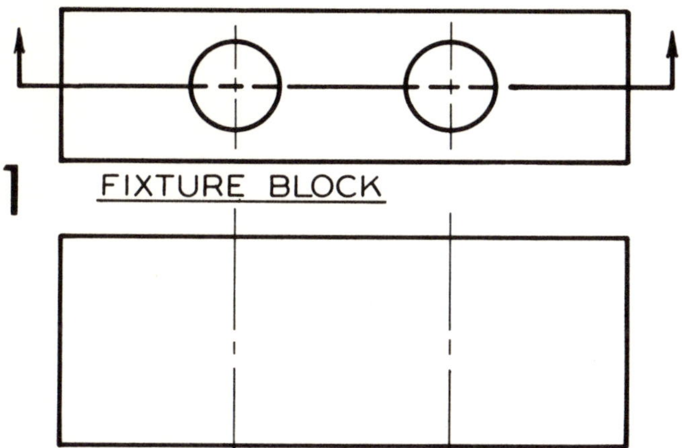

FULL SECTION

2 COMPLETE THE RIGHT SIDE VIEW AS A FULL SECTION.

BUSHING

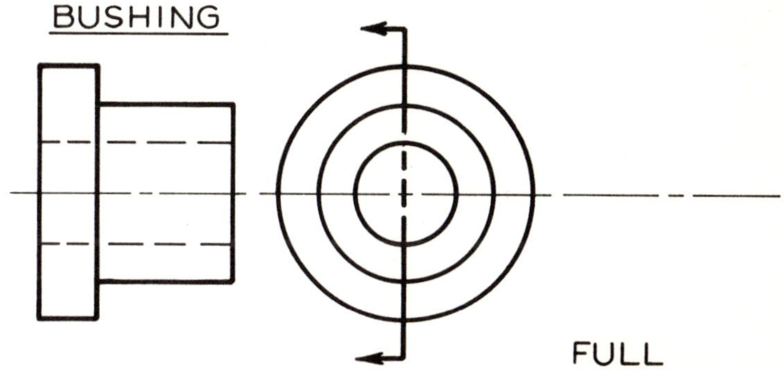

FULL SECTION

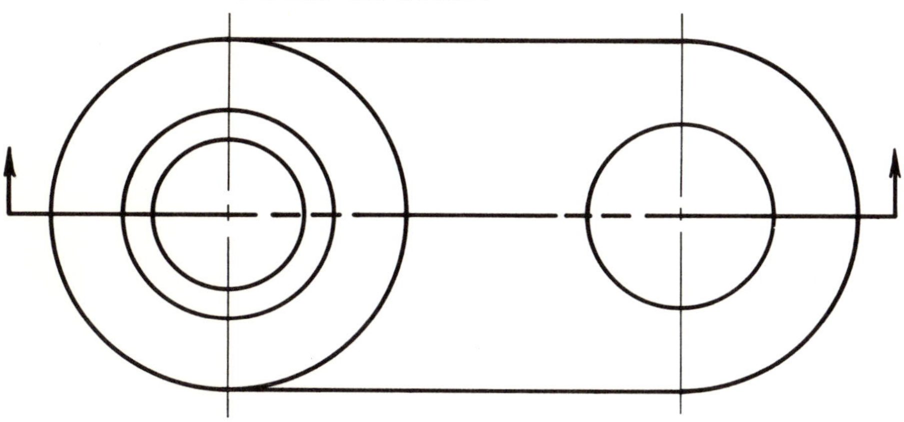

CLEVIS

3 COMPLETE THE FRONT VIEW AS A FULL SECTION.

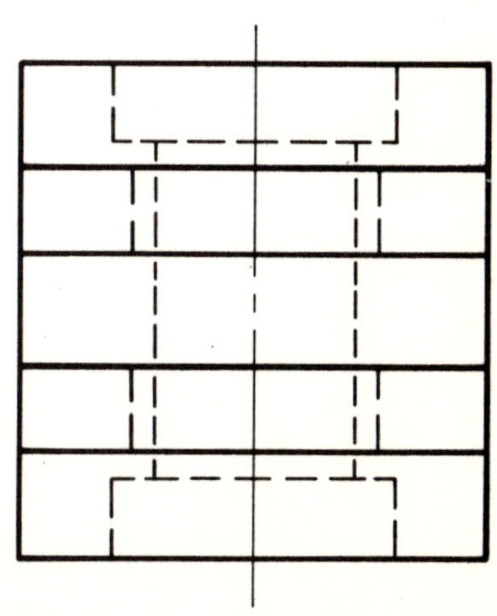

FULL SECTION

Drafting & Design ©James H. Earle	NAME FILE NO SEC DATE	grade	

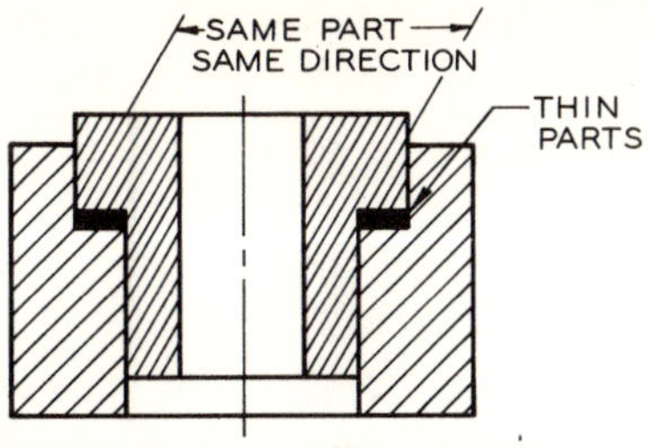

SECTION LINES ON THE SAME PART ARE DRAWN IN THE SAME DIRECTION. THIN PARTS ARE BLACKED IN. PARTS IN ASSEMBLIES ARE SECTIONED AT DIFFERENT ANGLES.

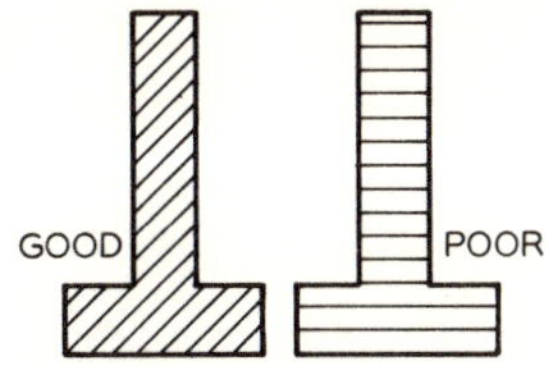

SECTION LINES SHOULD BE DRAWN AT AN ANGLE WITH THE OUTLINE OF THE PART; NOT PARALLEL OR PERPENDICULAR TO THE OUTLINE.

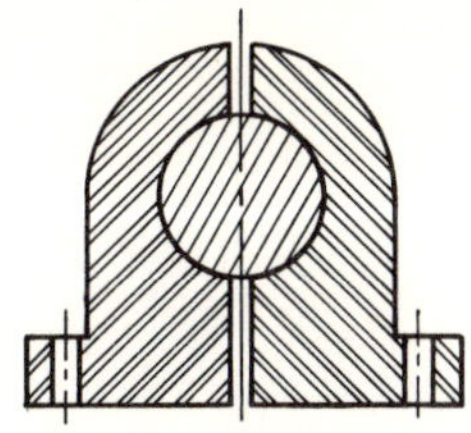

DIFFERENT SYMBOLS CAN BE USED TO REPRESENT DIFFERENT MATERIALS IN SECTIONS. CAST IRON SYMBOLS CAN BE USED FOR ALL MATERIALS.

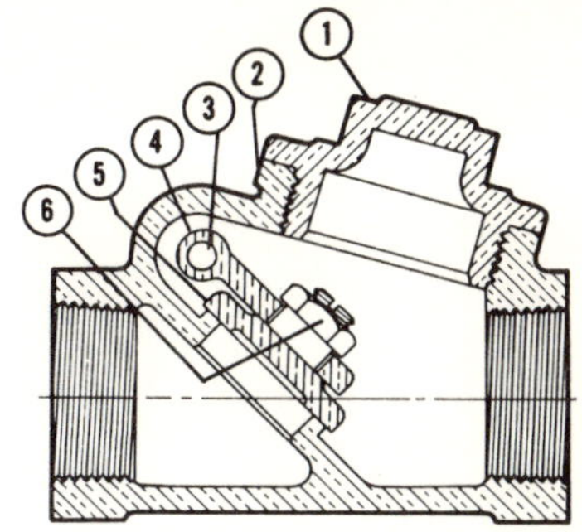

Courtesy of Nibco Inc.

1 COMPLETE THE FRONT VIEW AS AN OUTLINE SECTION.

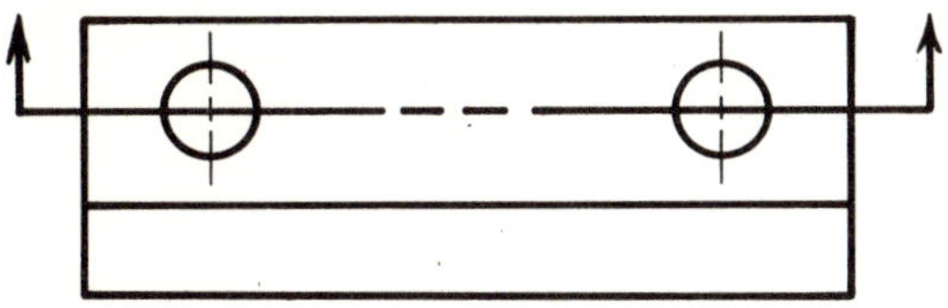

2 CROSSHATCH THE PARTS BELOW USING CAST IRON SYMBOLS.

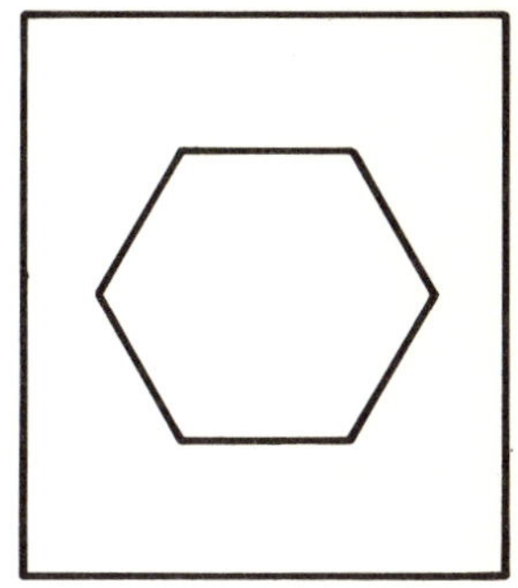

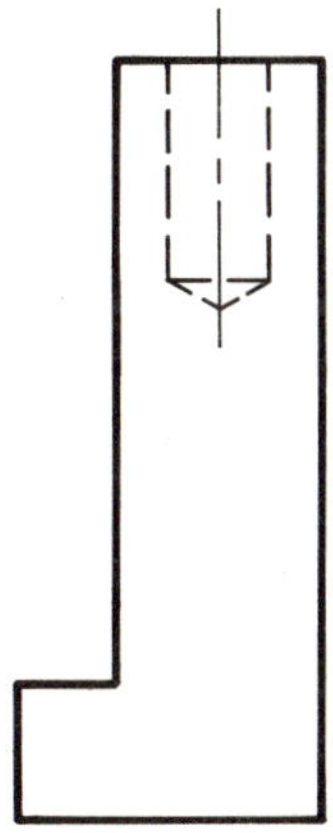

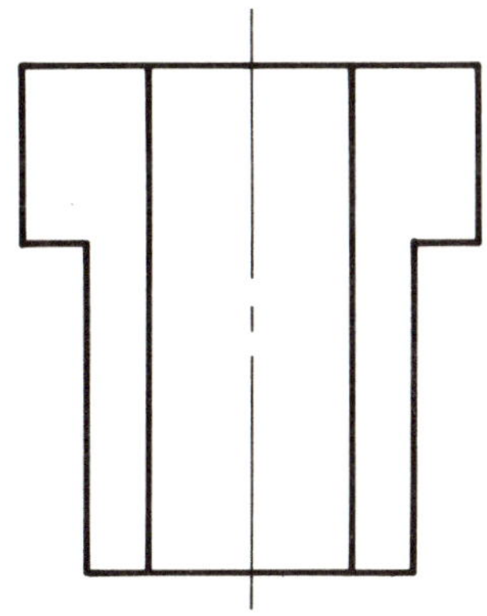

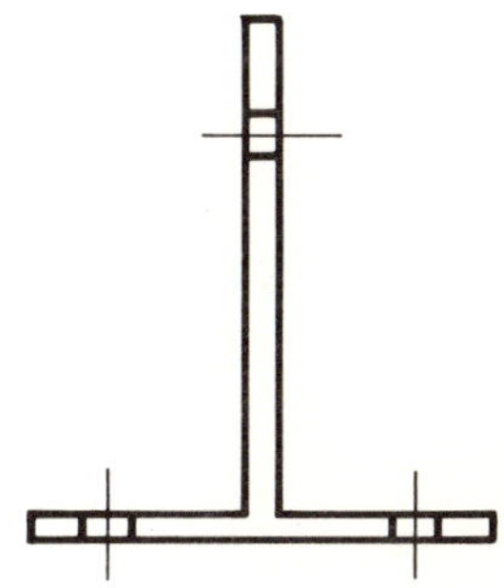

3 COMPLETE THIS ASSEMBLY AS A SECTION USING THE PROPER SYMBOLS.

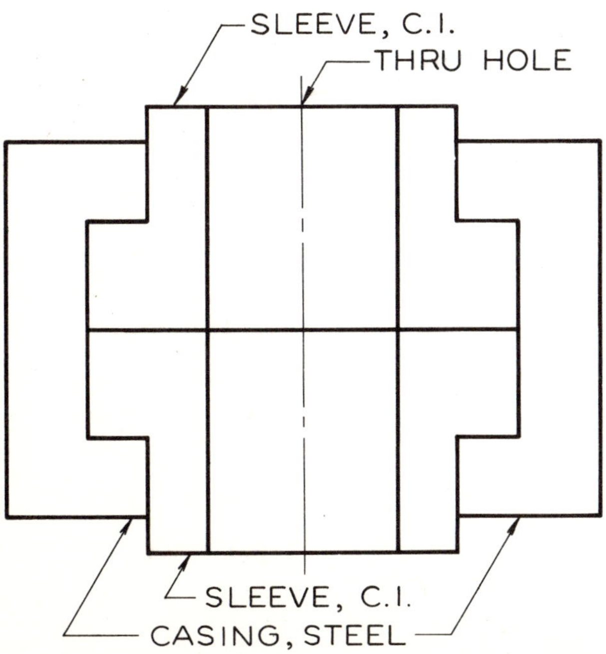

4 COMPLETE THE FRONT VIEW AS A SECTION USING THE SYMBOLS INDICATED. THE TOP AND SIDE VIEWS ARE PARTIAL VIEWS.

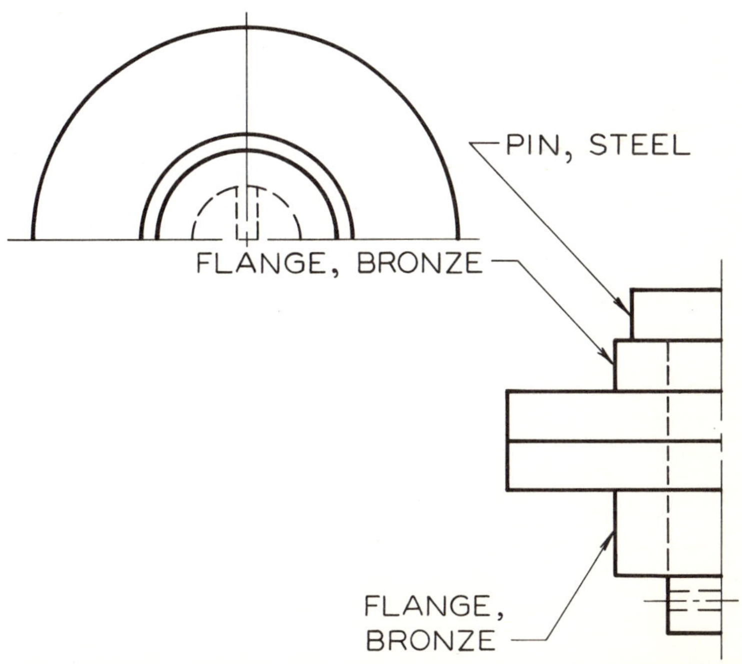

Drafting & Design

NAME

FILE NO. SEC. DATE

grade

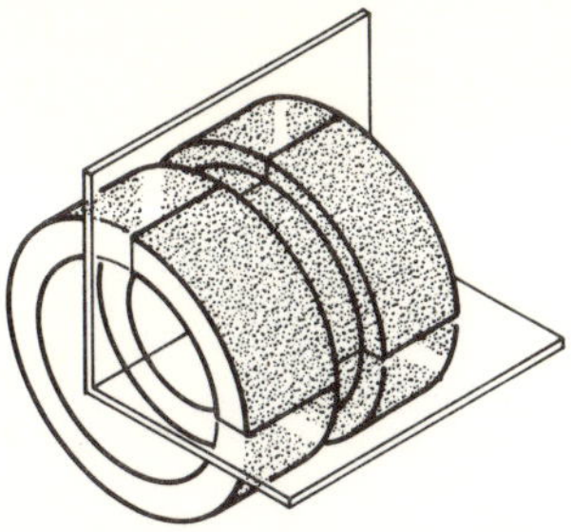

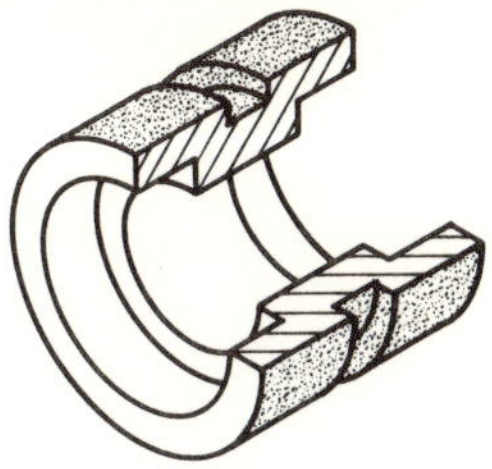

THE CUTTING PLANE IN A HALF SECTION PASSES HALFWAY THROUGH AN OBJECT AND A QUARTER IS REMOVED. THIS ENABLES BOTH INTERIOR AND EXTERIOR FEATURES TO BE SHOWN.

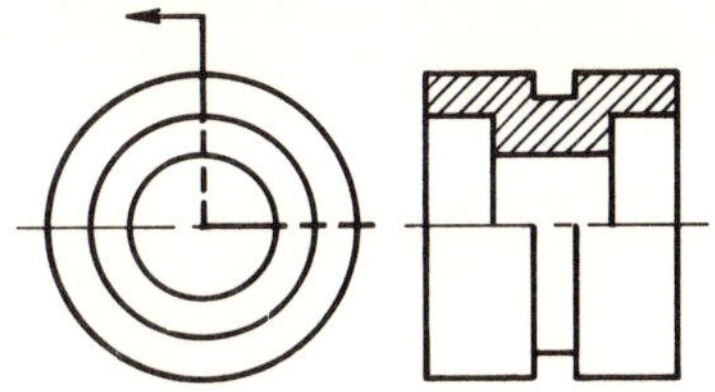

THE CUTTING PLANE IS SHOWN AS AN EDGE IN THE CIRCULAR VIEW; THE HALF SECTION IS SHOWN AT THE RIGHT. HIDDEN LINES ARE USUALLY OMITTED.

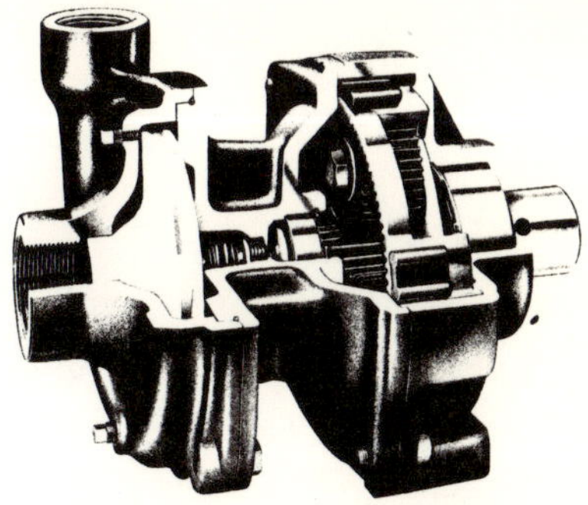

Courtesy of HYPRO of Lear Siegler, Inc.

COMPLETE THE FRONT VIEW AS A HALF SECTION.

1

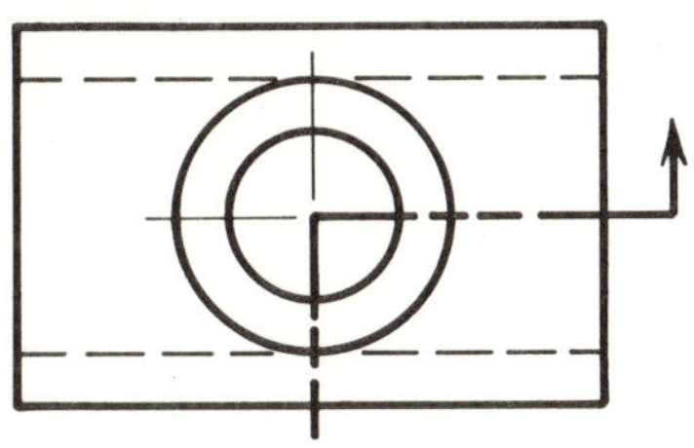

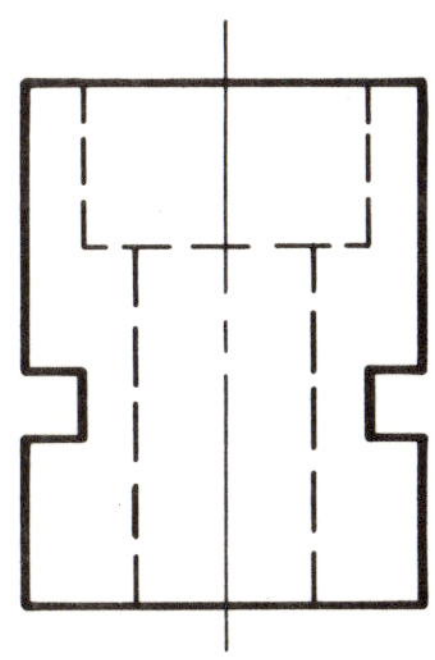

2 TWO PARTIAL VIEWS ARE GIVEN; COMPLETE THE FRONT VIEW AS A HALF SECTION.

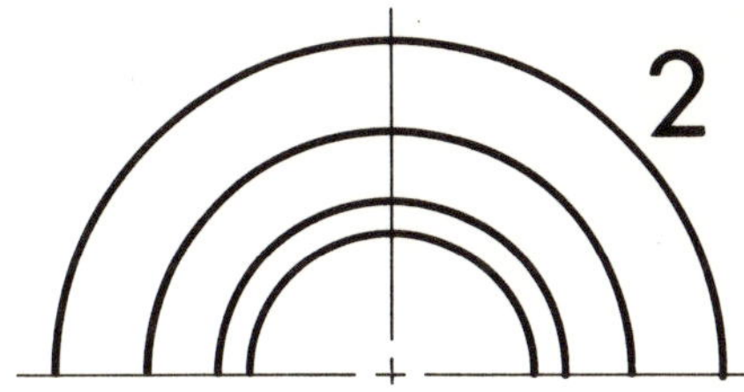

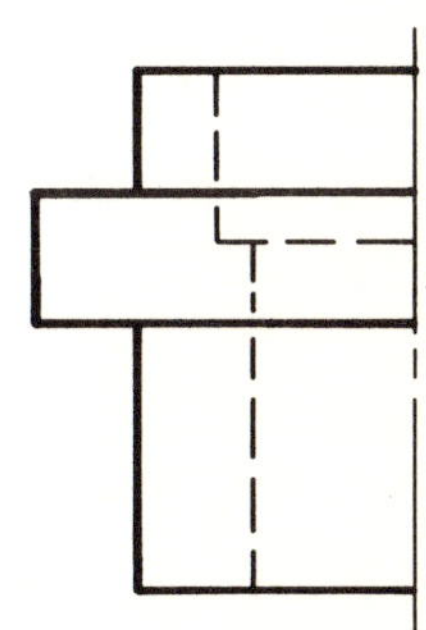

3 COMPLETE THE FRONT VIEW AS A HALF SECTION.

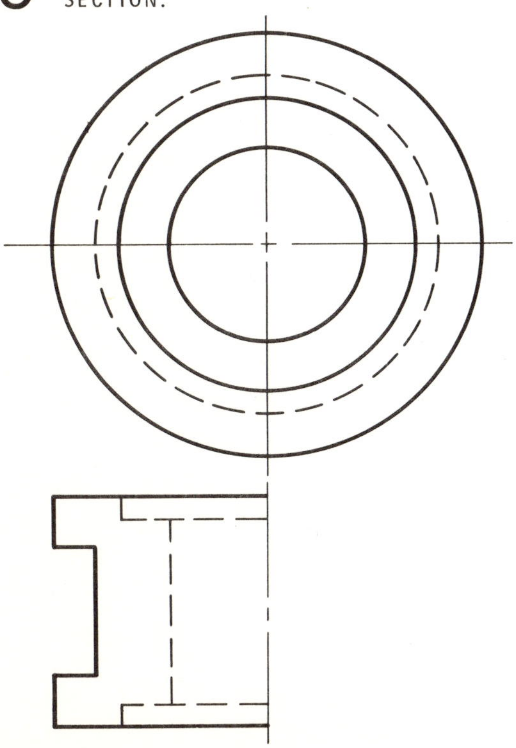

4 COMPLETE THE FRONT VIEW AS A HALF SECTION.

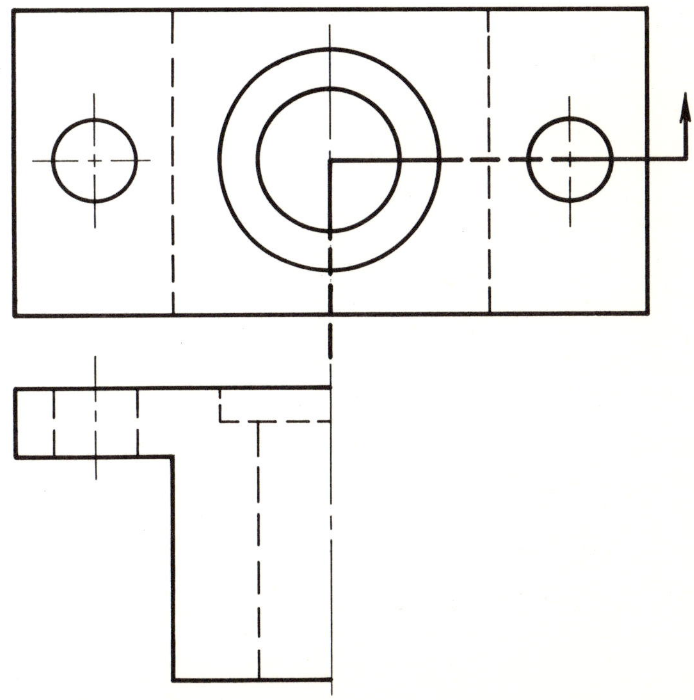

Drafting & Design © James H. Earle	NAME FILE NO SEC DATE	grade	

OFFSET SECTIONS

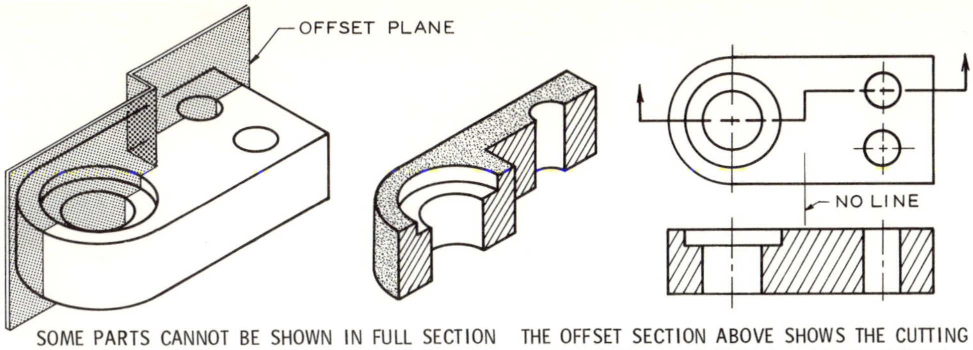

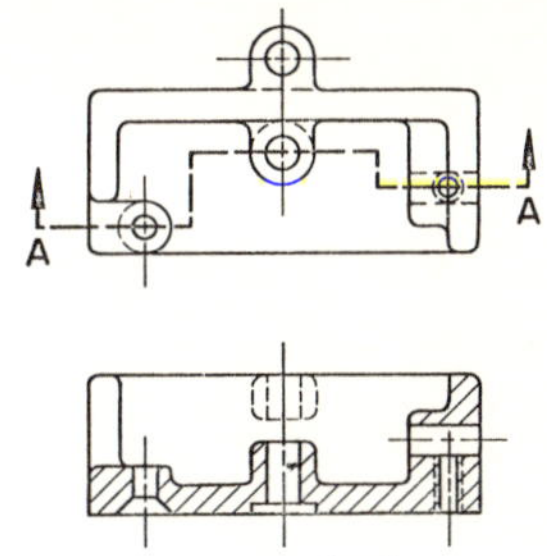

SECTION A-A

SOME PARTS CANNOT BE SHOWN IN FULL SECTION WITHOUT OFFSETTING THE CUTTING PLANE IN ORDER TO SHOW ITS MAJOR FEATURES.

THE OFFSET SECTION ABOVE SHOWS THE CUTTING PLANE PASSING THROUGH TWO HOLES. NOTICE THAT THE OFFSET IN THE CUTTING PLANE IS NOT SHOWN AS A LINE IN THE SECTIONAL VIEW.

1 COMPLETE THE OFFSET SECTION BELOW. THE HOLES ARE THROUGH HOLES.

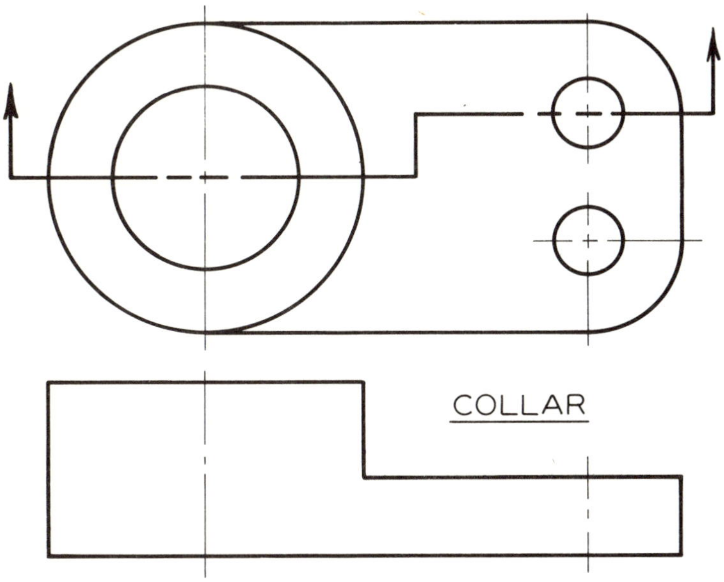

COLLAR

2 COMPLETE THE OFFSET SECTION BELOW. SHOW THE CUTTING PLANE IN THE TOP VIEW.

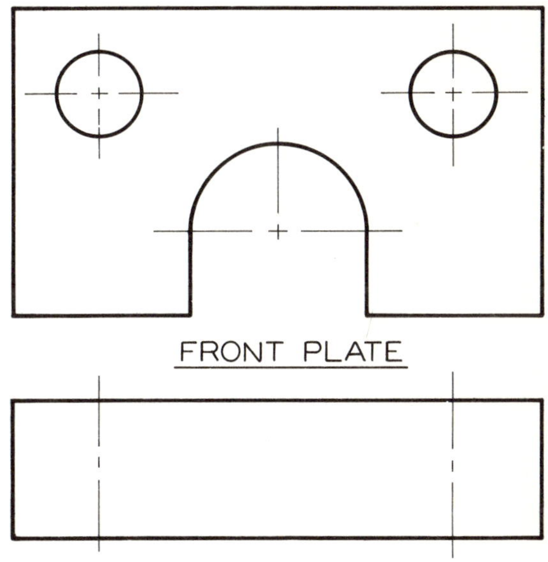

FRONT PLATE

3 CONSTRUCT THE FRONT VIEW AS AN OFFSET SECTION. SHOW THE CUTTING PLANE IN THE TOP VIEW.

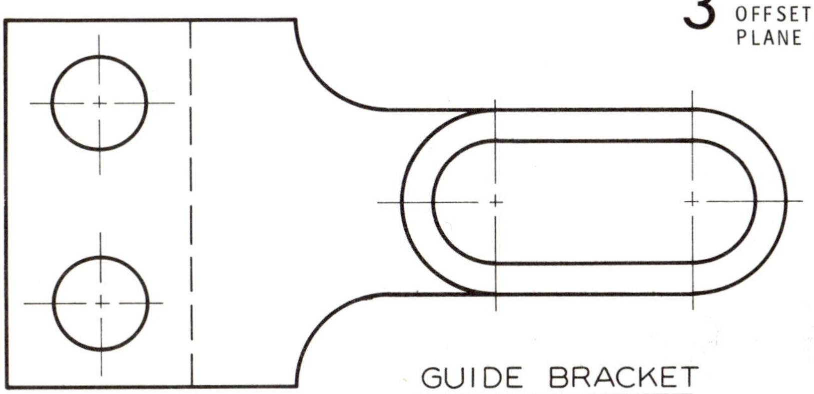

GUIDE BRACKET

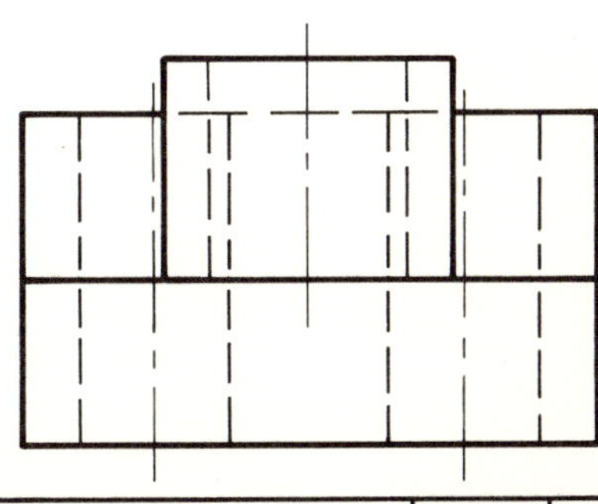

Drafting & Design ©James H. Earle	NAME FILE NO SEC DATE	grade	57

Drafting & Design
© James H. Earle

NAME		grade	
FILE NO	SEC	DATE	

BROKEN-OUT SECTIONS

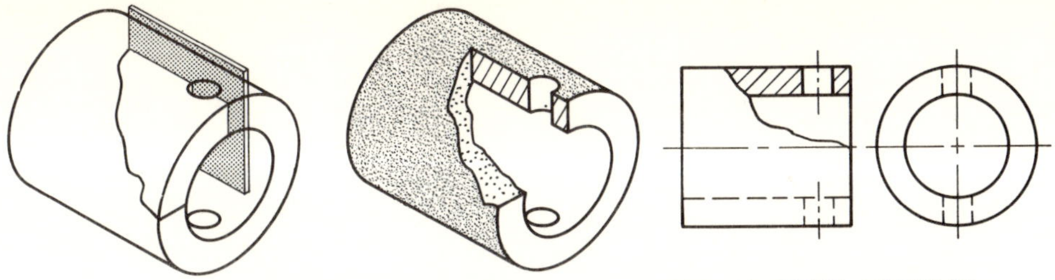

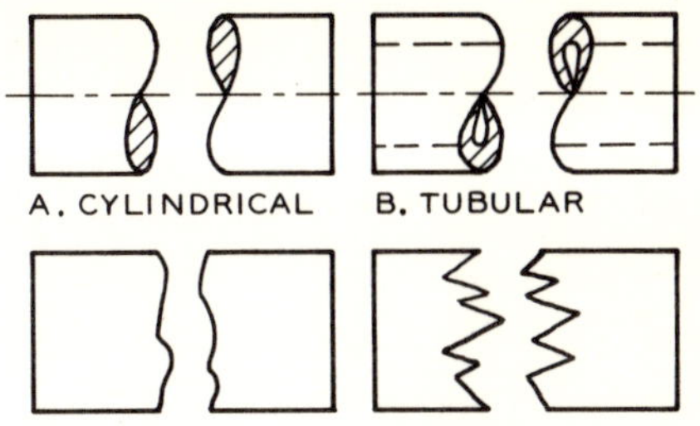

A BROKEN-OUT SECTION CAN BE USED TO SHOW INTERIOR DETAILS OF A PORTION OF A PART. CONVENTIONAL BREAKS ARE USED TO REPRESENT THE BROKEN PORTION. BREAK LINES FOR VARIOUS MATERIALS ARE SHOWN AT THE RIGHT.

1 COMPLETE THE RIGHT SIDE VIEW AS A BROKEN-OUT SECTION.

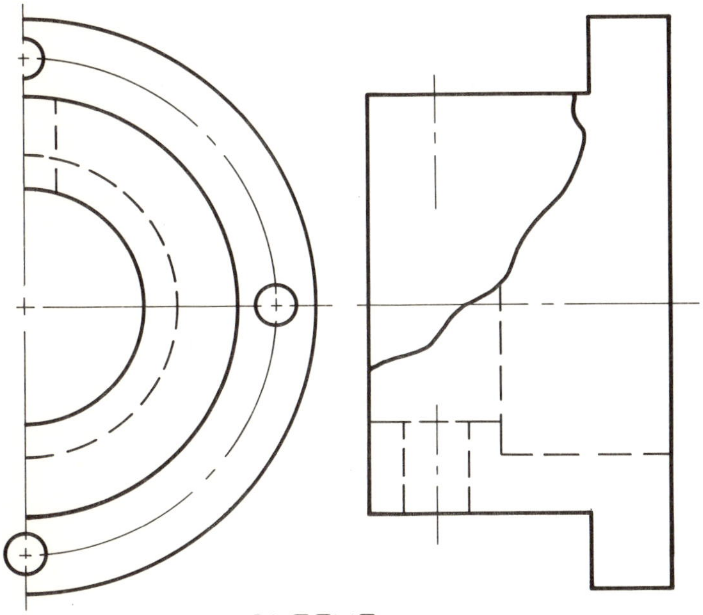

SLEEVE

2 COMPLETE THIS VIEW OF A SYMMETRICAL CYLINDRICAL PART. THE TOP PORTION IS IDENTICAL TO THE BOTTOM PORTION.

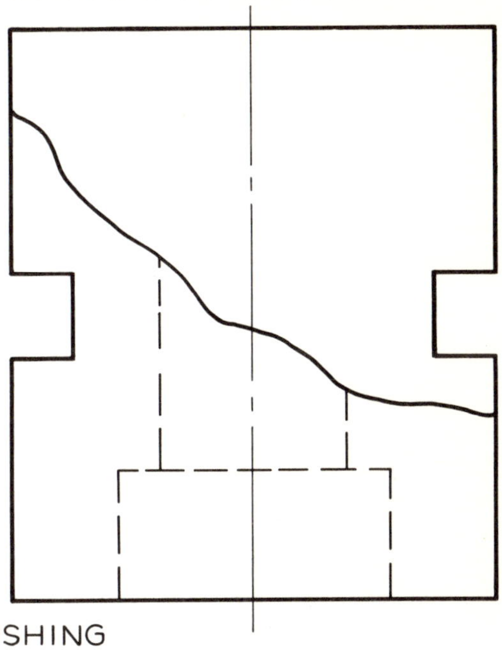

BUSHING

3 SHOW CONVENTIONAL BREAKS IN THE PARTS BELOW.

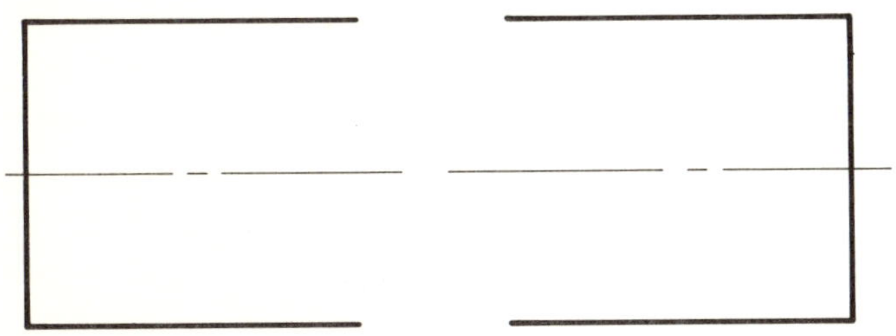

A. CYLINDRICAL – C.I.

C. RECTANGULAR – STEEL

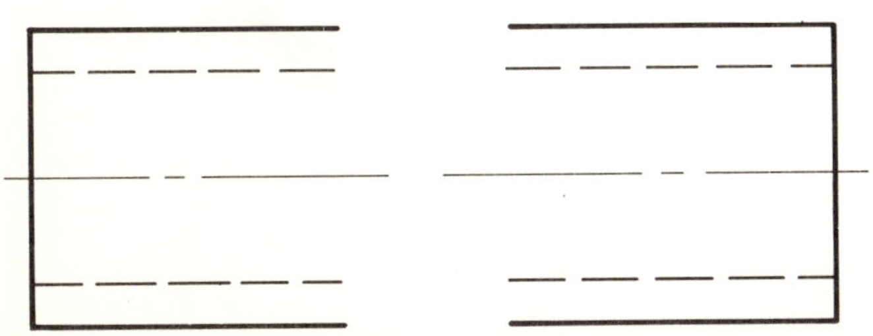

B. TUBULAR – BRASS

D. RECTANGULAR – WOOD

Drafting & Design

© James H. Earle

NAME

FILE NO

SEC

DATE

grade

REVOLVED SECTIONS

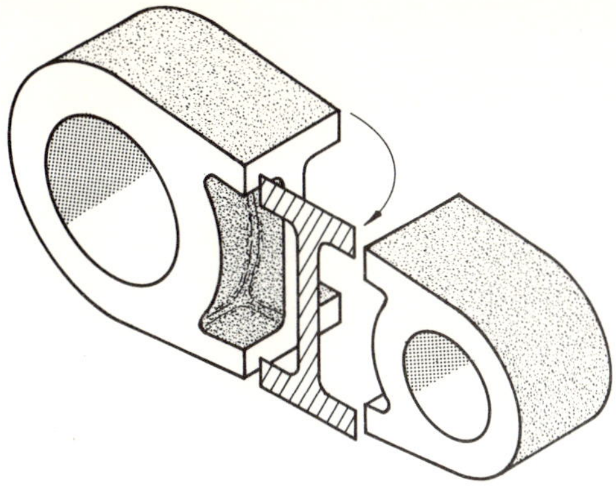

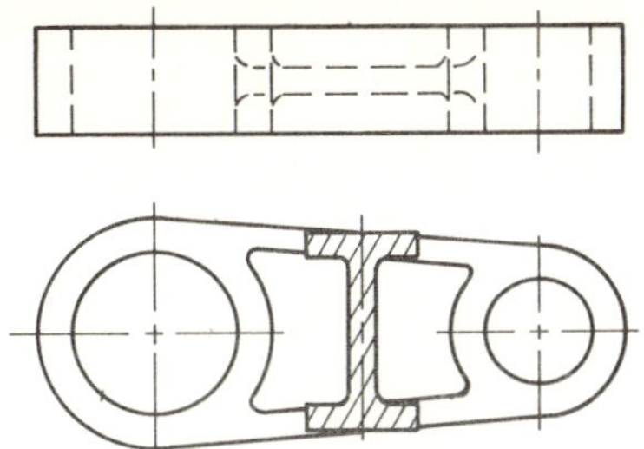

WITH BREAKS

A REVOLVED SECTION IS USED TO SHOW A CROSS SECTION THROUGH A PART THAT WILL DESCRIBE IT WITHOUT THE NEED FOR AN ADDITIONAL VIEW. IT CAN BE SUPERIMPOSED ON THE VIEW WHERE IT IS REVOLVED. NOTICE THAT OBJECT LINES DO NOT PASS THROUGH THE REVOLVED SECTION. THE REVOLVED SECTION CAN BE SEPARATED FROM THE VIEW BY USING CONVENTIONAL BREAKS AS SHOWN IN THE SECOND EXAMPLE.

1 SHOW REVOLVED SECTIONS WITHOUT CONVENTIONAL BREAKS BELOW.

2 SHOW REVOLVED SECTIONS WITH CONVENTIONAL BREAKS BELOW.

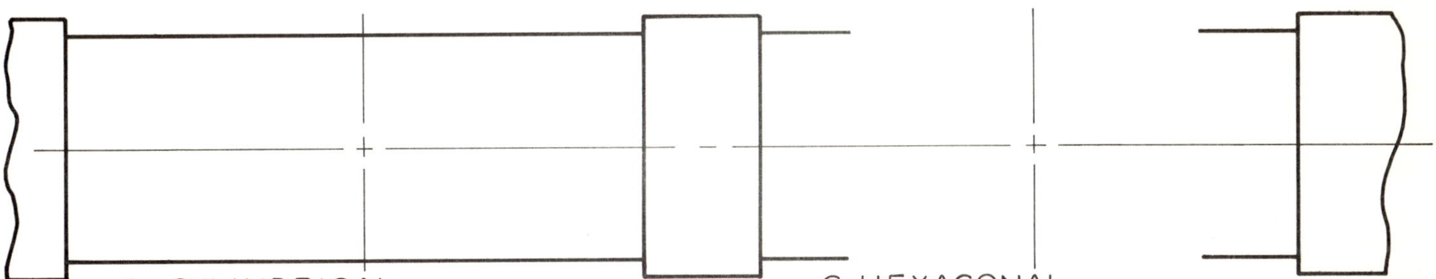

A. CYLINDRICAL

C. HEXAGONAL

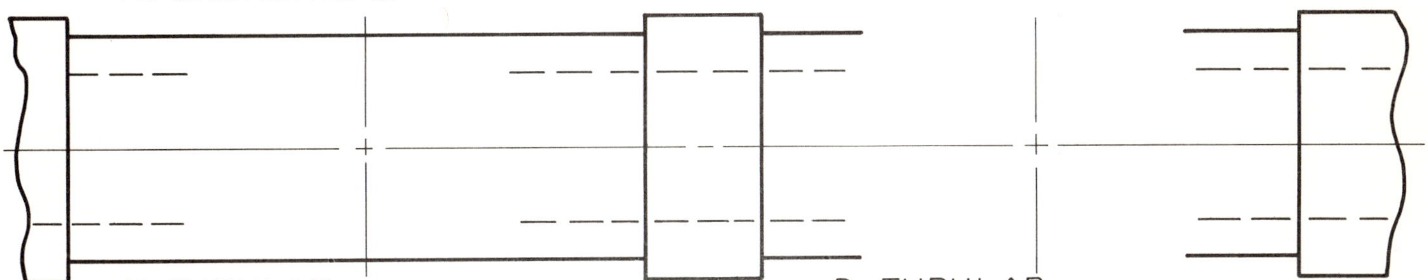

B. TUBULAR

D. TUBULAR

3 SHOW A REVOLVED SECTION IN THE FRONT VIEW WITHOUT CONVENTIONAL BREAKS.

4 SHOW A REVOLVED SECTION IN THE FRONT VIEW WITH CONVENTIONAL BREAKS.

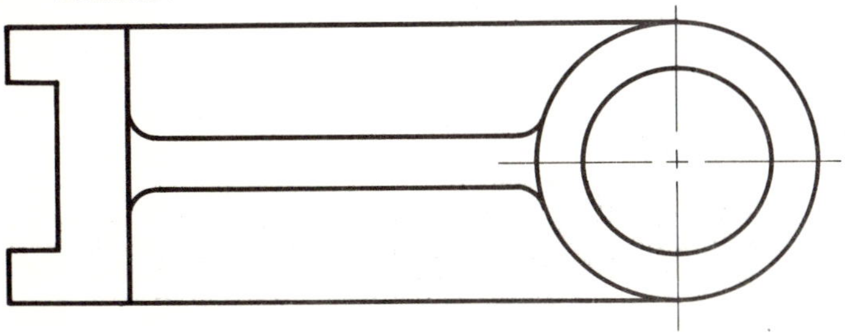

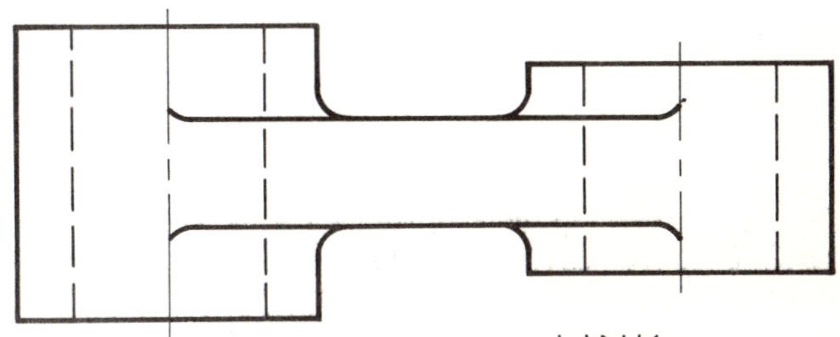

LINK

SHAFT LEVER

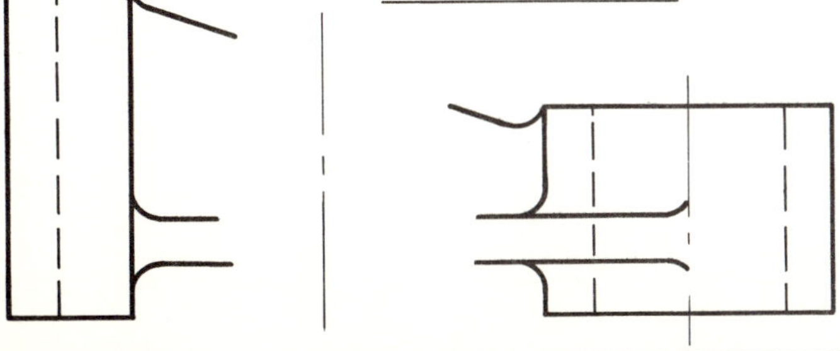

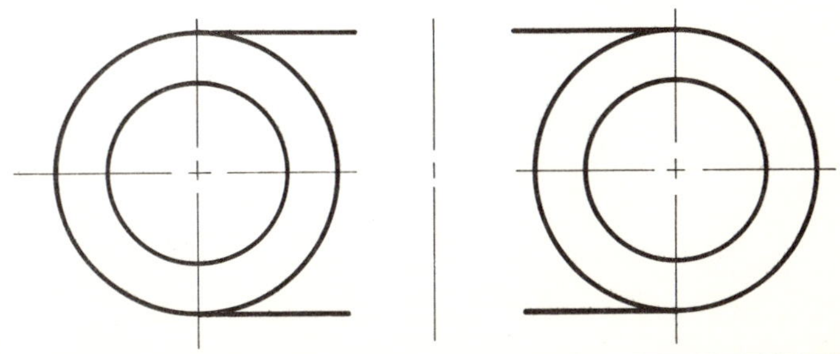

Drafting & Design © James H. Earle	NAME FILE NO SEC DATE	grade	

REMOVED SECTIONS

A REMOVED SECTION IS SECTION THAT IS LOCATED IN A REMOVED POSITION. IT MAY BE SHOWN ON A SEPARATE SHEET FROM THE CUTTING PLANE VIEW; CONSEQUENTLY THE SECTIONS ARE LABELED AS SHOWN.

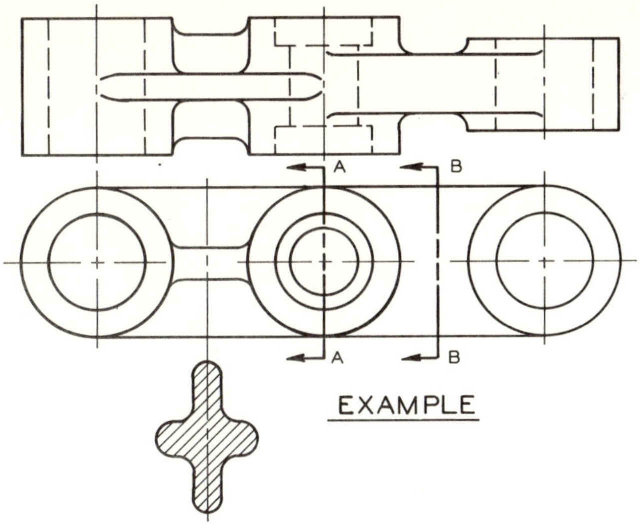

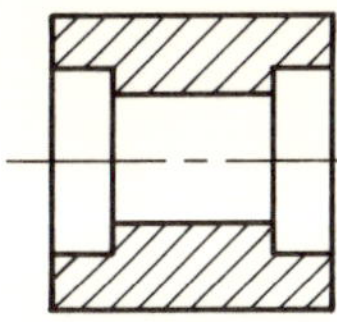

SECTION A-A

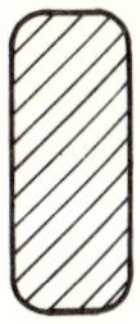

SECTION B-B

EXAMPLE

1 CONSTRUCT A REMOVED SECTION USING THE CENTER LINE GIVEN.

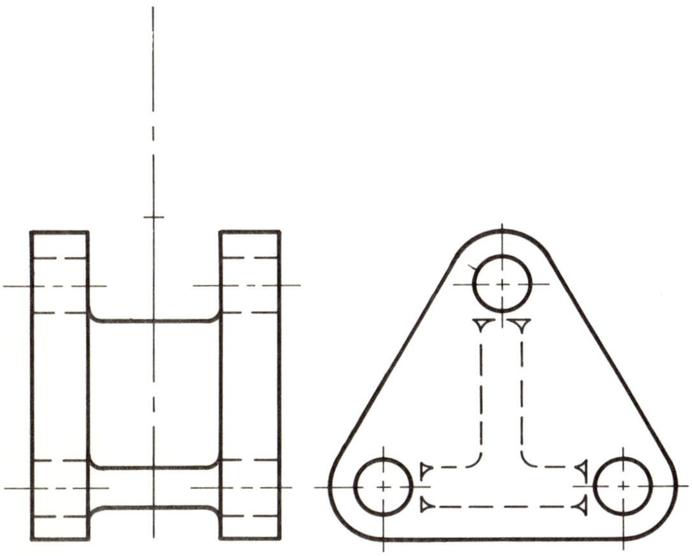

2 CONSTRUCT THE REMOVED SECTIONS INDICATED BY THE CUTTING PLANES.

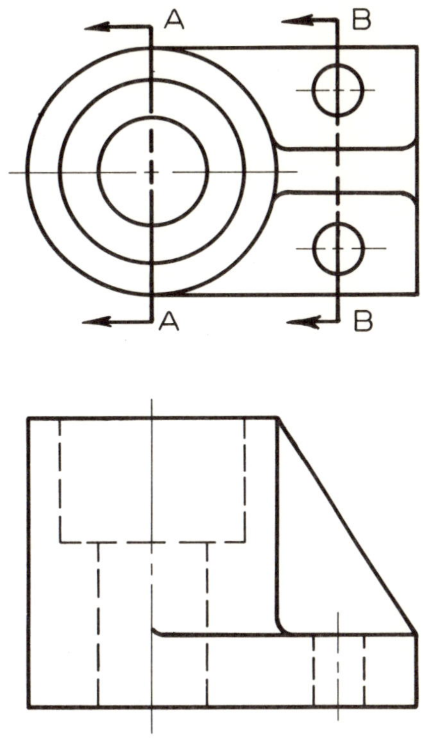

SECTION A-A

SECTION B-B

3 CONSTRUCT THE REMOVED SECTIONS INDICATED.

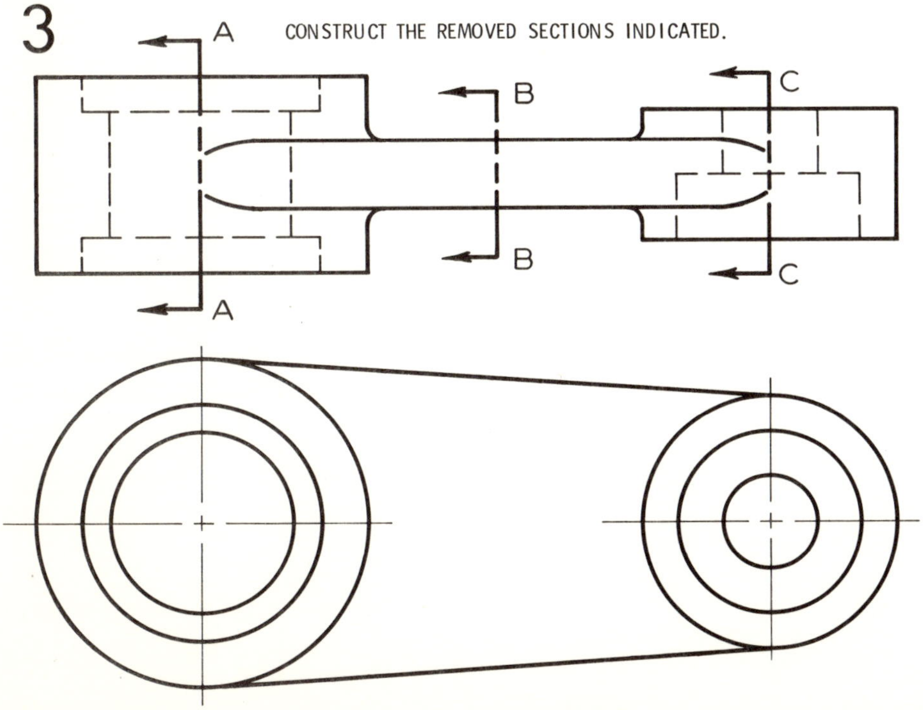

SECTION A-A

SECT B-B

SECTION C-C

Drafting & Design ©James H. Earle	NAME FILE NO SEC DATE	grade	60

Drafting & Design

NAME

FILE NO SEC DATE

grade

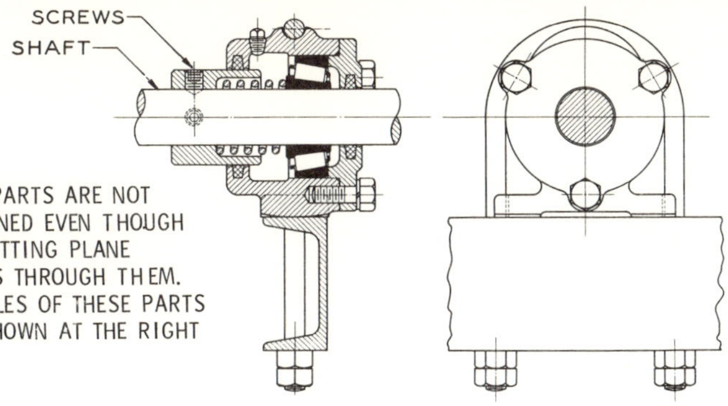

SOME PARTS ARE NOT SECTIONED EVEN THOUGH THE CUTTING PLANE PASSES THROUGH THEM. EXAMPLES OF THESE PARTS ARE SHOWN AT THE RIGHT

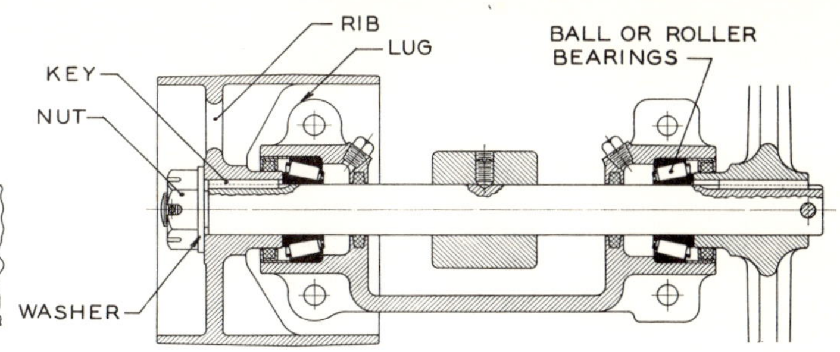

1 COMPLETE THE FRONT VIEW AS A FULL SECTION.

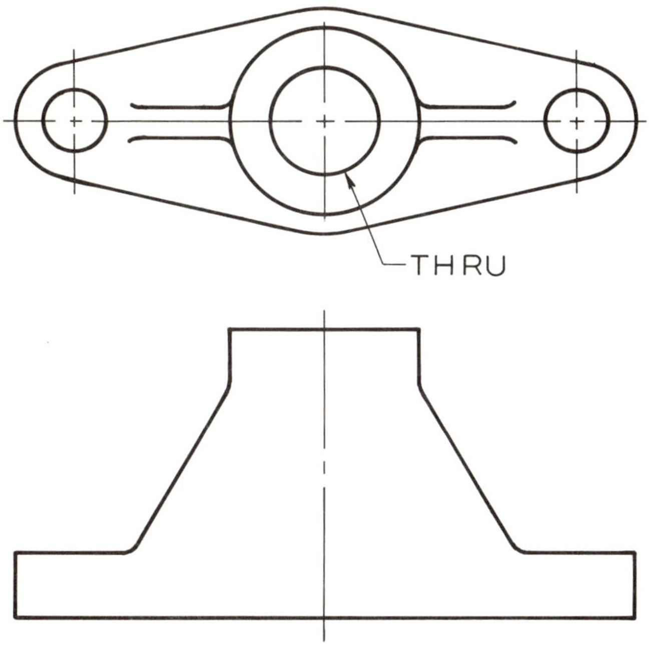

2 COMPLETE THE RIGHT SIDE VIEW AS A FULL SECTION.

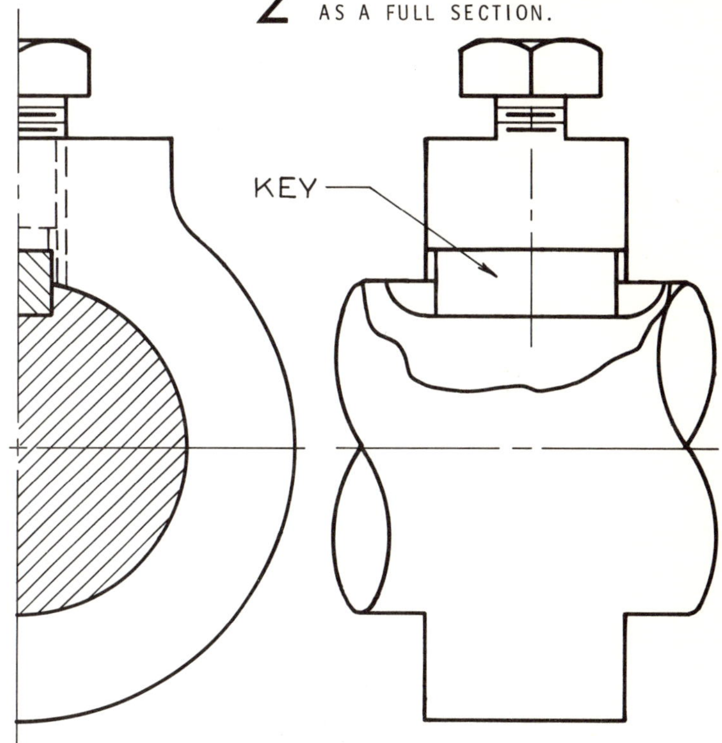

3 COMPLETE THE FRONT VIEW AS A PHANTOM SECTION.

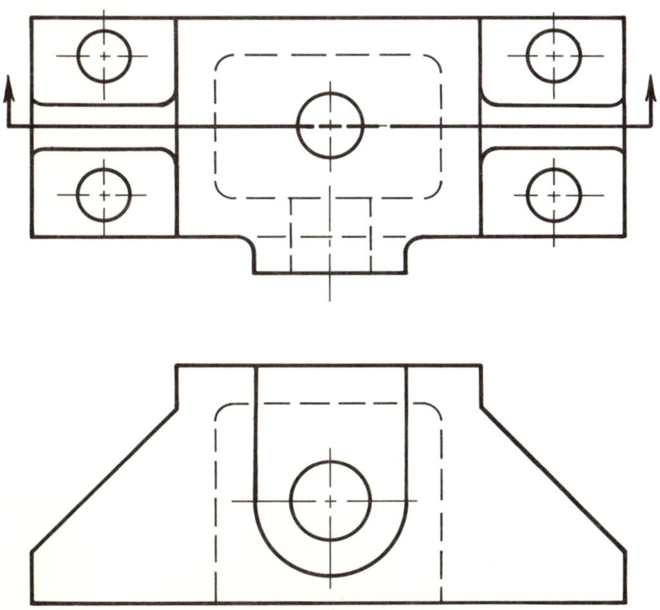

PHANTOM SECTION

4 COMPLETE THE FRONT VIEW AS A FULL SECTION.

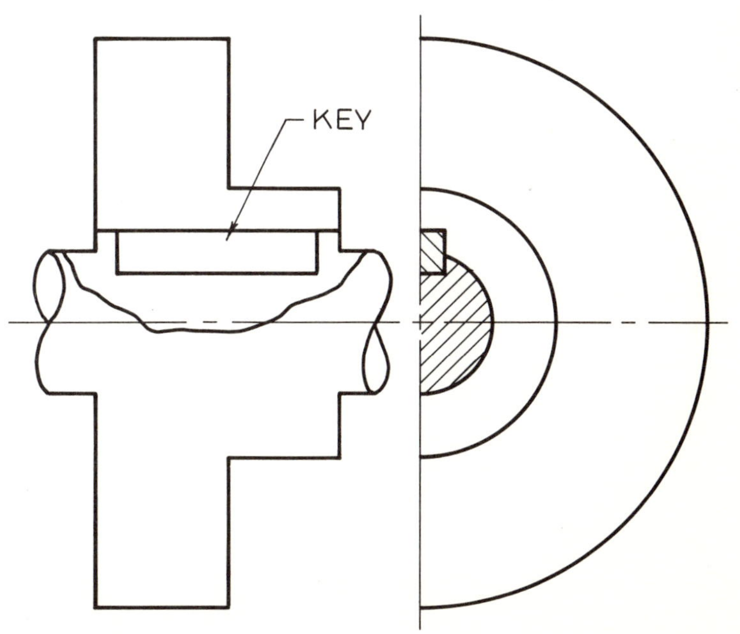

Drafting & Design © James H. Earle	NAME FILE NO SEC DATE	grade	

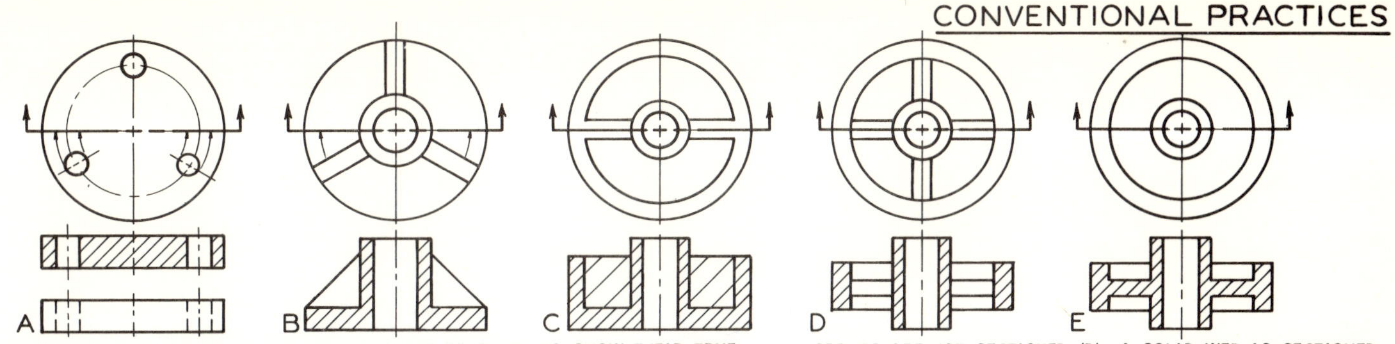

SYMMETRICALLY SPACED HOLES AND RIBS ARE REVOLVED TO SHOW THEIR TRUE SHAPES AND TRUE RADIAL DISTANCES FROM THE CENTER OF CIRCULAR PARTS IN BOTH VIEWS AND SECTIONS. RIBS AND WEBS ARE NOT SECTIONED WHEN THE CUTTING PLANE PASSES THROUGH THEM FLATWISE. RIBS MAY BE SECTIONED WITH ALTERNATE LINES TO CALL ATTENTION TO THEM (C).

SPOKES ARE NOT SECTIONED (D). A SOLID WEB IS SECTIONED WHEN THE CUTTING PLANE IS PASSED THROUGH IT AS SHOWN AT E.

1

COMPLETE THE FRONT VIEWS AS FULL SECTIONS.

2

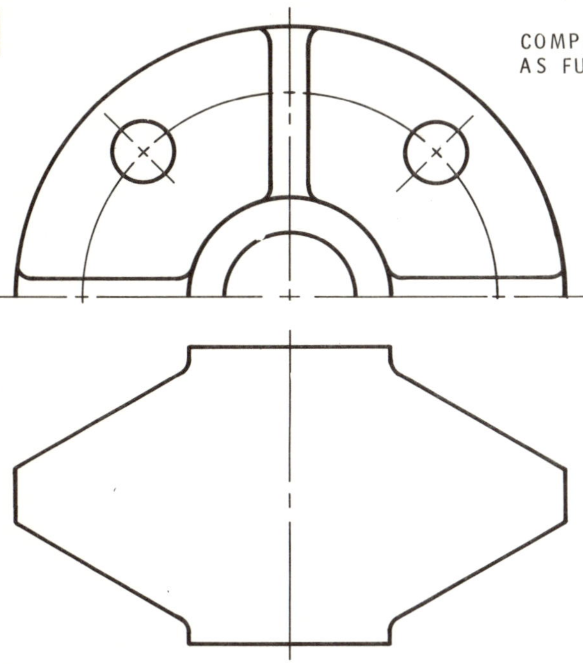

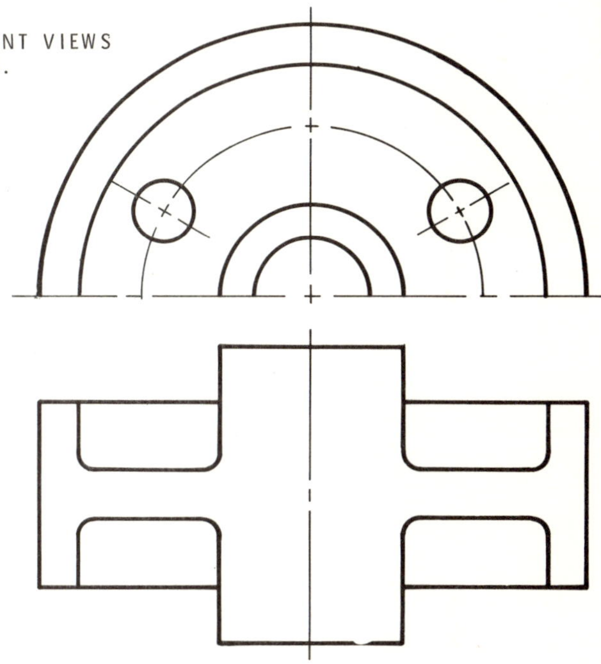

3 COMPLETE THE FRONT VIEW AS A FULL SECTION.

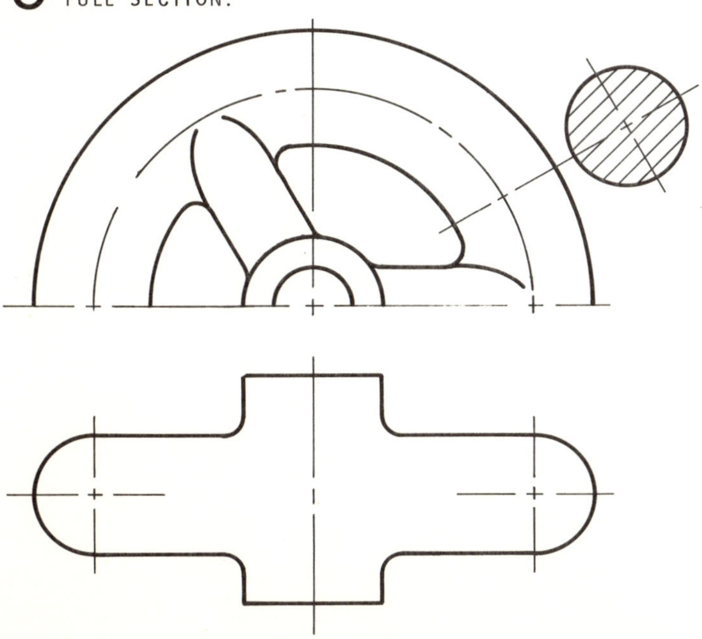

4 COMPLETE THE FRONT VIEW AS A HALF SECTION.

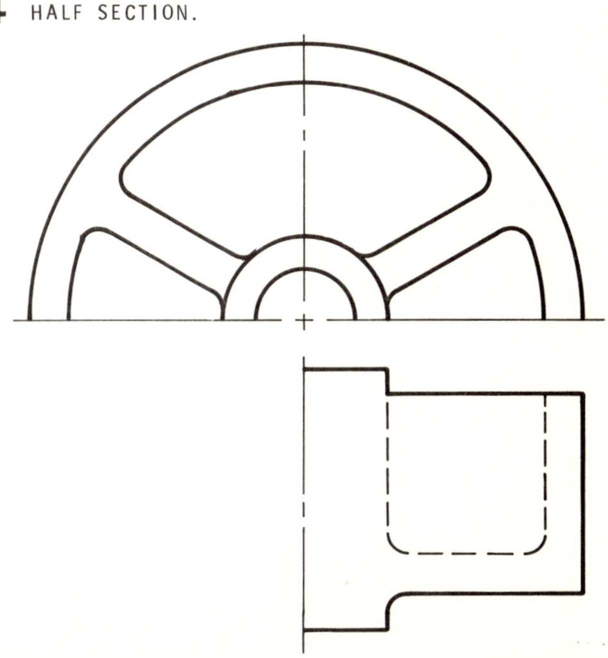

Drafting & Design

NAME
FILE NO SEC DATE
grade

Drafting & Design © James H. Earle	NAME FILE NO SEC DATE	grade	

SCHEMATIC THREADS

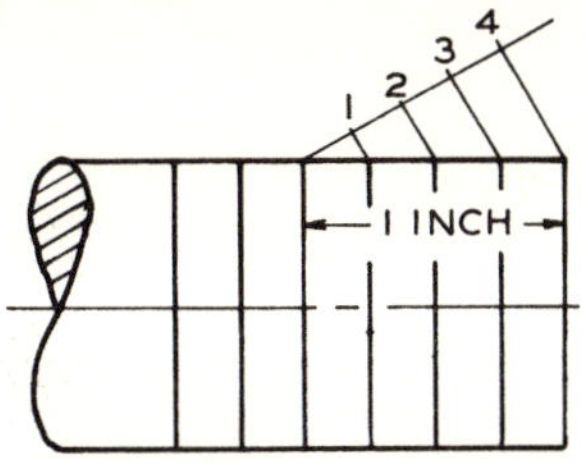

STEP 1: FIND THE SPACING BETWEEN CREST LINES BY DIVIDING 1" BY THE NUMBER OF THREADS PER INCH USING THREAD TABLES.

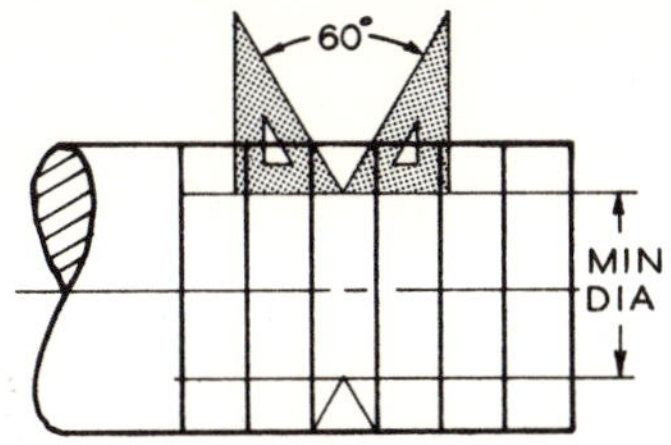

STEP 2: LOCATE THE MINOR DIAMETER BY USING A TRIANGLE AS SHOWN.

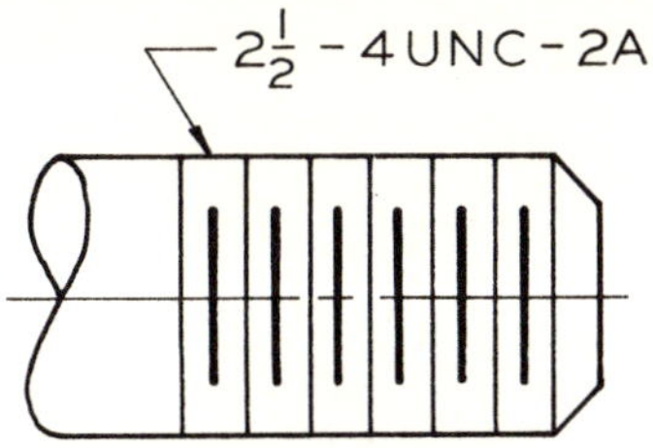

STEP 3: DRAW HEAVY LINES ACROSS THE MINOR DIAMETER FOR ROOT LINES. SHOW A 45° CHAMFER AND A THREAD NOTE.

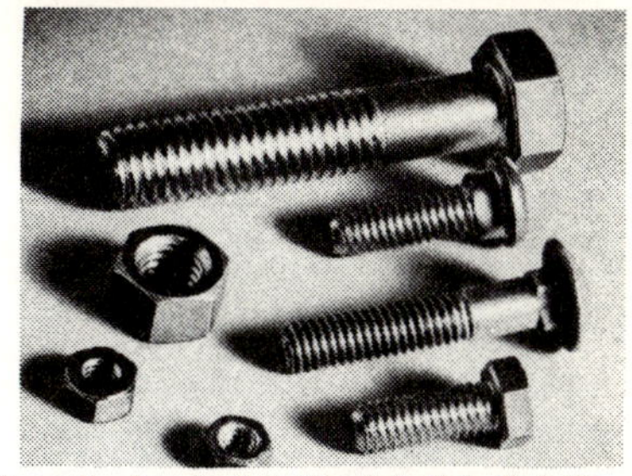

Russell, Burdsall & Ward Bolt & Nut Co.

1 COMPLETE THE SCHEMATIC THREADS. BY READING THE THREAD NOTES AT A & B, SUPPLY THE VALUES FOR EACH TERM LISTED BELOW.

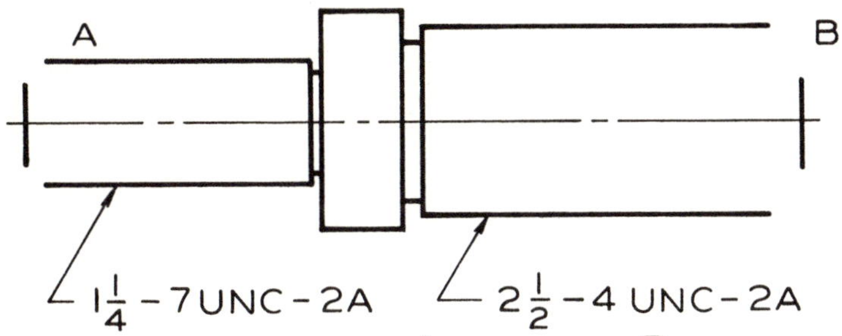

	A	B
MAJOR DIAMETER		
FORM OF THREAD		
CLASS OF FIT		
INTERNAL SYMBOL		
THREAD SERIES		
THREADS PER INCH		
EXTERNAL SYMBOL		

2 DRAW SCHEMATIC THREADS ON THE 1" DIA SCREW THAT IS THREADED 2" FROM END A. GIVE A THREAD NOTE FOR THE UNC CLASS 2 FIT THREAD.

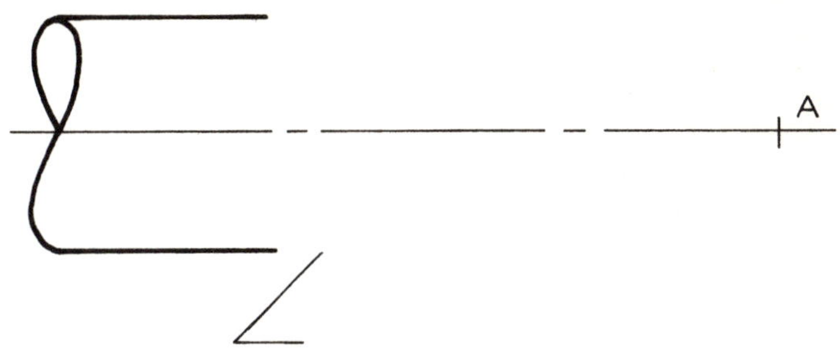

3 COMPLETE THE VIEW OF AN INTERNAL 3/4" DIA UNC THREAD WITH A CLASS 1 FIT THAT PASSES THROUGH THE PART USING SCHEMATIC SYMBOLS. GIVE A THREAD NOTE.

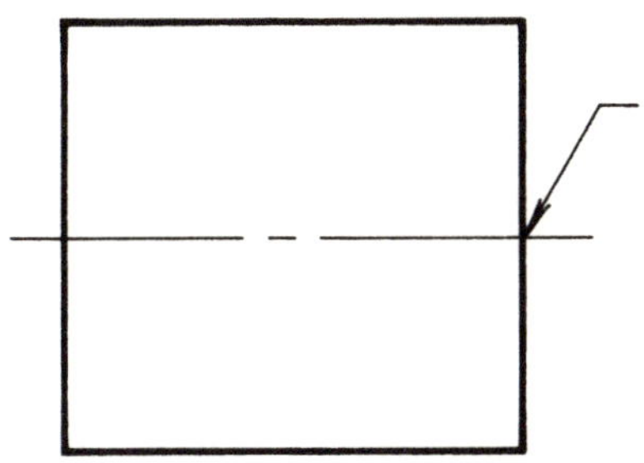

4 USING SCHEMATIC SYMBOLS, COMPLETE THE FRONT AND TOP VIEWS OF TWO 5/8" DIA INTERNAL UNC THREADS IN THE HALF SECTION. GIVE A THREAD NOTE.

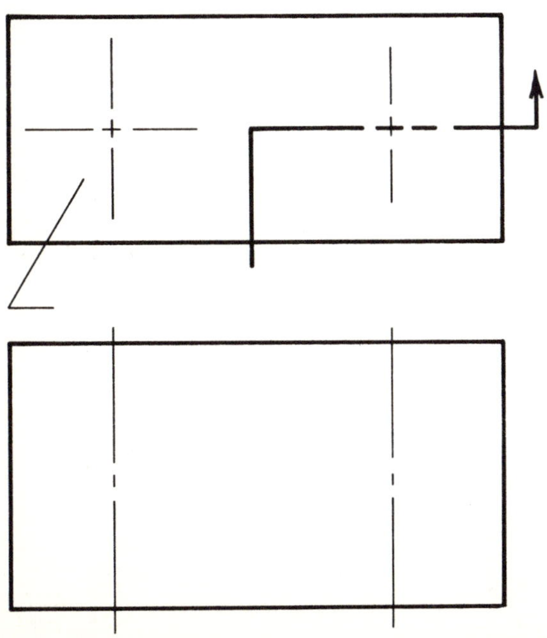

5 COMPLETE THE SCHEMATIC DRAWING OF THE NC THREADS AND GIVE A THREAD NOTE. IDENTIFY THE TYPES OF SCREW HEADS TO THE RIGHT OF EACH DRAWING.

TYPE OF HEAD

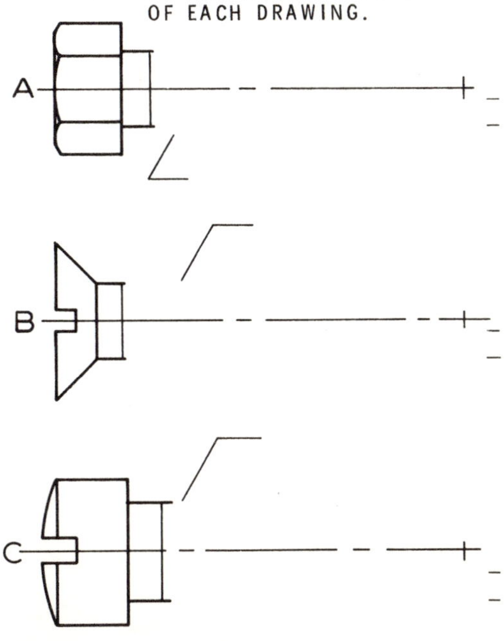

Drafting & Design

NAME
FILE NO SEC DATE
grade

SIMPLIFIED THREADS

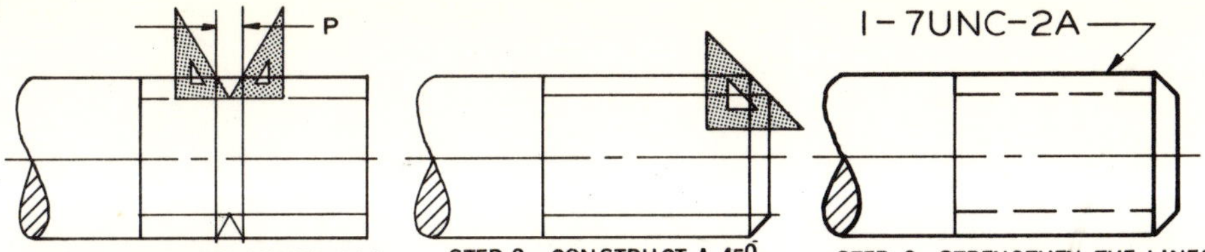

STEP 1: FIND THE MINOR DIA BY CONSTRUCTING A 60° ANGLE BETWEEN THE PITCH SPACING OR BY ESTIMATING BY EYE.

STEP 2: CONSTRUCT A 45° CHAMFER FROM THE MINOR DIAMETER.

STEP 3: STRENGTHEN THE LINES ADD A NOTE AND DRAW DASHED LINES TO REPRESENT THE MINOR DIAMETER.

1 COMPLETE THE SIMPLIFIED UNC. CLASS 2 FIT THREADS AND SUPPLY THREAD NOTES.

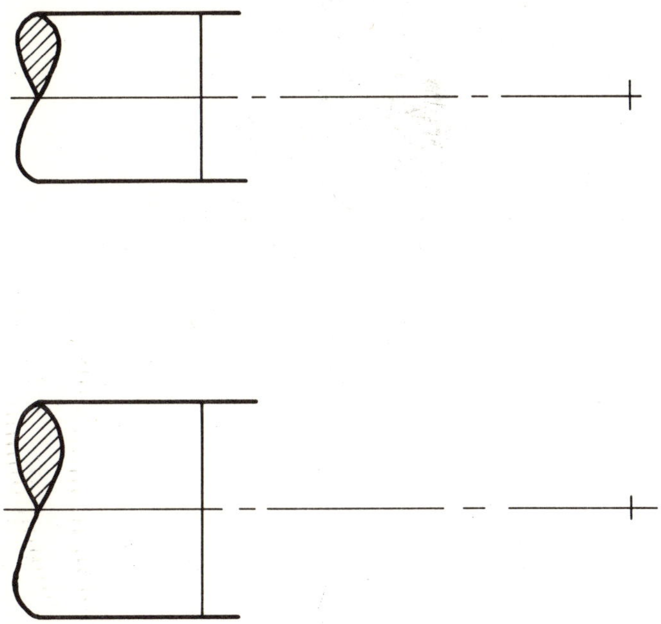

2 COMPLETE THE FRONT VIEW AS A FULL SECTION THROUGH A HEX HEAD BOLT FOR A 1-3/4" DIA BOLT. USE SIMPLIFIED SYMBOLS AND SUPPLY A THREAD NOTE.

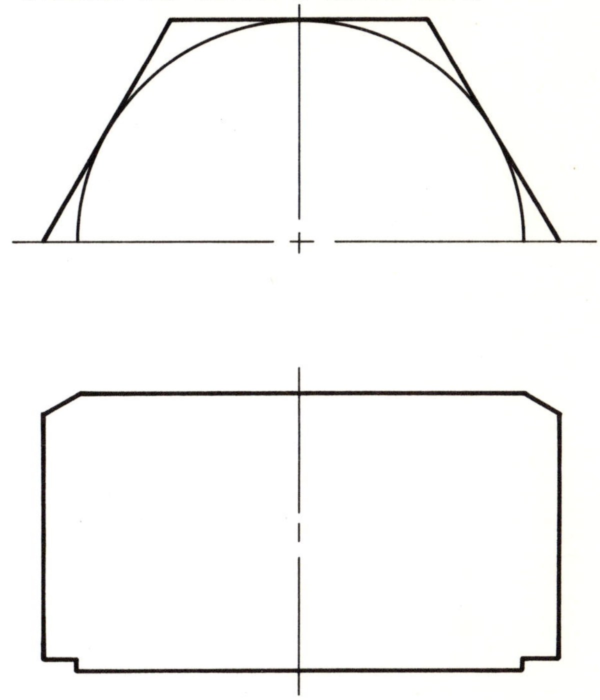

3 COMPLETE THE SIMPLIFIED THREADS BELOW AND SUPPLY THREAD NOTES. IDENTIFY THE TYPES OF HEADS AT THE RIGHT OF EACH LETTER.

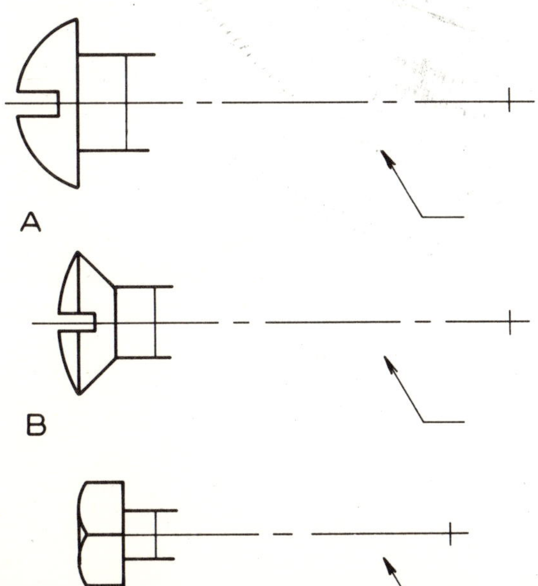

A

B

C

4 COMPLETE THE FRONT VIEW AS A HALF SECTION. EACH BOSS IS THREADED WITH AN INTERNAL 3/4" DIAMETER THREADS. SUPPLY NOTES.

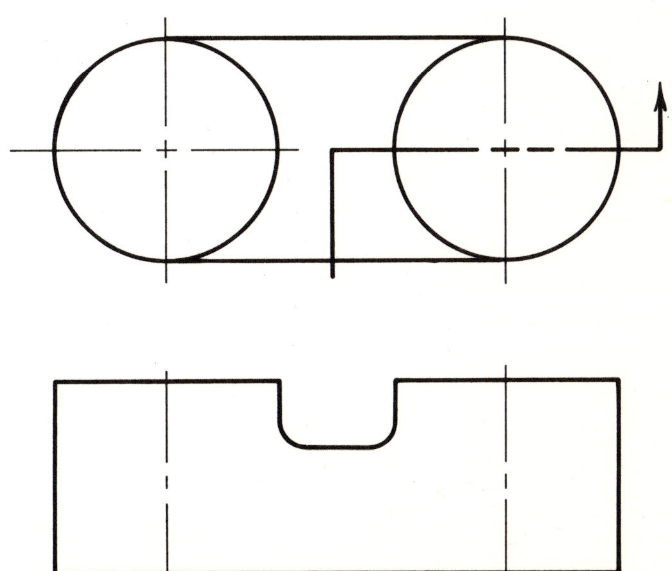

Drafting & Design © James H. Earle	NAME FILE NO SEC DATE	grade	64

Drafting & Design © James H. Earle	NAME FILE NO SEC DATE	grade	

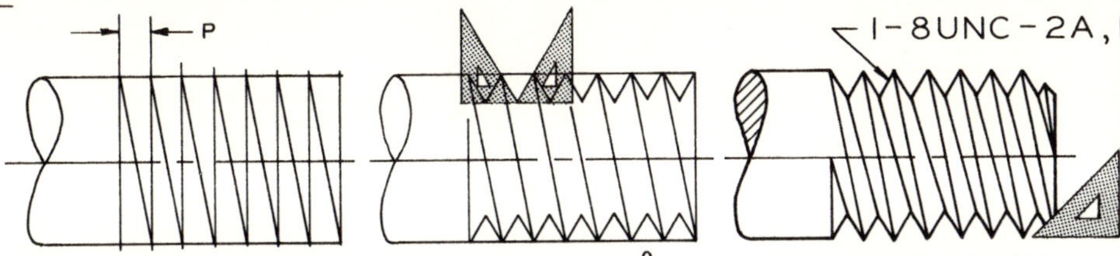

STEP 1: DETERMINE THE PITCH AND LOCATE THE SLOPING CREST LINES AS SHOWN FOR RIGHT-HAND, DOUBLE THREADS.

STEP 2: CONSTRUCT 60° V's BETWEEN THE CREST LINES.

STEP 3: CONNECT THE ROOT LINES AND CHAMFER AND STRENGTHEN THE LINES.

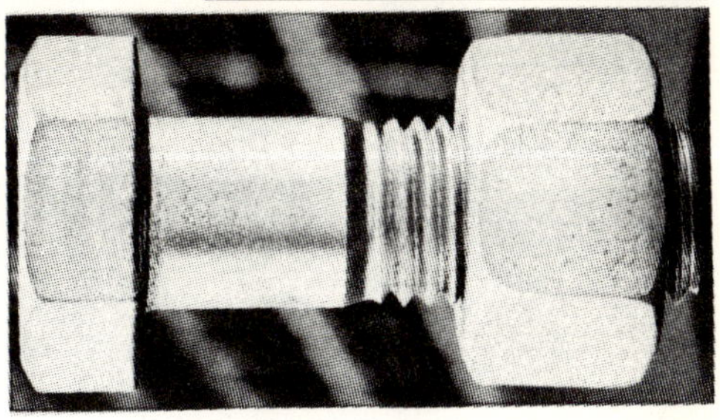

Courtesy of Russell, Burdsall & Ward Bolt and Nut Company

1 COMPLETE DETAILED THREADS FOR THE UNC, CLASS 2 FIT, RIGHT-HAND, DOUBLE THREADS. THE SCREW IS THREADED 3" FROM END A. COMPLETE THE NUT AS A FULL SECTION. SUPPLY THREAD NOTES FOR BOTH.

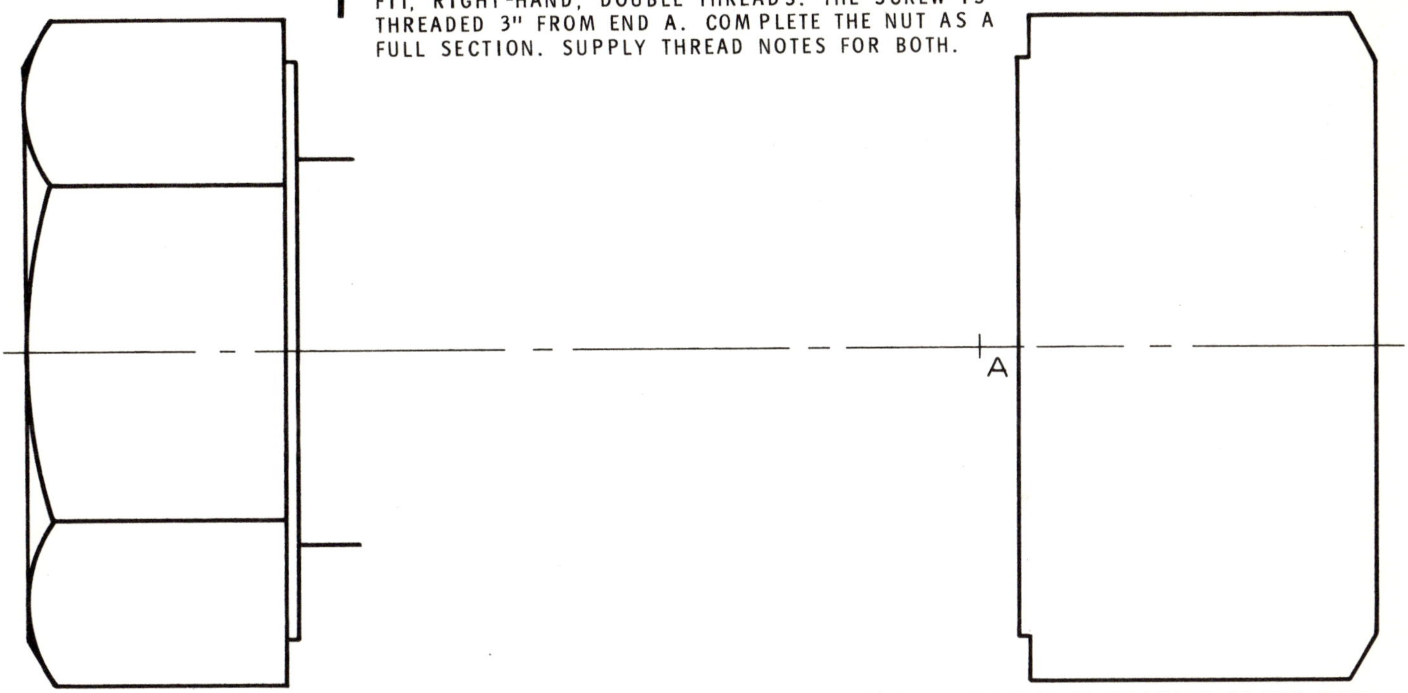

2 COMPLETE BOTH VIEWS OF THE SQUARE NUT FOR A 1-1/2" DIA SCREW WITH TRIPLE THREADS USING DETAILED SYMBOLS. GIVE A THREAD NOTE.

3 COMPLETE THE DETAILED DRAWING OF THE STUD WITH RIGHT-HAND SINGLE THREADS FROM A TO B AND LEFT-HAND SINGLE THREADS FROM C TO D. GIVE A THREAD NOTE FOR EACH END.

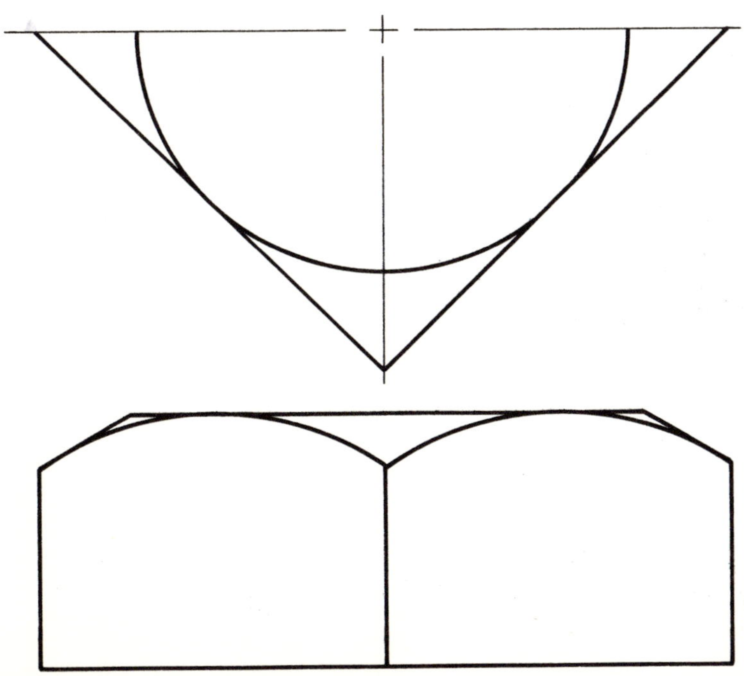

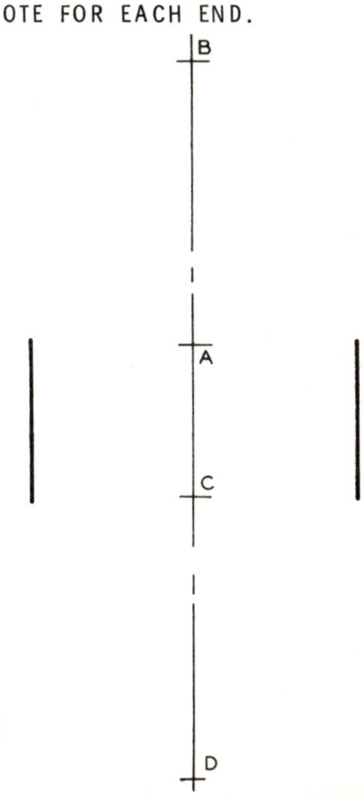

Drafting & Design © James H. Earle	NAME FILE NO SEC DATE	grade	

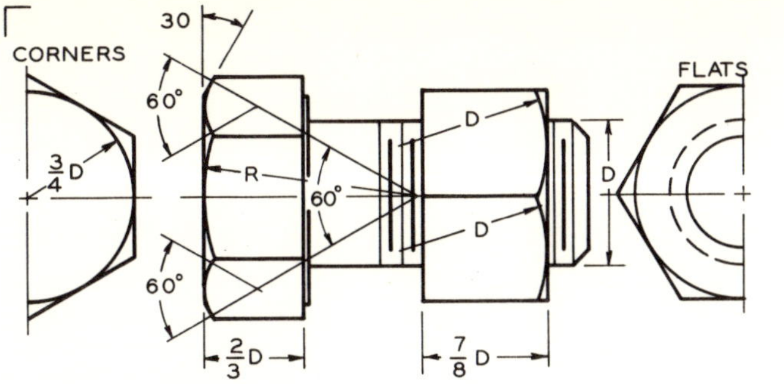

HEXAGON BOLTS AND NUTS ARE DRAWN USING THE CONSTRUCTION SHOWN ABOVE.

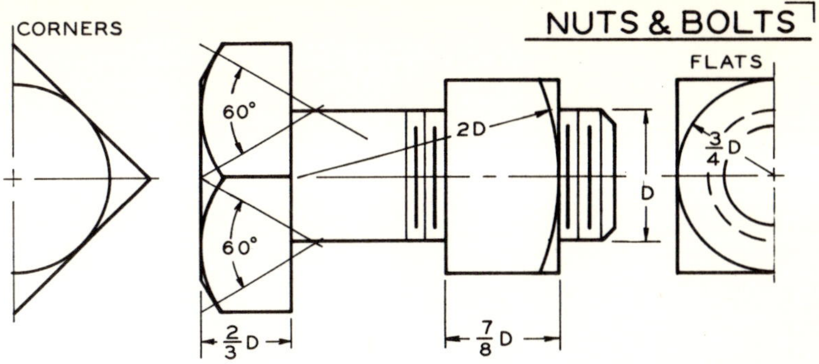

SQUARE BOLTS AND NUTS ARE DRAWN USING THE CONSTRUCTION SHOWN ABOVE.

1 CONSTRUCT A HEXAGON HEAD BOLT (HEAD AT LEFT) WITH A HEXAGON NUT (NUT AT RIGHT). SHOW THE NUT ASSEMBLED ON THE BOLT THAT IS THREADED FROM A TO B. COMPLETE BOTH END VIEWS AND SHOW THREAD NOTES.

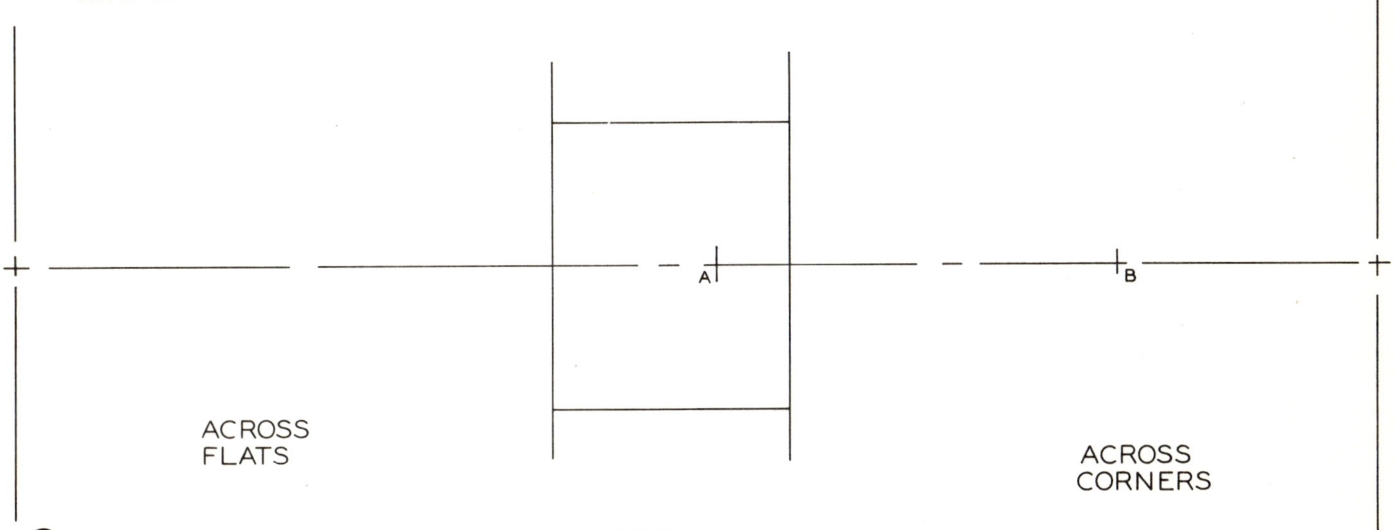

2 CONSTRUCT A SQUARE HEAD BOLT AND NUT (HEAD AT LEFT AND NUT AT RIGHT). SHOW THE NUT ASSEMBLED ON THE BOLT THAT IS THREADED FROM A TO B. COMPLETE BOTH END VIEWS AND SHOW THREAD NOTES.

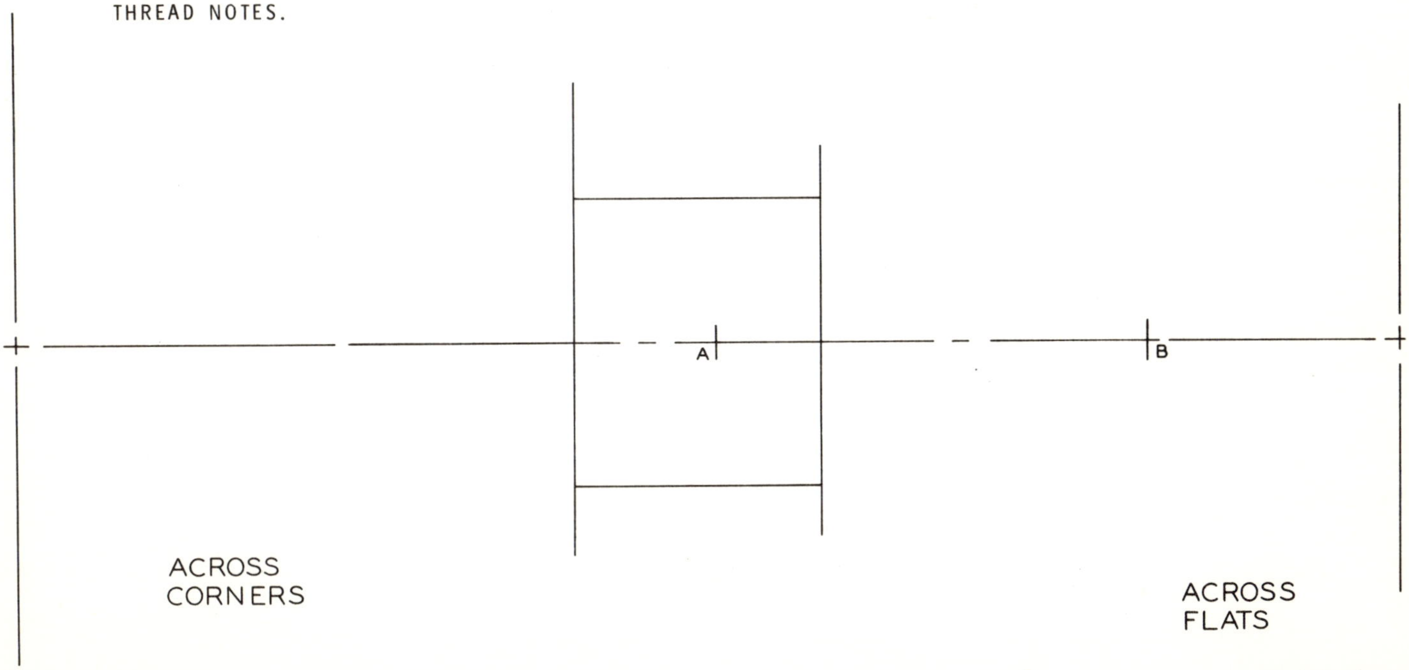

Drafting & Design © James H. Earle	NAME FILE NO SEC DATE	grade	

DIMENSIONING

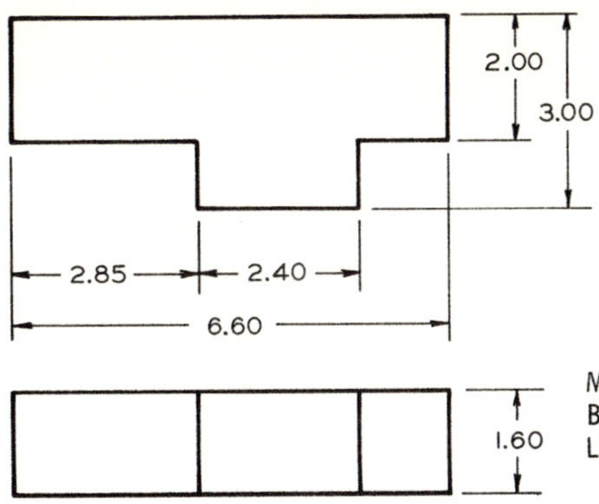

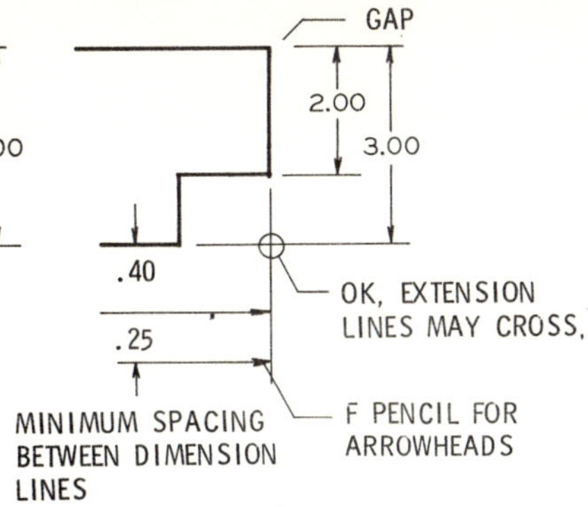

DIMENSIONS ARE USED TO INDICATE THE SIZE OF A PART ONCE IT HAS BEEN DRAWN. DIMENSION AND EXTENSION LINES ARE DRAWN WITH A 2H-4H PENCIL AS THIN LINES. A TYPICAL APPLICATION OF DIMENSIONS IS SHOWN AT THE LEFT IN THE EXAMPLE.

REQUIRED: DRAW AND DIMENSION THE TWO VIEWS OF THE STEP FIXTURE KEY IN THE SPACE BELOW. DRAW THE PART HALF SIZE USING THE DIMENSIONS GIVEN IN THE EXAMPLE BELOW.

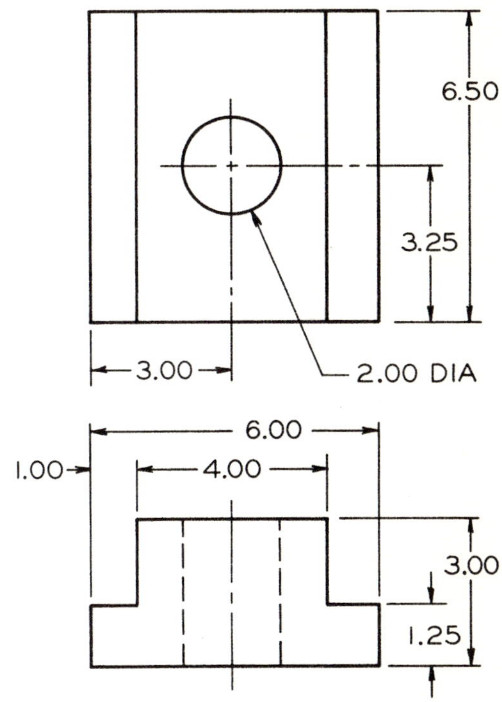

Drafting & Design © James H. Earle	NAME FILE NO SEC DATE	grade	

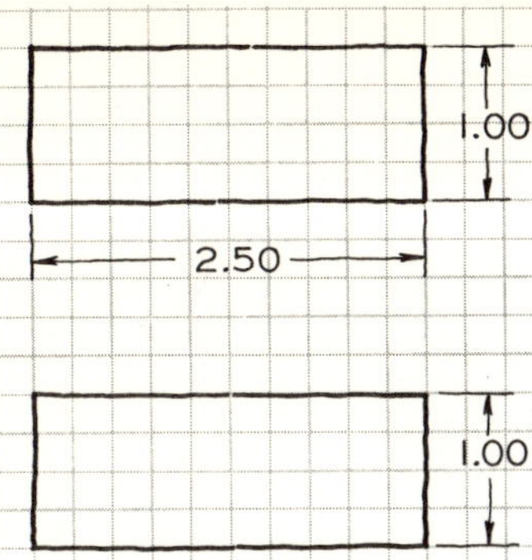

THE METHOD OF DIMENSIONING A SIMPLE BLOCK.

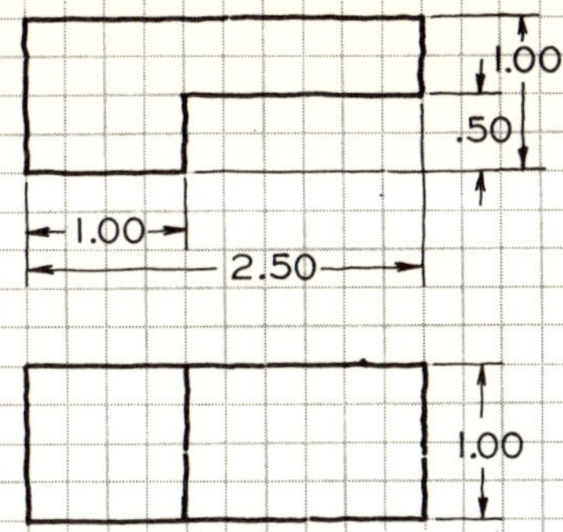

PLACEMENT OF DIMENSIONS ON A BLOCK WITH A NOTCH.

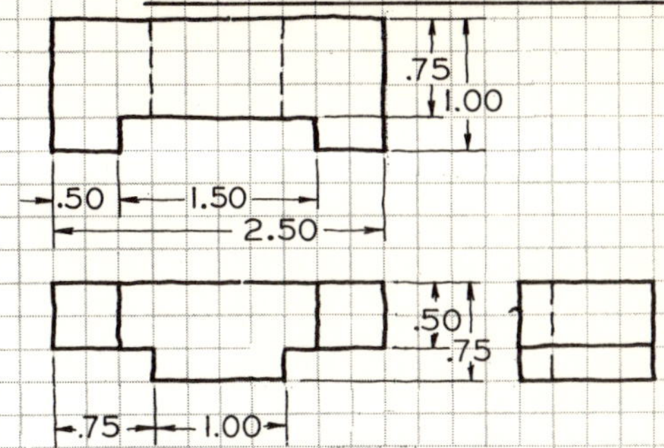

DIMENSIONS ARE PLACED ON THE MOST REPRESENTATIVE VIEWS.

REQUIRED: DIMENSION THE FULL-SIZE PARTS. EITHER SKETCH, OR USE INSTRUMENTS AS ASSIGNED.

1 GUIDE

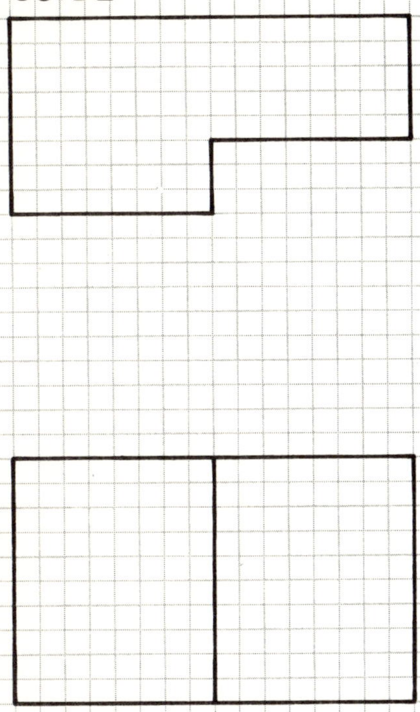

2 END BLOCK

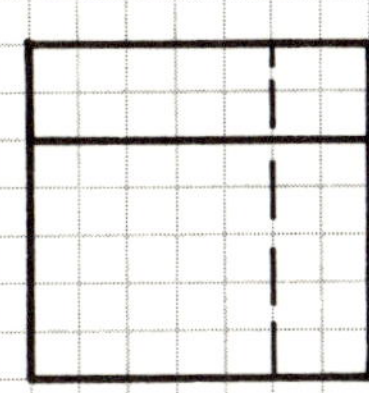

3 SEAT

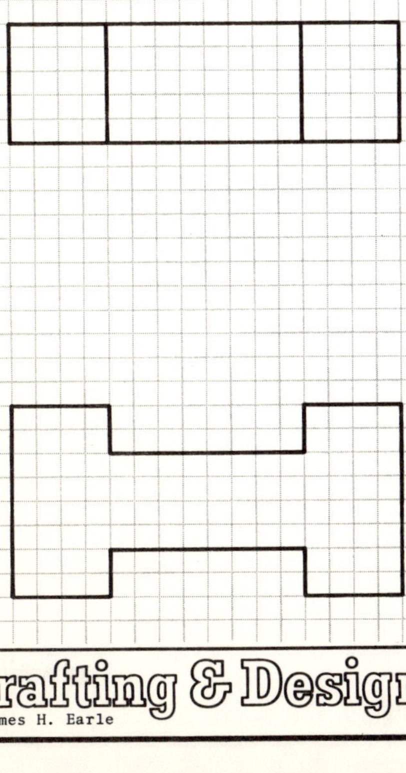

4 TONGUE

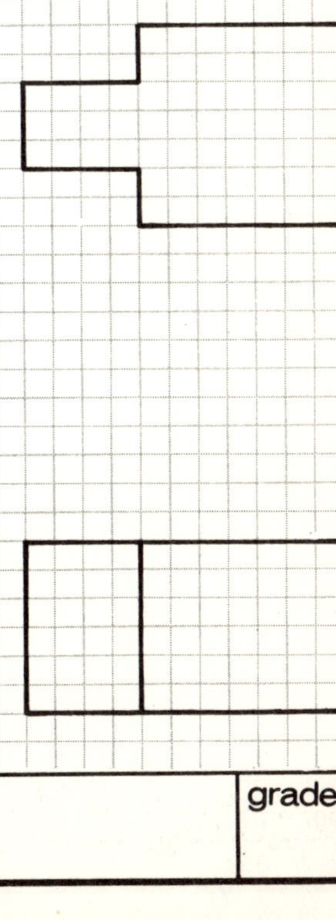

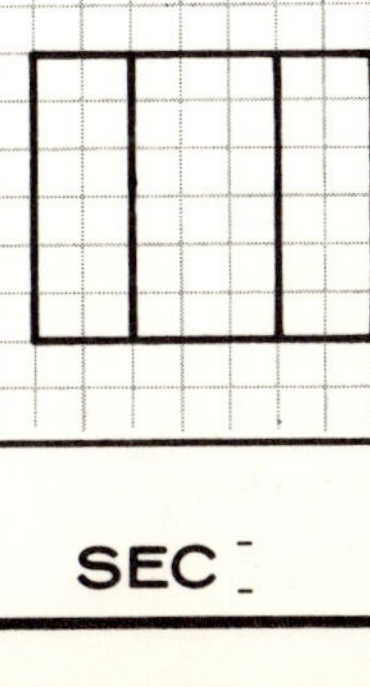

NAME

FILE NO. SEC. DATE

grade

Drafting & Design ©James H. Earle	NAME FILE NO SEC DATE	grade	

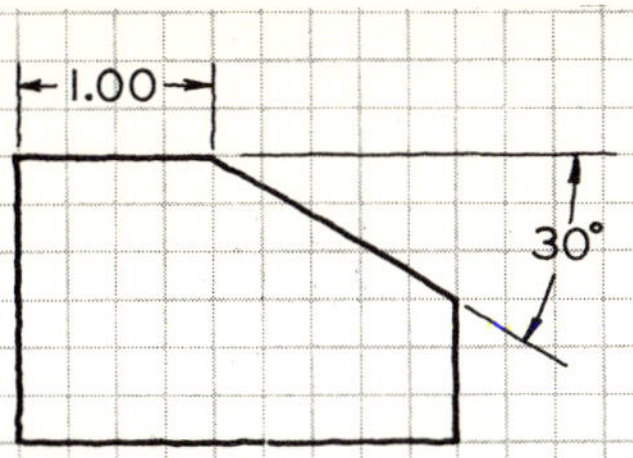

DIMENSIONING AN ANGLE USING DEGREES.

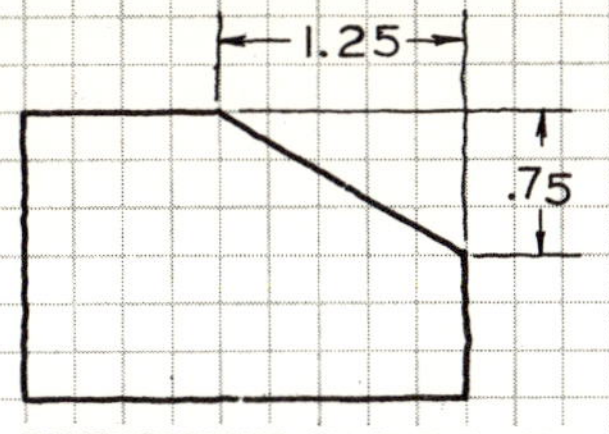

DIMENSIONING AN ANGLE USING COORDINATES.

REQUIRED: DIMENSION THE FULL-SIZE PARTS BELOW. SKETCH OR USE INSTRUMENTS AS ASSIGNED.

1 LIFTER

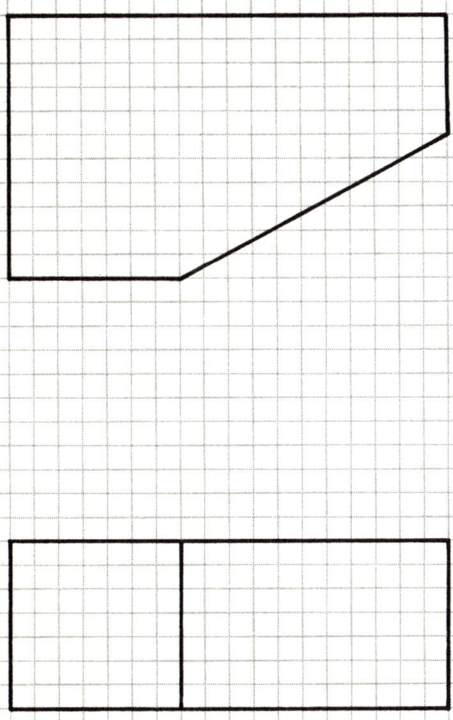

2 WEDGE

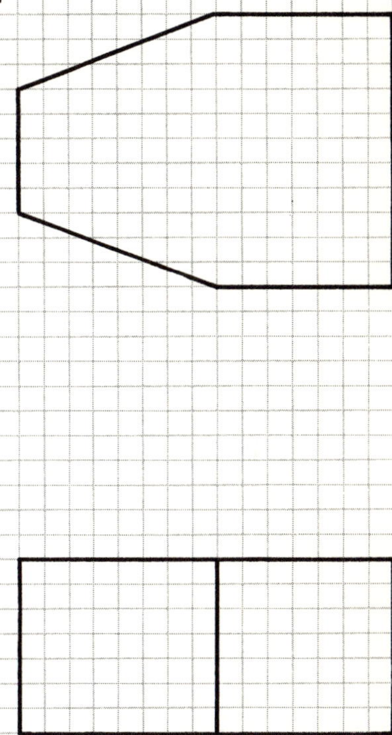

3 FIXTURE BASE

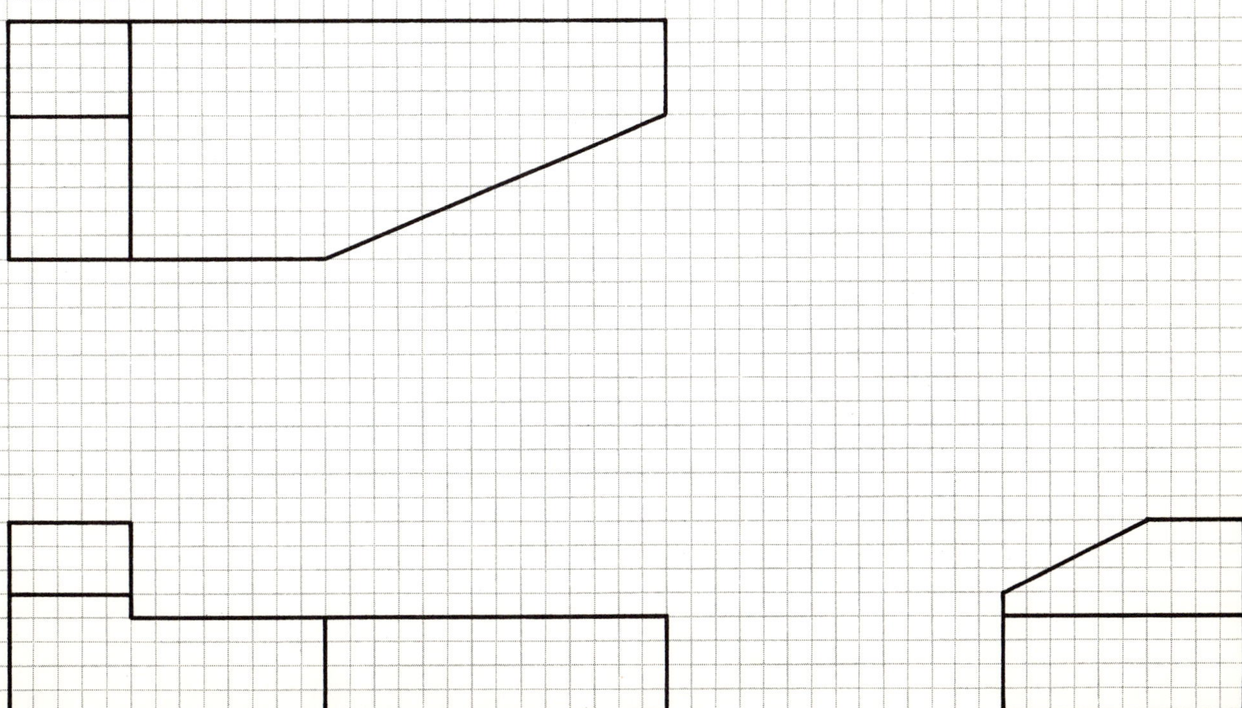

NAME
FILE NO. SEC. DATE

grade

Drafting & Design

NAME

FILE NO SEC DATE

grade

DIMENSIONING CYLINDERS

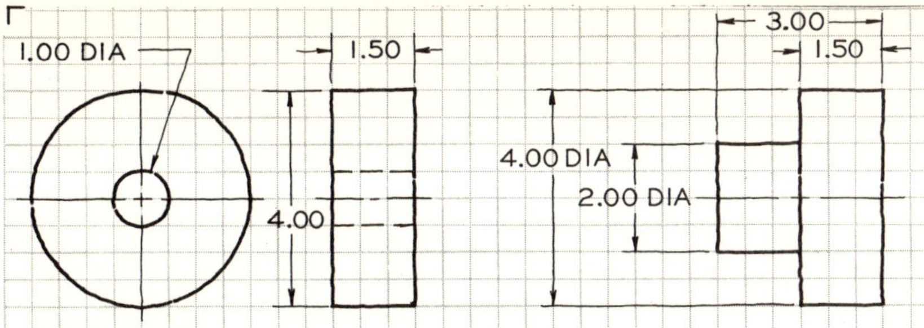

EXAMPLES OF DIMENSIONED CYLINDERS ARE SHOWN AT THE LEFT. DIMENSIONS ARE PLACED ON THE RECTANGULAR VIEW USING DIAMETERS INSTEAD OF RADII. SMALL HOLES ARE DIMENSIONED WITH A NOTE IN THE CIRCULAR VIEW. THE CIRCULAR VIEW CAN BE OMITTED WHEN DIMENSIONING CYLINDERS IF "DIA" IS PLACED AFTER EACH DIMENSIONED DIAMETER IN THE RECTANGULAR VIEW.

1 DIMENSION THE FULL-SIZE CYLINDRICAL PART BELOW. THE TOP VIEW IS A HALF VIEW.

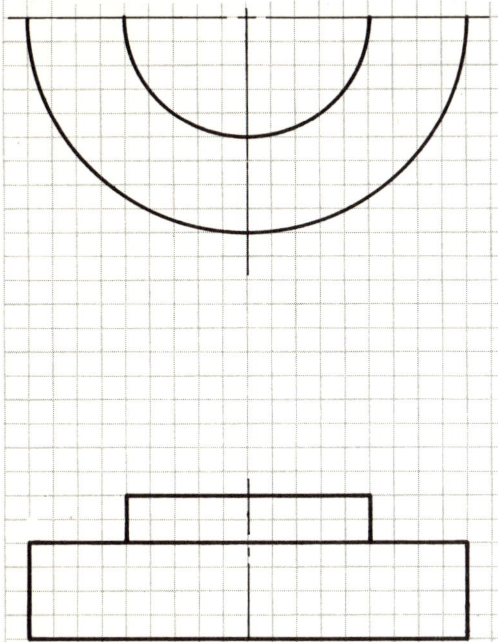

2 DIMENSION THE FULL-SIZE CYLINDRICAL PART. THE CIRCULAR VIEW HAS BEEN OMITTED.

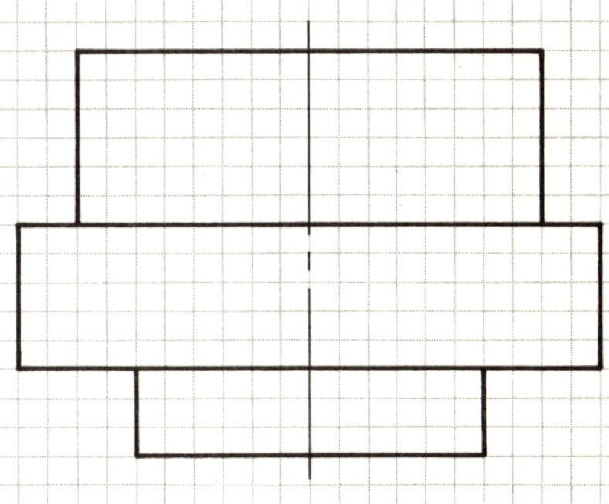

3 DIMENSION THE FULL-SIZE CYLINDRICAL PART SHOWN IN THE HALF SECTION.

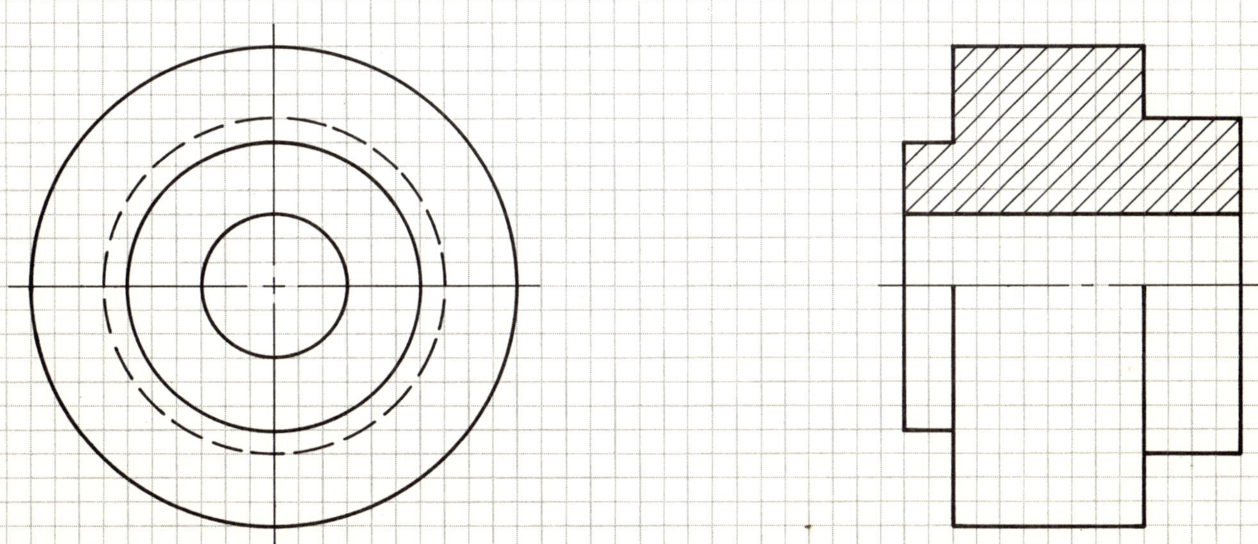

Drafting & Design

NAME

FILE NO SEC DATE

grade

Drafting & Design © James H. Earle	NAME FILE NO SEC DATE	grade	

DIMENSIONING CONES

TWO EXAMPLES OF DIMENSIONED CONES ARE SHOWN AT THE LEFT. NOTICE THAT THE DIMENSIONS ARE PLACED ON THE TRIANGULAR VIEWS.

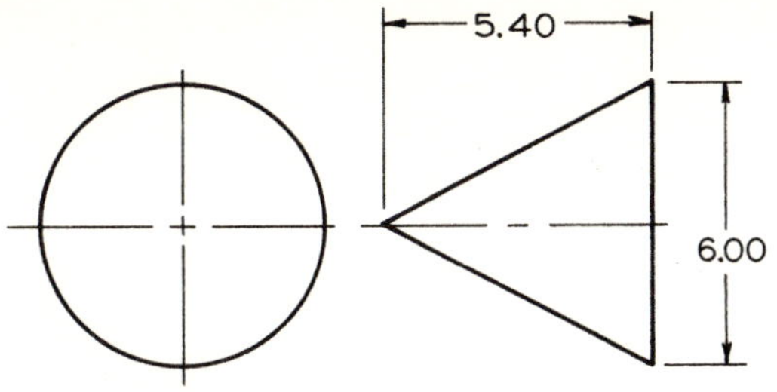

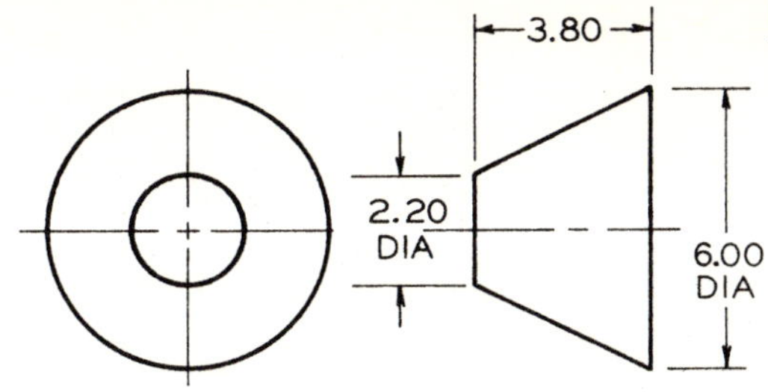

DIMENSION THE FULL-SIZE CONICAL PARTS SHOWN BELOW.

1 INSERT

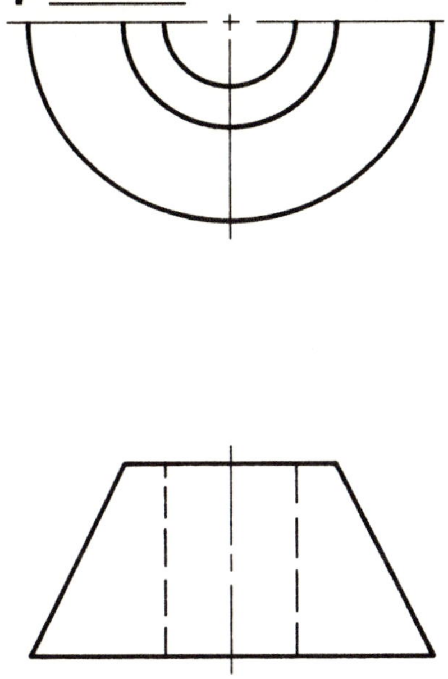

2 BEARING

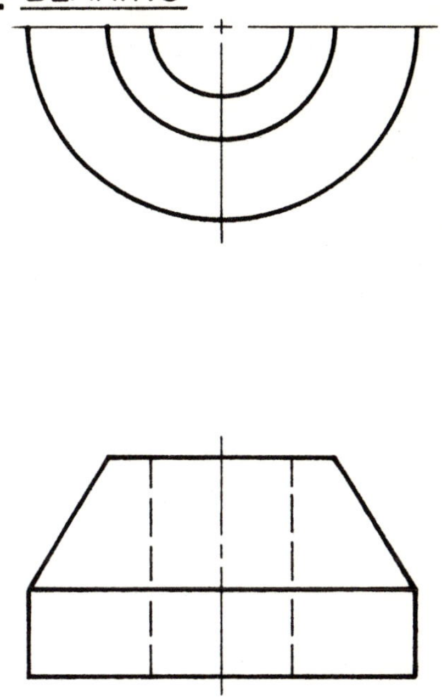

3 HUB

NAME
FILE NO SEC DATE
grade

Drafting & Design ©James H. Earle	NAME FILE NO SEC DATE	grade	

DIMENSIONING ARCS

TYPICAL METHODS OF DIMENSIONING ARCS ARE SHOWN AT THE LEFT. NOTICE THAT A RADIUS IS USED WHEN THE ARC IS LESS THAN A FULL CIRCLE. NOTES CAN BE USED TO SPECIFY FILLETS AND ROUNDS TO REDUCE REPETITIVE DIMENSIONS.

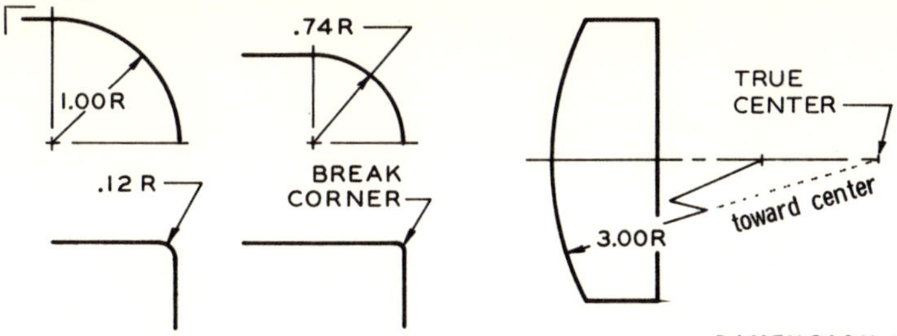

NOTES

ALL FILLETS & ROUNDS .24R

FILLETS & ROUNDS .24R UNLESS OTHERWISE SPECIFIED

DIMENSION THE PARTS BELOW.

1

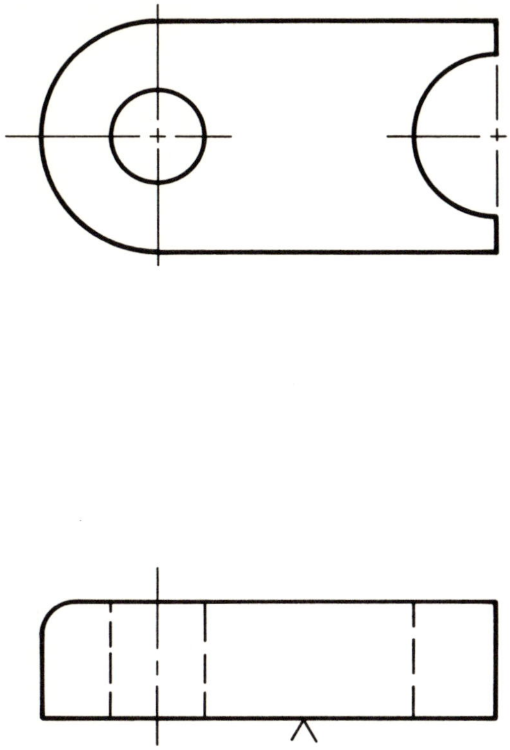

2

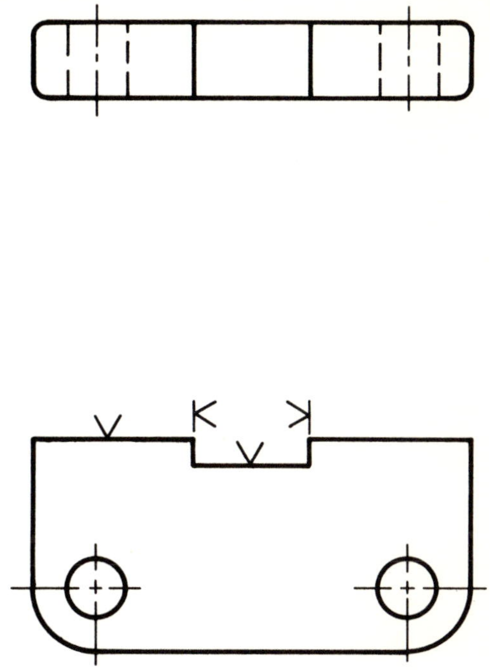

3

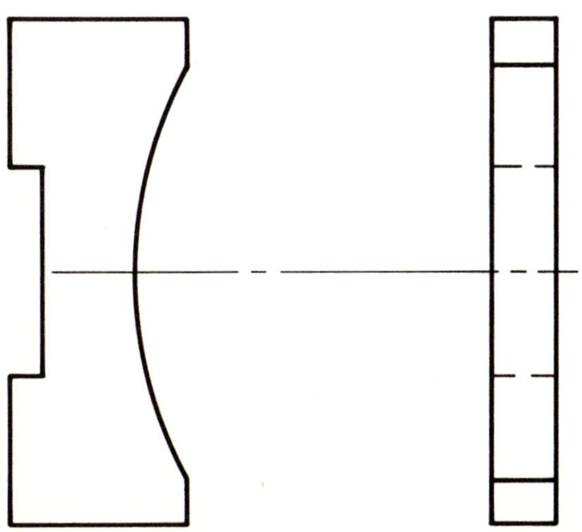

4

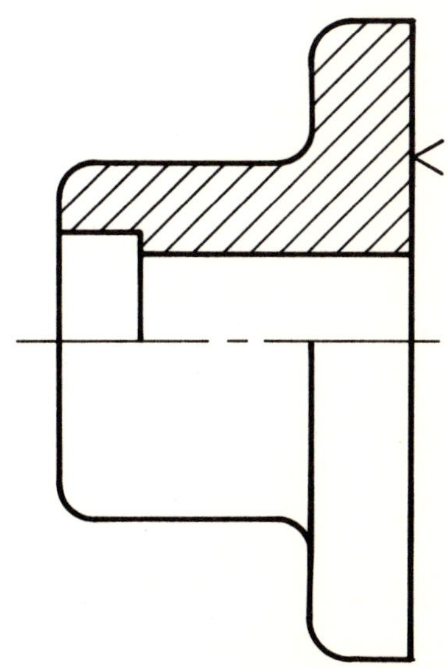

Drafting & Design © James H. Earle	NAME FILE NO SEC DATE	grade	

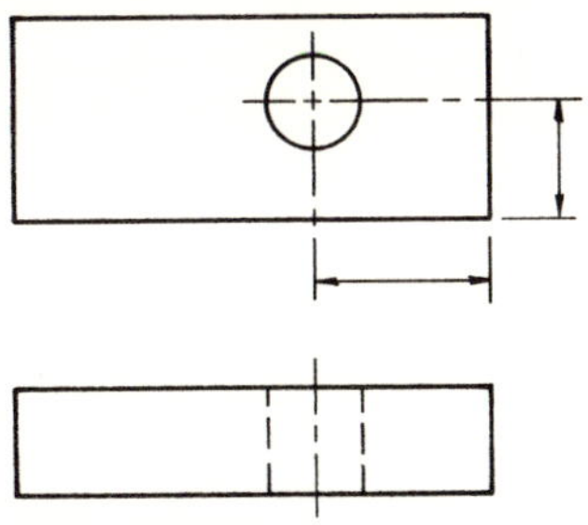

HOLES SHOULD BE LOCATED IN THE CIRCULAR VIEW WITH TWO DIMENSIONS.

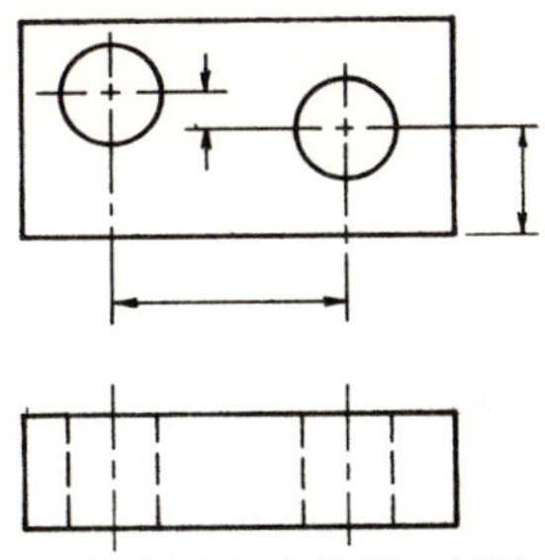

HOLES SHOULD BE LOCATED FROM CENTER TO CENTER WHEN MORE THAN ONE HOLE IS GIVEN.

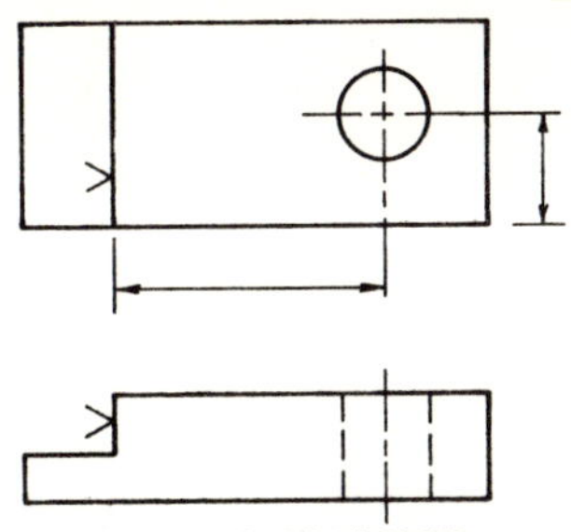

HOLES SHOULD BE LOCATED FROM FINISHED SURFACES FOR GREATER ACCURACY.

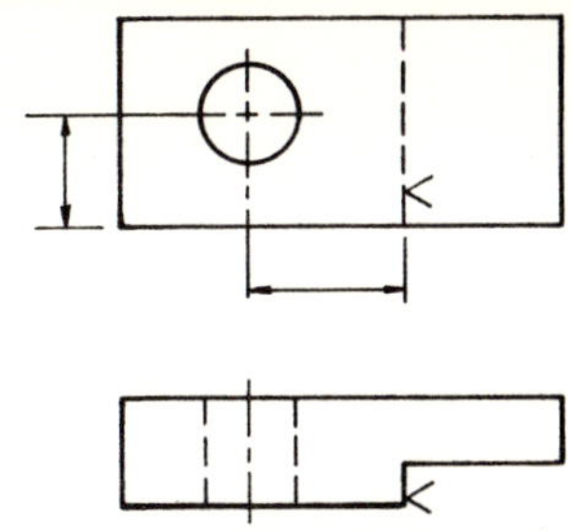

HOLES SHOULD BE LOCATED FROM FINISHED SURFACES EVEN IF THE SURFACE IS HIDDEN.

COMPLETELY DIMENSION THE FULL-SIZE PARTS BELOW-- LOCATION AND SIZE DIMENSIONS.

1 GUIDE

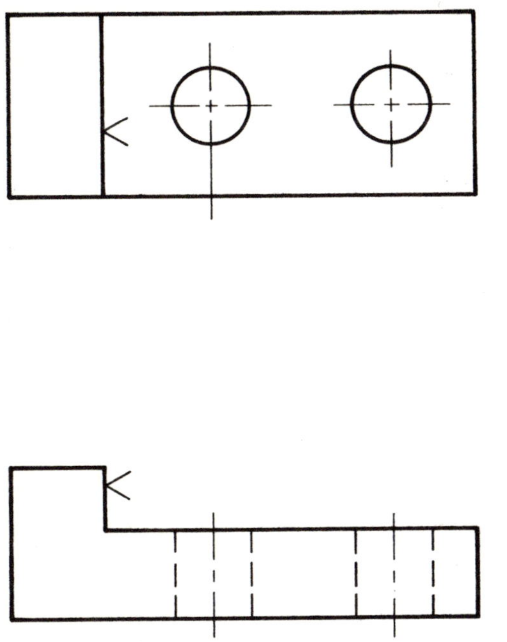

2 ADAPTER

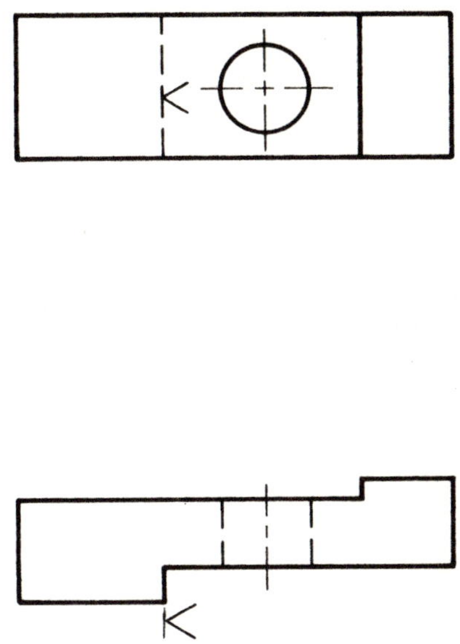

3 FLANGE

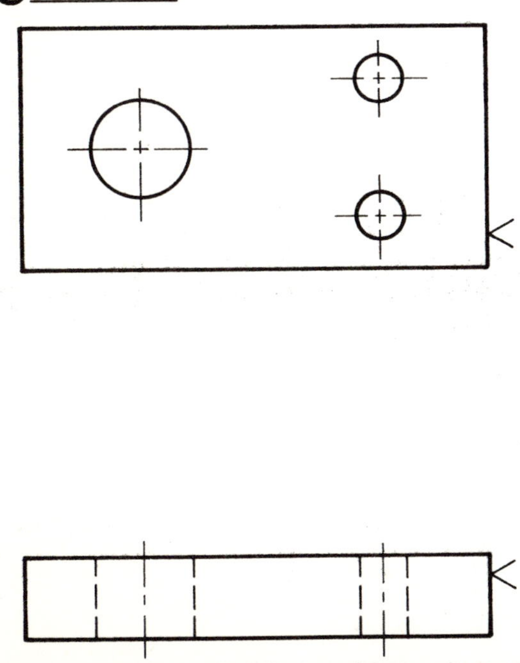

4 CASE

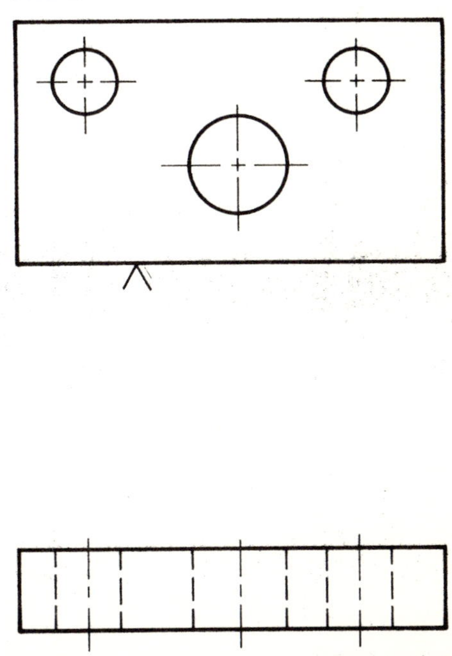

NAME
FILE NO
SEC
DATE
grade

Drafting & Design © James H. Earle	NAME FILE NO SEC DATE	grade	

LOCATION DIMENSIONS

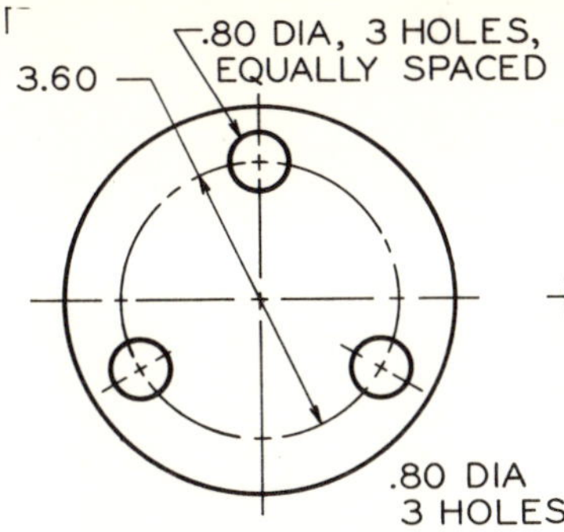

HOLES CAN BE LOCATED BY DIMENSIONING THE CIRCLE OF CENTERS AND WITH A NOTE.

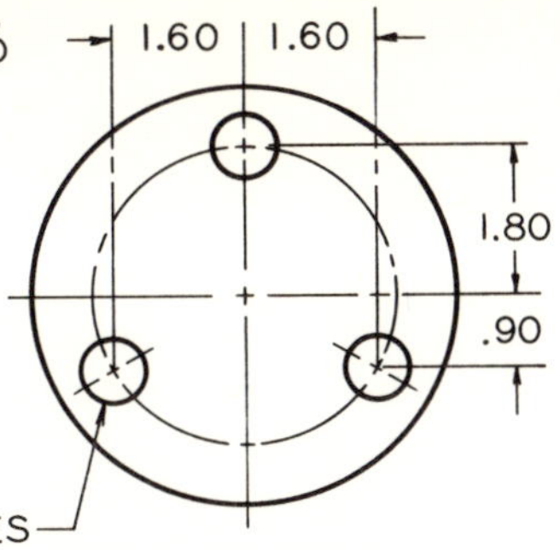

HOLES CAN BE LOCATED WITH COORDINATE DIMENSIONS FROM THE CENTER LINES.

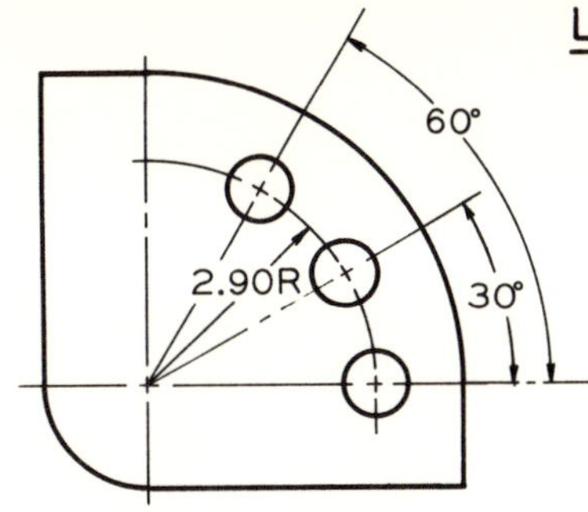

HOLES CAN BE LOCATED WITH ANGULAR DIMENSIONS AND THE RADIUS FROM A POLE POINT.

1

2

LOCATE THE HOLES USING THE CIRCLE OF CENTERS METHOD FOR PROBLEM 1 AND THE COORDINATE METHOD FOR PROBLEM 2. GIVE HOLE NOTES.

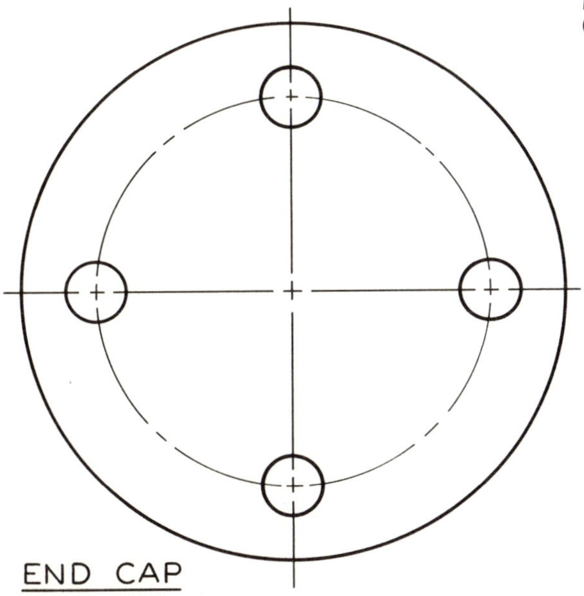

END CAP
HALF SIZE

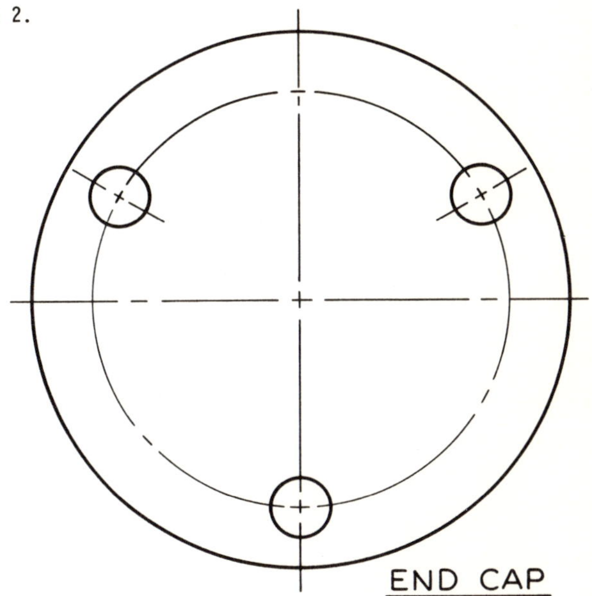

END CAP
HALF SIZE

3 COMPLETELY DIMENSION THE PART BELOW.

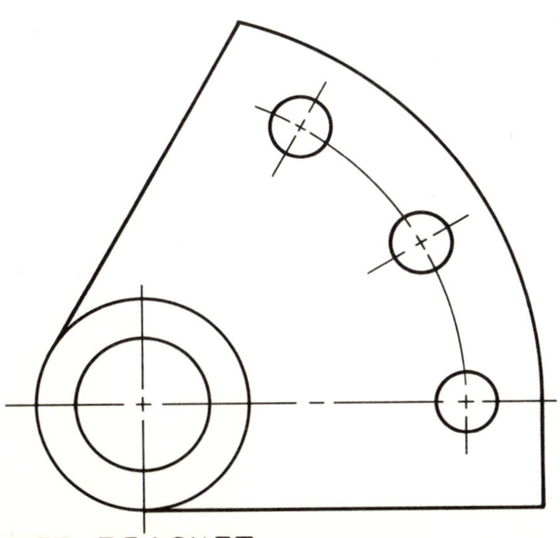

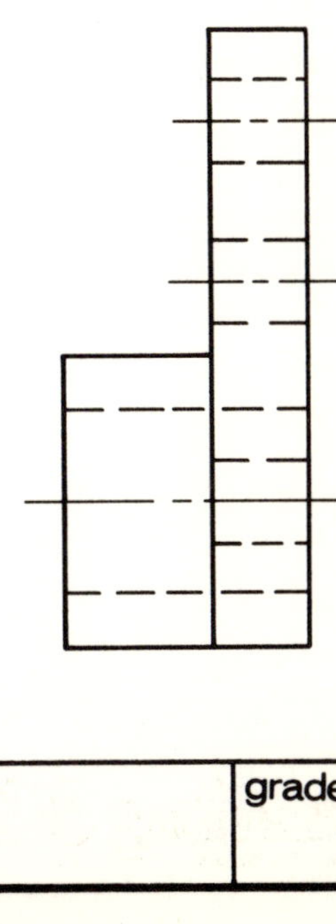

SHAFT BRACKET HALF SIZE

Drafting & Design © James H. Earle	NAME FILE NO SEC DATE	grade	74

Drafting & Design © James H. Earle	NAME FILE NO SEC DATE	grade	

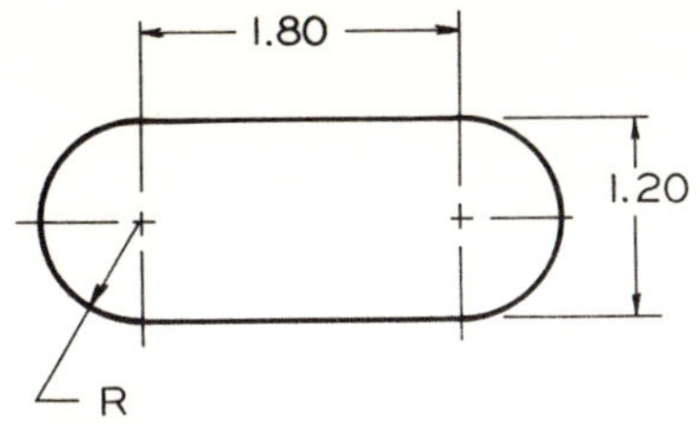

PARTS WITH ROUNDED ENDS SHOULD BE DIMENSIONED WITH AN OVERALL DIMENSION. RADIUS R INDICATES THAT THE ENDS ARE SEMICIRCULAR.

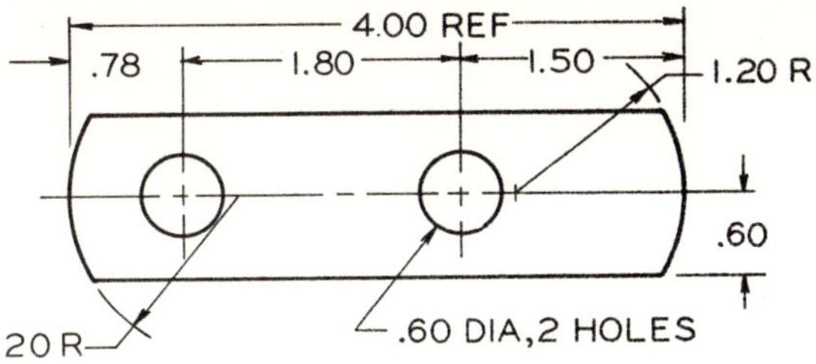

PARTS WITH ENDS THAT ARE NOT FULL SEMICIRCLES SHOULD BE DIMENSIONED AS SHOWN HERE. THE DIMENSIONS OF THE RADII MUST BE SPECIFIED.

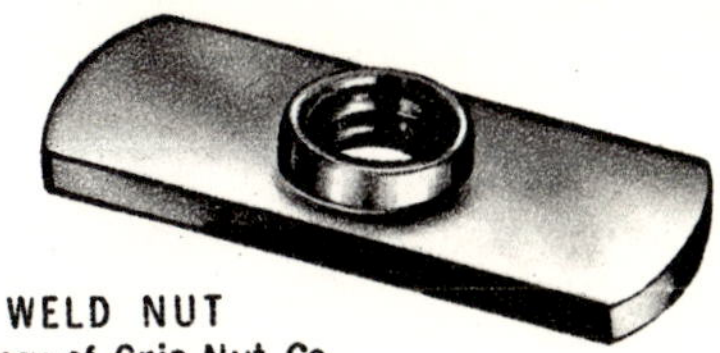

TAB WELD NUT
Courtesy of Grip Nut Co.

COVER PLATE
SCALE: HALF SIZE

1 DIMENSION THE PART BELOW.

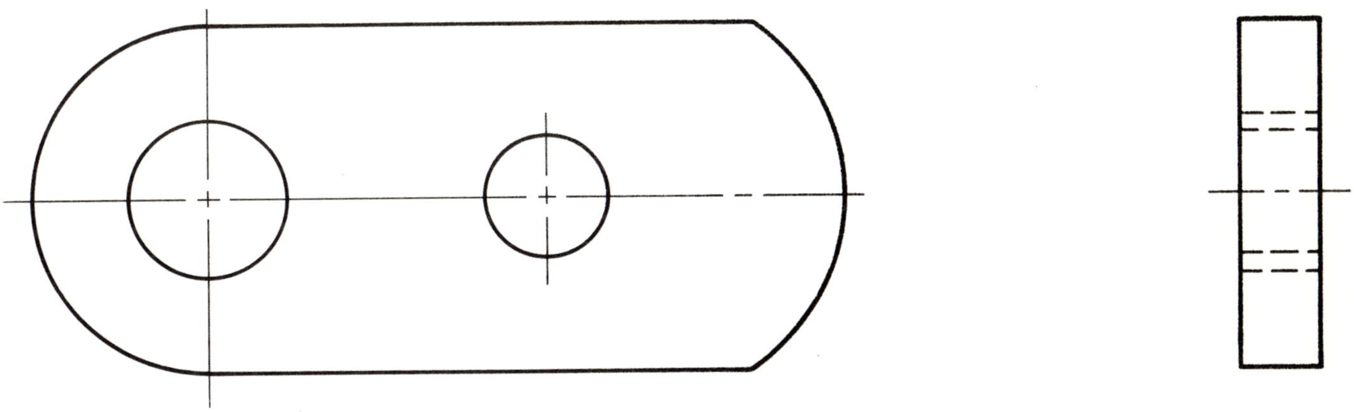

2 DIMENSION THE PART BELOW.

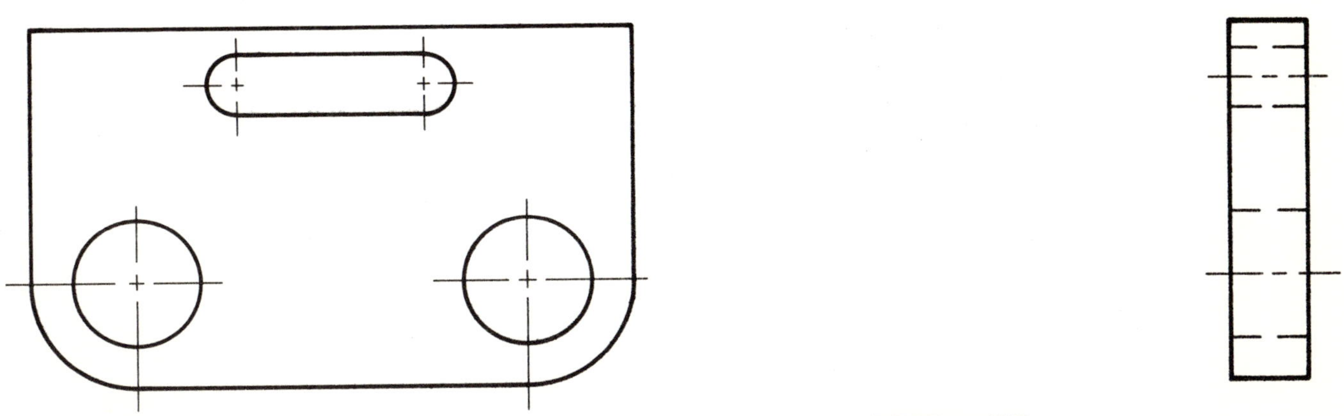

RETAINER
SCALE: HALF SIZE

Drafting & Design © James H. Earle	NAME FILE NO SEC DATE	grade	

MACHINED HOLES

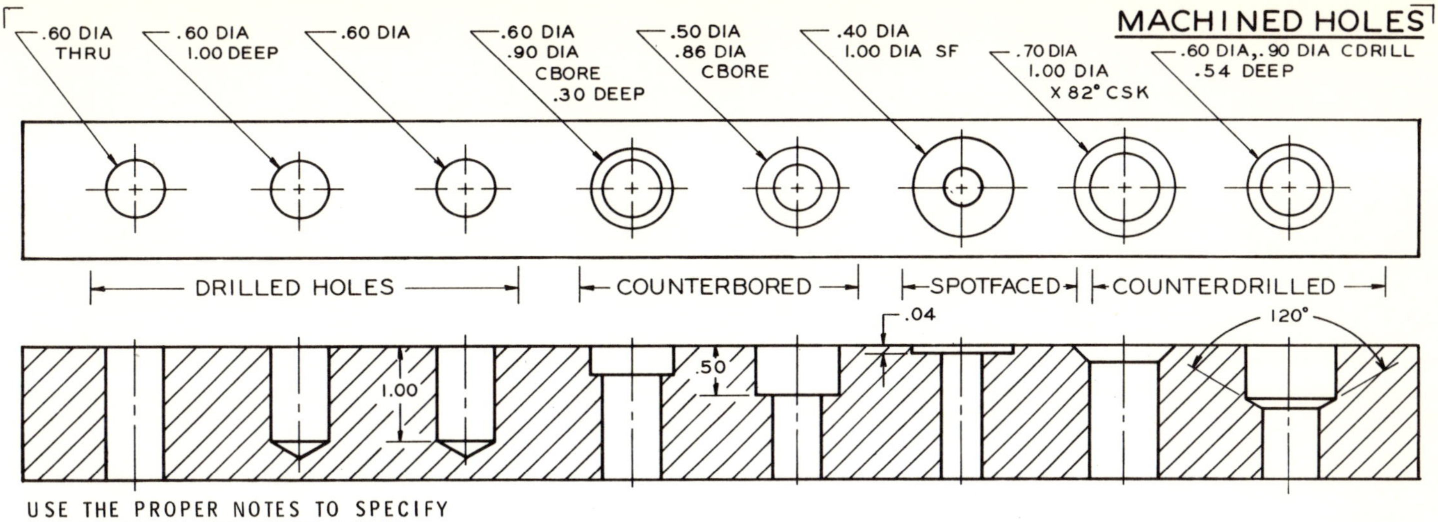

USE THE PROPER NOTES TO SPECIFY THE HOLES IN THE PARTS BELOW.

1

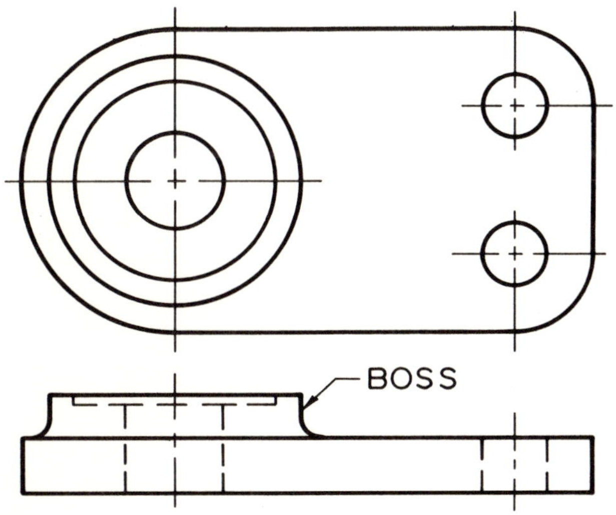

2

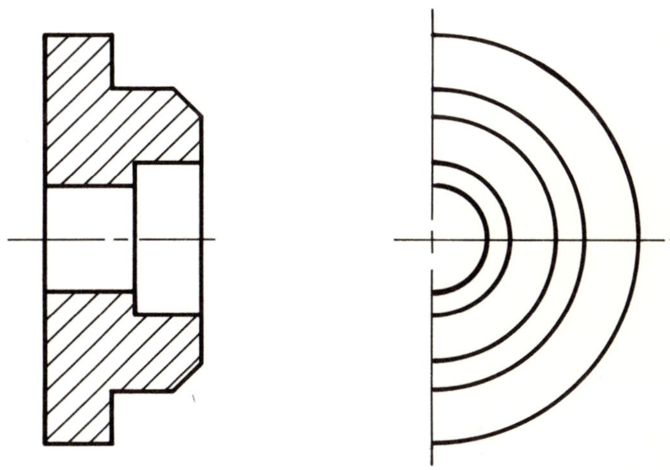

3

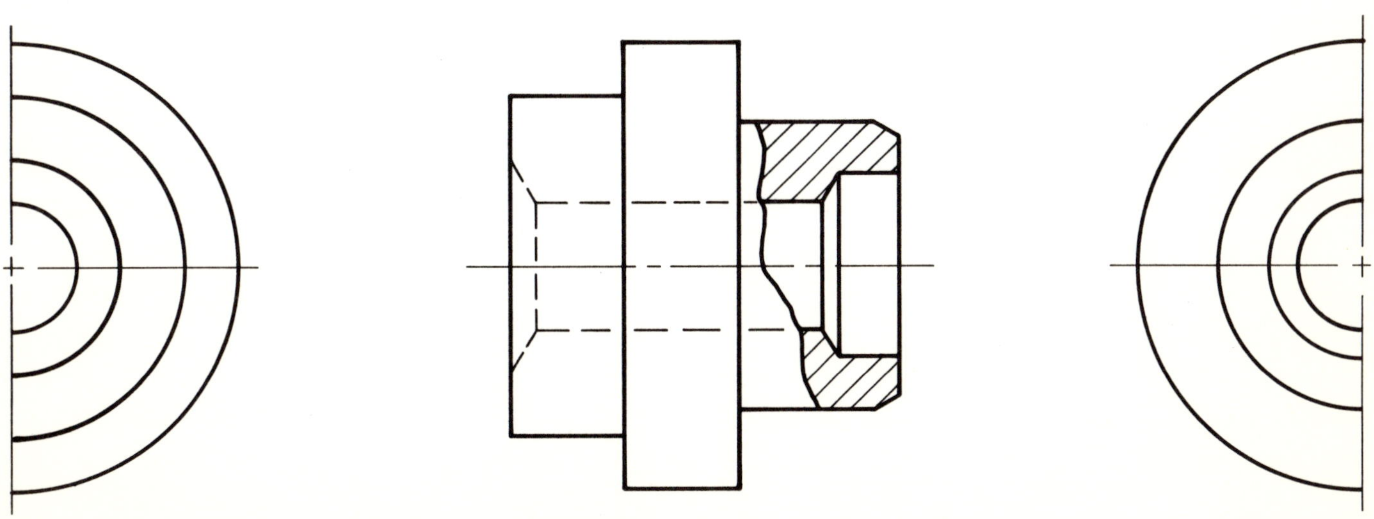

Drafting & Design

NAME

FILE NO SEC DATE

grade

Drafting & Design

NAME
FILE NO SEC DATE

grade

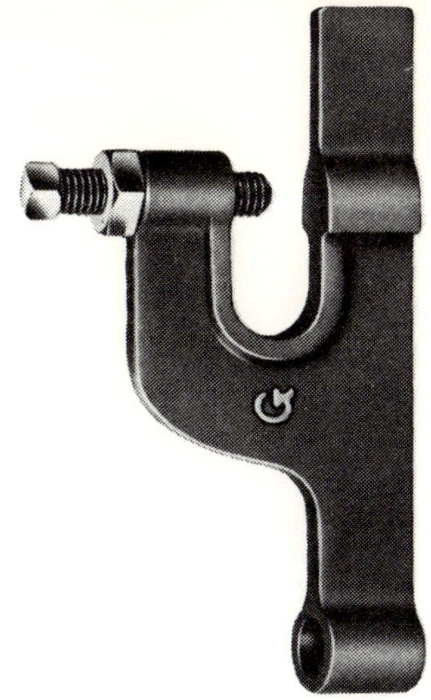

Courtesy of Grinnell Corp.

THE EXTENSION C-CLAMP SHOWN BELOW IS USED TO SUSPEND PIPES FROM OVERHEAD I-BEAMS. TWO VIEWS OF THE BODY OF ONE OF THESE CLAMPS ARE GIVEN. DIMENSION THESE VIEWS COMPLETELY TO FULLY DESCRIBE THEM

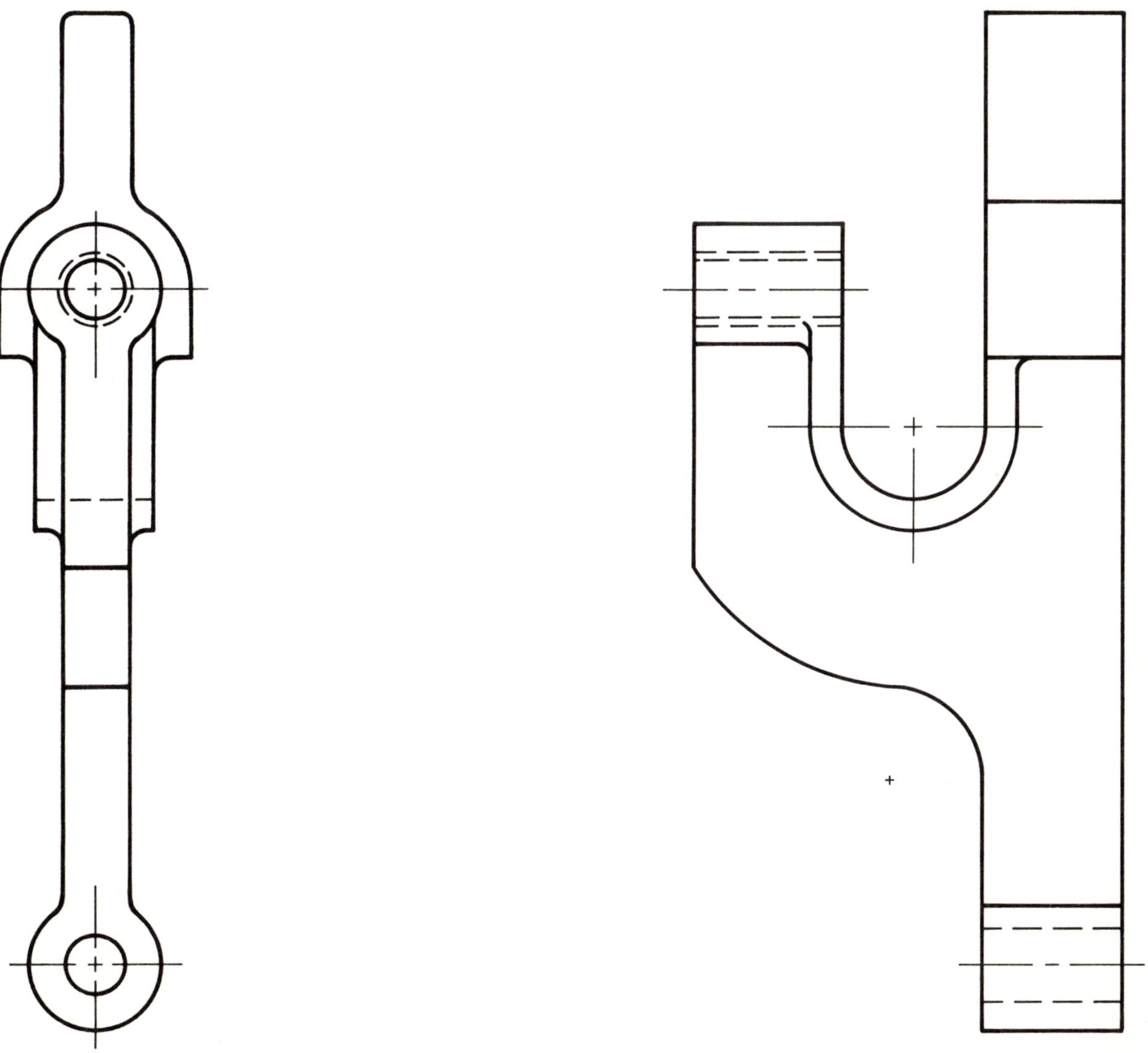

EXTENSION C-CLAMP

FULL SIZE

Drafting & Design © James H. Earle	NAME FILE NO SEC DATE	grade	

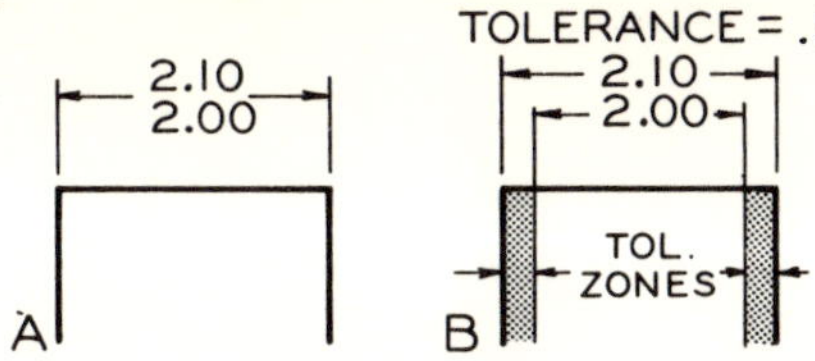

TOLERANCES ARE APPLIED TO DIMENSIONS TO SPECIFY THE VARIATION IN SIZE THAT IS ALLOWABLE WHEN A PART IS MADE. THE TOLERANCE HERE IS .10.

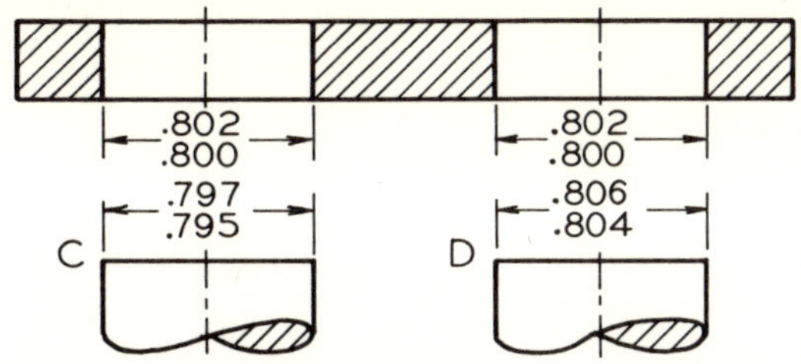

WHEN TWO PARTS ARE TOLERANCED THE TIGHTEST FIT BETWEEN THE ASSEMBLED PARTS IS THE ALLOWANCE. PARTS MAY ASSEMBLE WITH A CLEARANCE OR AN INTERFERENCE. THE ALLOWANCE AT C IS +.003 (CLEARANCE) AND AT D -.006 (INTERFERENCE).

E ← 3.80 / 3.74 LIMIT TOL

F ← 2.500 ± .002 BILATERAL

G ← 2.500 $^{+.000}_{-.003}$ UNILATERAL

METHODS OF DIMENSIONING TOLERANCES ARE GIVEN AT THE LEFT. LIMITS MAY BE GIVEN OR A BASIC DIMENSION WITH PLUS AND MINUS LIMITS MAY BE USED.

1 ANSWER THE QUESTIONS BELOW IN THE TABLE BY REFERRING TO THE DIMENSIONED PART.

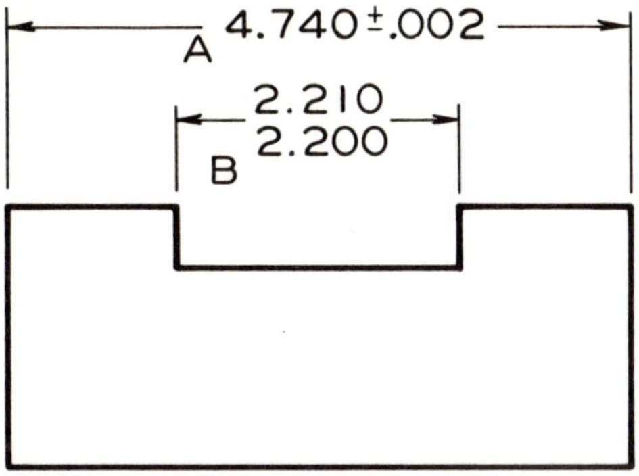

	A	B
NOMINAL SIZE:		
TOLERANCE:		
LARGEST SIZE:		

2 ANSWER THE QUESTIONS BELOW IN THE TABLE BY REFERRING TO DIMENSIONED PARTS.

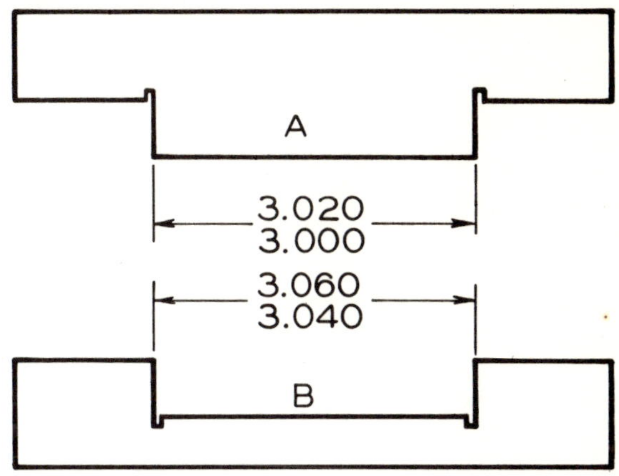

TOLERANCE AT A: ___ AT B: ___

ALLOWANCE: ___

MAXIMUM CLEARANCE: ___

3 DIMENSION THE PART TO FIT INTO THE SLOT SO IT WILL HAVE A TOLERANCE OF .010 AND A CLEARANCE FIT WITH AN ALLOWANCE OF .012.

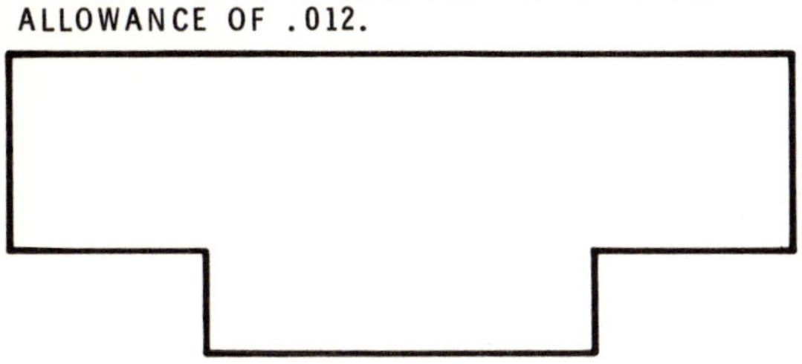

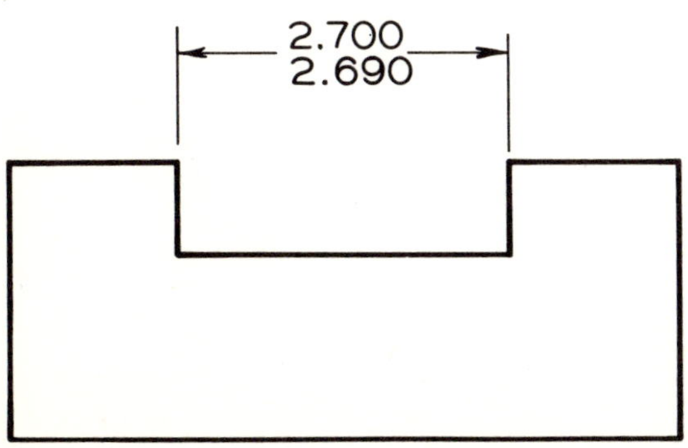

4 DIMENSION THE SHAFT TO HAVE A TOLERANCE OF .004 AND A CLEARANCE FIT WITH AN ALLOWANCE OF .006.

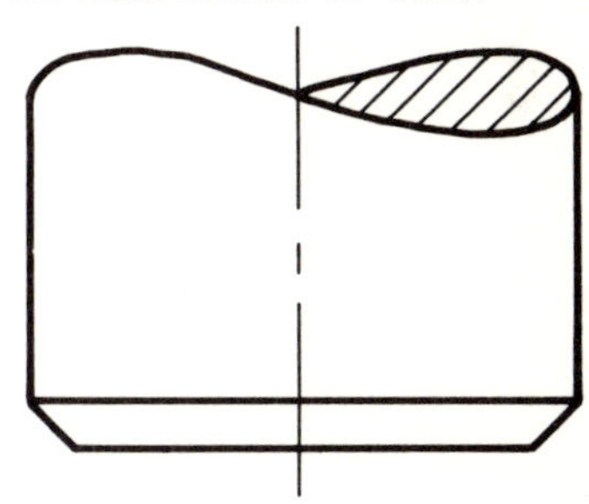

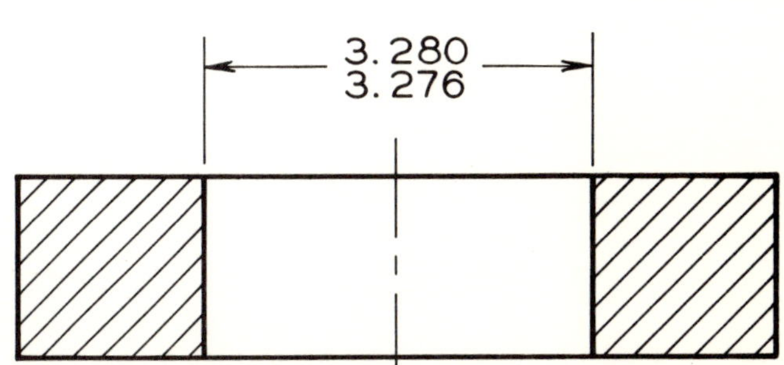

Drafting & Design © James H. Earle	NAME FILE NO SEC DATE	grade	

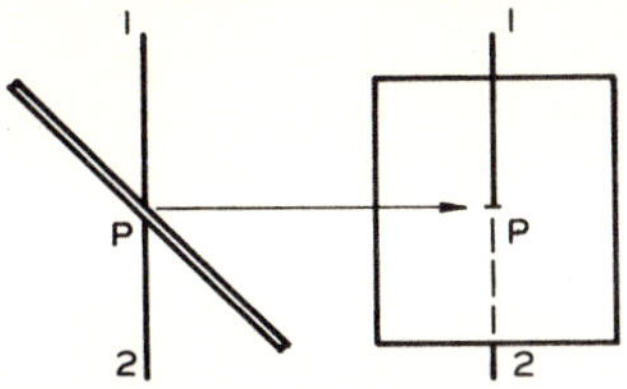

THE INTERSECTION BETWEEN A LINE AND A PLANE CAN BE FOUND IN THE LEFT-SIDE VIEW WHERE THE PLANE IS AN EDGE AND IS PROJECTED TO THE FRONT VIEW.

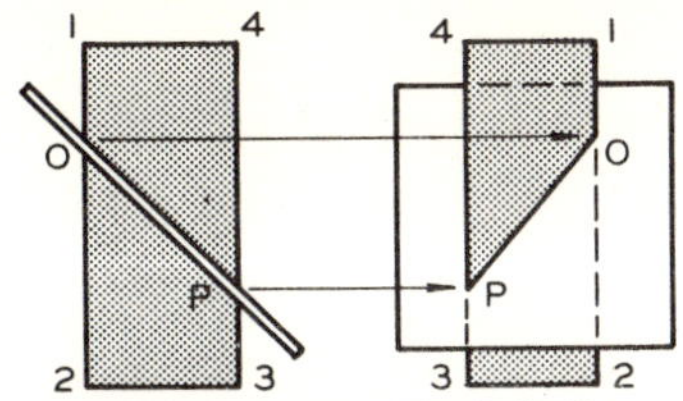

THE INTERSECTION BETWEEN PLANES IS FOUND BY LOCATING THE POINTS OF INTERSECTION OF TWO LINES (1-2 AND 3-4) ON THE PLANE.

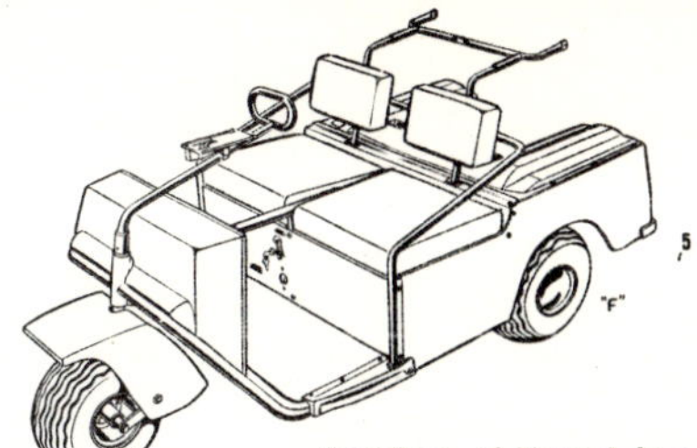

Courtesy of Versal Inc.

1 FIND THE POINTS OF INTERSECTION FOR LINES 1-2 AND 3-4.

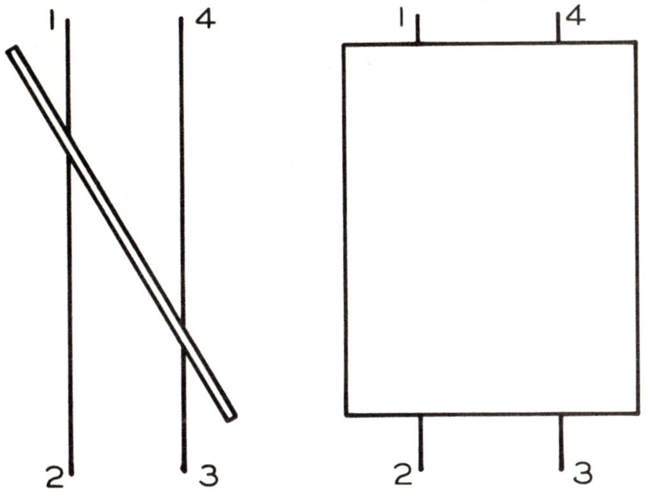

2 FIND THE LINE OF INTERSECTION BETWEEN THE TWO PLANES.

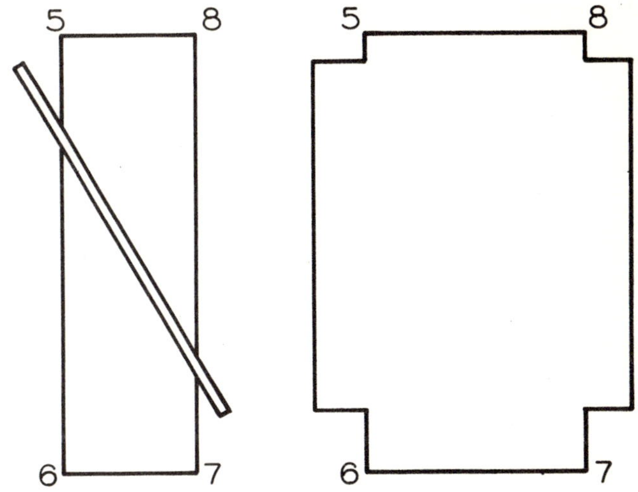

3 FIND THE LINE OF INTERSECTION BETWEEN THE PRISM AND PLANE.

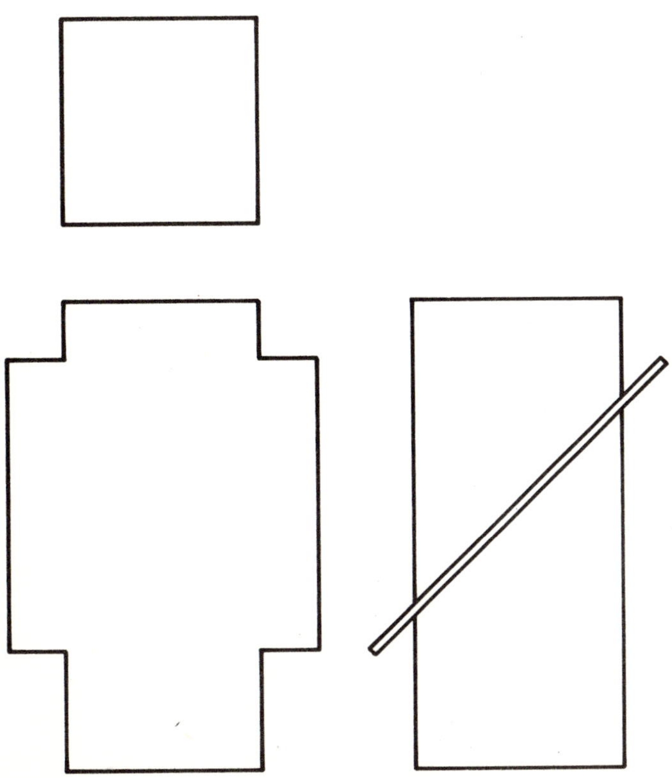

4 FIND THE LINE OF INTERSECTION BETWEEN THE PRISM AND PLANE.

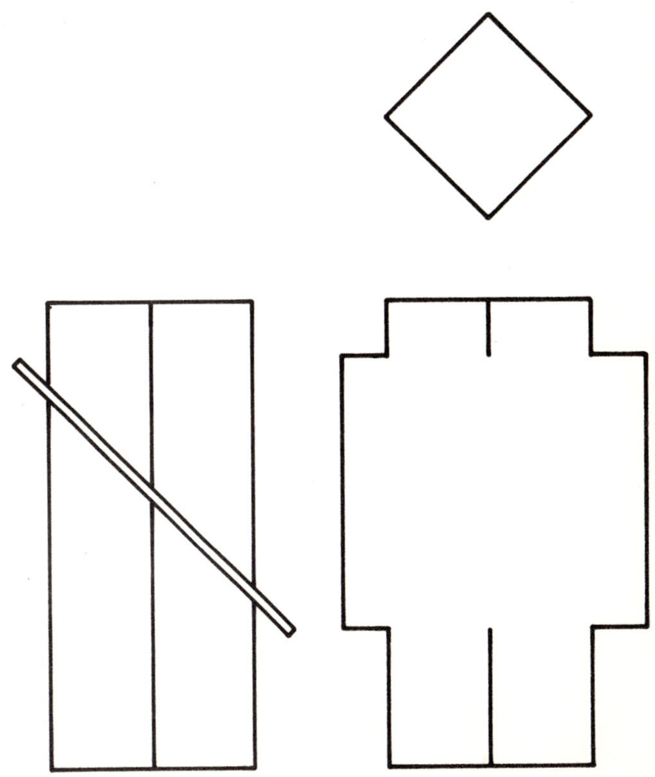

Drafting & Design ©James H. Earle	NAME FILE NO SEC DATE	grade	83

Drafting & Design © James H. Earle	NAME FILE NO SEC DATE	grade	

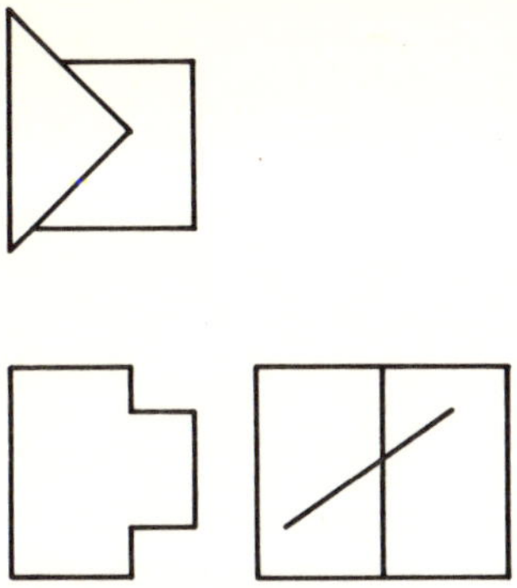

REQUIRED: FIND THE LINE OF INTERSECTION BETWEEN THE PLANE AND THE PRISM.

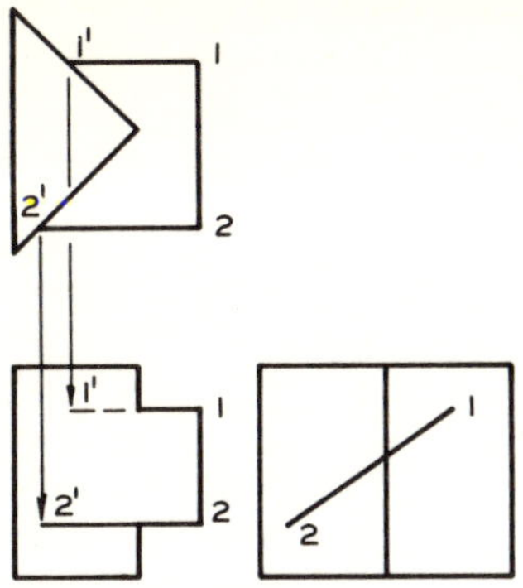

STEP 1: PIERCING POINTS 1' & 2' ARE FOUND IN THE TOP AND FRONT VIEWS.

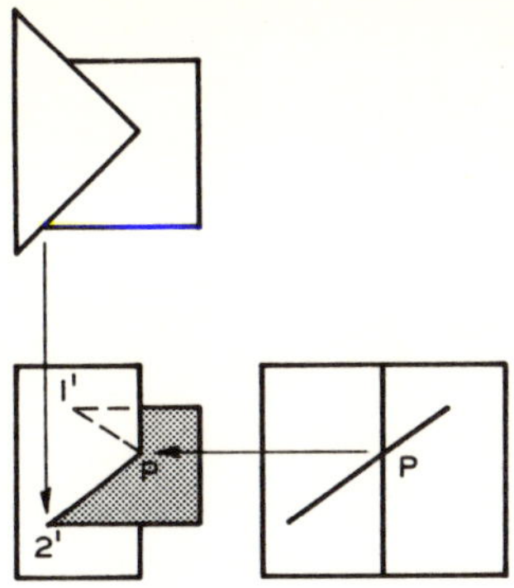

STEP 2: POINT P IS PROJECTED TO THE FRONT VIEW. POINTS 1', 2' AND P ARE CONNECTED.

Courtesy of Pan American Petroleum Co.

1 FIND THE INTERSECTION BETWEEN THE PLANE AND PRISM

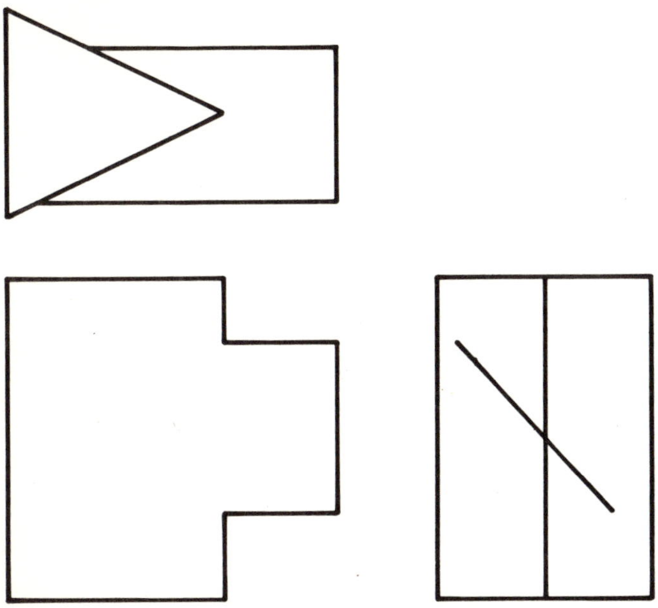

2 FIND THE INTERSECTION BETWEEN THE TWO PRISMS.

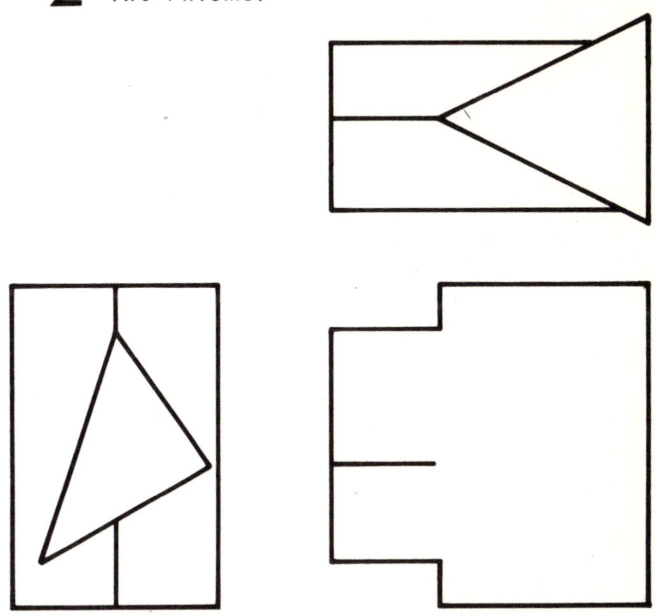

3 FIND THE INTERSECTION BETWEEN THE TWO PRISMS.

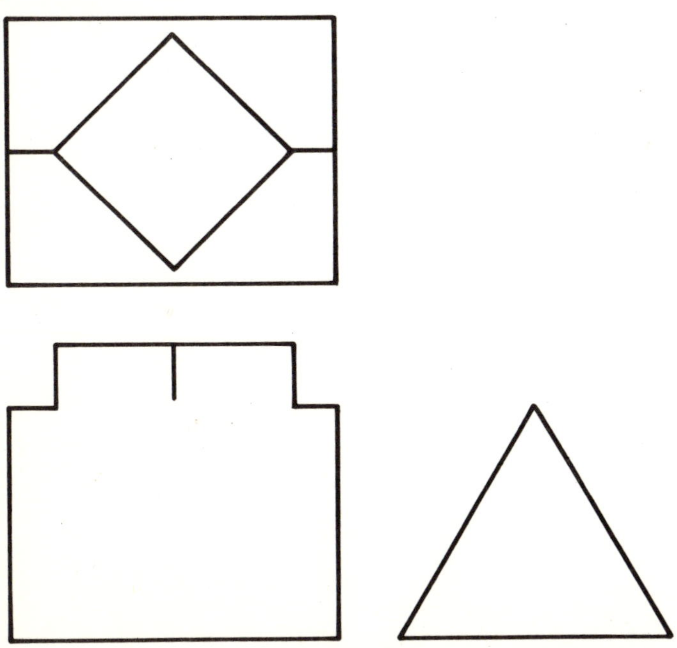

4 FIND THE INTERSECTION BETWEEN THE TWC PRISMS.

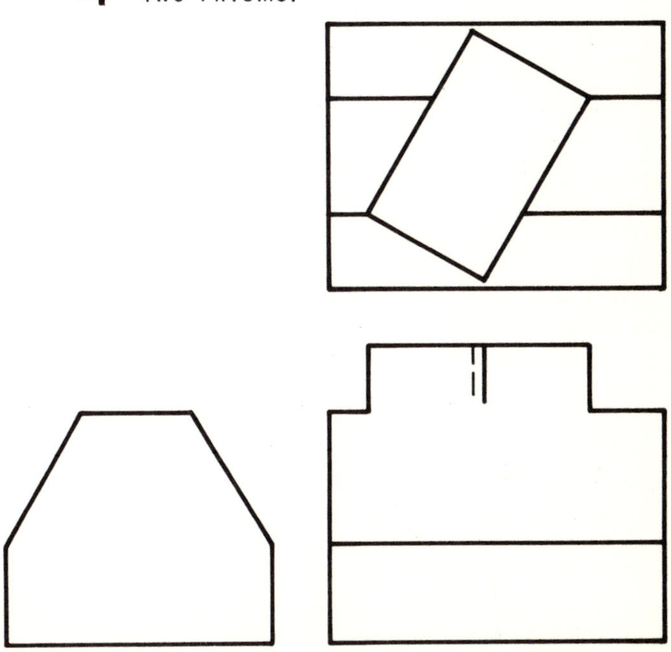

Drafting & Design © James H. Earle	NAME FILE NO SEC DATE	grade	

INTERSECTIONS

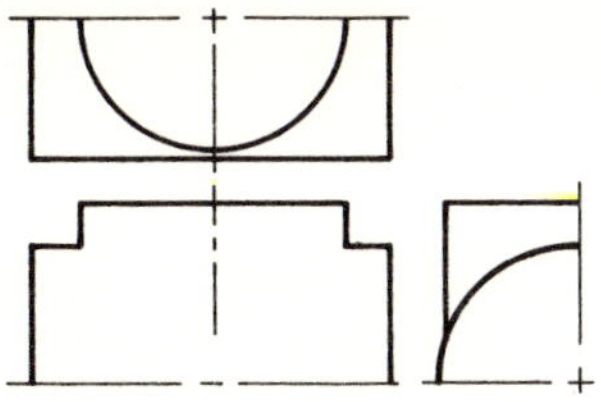

REQUIRED: FIND THE LINE OF INTERSECTION BETWEEN THE TWO CYLINDERS.

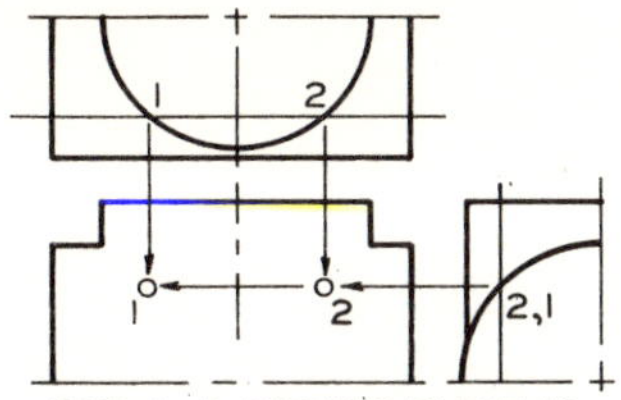

STEP 1: A CUTTING PLANE IS PASSED THROUGH THE TOP AND SIDE VIEWS. POINTS 1 & 2 ARE PROJECTED TO THE FRONT. VIEW.

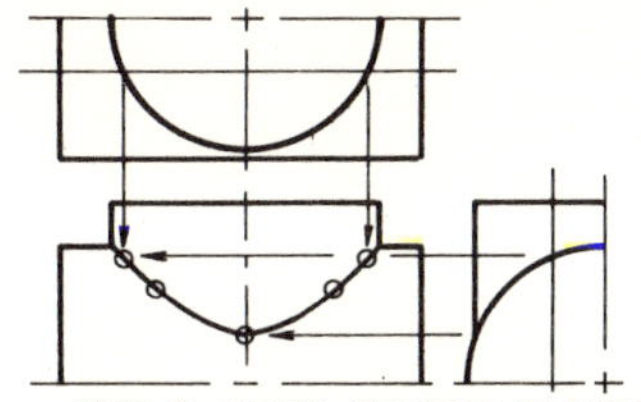

STEP 2: OTHER CUTTING PLANES LOCATE OTHER POINTS ON THE LINE OF INTERSECTION. THESE POINTS ARE CONNECTED WITH A SMOOTH CURVE.

courtesy of Cameron Iron Works

1 FIND THE LINE OF INTERSECTION BETWEEN THE TWO CYLINDERS.

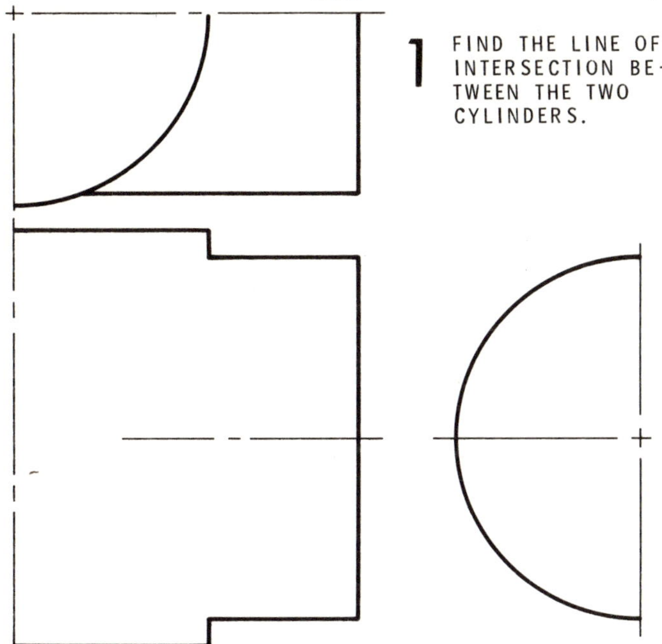

2 FIND THE LINE OF INTERSECTION BETWEEN THE PLANE AND CYLINDER.

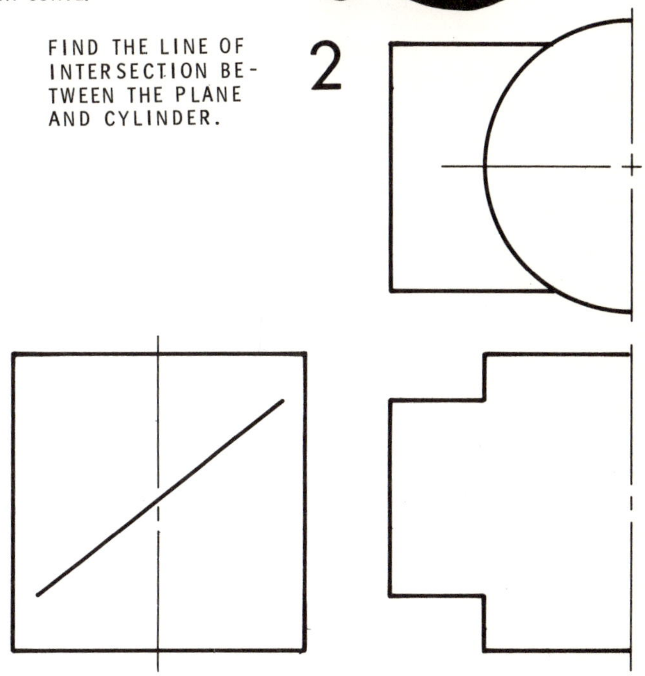

3 FIND THE LINE OF INTERSECTION BETWEEN THE TWO CYLINDERS.

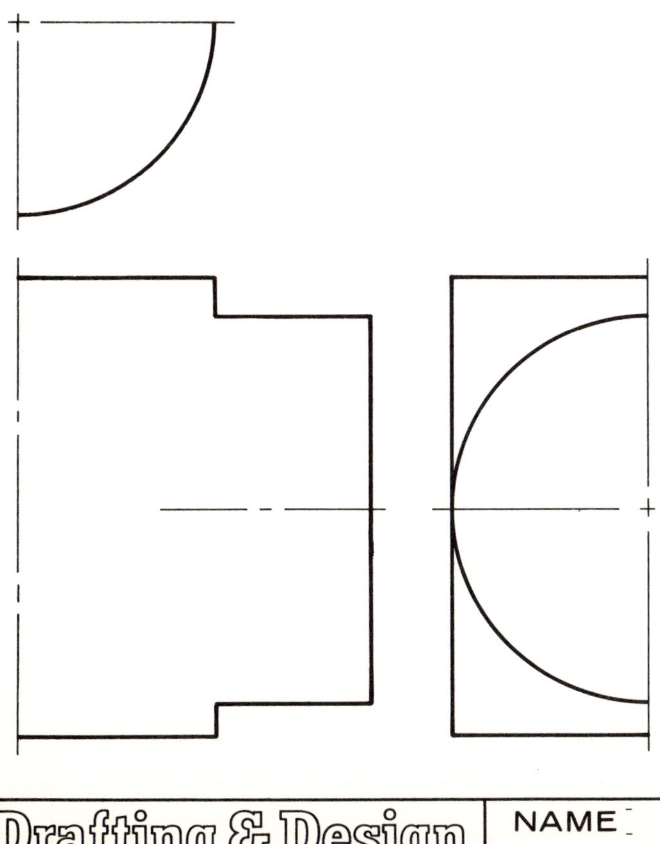

4 FIND THE LINE OF INTERSECTION BETWEEN THE PRISM AND CYLINDER.

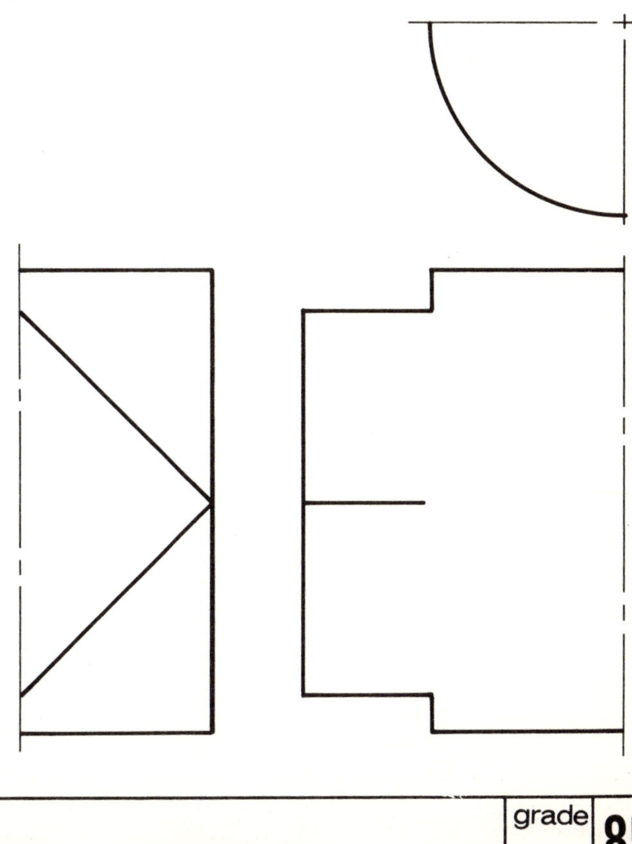

NAME ____
FILE NO ____ SEC ____ DATE ____

grade

Drafting & Design © James H. Earle	NAME FILE NO. SEC. DATE	grade	

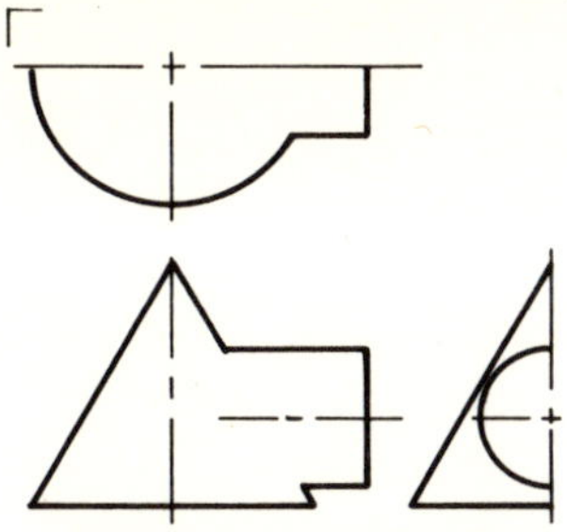

REQUIRED: FIND THE INTERSECTION BETWEEN THE CONE AND THE CYLINDER.

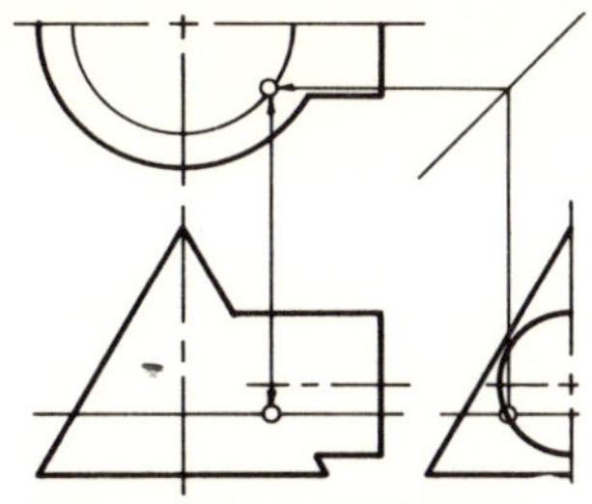

STEP 1: PASS A HORIZONTAL CUTTING PLANE THROUGH THE CONE AND CYLINDER TO LOCATE A POINT ON THE LINE OF INTERSECTION.

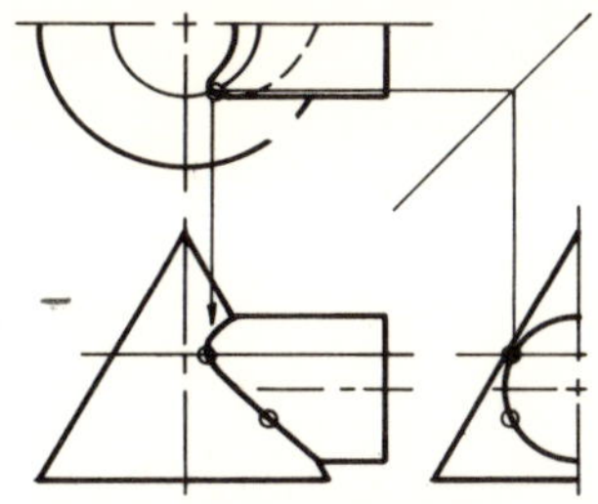

STEP 2: OTHER HORIZONTAL CUTTING PLANES ARE USED TO FIND OTHER POINTS TO ESTABLISH THE LINE OF INTERSECTION

Courtesy of Ridge Runner, Inc.

1 FIND THE INTERSECTION BETWEEN THE CONE AND CYLINDER. THESE ARE PARTIAL VIEWS.

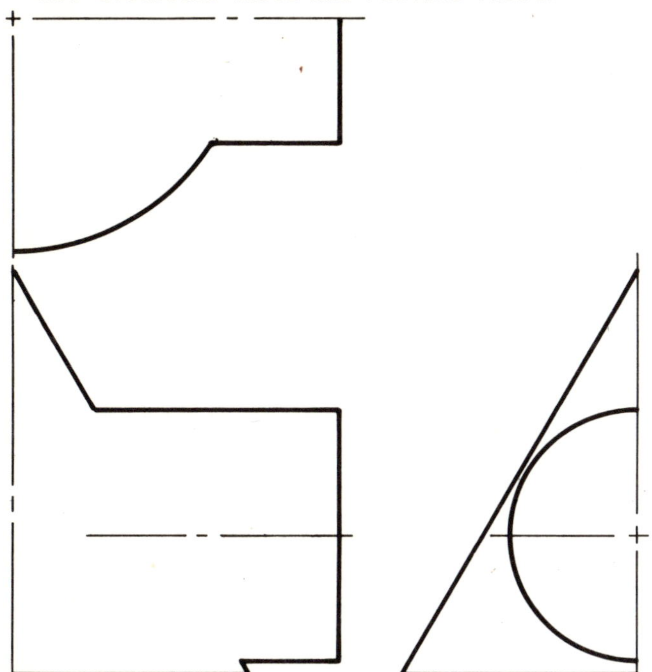

2 FIND THE INTERSECTION BETWEEN THE CONE AND PLANE. THESE ARE PARTIAL VIEWS.

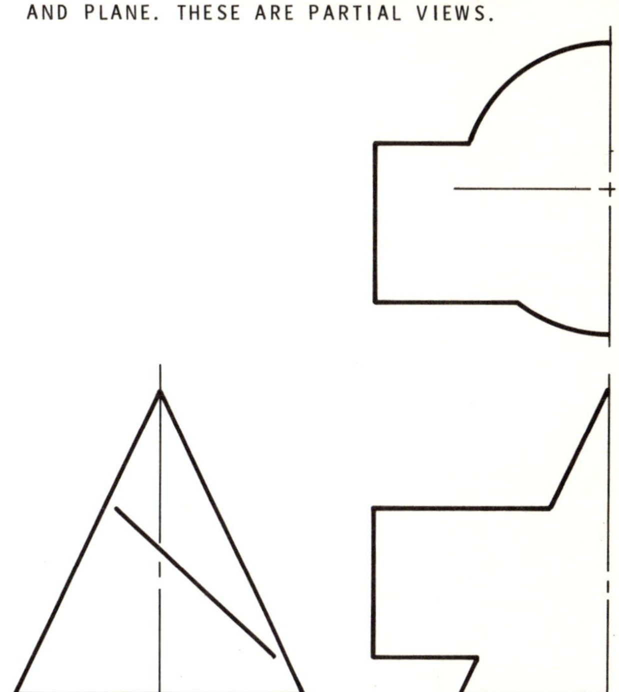

3 FIND THE INTERSECTION BETWEEN THE CONE AND PRISM. THESE ARE PARTIAL VIEWS.

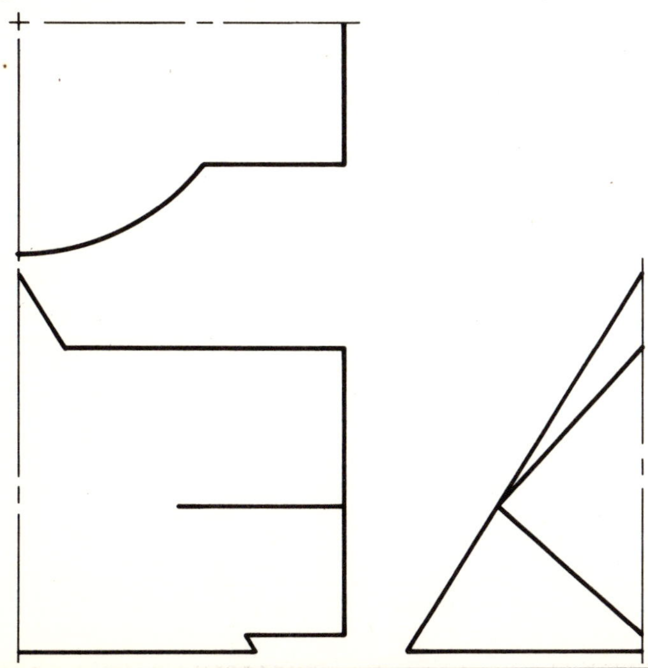

4 FIND THE INTERSECTION BETWEEN THE PRISM AND PYRAMID. THESE ARE PARTIAL VIEWS.

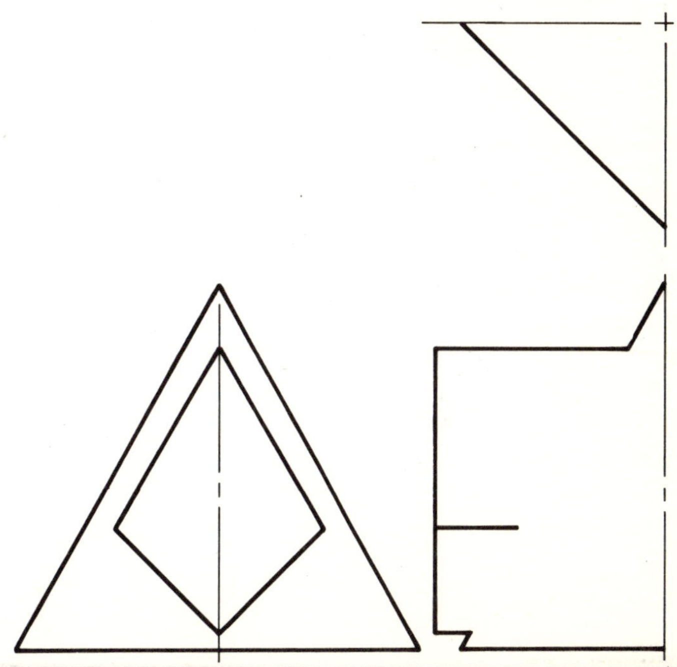

Drafting & Design © James H. Earle	NAME FILE NO SEC DATE	grade	

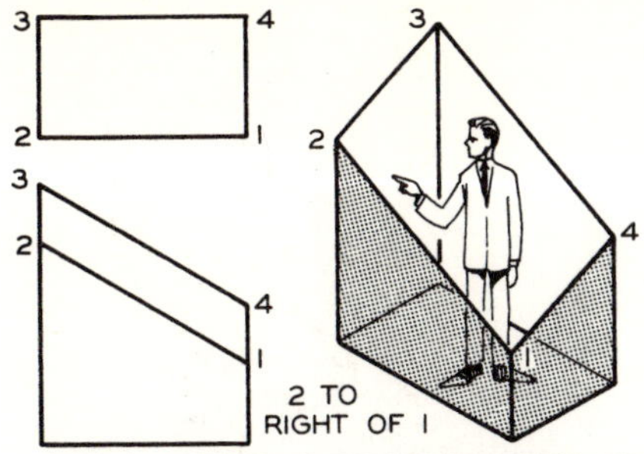

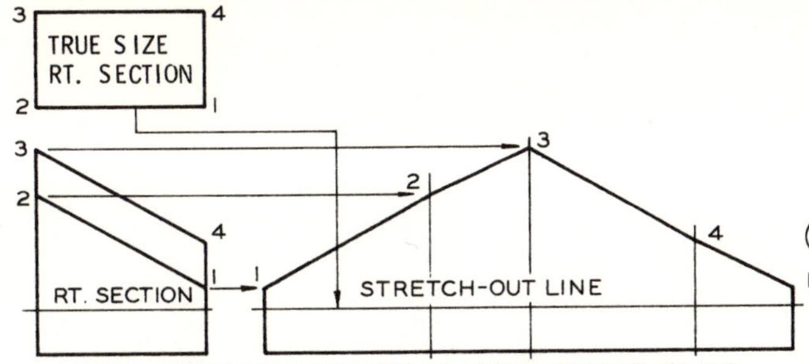

STEP 1: DETERMINE THE ORDER OF POINTS THAT WILL GIVE AN INSIDE PATTERN. SINCE IT WILL BE LAID OUT TO THE RIGHT FIND THE POINT TO THE RIGHT OF 1 IMAGINING THAT YOU ARE INSIDE THE PRISM. THE SEAM IS LOCATED THROUGH 1 SINCE IT IS THE SHORTEST AND MOST ECONOMICAL CONNECTION.

STEP 2: THE STRETCH-OUT LINE IS DRAWN PARALLEL TO THE EDGE VIEW OF THE RIGHT SECTION. TRUE LENGTH MEASUREMENTS BETWEEN THE CORNERS ARE TRANSFERRED FROM THE TOP VIEW TO THE STRETCH-OUT LINE. THE ENDS OF EACH CORNER LINE ARE PROJECTED TO THESE FOLD LINES WHICH ARE DRAWN AS THIN, SHARP LINES.

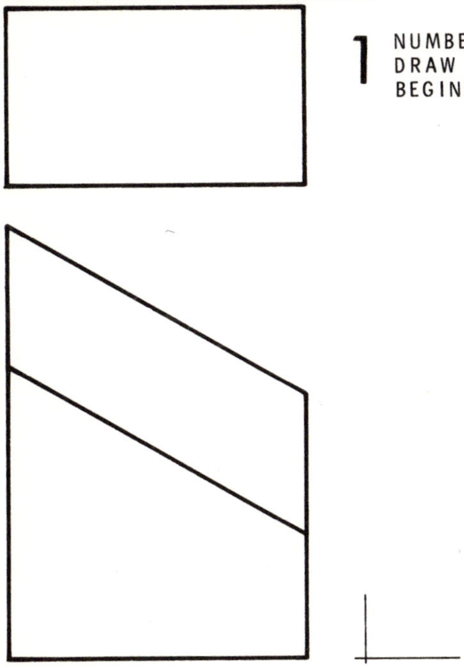

1 NUMBER THE POINTS IN BOTH VIEWS AND DRAW AN INSIDE PATTERN AT THE RIGHT BEGINNING WITH THE SHORTEST LINE.

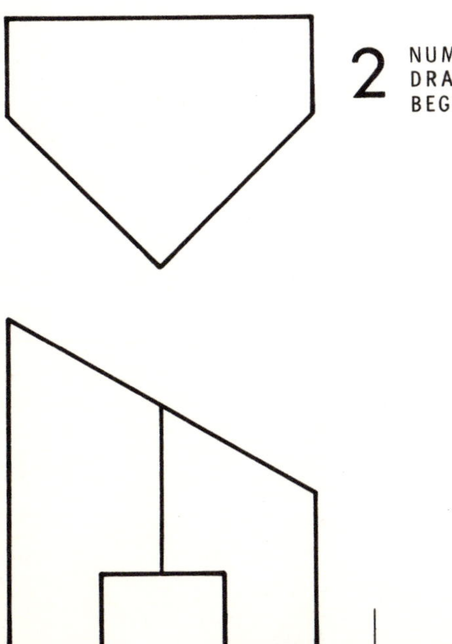

2 NUMBER THE POINTS IN BOTH VIEWS AND DRAW AN INSIDE PATTERN AT THE RIGHT BEGINNING WITH THE SHORTEST LINE.

NAME
FILE NO. SEC. DATE
grade

Drafting & Design

NAME

FILE NO SEC DATE

grade

Courtesy of International Harvester

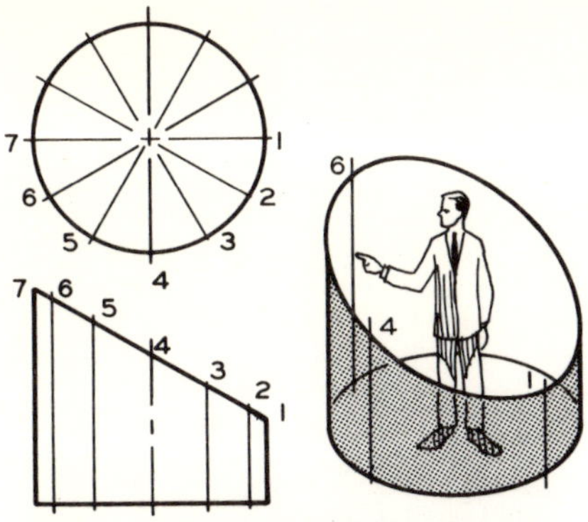

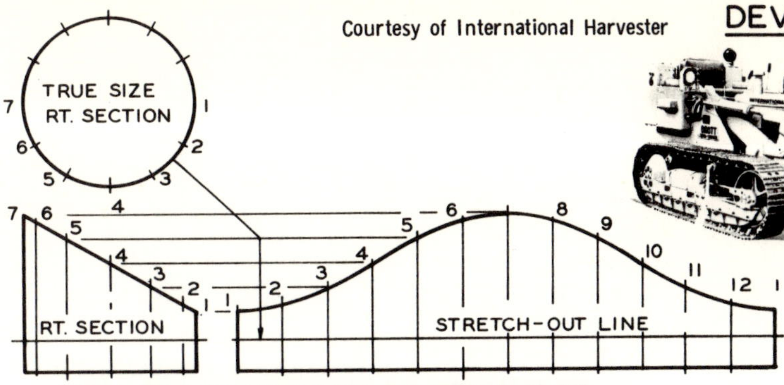

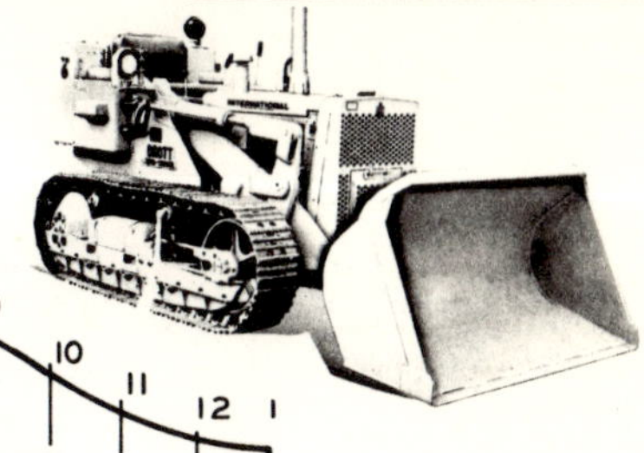

STEP 1: DIVIDE THE CIRCULAR VIEW INTO EQUAL ARCS TO FIND ELEMENTS ON THE CYLINDER. SINCE THE PATTERN IS TO BE LAID OUT TO THE RIGHT BEGINNING WITH THE SHORTEST ELEMENT THROUGH 1, IMAGINE THAT YOU ARE INSIDE THE CYLINDER. POINTS 2, 3, ETC. ARE TO THE RIGHT FOR AN INSIDE PATTERN.

STEP 2: DRAW THE STRETCH-OUT LINE PARALLEL TO THE EDGE VIEW OF THE RIGHT SECTION. TRUE CHORDAL DISTANCES ARE TRANSFERRED FROM THE TOP VIEW TO THE STRETCH-OUT LINE TO LOCATE ELEMENTS WHOSE LENGTHS ARE FOUND BY PROJECTING FROM THE FRONT VIEW.

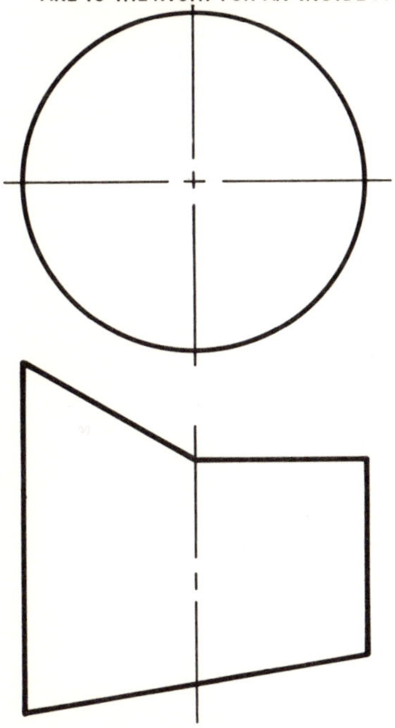

1 NUMBER THE POINTS IN BOTH VIEWS AND DRAW AN INSIDE PATTERN BY STARTING WITH THE SHORTEST ELEMENT.

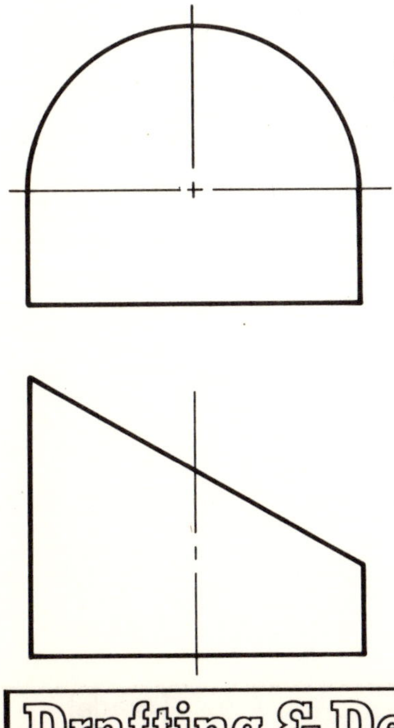

2 NUMBER THE POINTS IN BOTH VIEWS AND DRAW AN INSIDE PATTERN BY STARTING WITH THE SHORTEST ELEMENT.

NAME

FILE NO. SEC. DATE

grade

Drafting & Design

NAME

FILE NO SEC DATE

grade

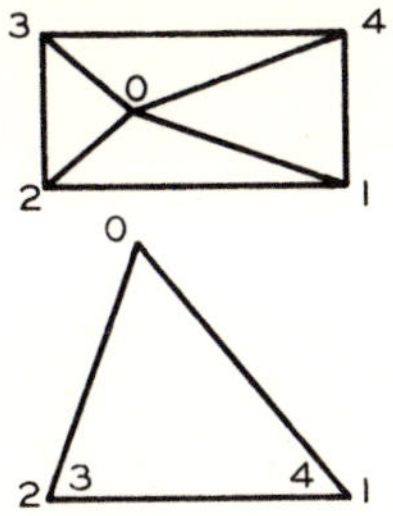

REQUIRED: CONSTRUCT AN INSIDE PATTERN OF THE PYRAMID.

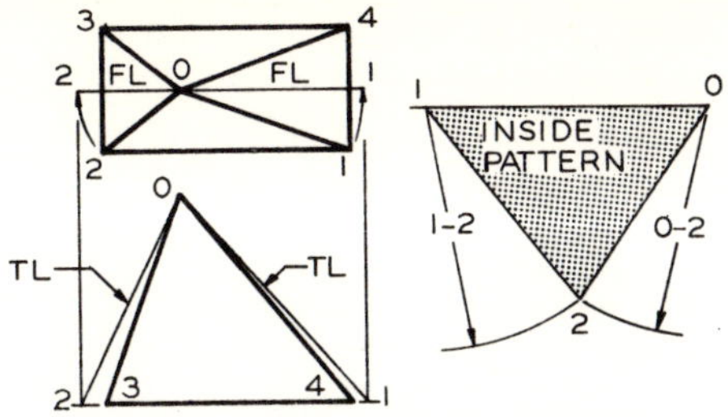

STEP 1: FIND CORNER LINES 0-1 AND 0-2 TRUE LENGTH. 1-2 IS TRUE LENGTH IN THE TOP VIEW. CORNERS 0-1, 0-2 AND 1-2 ARE USED TO FIND PLANE 0-1-2 BY TRIANGULATION. POINT 2 IS THE RIGHT OF 1 FOR AN INSIDE PATTERN.

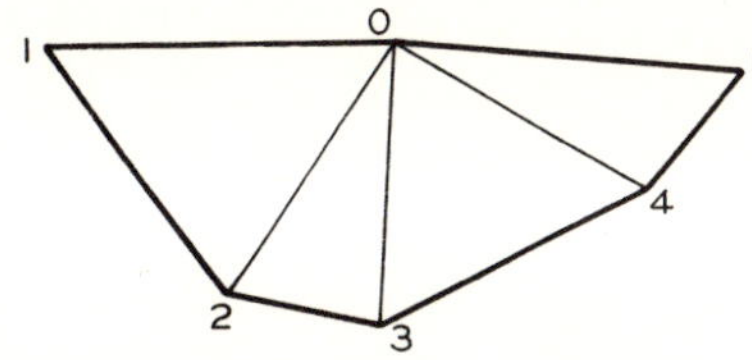

STEP 2: OTHER CORNERS ARE USED TO FIND THE REMAINING TRIANGULAR PLANES IN SEQUENCE. ALL LINES OF THE PATTERN MUST BE TRUE LENGTH. THE LINES ARE CONNECTED TO COMPLETE THE PATTERN.

LAY OUT INSIDE PATTERNS FOR TWO OF THE PARTS ASSIGNED BEGINING WITH LINE 0-1. DOUBLE THE GIVEN DIMENSIONS. NUMBER ALL POINTS ON THE GIVEN VIEWS AND THE PATTERN.

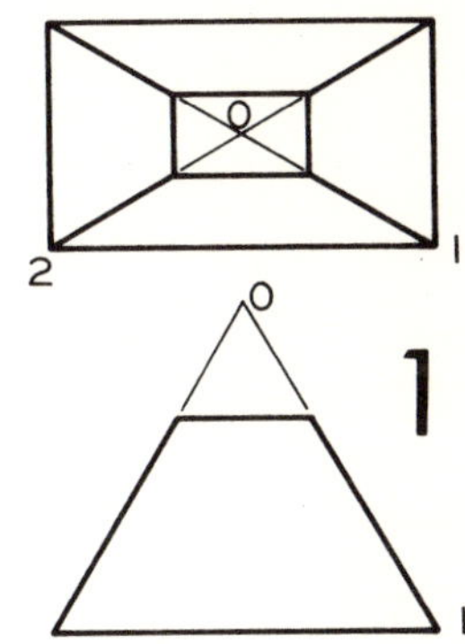

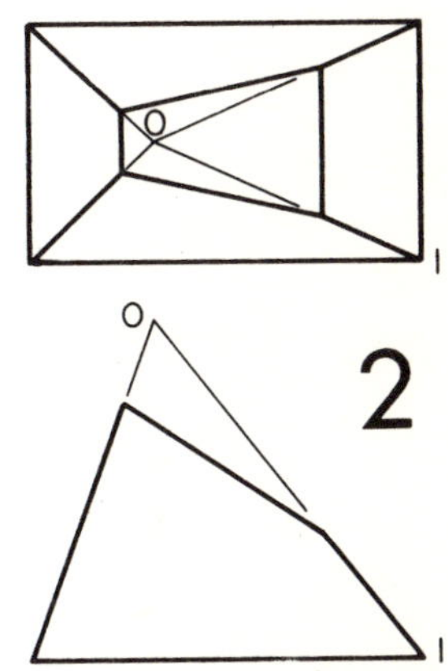

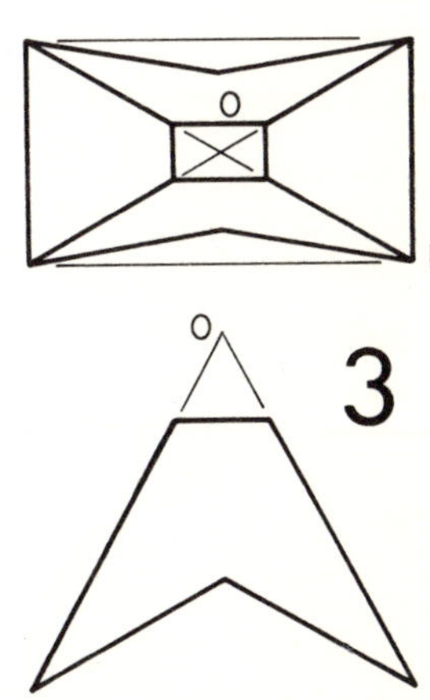

Drafting & Design © James H. Earle	NAME FILE NO SEC DATE	grade	

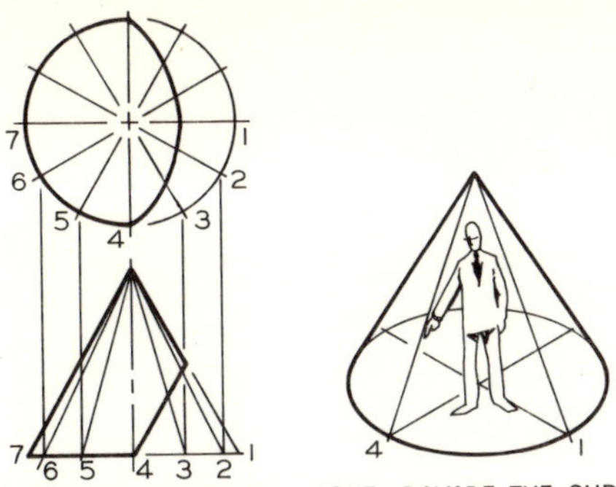

STEP 1: TO DEVELOP A CONE, DIVIDE THE SURFACE INTO EQUALLY SPACED ELEMENTS. IMAGINE THAT YOU ARE INSIDE THE CONE TO VISUALIZE AN INSIDE PATTERN. 4 IS TO THE RIGHT OF 1.

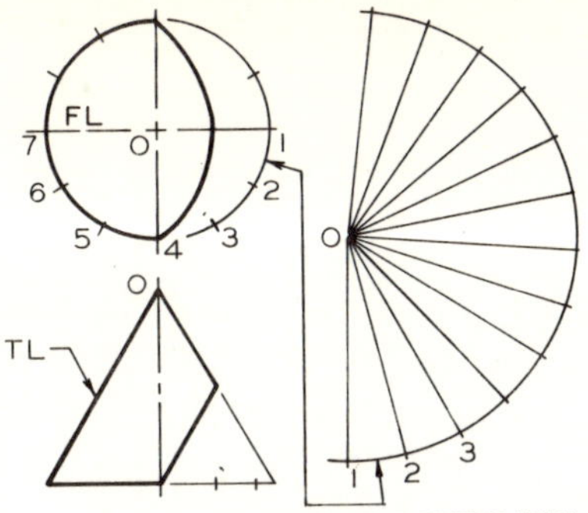

STEP 2: THE OUTSIDE ELEMENT WILL BE TRUE LENGTH SINCE IT IS A FRONTAL LINE. THIS LENGTH IS USED AS THE RADIUS FOR THE PATTERN. TRANSFER ARC LENGTHS FROM THE TOP VIEW TO THE PATTERN.

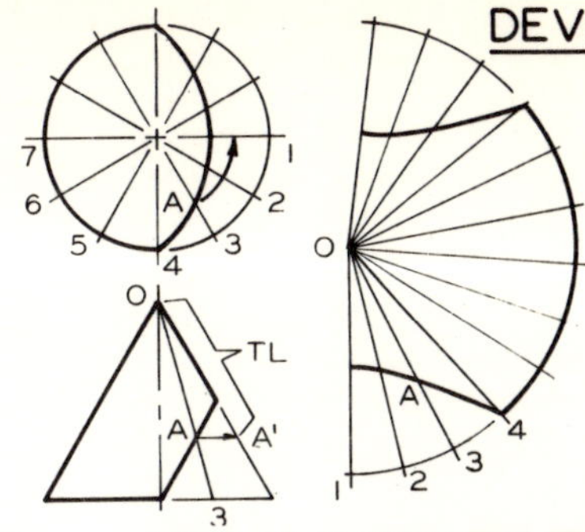

STEP 3: OA IS FOUND TRUE LENGTH BY REVOLUTION IN THE TOP AND BY PROJECTING HORIZONTALLY IN THE FRONT VIEW TO THE OUTSIDE ELEMENT. OA IS MEASURED ALONG ELEMENT O-3 TO LOCATE POINT A. FIND OTHER POINTS IN THIS MANNER.

1

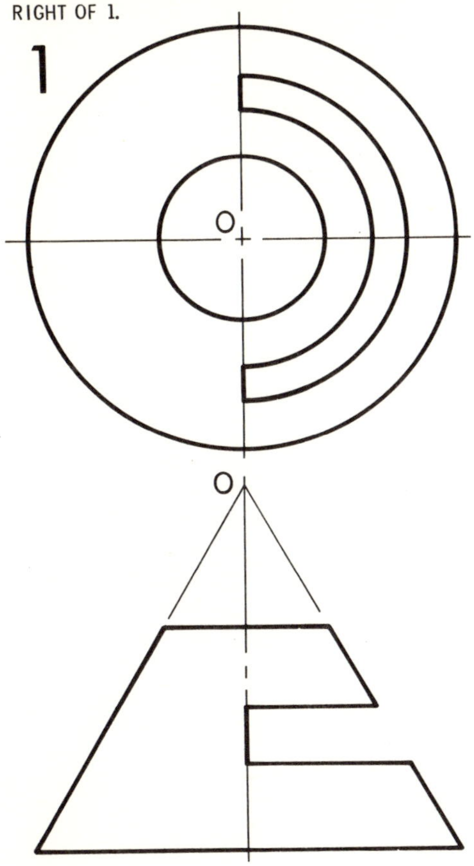

LAY OUT AN INSIDE PATTERN OF EACH OF THESE CONICAL PARTS. BEGIN WITH THE SHORTEST ELEMENT ON EACH. LETTER THE POINTS IN ALL VIEWS AND ON THE PATTERN.

2

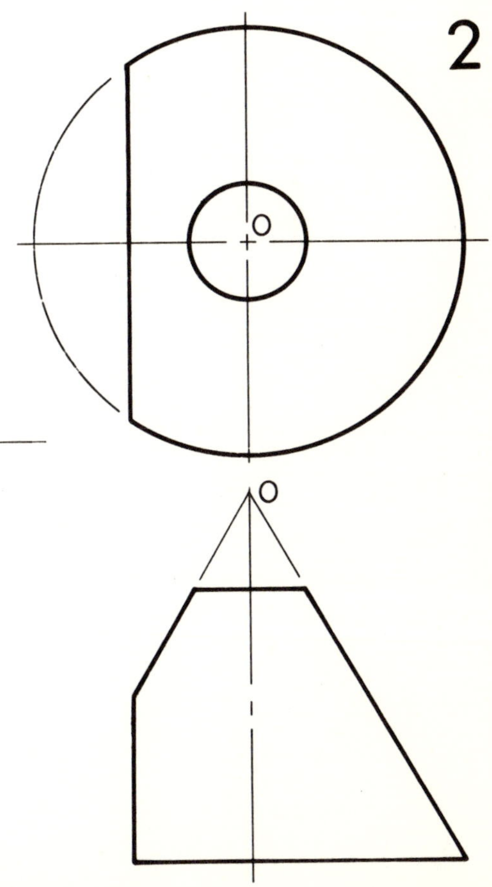

Drafting & Design © James H. Earle	NAME FILE NO SEC DATE	grade	

DESIGN

GENERAL

These problems have been designed to encourage you to apply graphical techniques to the development of an original solution to a design problem. Your solution will involve freehand sketches, notes and preliminary ideas. The completion of the problems will require detailed, dimensioned working drawings that specify the final solution from which the design can be constructed. Utilize any graphical technique that will aid you in presenting your solution.

Your solutions should be presented on 11" x 15" tracing paper similar to that provided at the rear of the book. Adequate notes, specifications and pictorials should be included to clearly describe your ideas without additional explanation.

These problems listed below may suggest other problems similar to these that you would like to work on with the approval of your instructor.

1. BICYLE RACK

Design a bicycle rack for your campus and determine its most advantageous location. You may wish to have several at different locations or just one single rack. It may be a permanent rack or a portable rack that would allow it to be moved as its usage varied.

2. OUTDOOR GRILL

Design and detail an outdoor grill for broiling steaks over charcoal. Consider all of the features that are necessary for this grill to be a successful product -- economical, efficient, portable and attractive. Begin by inspecting those that are presently on the market.

3. WALL-SUPPORT FOR A TV

Design and detail a support bracket that can be used fo attaching a portable TV to a vertical wall. This device should permit the set to be adjusted to reduce reflections and glare.

4. TRASH CONTAINER

Design and detail an attractive recepticle that could be manufactured and installed on your campus in which wrappers and other scrap paper could be deposited. Determine where these should be located and how they will be emptied and serviced.

5. BICYCLE LUGGAGE RACK

Design and detail a luggage carriage that can be attached to a bicycle for carrying packages, books or similar items while riding a bicycle. The design should be simple but functional and easy to attach and remove from a bicycle. The design should be begun only after studying the structure of the bicycle to which it will be attached.

6. LOCKER SYSTEM

Design and detail a locker (storage) system that can be used in your drafting classroom for storing student supplies, instruments and drawings. Determine where the units will be located and how they will be used.

7. SALABLE PRODUCT

Can you think of a product that could be mass-produced in your school shop that could be sold to the student body to raise money for club activities? Make a list of you ideas with sketches of as many as you can think of. Make the necessary detail drawings and specifications to communicate the best idea. Determine the selling price and the profit margin that you would recommend.

8. PRODUCT REDESIGN

Select a product from a catalog or an advertisement and redesign it into what you consider is as better design. Explain why your modifications have improved the product.

9. RIFLE REST

A rifle rest is sometimes used in target practice for shooting from a sitting or prone position. Design and detail a rifle rest that is adjustable, portable and economical for target shooters.

10. BASKETBALL GOAL AND GYM UNIT

Design and detail a portable basketball goal that can be disassembled easily and removed for storage. Consider other uses for the support structure that could be used for exercise and body building. Suggestions are: chinning bars, punching bag, parallel bars, etc.

11. PROJECTOR CABINET

Design and detail a projector cabinet that will contain a 35mm slide projector and a series of slide trays that could be used as a piece of furniture in a living room. This would reduce the set-up time when the projector is to be used. The cabinet should have a power source for operating the projector and adjustments that would allow the image to be projected

THE DESIGN DRAFTSMAN MUST BE ABLE TO WORK FROM A DESIGNER'S ROUGH SKETCHES AND CONVERT THESE IDEAS INTO FINAL WORKING DRAWINGS. THE FREEHAND SKETCHES BELOW REPRESENT THE PARTS OF A SMALL DRILL VISE THAT IS DRAWN ON A 1/4" GRID. THERE ARE OMISSIONS IN NOTES AND DIMENSIONS ON THESE DRAWINGS. EACH SPECIFICATION SHOULD BE CHECKED TO ENSURE ITS CORRECTNESS AND CHANGED IF WRONG. SHOW FILLETS, ROUNDS AND RUNOUTS WHERE THEY SHOULD BE SHOWN. MAKE ANY MODIFICATION THAT WILL IMPROVE THE DESIGN THAT YOU DESIRE PROVIDED THE GENERAL DIMENSIONS AND THE FUNCTION OF THE VISE IS NOT CHANGED.

THE FOLLOWING PROBLEMS MAY BE ASSIGNED:

1. COMPLETE THE DETAIL DRAWINGS OF THE DRILL PRESS VISE ON THE TWO 11X 15 TRACING PAPER SHEETS THAT FOLLOW PAGE 98. THESE SHEETS ARE PARTIALLY LAID OUT.
2. CONSTRUCT AN ASSEMBLY DRAWING OF THE VISE ON THE THIRD SHEET OF TRACING PAPER SIMILAR TO ONE SHOWN ON PAGE 94. COMPLETE THE PARTS LIST.
3. MAKE PRINTS OF THE COMPLETED DRAWINGS AND EXCHANGE THEM WITH A CLASSMATE AND CHECK EACH OTHER'S DRAWINGS FOR ERRORS USING A COLORED PENCIL.

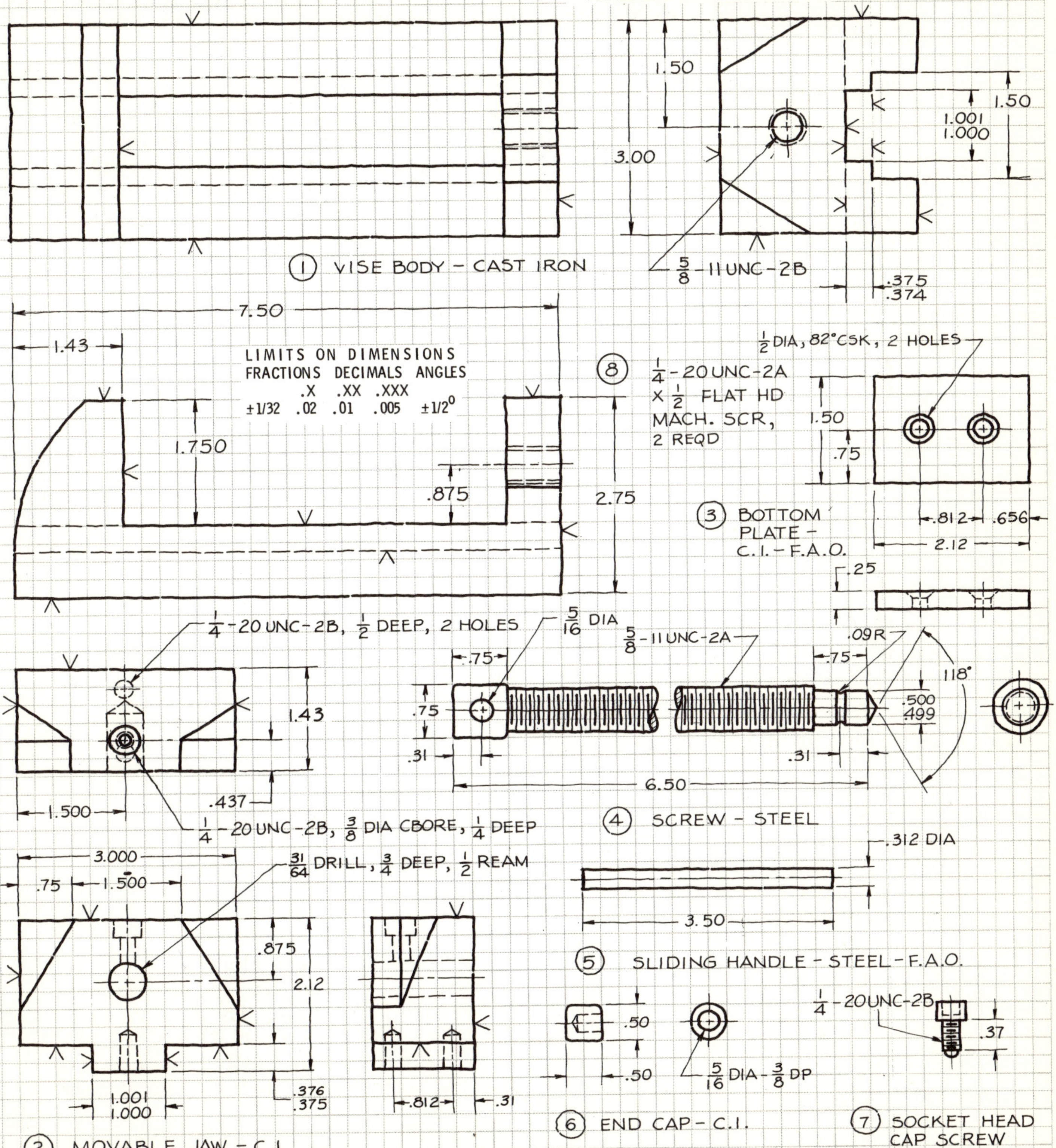

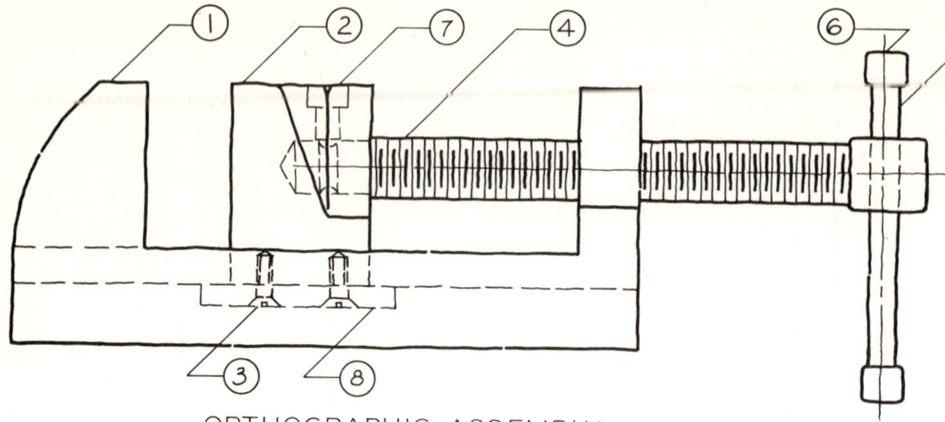

ORTHOGRAPHIC ASSEMBLY

THE ASSEMBLIES SHOWN ON THIS SHEET DESCRIBE HOW THE PARTS OF THE DRILL VISE ARE TO BE ASSEMBLED. REFER TO THE DETAILS OF EACH PART ON THE REVERSE SIDE OF THIS SHEET TO BETTER UNDERSTAND THE DETAILS OF THE PARTS.

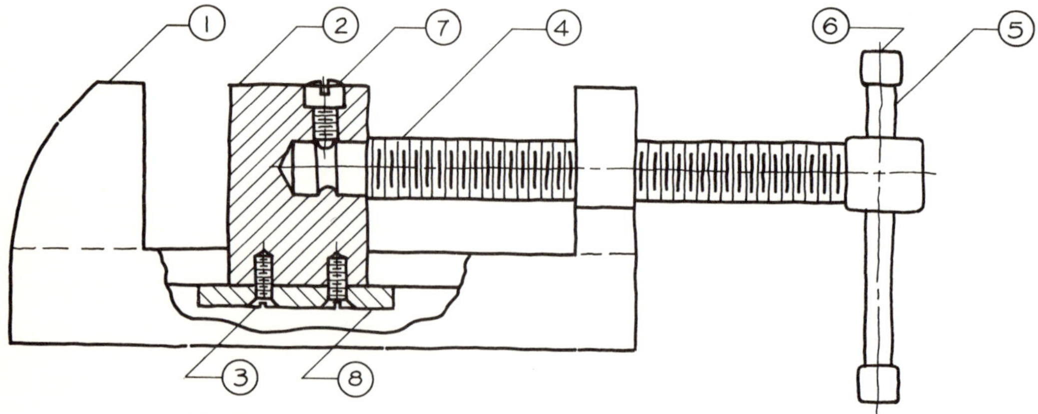

SECTIONED, ORHOGRAPHIC ASSEMBLY

ASSEMBLIES ARE NECESSARY TO EXPLAIN HOW PARTS FIT TOGETHER AFTER THEY HAVE BEEN MADE AS INDIVIDUAL UNITS. THE ASSEMBLY CAN BE DRAWN IN A NUMBER OF WAYS AND STILL BE EFFECTIVE IN EXPLAINING THE RELATIONSHIP BETWEEN THE PARTS.

THE THREE EXAMPLES OF ASSEMBLIES SHOWN ON THIS SHEET ARE:

1. AN ORTHOGRAPHIC ASSEMBLY
2. A PARTIALLY SECTIONED ORTHOGRAPHIC ASSEMBLY
3. AN EXPLODED, ISOMETRIC ASSEMBLY

MANY DRAWING TECHNIQUES CAN BE USED TO PRESENT AN ASSEMBLY. THE PARTS CAN BE COMPLETELY EXPLODED, PARTIALLY EXPLODED, SECTIONED, SHOWN ORTHOGRAPHICALLY OR PICTORIALLY.

NOTICE THAT CALL-OUT NUMBERS ARE GIVEN FOR EACH PART TO MAKE IT CONVENIENT TO CROSS-REFERENCE THE PARTS WITH THE PARTS LIST AND THE DETAIL DRAWING FROM WHICH THE PARTS WERE MADE.

THE EXAMPLES ON THIS SHEET WERE SKETCHED FREEHAND, BUT MOST ASSEMBLIES ARE DRAWN WITH INSTRUMENTS.

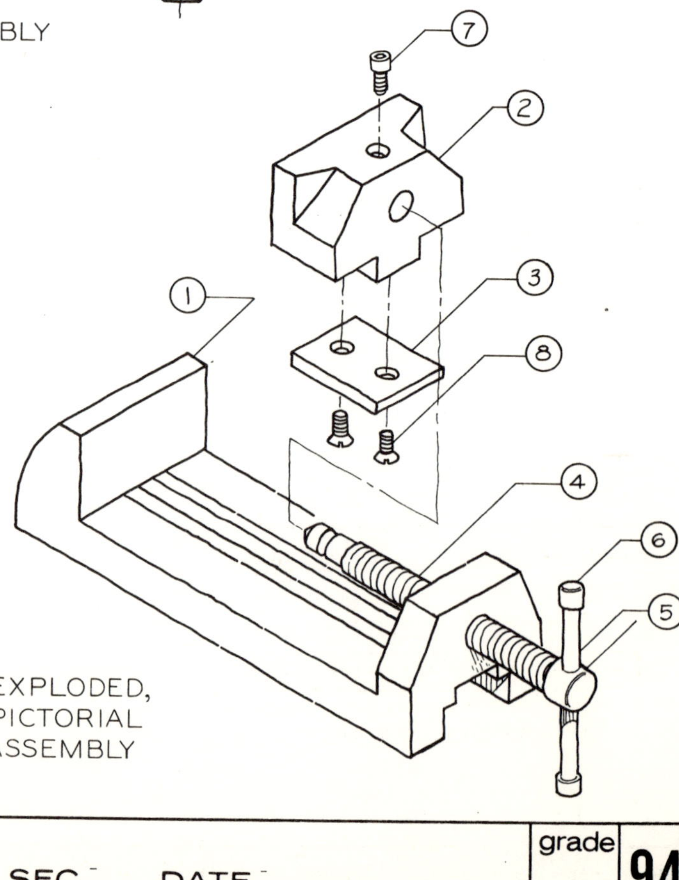

EXPLODED, PICTORIAL ASSEMBLY

Drafting & Design © James H. Earle	NAME FILE NO SEC DATE	grade	94

DESIGN & WORKING DRAWINGS

ASSUME THAT A DESIGNER HAS COMPLETED THE PRELIMINARY SKETCHES FOR THE PARTS OF A WOODWORKING VISE SHOWN HERE. YOU ARE TO PERFORM THE ROLE OF A DESIGN DRAFTSMAN AND ARE TO CONVERT THESE SKETCHES INTO A FINISHED WORKING DRAWING ADDING ANY OMITTED SPECIFICATIONS AND CORRECTING ANY THAT ARE INCORRECT.

1. PREPARE FINISHED DETAIL DRAWINGS ON THE BLANK 11" X 15" TRACING PAPER SHEETS.
2. PREPARE AN ASSEMBLY DRAWING SHOWING HOW THE PARTS ARE ASSEMBLED. REFER TO SHEET 94 AS AN EXAMPLE.
3. MAKE PRINTS OF THE COMPLETED DRAWINGS AND EXCHANGE THEM WITH A CLASSMATE AND CHECK EACH OTHER'S DRAWINGS FOR ERRORS USING A COLORED PENCIL.

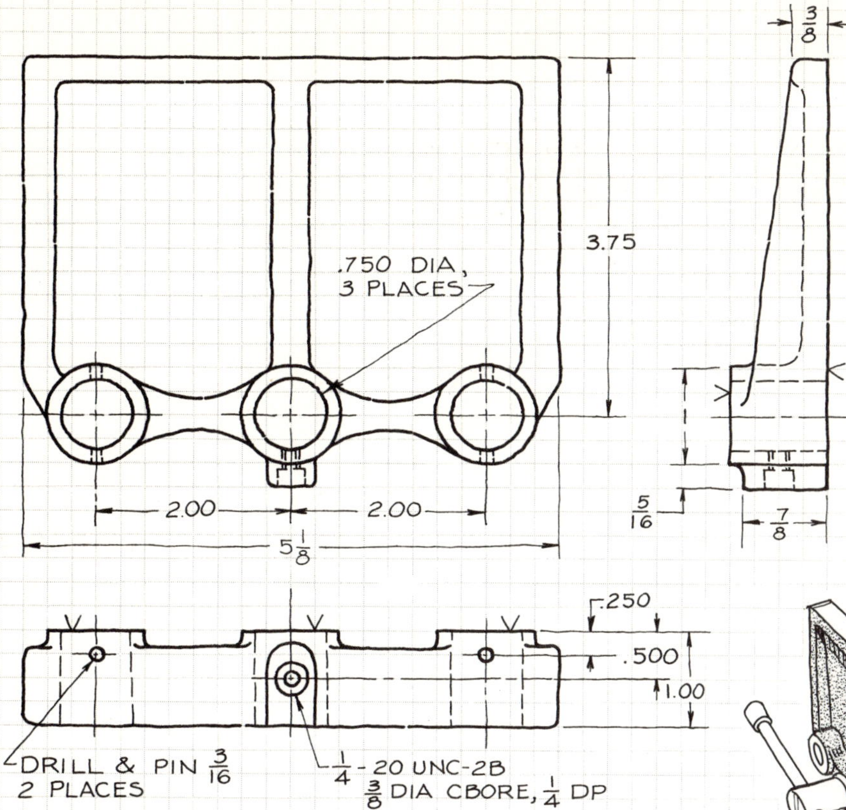

(1) FRONT JAW, C.I.

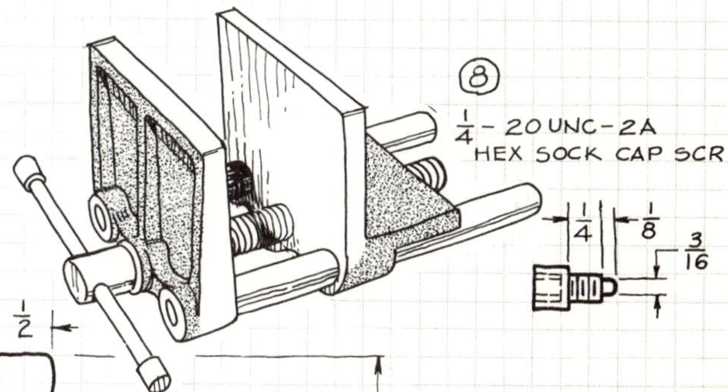

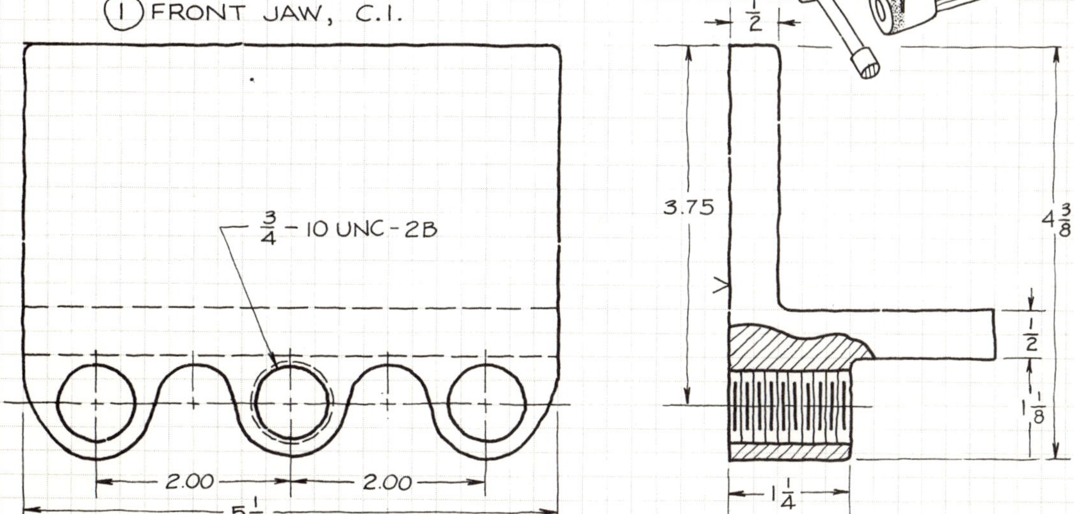

(2) FIXED JAW, C.I.

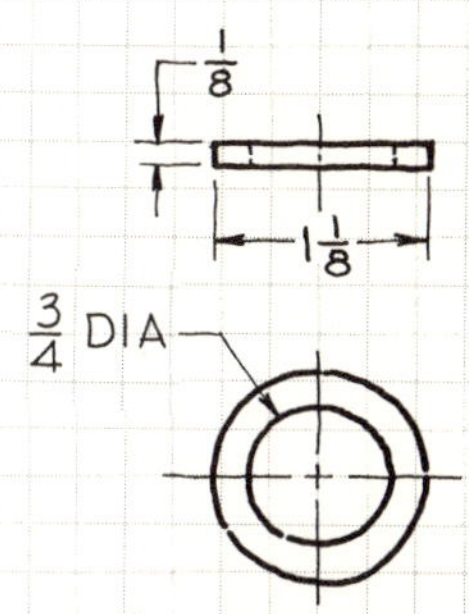

(4) WASHER, STEEL

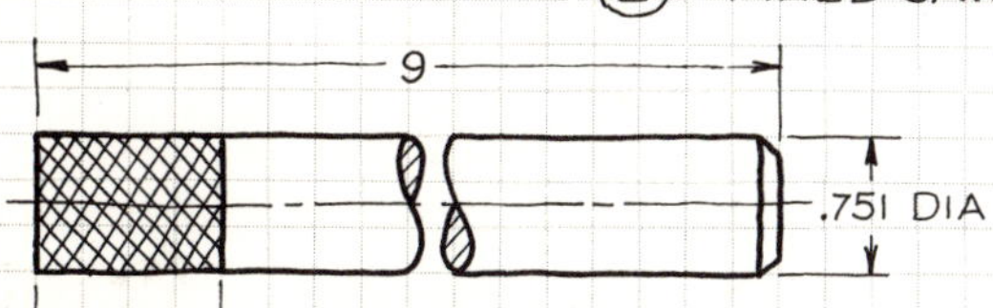

(5) RAILS, 2 REQ'D, STEEL

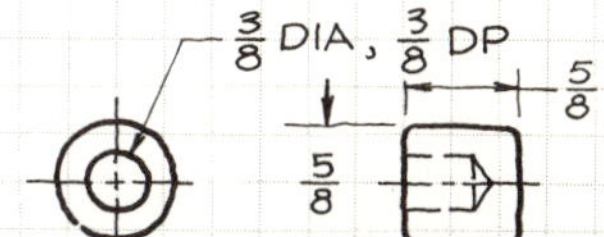

(6) HANDLE CAPS, STL

(7) HANDLE, STEEL

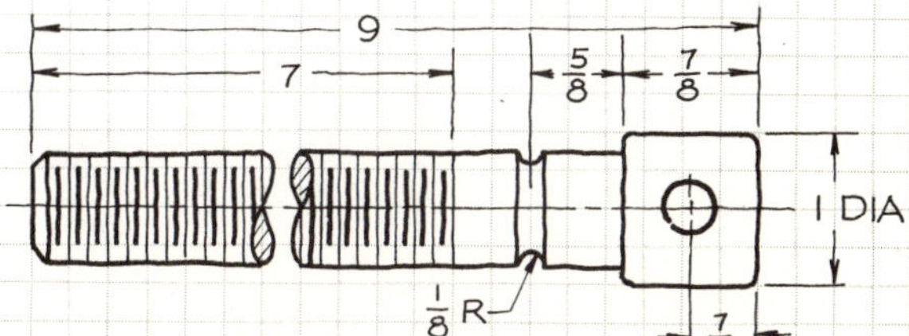

(3) LEAD SCREW, STEEL

DESIGN & WORKING DRAWINGS

BLOCK PLANE

THE PARTS OF TWO ASSEMBLIES ARE SHOWN ON THIS SHEET-- A BLOCK PLANE AND A PAPER PUNCH. THE DESIGNER HAS SKETCHED DETAILED VIEWS OF THE PARTS ON A 1/4" GRID. SINCE THESE ARE PRELIMINARY IDEAS MANY DIMENSIONS ARE OMITTED AND SOME DIMENSIONS AND NOTES MAY BE INCORRECT. YOU ARE TO PERFORM THE ROLE OF A DESIGN DRAFTSMAN AND ARE TO CONVERT THESE SKETCHES INTO A FINISHED WORKING DRAWING ADDING ANY OMITTED SPECIFICATIONS AND CORRECTING ANY THAT ARE INCORRECT.

1. PREPARE FINISHED DETAIL DRAWINGS ON THE BLANK 11" X 15" TRACING PAPER SHEETS.
2. PREPARE AN ASSEMBLY DRAWING SHOWING HOW THE PARTS ARE ASSEMBLED. REFER TO SHEET 94 FOR AN EXAMPLE.
3. MAKE PRINTS OF THE COMPLETED DRAWINGS AND EXCHANGE THEM WITH A CLASSMATE AND CHECK EACH OTHER'S DRAWINGS FOR ERRORS USING A COLORED PENCIL.

BLOCK PLANE

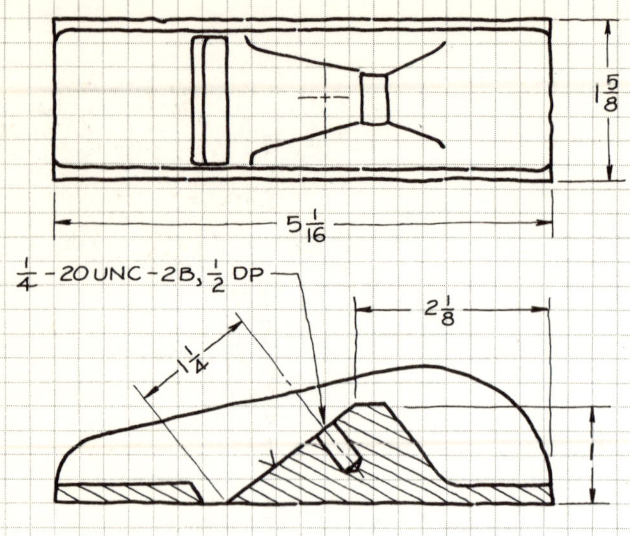

① BODY, CAST IRON

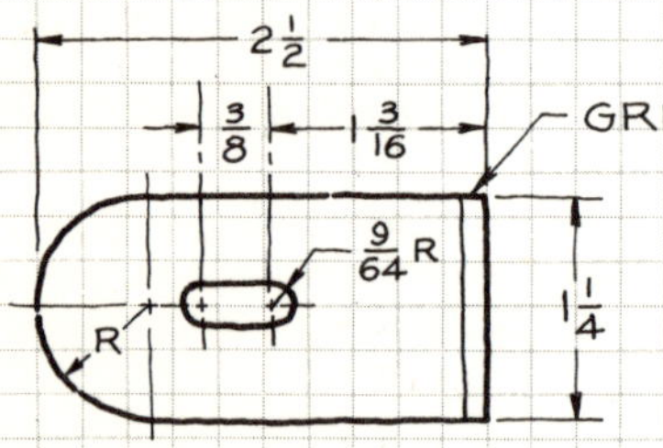

② PLANE IRON, STL
1/8 THICK

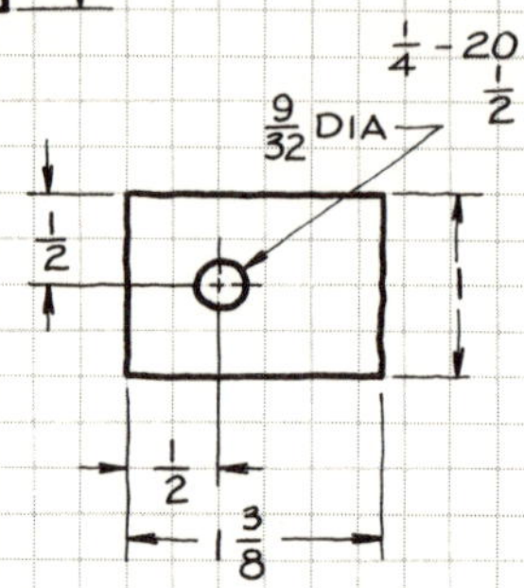

③ CAP IRON, STL
1/8 THICK

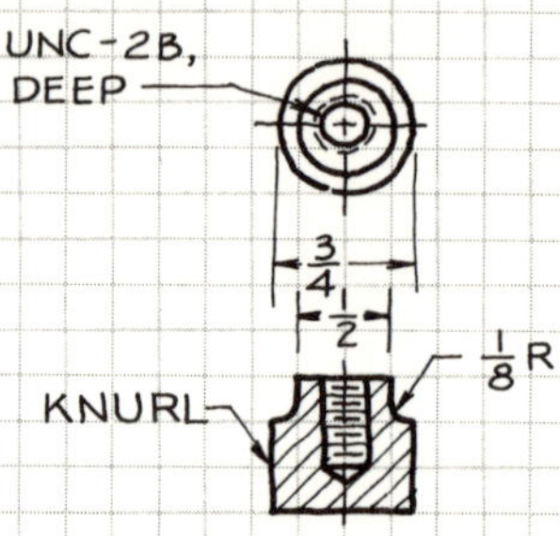

④ SCREW CAP, C.I.

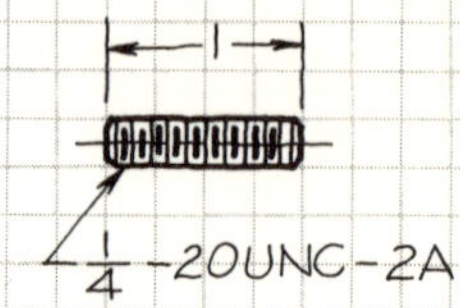

⑤ STUD, STL

PAPER PUNCH

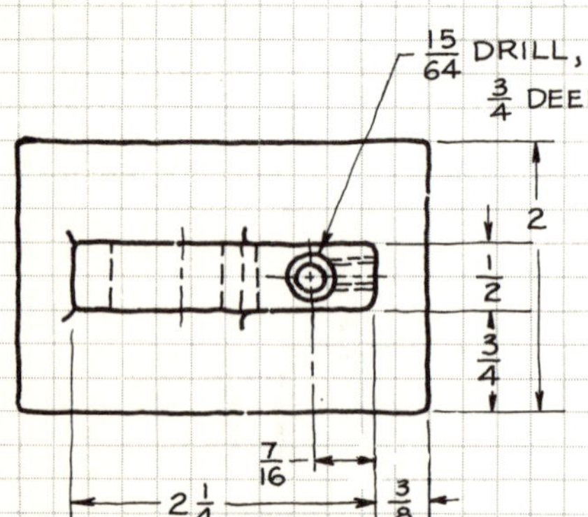

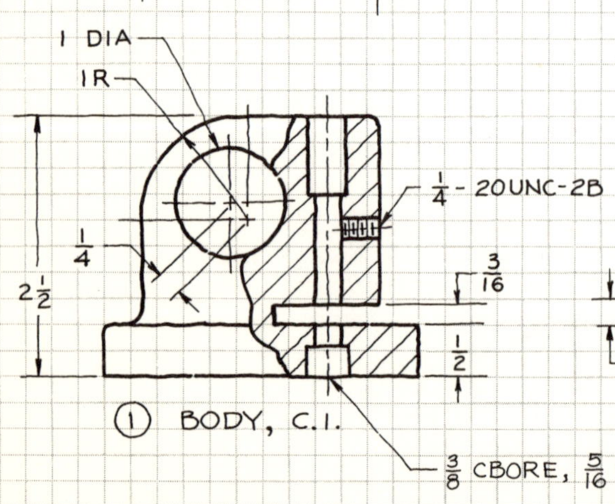

① BODY, C.I.

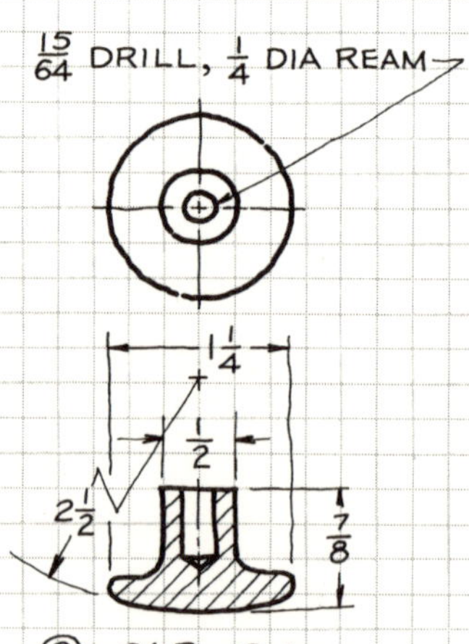

② CAP, C.I.
DRILL & PIN TO ③

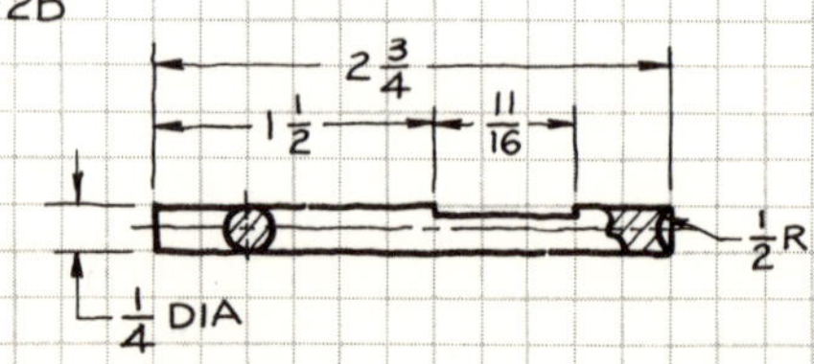

③ PUNCH, STL

④ 3/16 DIA X 1/2 LG COMPRESSION SPRING

⑤ 1/4 - 20 UNC-2A X 3/8 SOCK FULL DOG PT SET SCR

These details were made available by Genevro Machine Co. Garden Grove, California. Unfinished casting for shop projects may be purchased from them.

NAME
FILE NO. SEC. DATE
grade

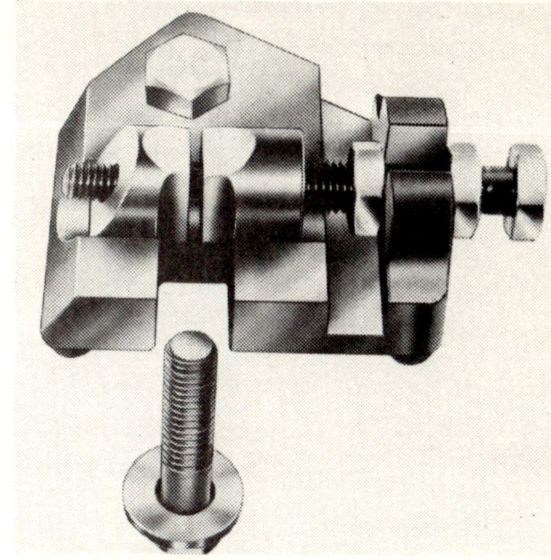

Courtesy of Thomson Industries Inc.
Manhasset, L. I., NY

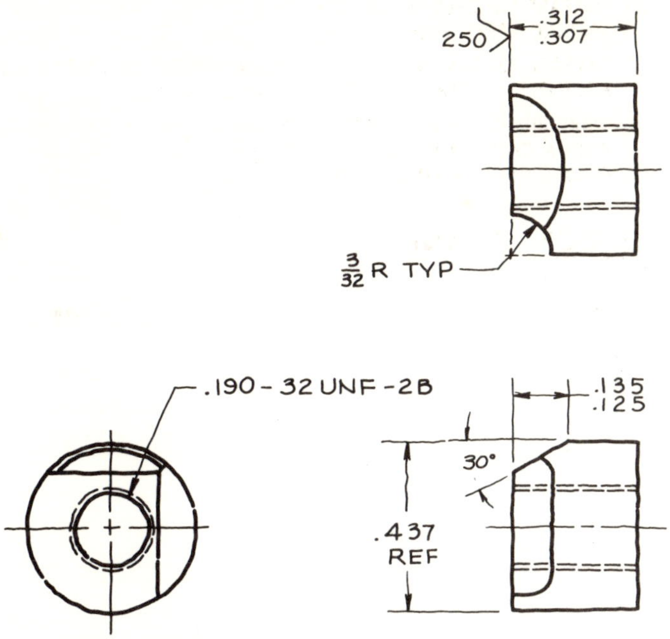

② RIGHT HAND BEARING BLOCK
52100 STL , NO. R180A

THE PARTS SHOWN ON BOTH SIDES OF THIS SHEET DESCRIBE THE DETAILS OF THE PARTS OF A WAYMOUNT THAT IS USED TO SUPPORT SHAFTS (CALLED WAYS) ON WHICH CARRIAGES ARE SUPPORTED BY BALL BEARING UNITS ALLOWING FOR LINEAR MOTION ALONG THE SHAFTS. CHECK THE DIMENSIONS, NOTES AND VIEWS SKETCHED HERE AND COMPLETE THE FOLLOWING ASSIGNMENTS. USE ANY GRAPHICAL TECHNIQUES AVAILABLE TO YOU THAT WOULD HELP YOU EXPLAIN THESE PARTS OF THE ASSEMBLY.

1. PREPARE FINISHED DETAIL DRAWINGS ON BLANK 11" X 15" TRACING PAPER SHEETS.
2. PREPARE AN ASSEMBLY DRAWING SHOWING HOW THE PARTS ARE ASSEMBLED. REFER TO SHEET 94 FOR EXAMPLES.
3. MAKE PRINTS OF THE COMPLETED DRAWINGS AND EXCHANGE THEM WITH A CLASSMATE AND CHECK EACH OTHER'S DRAWINGS FOR ERRORS USING A COLORED PENCIL.

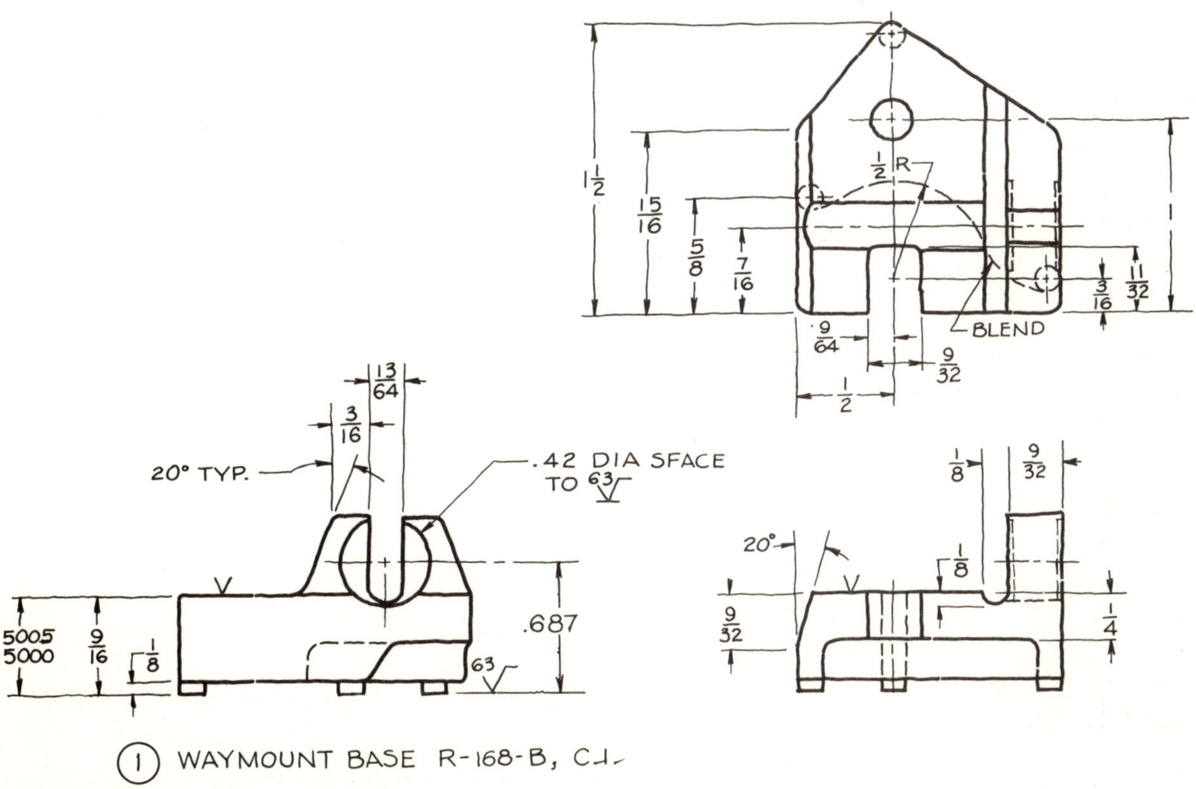

① WAYMOUNT BASE R-168-B, C.I.

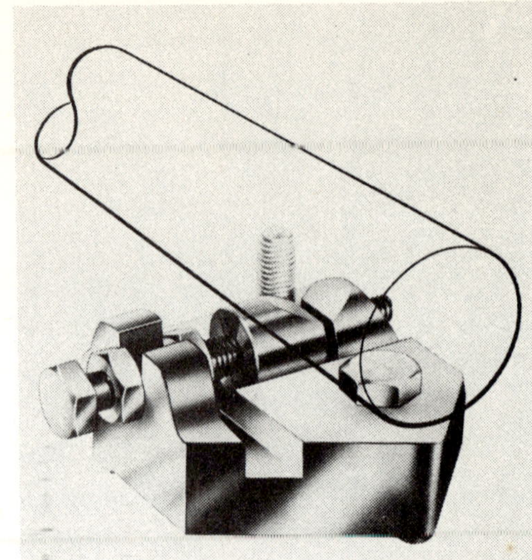

Courtesy of Thomson Industries, Inc.

TOLERANCES UNLESS OTHERWISE NOTED
FRACTIONAL ±.010
DECIMAL ±.005
ANGULAR ±1/2°

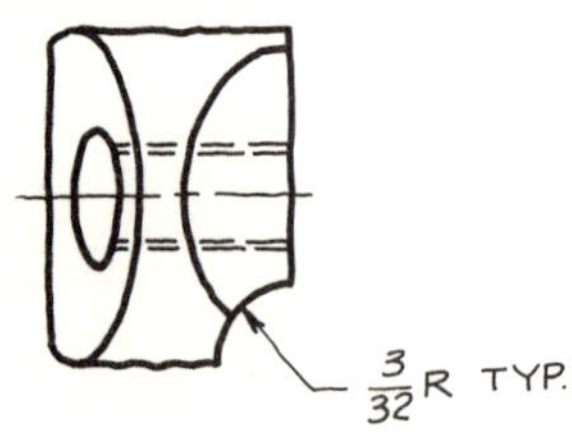

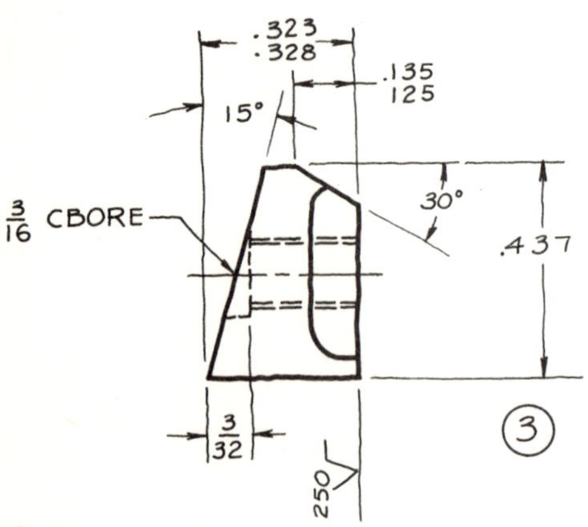

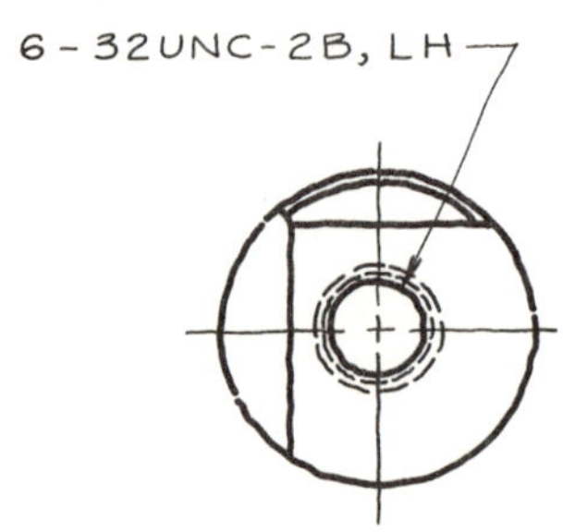

(3) LH BEARING BLOCK
NO. R-246A. 52100 STL

(5) #10-32UNF-2B HEX NUT NO. 2101-7, 2 REQD

(6) FLAT WASHER, 11/64 ID X 3/8 OD X .030-.040 TH, 2 REQD, NO. 2301-7

(7) #8-32UNF-2A, HEX HD SCR NO. 2007-6

(8) FLAT WASHER, 11/64 ID X 1/2 OD X .050-.060 TH.

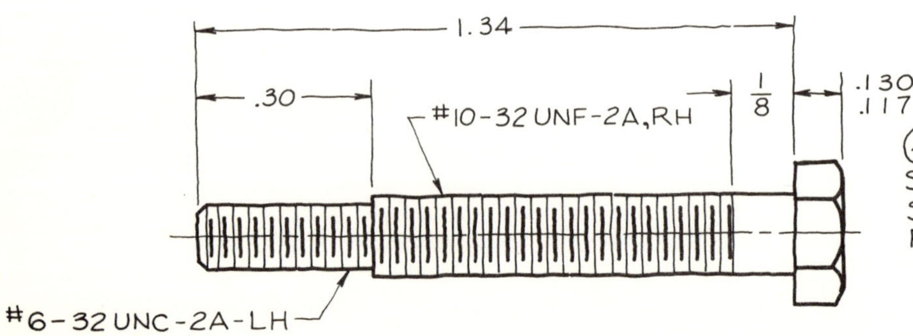

(4) NO. R172A LEAD SCREW
STANDARD HEX SCREW 3/8 ACROSS FLATS

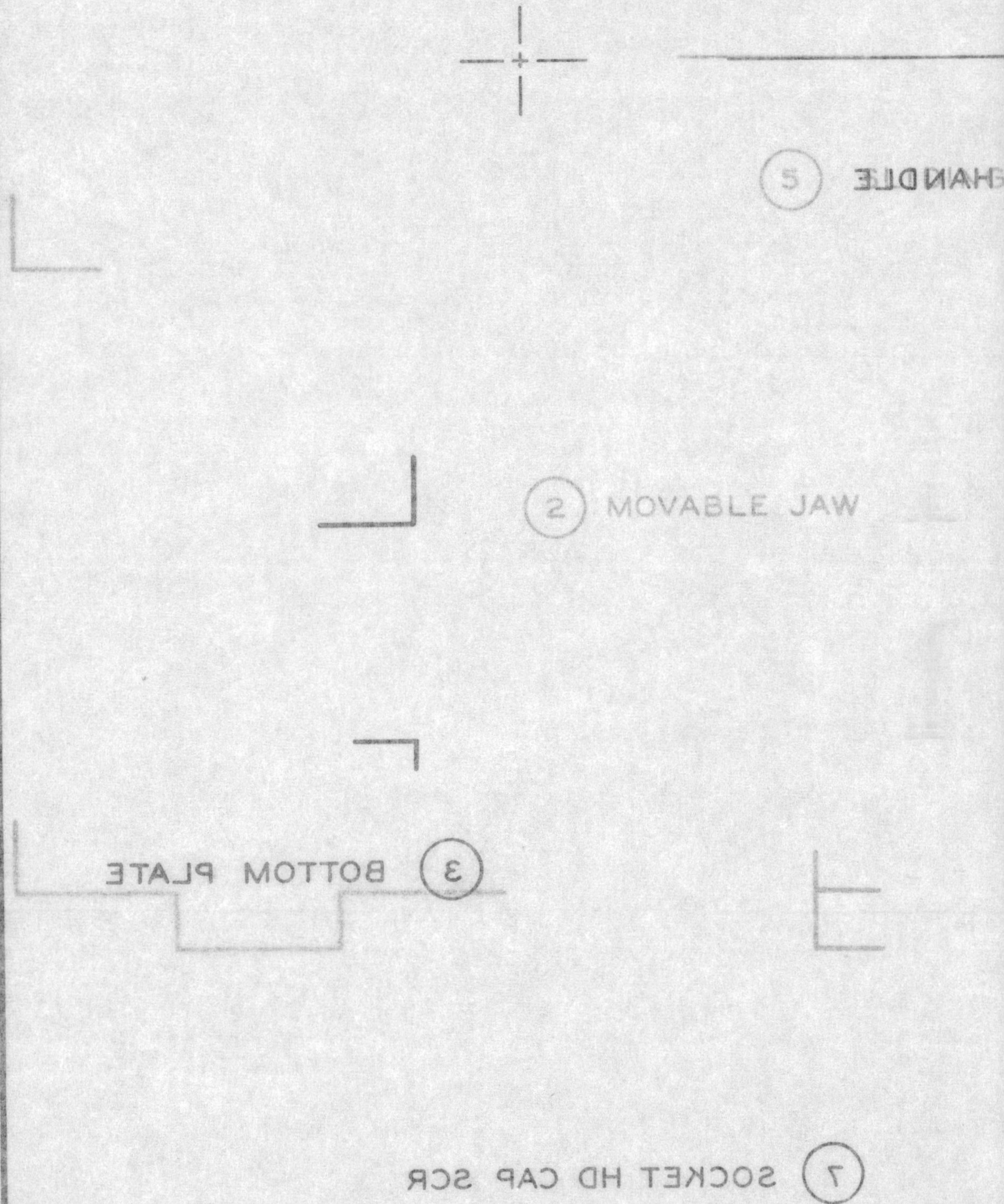

DRILL PRESS VISE

BY: SECTION:

DATE: SHEET:

SCALE: OF SHEETS

3 BOTTOM PLATE

7 SOCKET HD CAP SCR

DRILL PRESS VISE	
BY:	SECTION:
DATE:	SHEET:
SCALE:	OF SHEETS

NO	PART NAME	REQD	MAT'L

PARTS LIST

DRILL PRESS VISE - ASSEMBLY

BY: SECTION:

DATE: SHEET:

SCALE: OF SHEETS

NO	PART NAME	REQD	MAT'L

PARTS LIST

DRILL PRESS VISE - ASSEMBLY

BY:	SECTION:
DATE:	SHEET:
SCALE:	OF SHEETS

BY: SECTION:

DATE: SHEET:

SCALE: SHEETS OF

BY:	SECTION:
DATE:	SHEET:
SCALE:	OF SHEETS

BY:	SECTION:
DATE:	SHEET:
SCALE:	OF SHEETS

BY:	SECTION:
DATE:	SHEET:
SCALE:	OF SHEETS

BY:	SECTION:
DATE:	SHEET:
SCALE:	OF SHEETS

BY:	SECTION:
DATE:	SHEET:
SCALE:	OF SHEETS

BY:	SECTION:
DATE:	SHEET:
SCALE:	OF SHEETS

BY:	SECTION:
DATE:	SHEET:
SCALE:	OF SHEETS

BY: SECTION:

DATE: SHEET:

SCALE: OF SHEETS

BY:	SECTION:
DATE:	SHEET:
SCALE:	OF SHEETS

NAME: SECTION: GRADE:

QUIZ 1: INSTRUMENTS, SCALES, AND GEOMETRIC CONSTRUCTION (1-19)

1. Scale the lines below and give their dimensions in the blanks at the left of each item. (3 pts each)

_______ A. SCALE: 1/2" = 1'-0"

_______ B. SCALE: 3/4" = 1'-0"

_______ C. SCALE: 1" = 200'

_______ D. SCALE: 1" = 30'

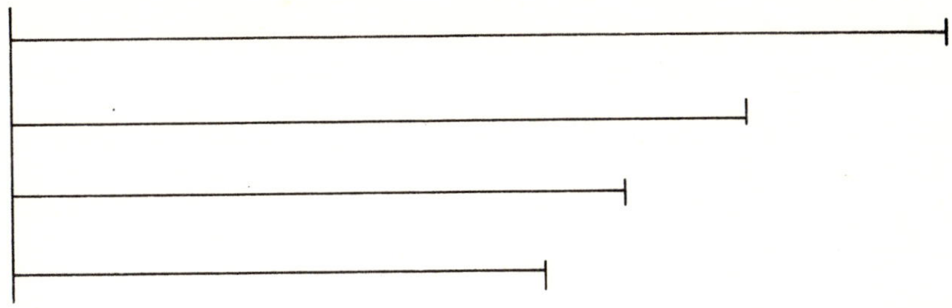

2. Construct a pentagon inscribed in the circle below. Show construction. (10 pts)

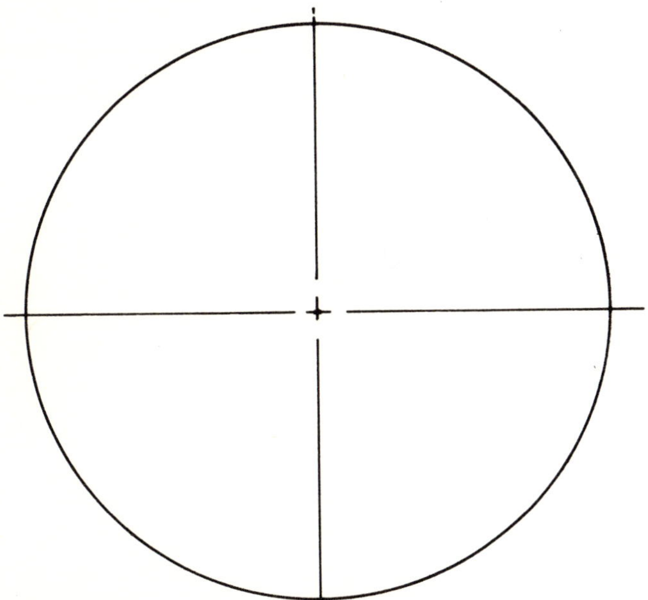

3. Divide line AB into 5 equal parts by using geometric construction. Show construction. (10 pts)

4. Construct 2 lines from point A that are tangent the the circle. Show construction. (10 pts)

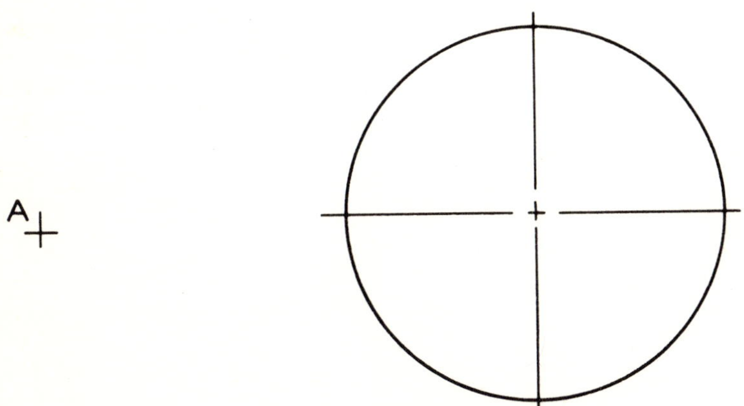

5. Bisect both the angle and line. Show construction. (4 pts each)

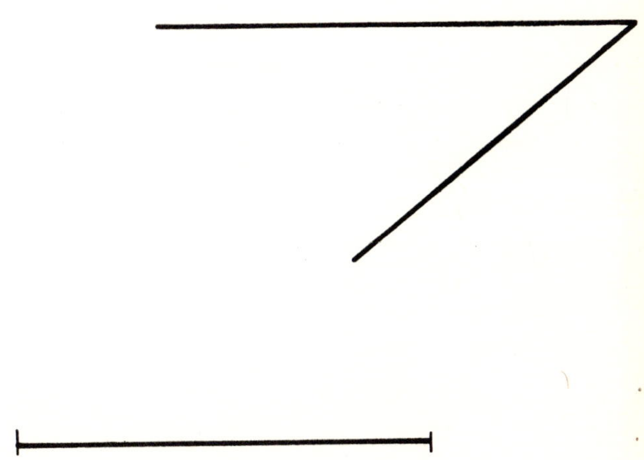

6. Construct an arc with radius R that is tangent to the two lines. Mark points of tangency and show construction. (10 pts)

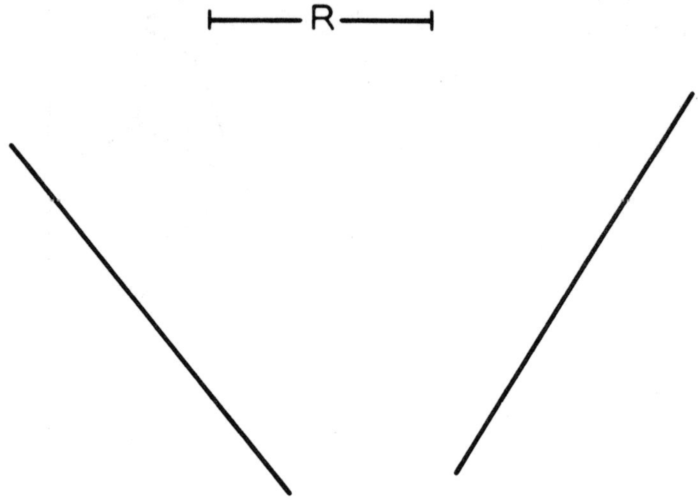

7. Construct an arc with radius R that is tangent to the two lines. Mark points of tangency and show construction. (10 pts)

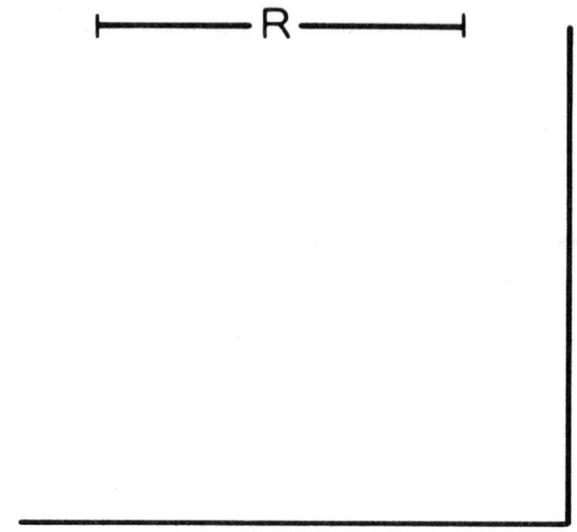

8. Construct a helix with a lead equal to the height of the cylinder. Show construction. (15 pts)

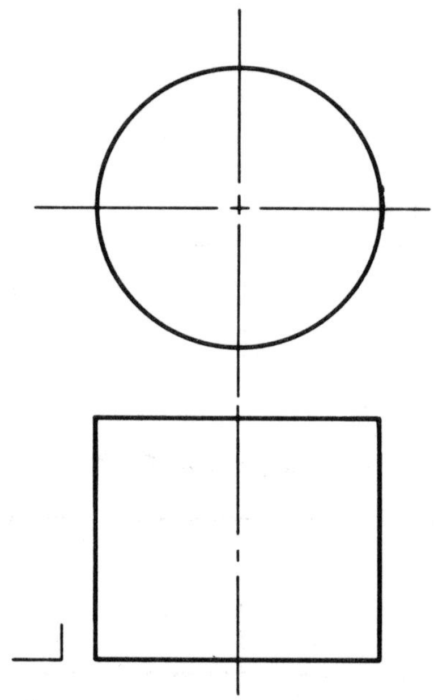

9. Find the elliptical view of the circle when it is revolved 60° from the vertical. (15 pts)

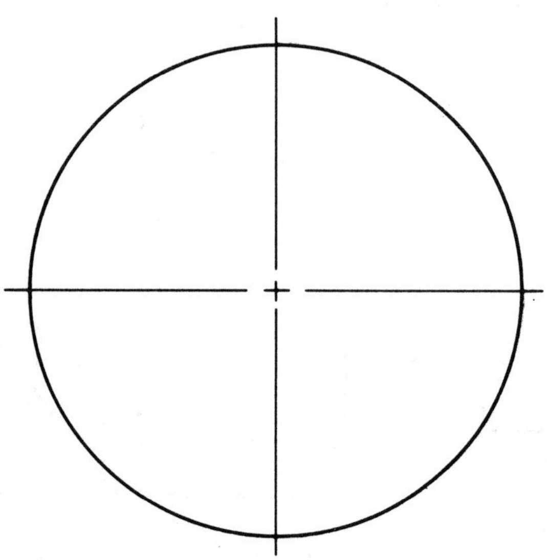

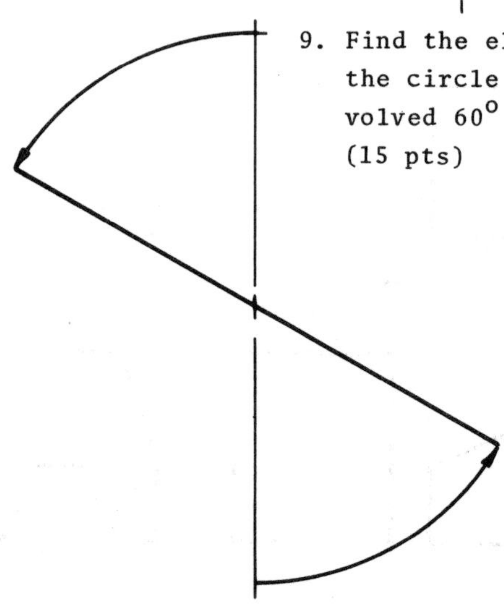

NAME: SECTION: GRADE:

QUIZ 2: ORTHOGRAPHIC PROJECTION (20-38)

1. Construct 3 orthographic views of the part shown in the pictorial. Label the views and show overall dimensions H, W and D. (15 pts)

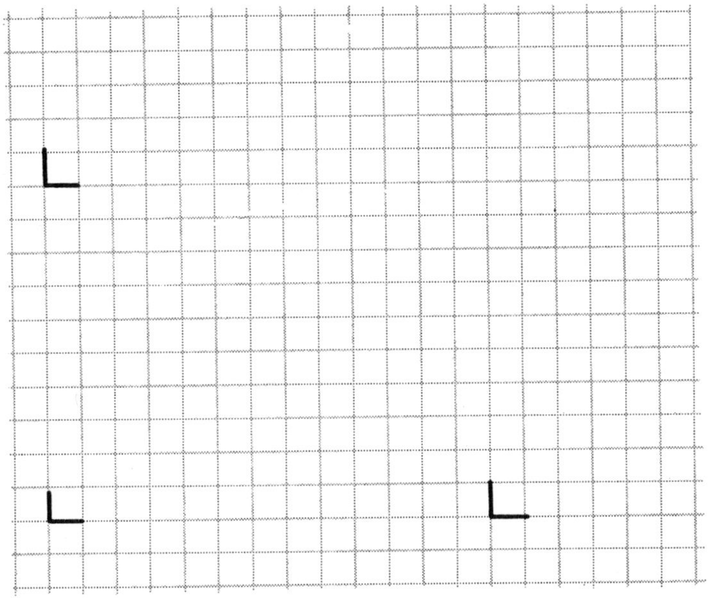

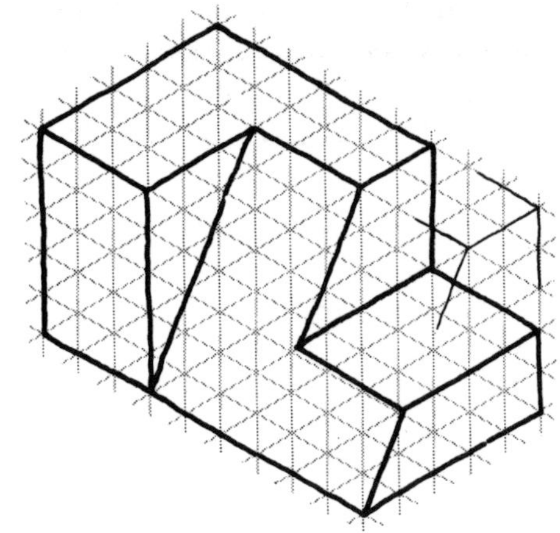

2. Complete the runouts below in the front view. Show construction. (16 pts)

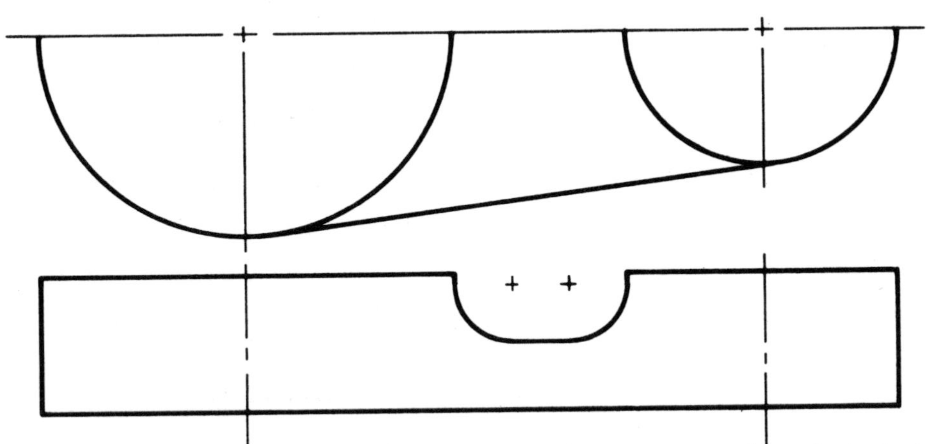

3. Complete the views. Lines may be missing in all views. (5 pts each)

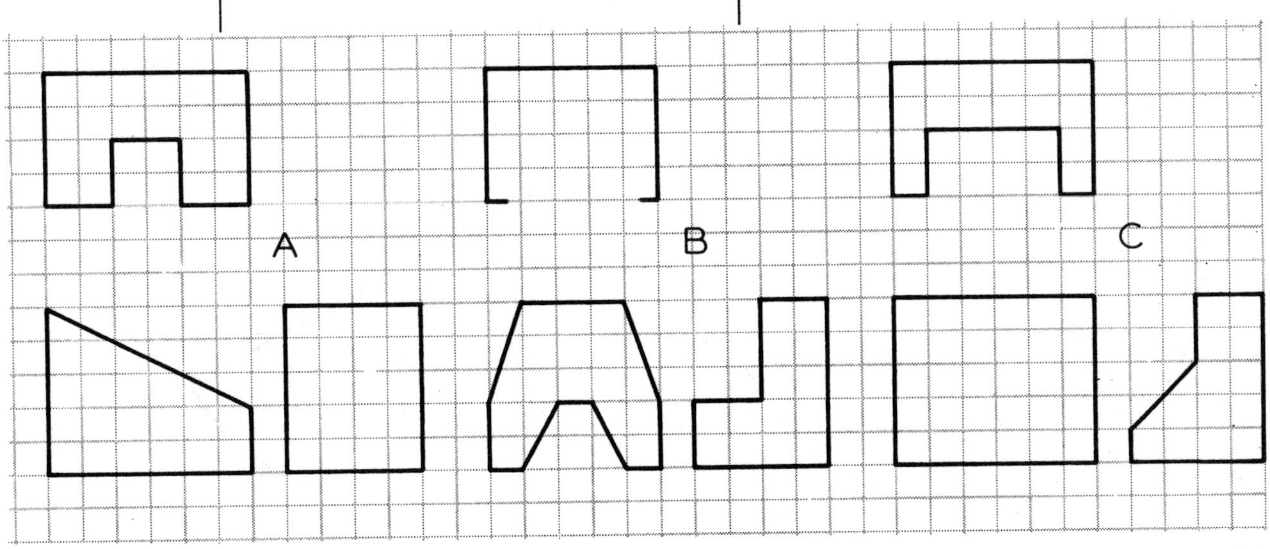

4. Identify the lines in the drawing by placing letters in the blanks at the left of each type of line. (3 pts each)

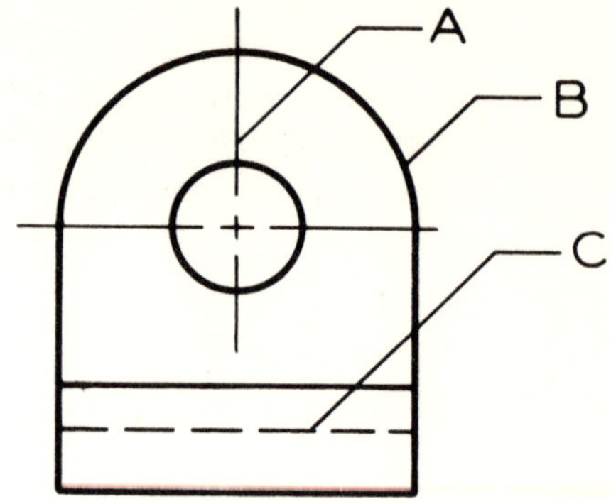

_____ HIDDEN LINE

_____ OBJECT LINE (VISIBLE)

_____ CENTERLINE

5. Complete the missing views and given views. (5 pts each)

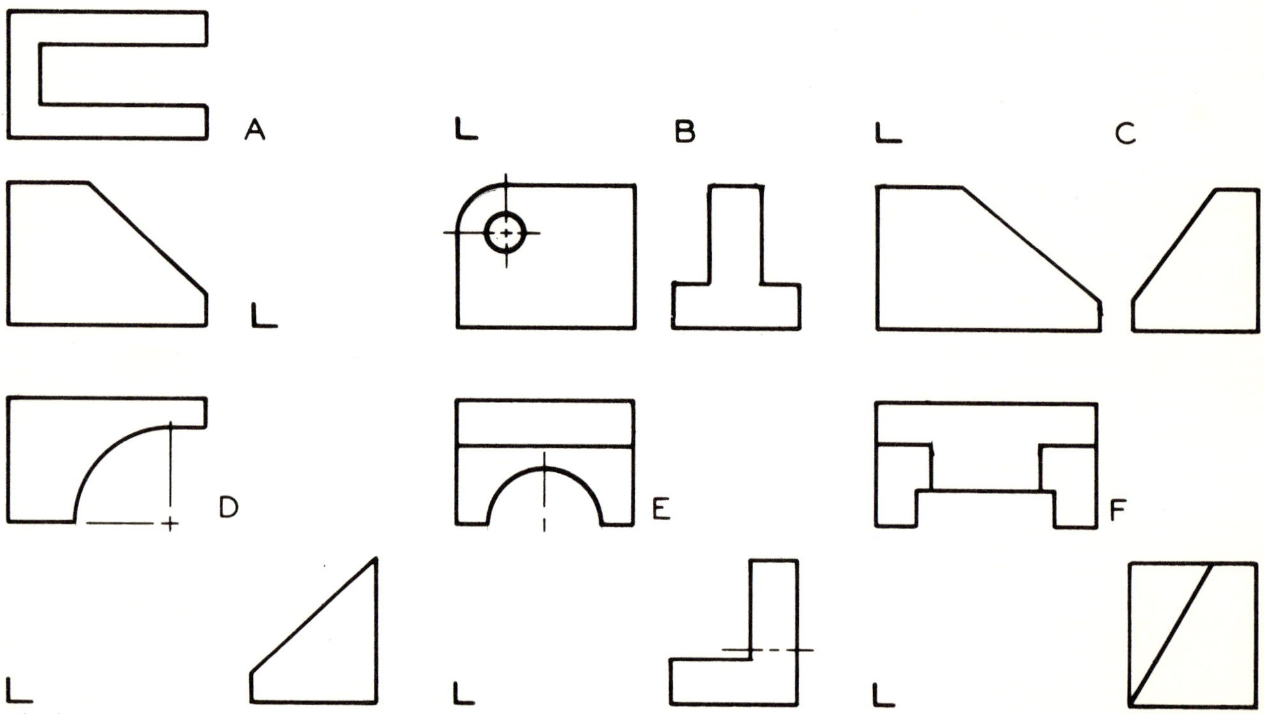

6. Construct six orthographic views to describe the object shown in the pictorial. Begin the views using the corners given. (15 pts)

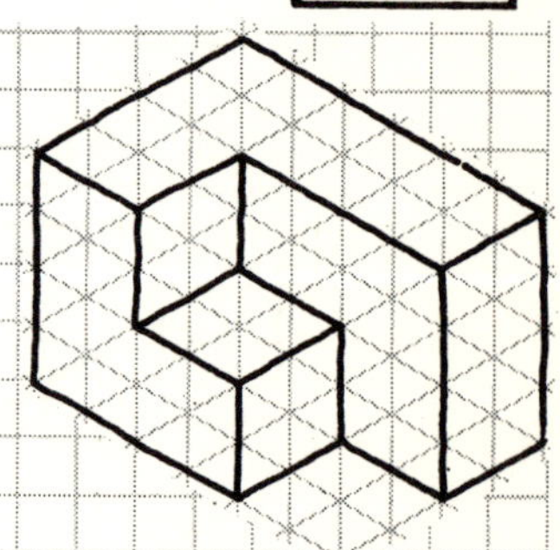

NAME: SECTION: GRADE:

QUIZ 3: PICTORIALS (39-48)

1. Construct an isometric of the object beginning with point O. Double the orthographic grid. (16 pts)

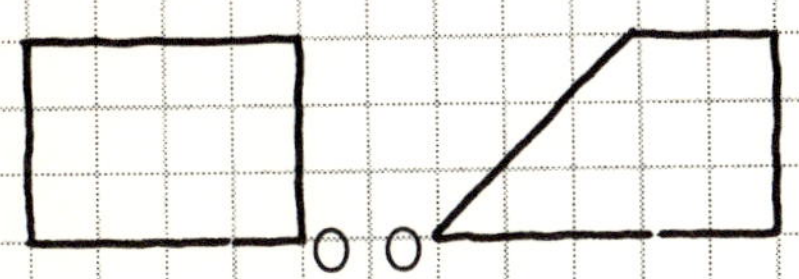

2. Using instruments and the four-center ellipse method, construct an isometric of cylinder. Double the orthographic grid. (16 pts)

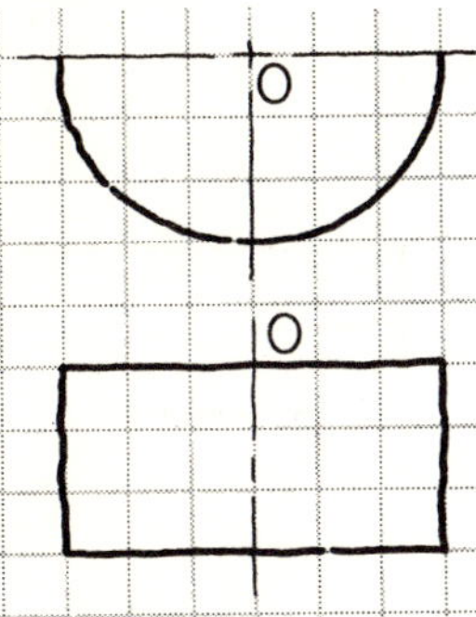

3. Using instruments, construct an isometric of the part below. Double the orhtographic grid. (18 pts)

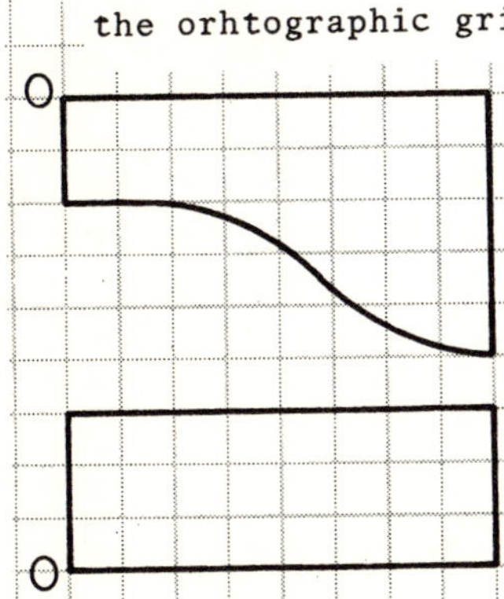

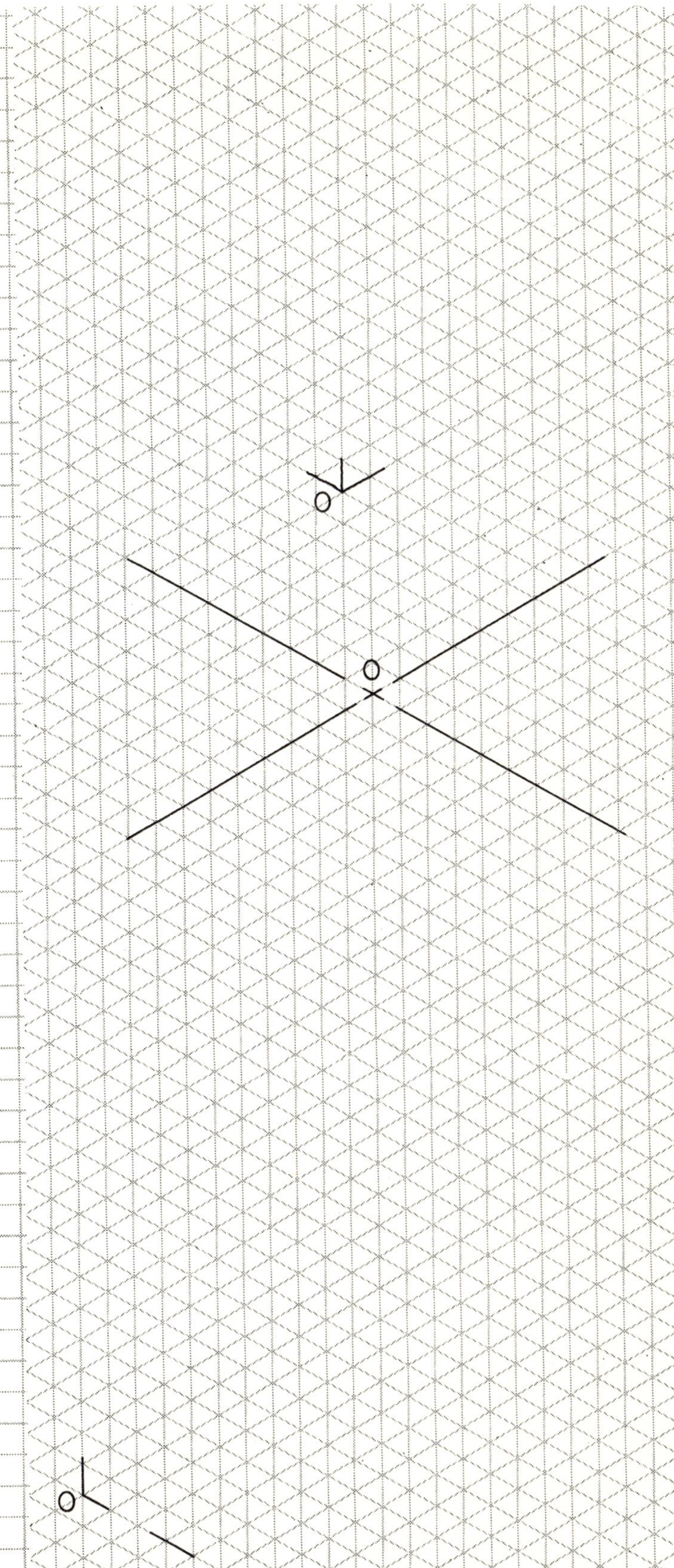

4. Construct a cavalier oblique of the part below in the space at the right. Double the dimensions with your dividers. (16 pts)

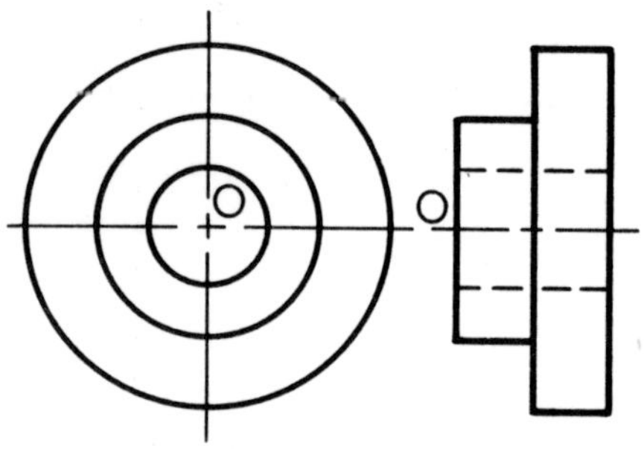

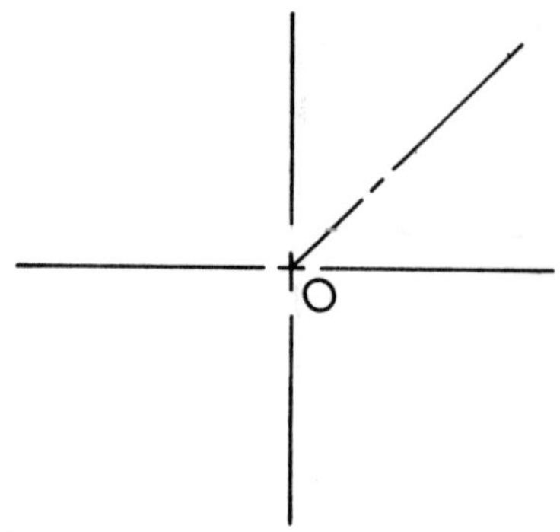

5. Construct a cavalier oblique of the part below at the right. Double the dimensions with your dividers. (18 pts)

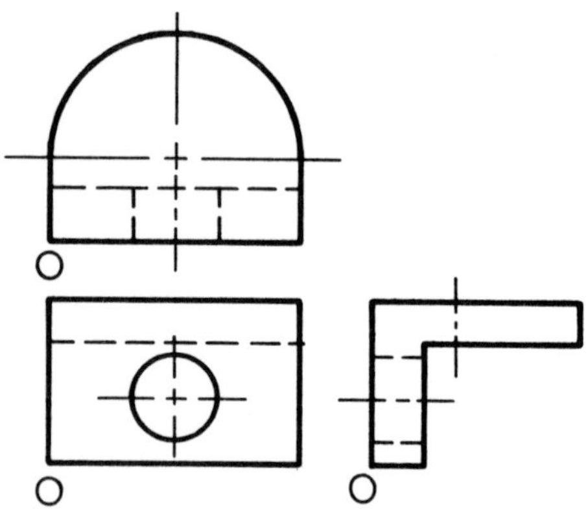

6. Construct a cabinet oblique of the part below in the space at the right. Double the dimensions with your dividers. (16 pts)

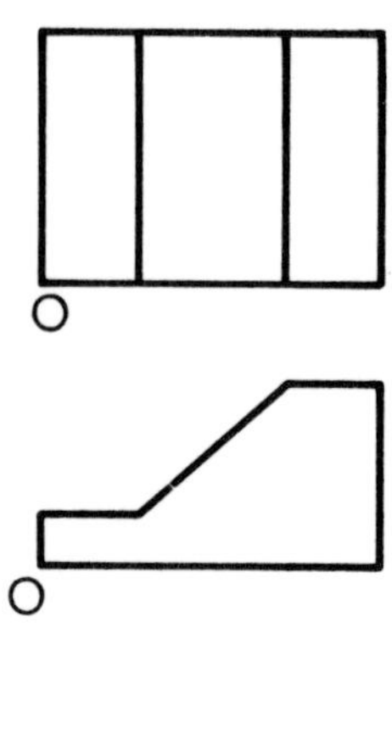

NAME: SECTION: GRADE:

QUIZ 4: AUXILIARY VIEWS AND REVOLUTIONS (49-53)

1. Find an auxiliary view of the inclined surface that shows it true shape. Label the reference plane. (14 pts)

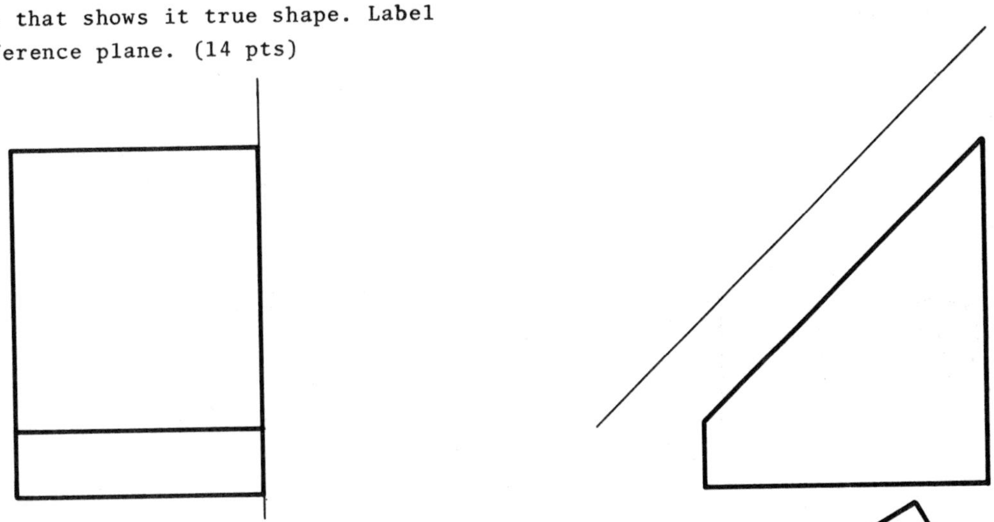

2. Find an auxiliary view that shows the inclined surface true size. This end is similar to the left end given. (18 pts)

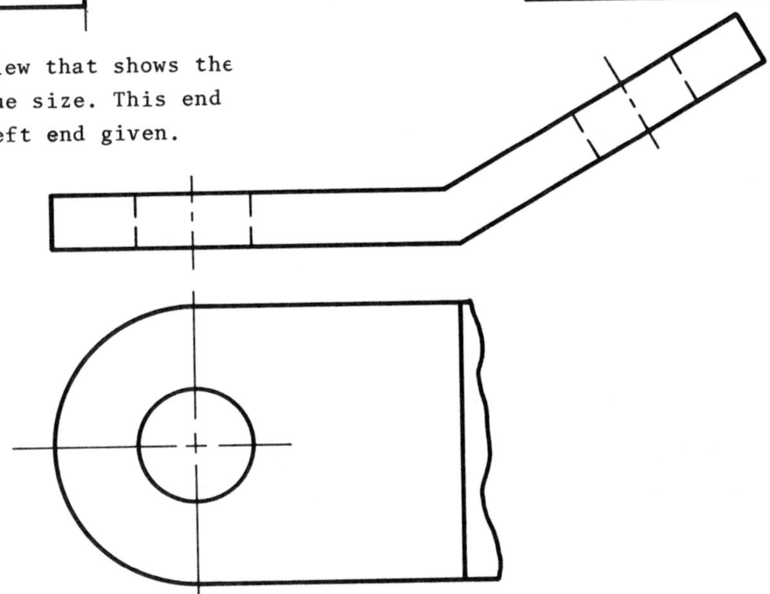

3. Complete the front view as a true-size view by revolution of the top view. (18 pts)

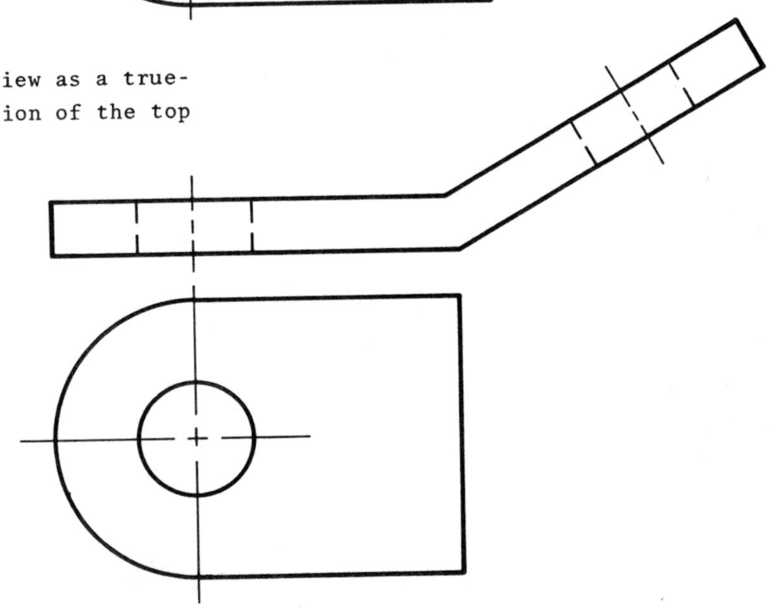

4. Find the inclined surface true size in the right-side view by revolving the front view about the axis shown. (14 pts)

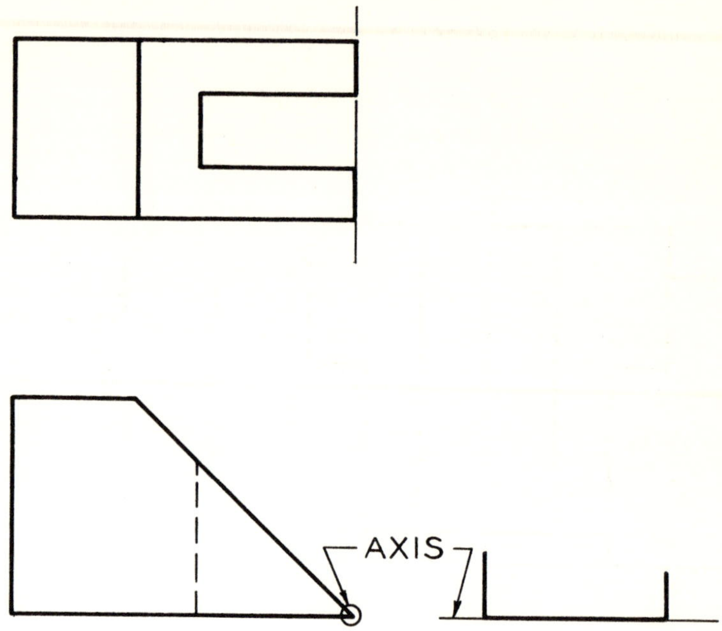

5. Find the inclined surface true size by an auxiliary view. (18 pts)

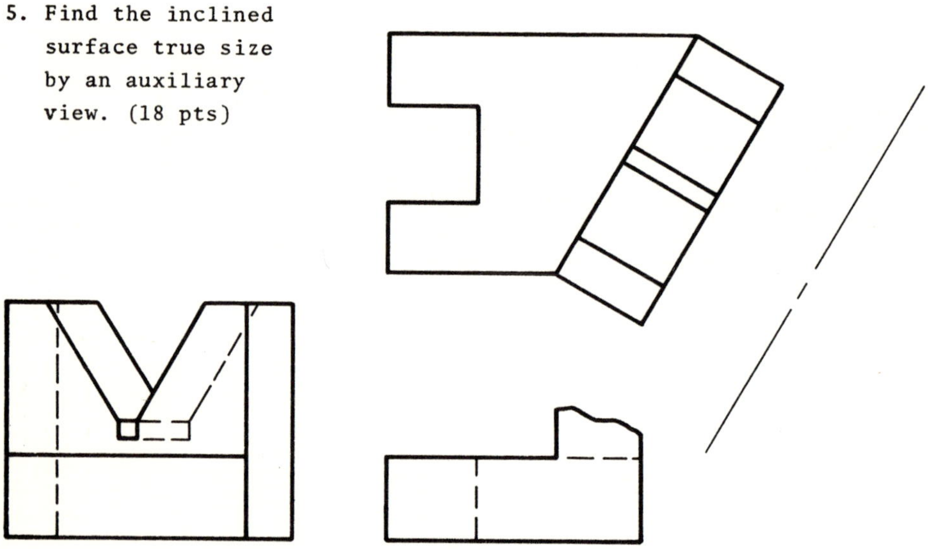

6. Find the inclined surface true size by an auxiliary view as indicated by the line of sight. (18 pts)

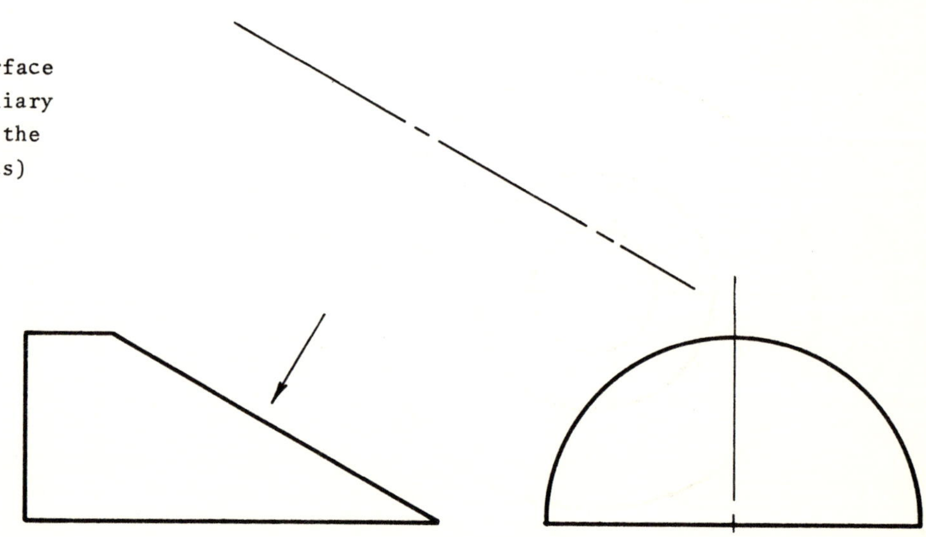

NAME: SECTION: GRADE:

QUIZ 5: SECTIONING (54-62)

1. Crosshatch the two assembled parts as a section. (10 pts)

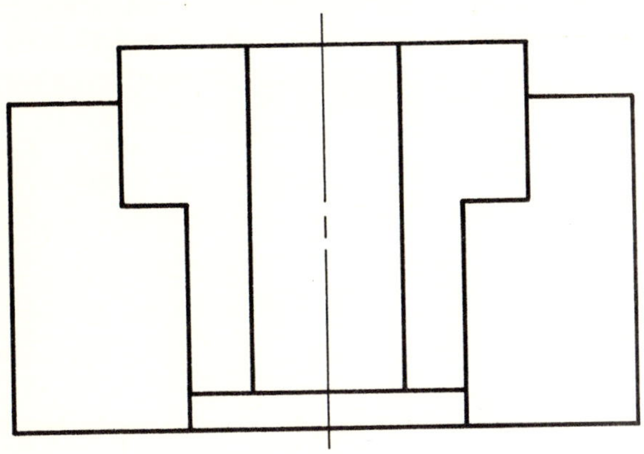

2. Complete the full section. (10 pts)

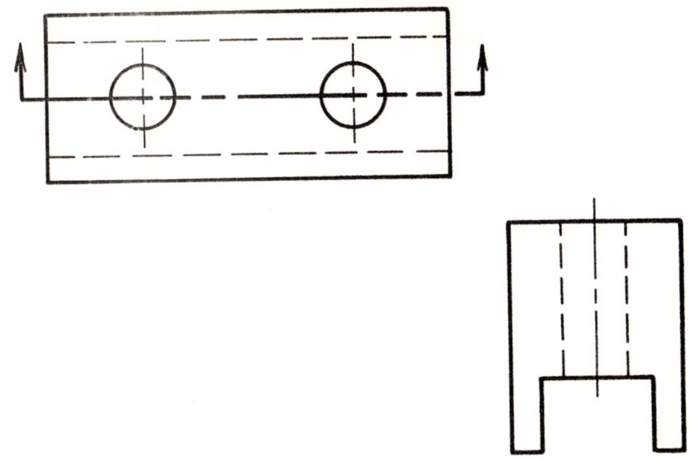

3. Complete the front view as a half section.(10 pts)

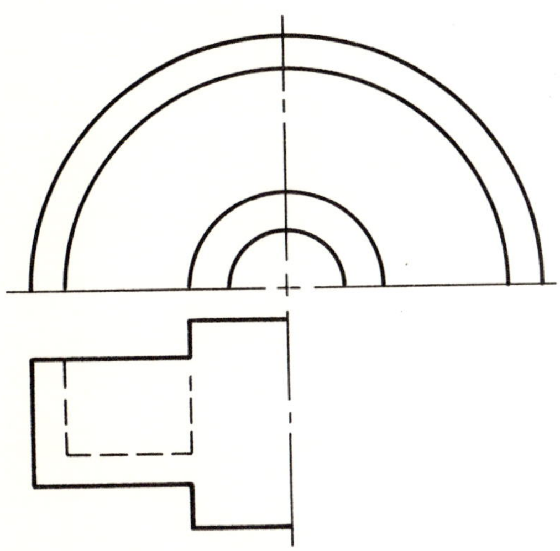

4. Complete the front view as an offset section. Show cutting plane. (10 pts)

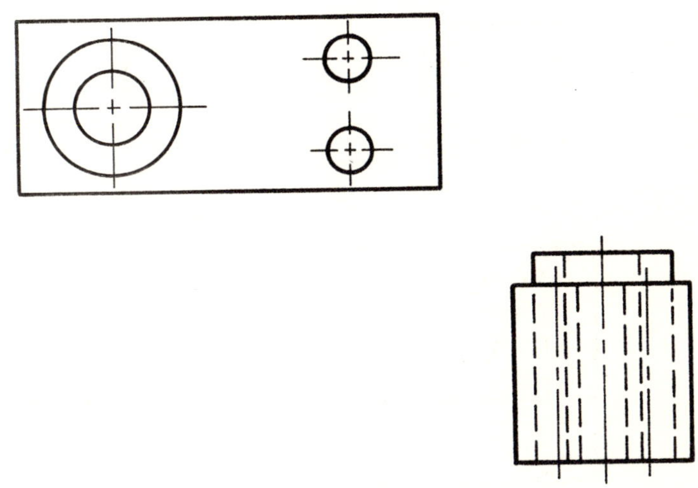

5. Complete the right-side view as a broken-out section. (10 pts)

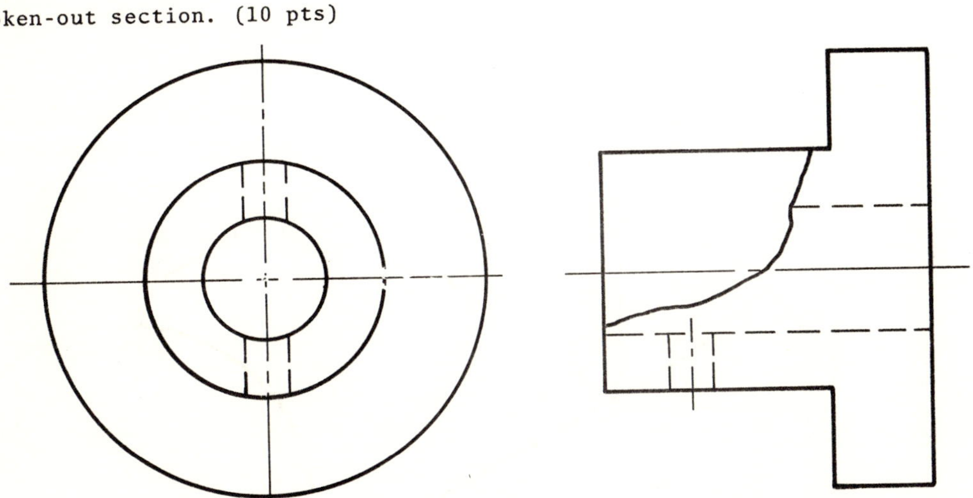

6. Construct a revolved section between the ends of the crank arm. This will be a hexagonal section. (10 pts)

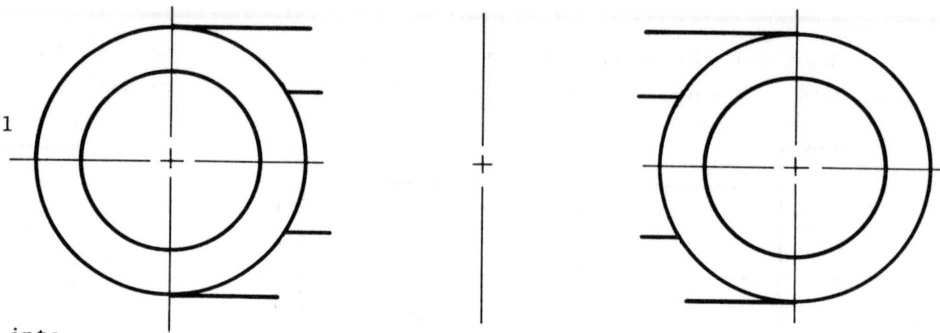

7. Convert the front view into a full section. (10 pts)

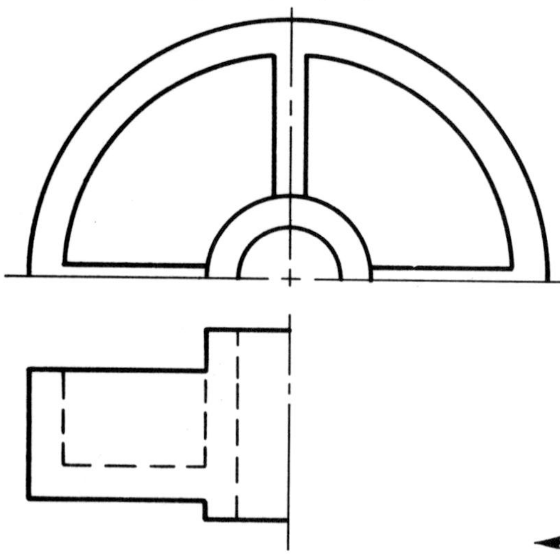

8. Convert the front view into a full section. (10 pts)

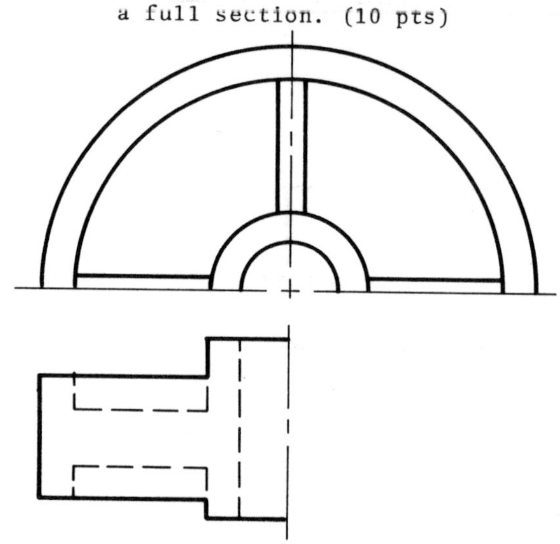

9. Convert the front view into a full section. (10 pts)

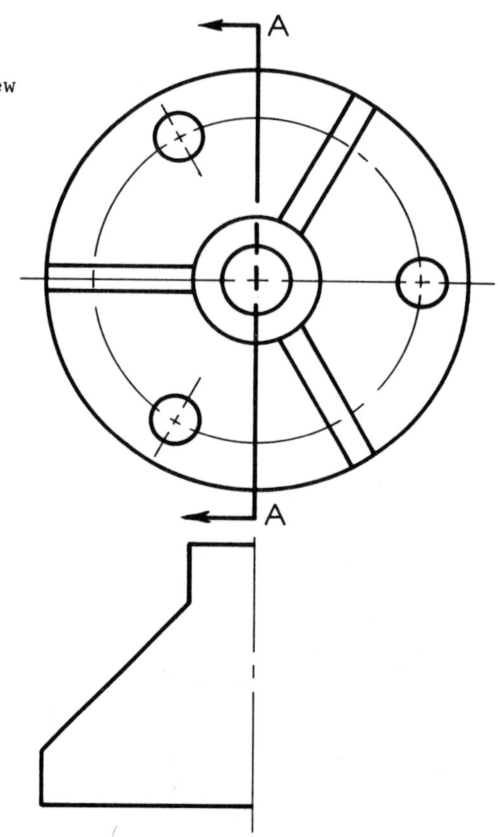

10. Complete removed section A-A. (10 pts)

SECTION A–A

NAME: SECTION: GRADE:

QUIZ 6: FASTENERS AND DIMENSIONING (63-78)

1. Complete the schematic drawing of the 3/4 - 10 UNC - 2A thread. (10 pts)

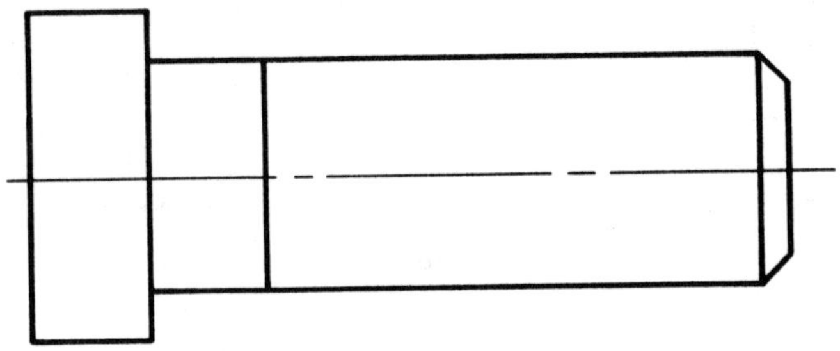

2. Complete the simplified drawing of the internal threads and give a thread note. 1 - 8 NC - 2 (10 pts)

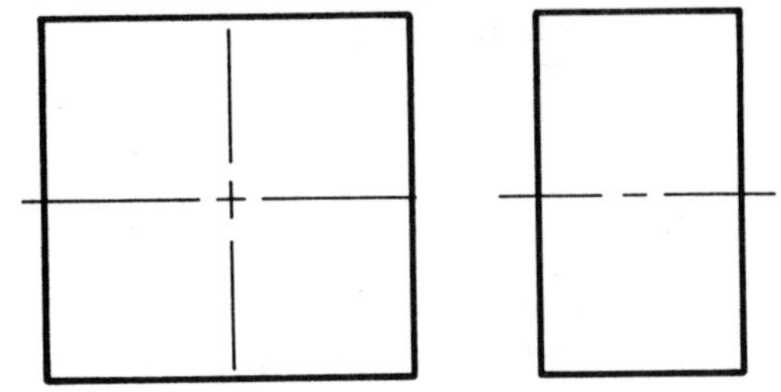

3. Dimension the full-size object. (15 pts)

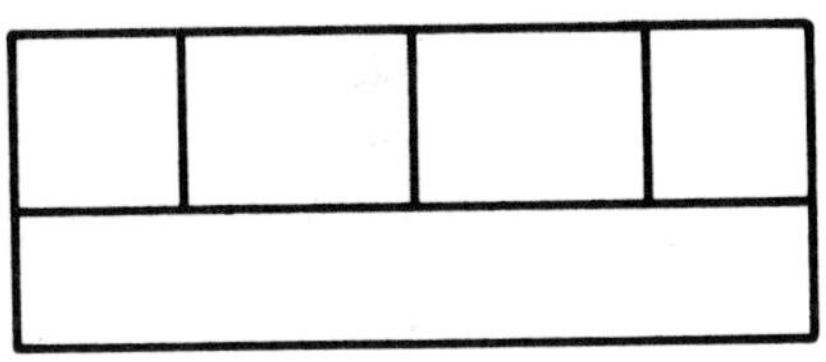

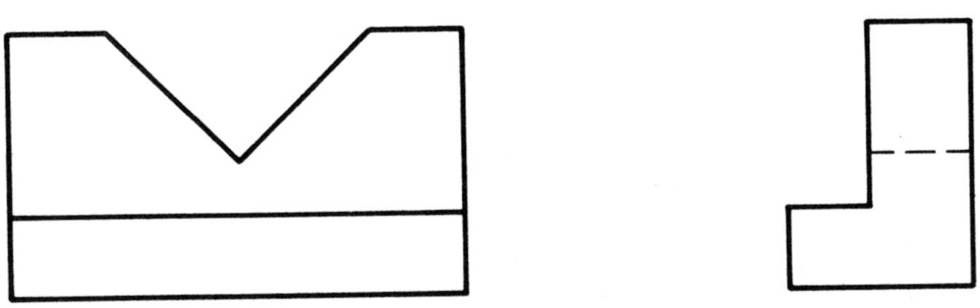

4. Dimension the full-size object. (15 pts)

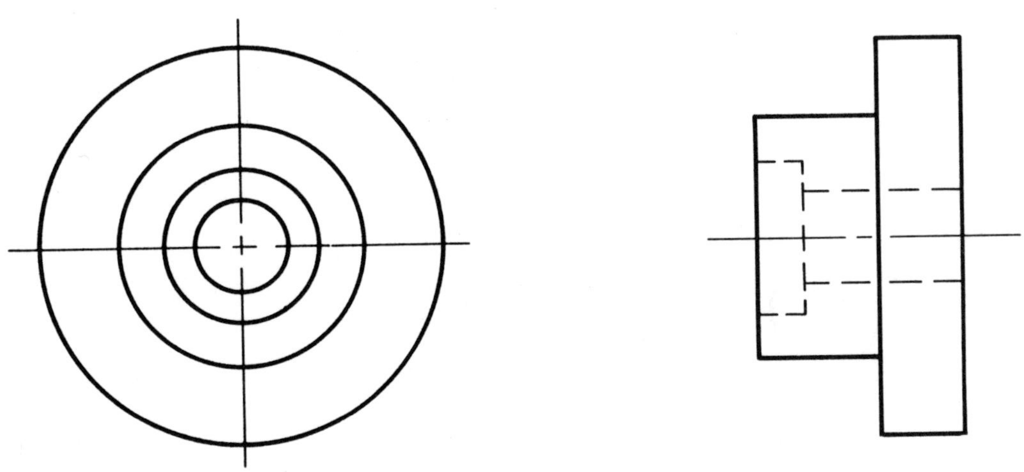

5. Dimension the full-size link.
   (14 pts)

6. Dimension the shaft and the hole to have a ± .002 tolerance and an allowance of +.005. The basic diameter of the the shaft is 1.600". (18 pts)

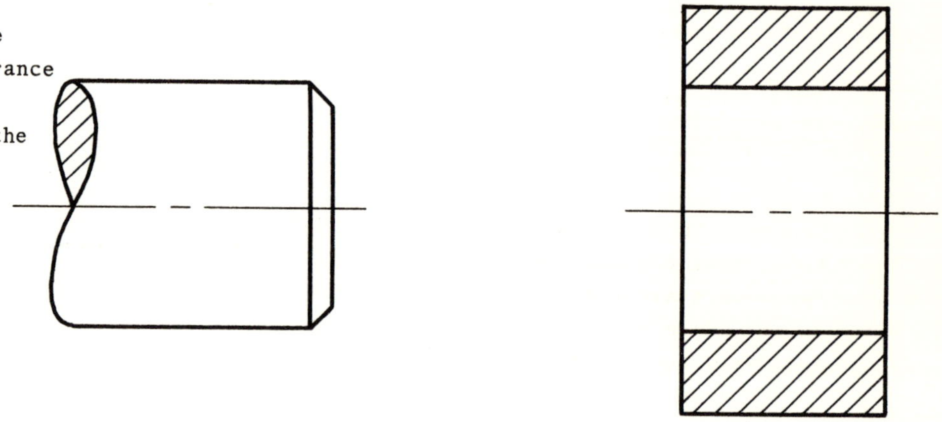

7. Complete the right-side view and dimension the full-size disc. (18 pts)

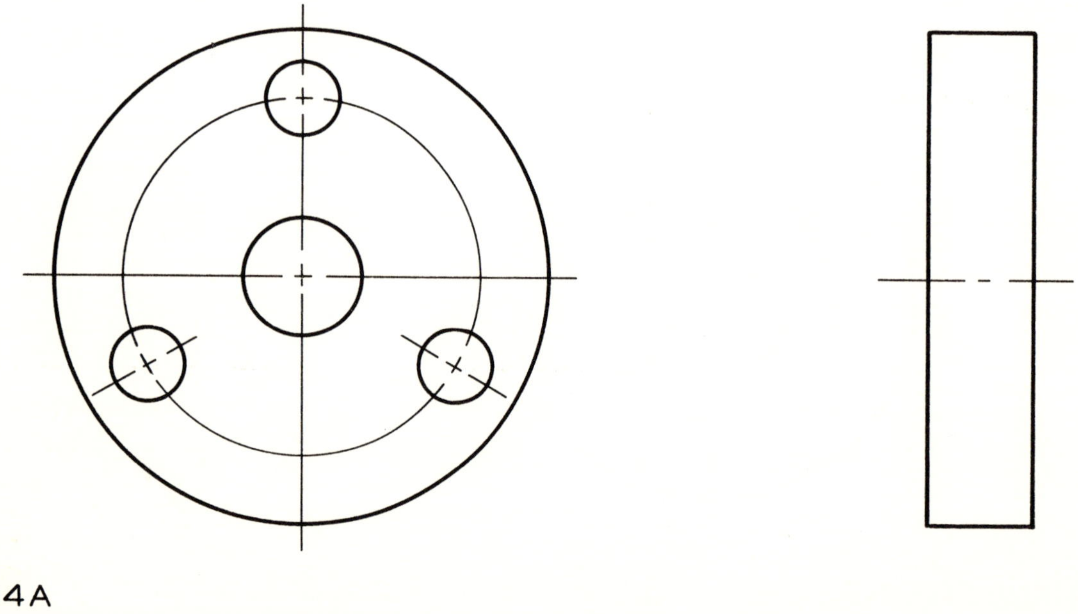

NAME: SECTION: GRADE:

QUIZ 7: GRAPHS (79-82)

1. Construct a bar graph (with horizontal bars) to show the data below. This data shows the sales in thousands of dollars for a company during four years at 10 year intervals.

   Smith Company Sales
   1940-1970

1940	$520
1950	750
1960	820
1970	980

   Label the graph completely. (25 pts)

2. Construct a line graph that shows the data below. Place days along the X-axis and pounds along the Y-axis. This data compare the weight lost by two people during a 10 day regimen.

   Pounds lost--10 days diet

Day	Mr. A	Mr. B
0	0	0
2	3	2.5
4	4	4.5
6	7	8
8	7.2	8.6
10	8	9.5

   Label the graph completely (25 pts)

3. Graph the data below as a circle graph and completely label and title it. (25 pts)

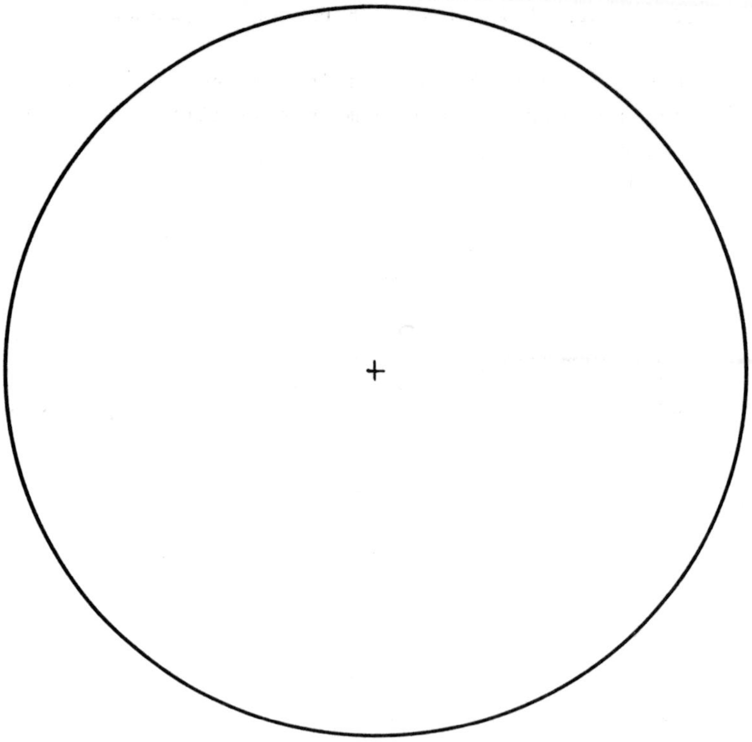

The Brown Company had $100,000 office expenses during 1973. The categories of these expenses were:

Category	Expense
Wages	$52,000
Rent	10,000
Utilities	3,000
Equipment	35,000
	$100,000

4. Convert the bar below to represent the percentages of students participating in the sports listed below during a particular school year.

1973 PARTICIPATION IN SPORTS--500 Students

Sports	Number
Football	200
Basketball	50
Track	150
Baseball	100

(25 pts)

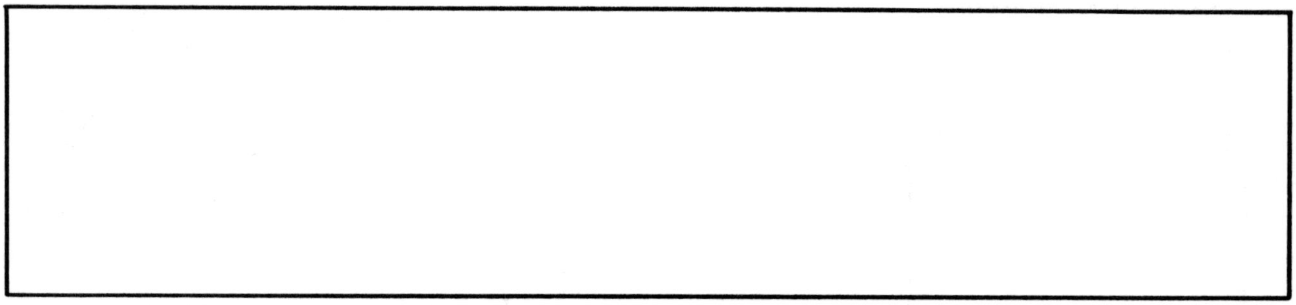

NAME: SECTION: GRADE:

QUIZ 8: INTERSECTIONS AND DEVELOPMENTS (83-90)

1. Find the line of intersection between the two planes and determine visibility. (10 pts.

2. Find the intersection between the prisms. (10 pts)

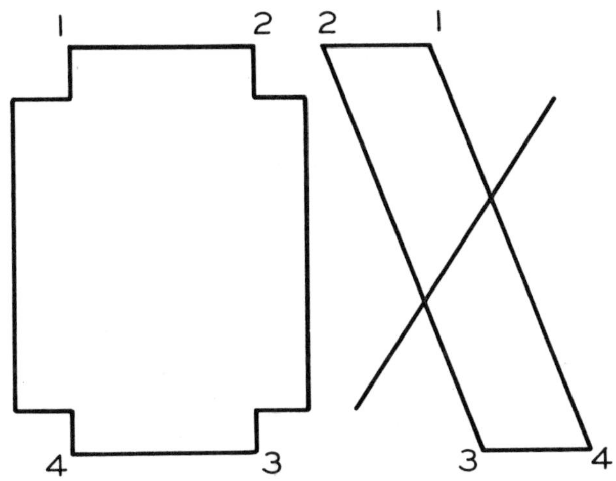

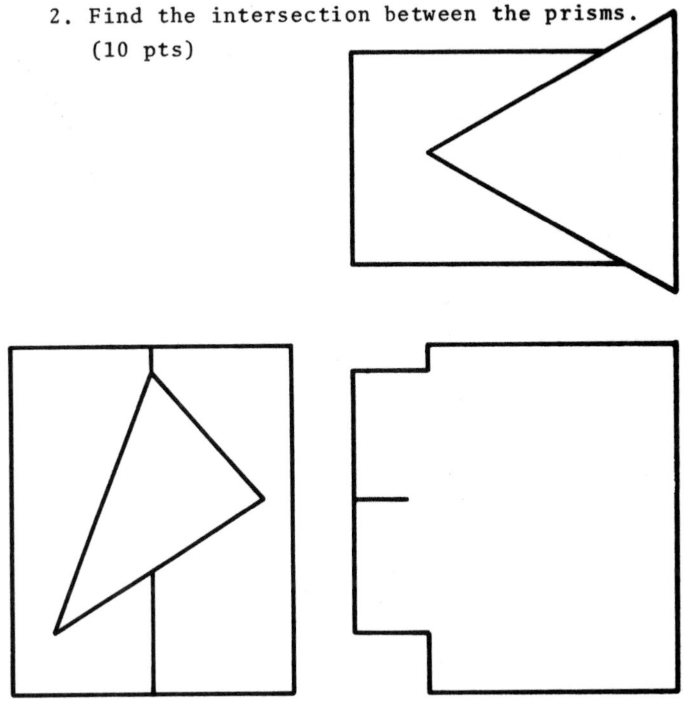

3. Find the intersection between the two cylinders. (15 Pts)

4. Find the intersection between the cone and cylinder. (15 pts)

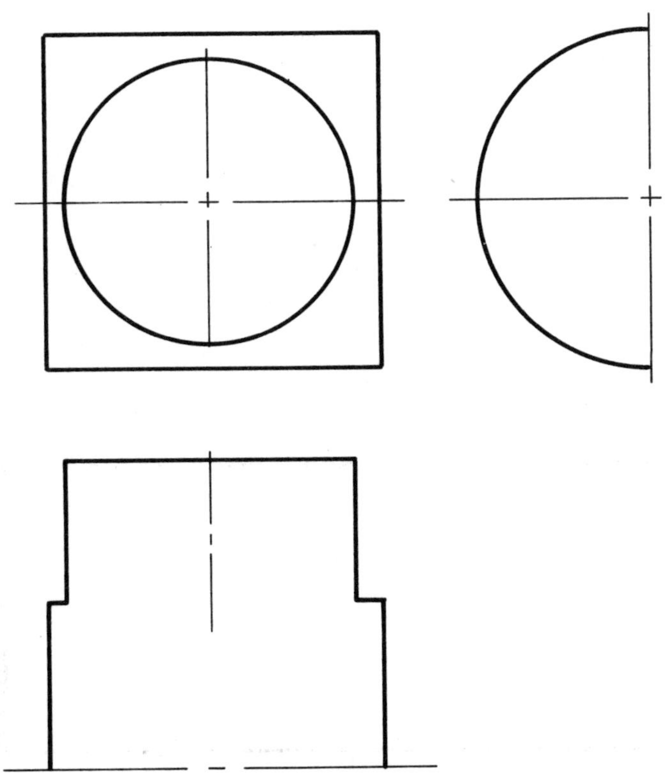

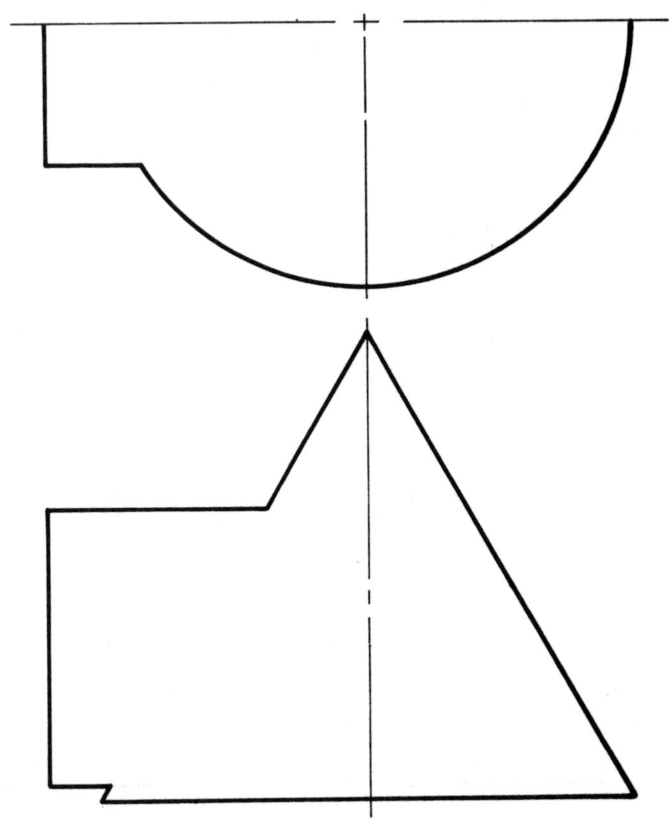

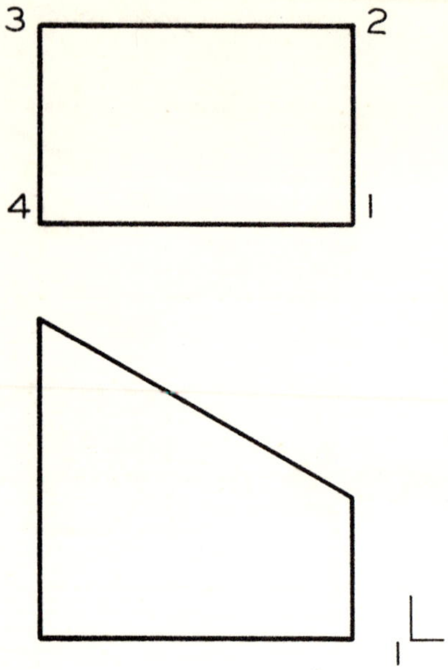

5. Letter the points in both views and construct and inside development of the prism beginning with the shortest fold line. (14 pts)

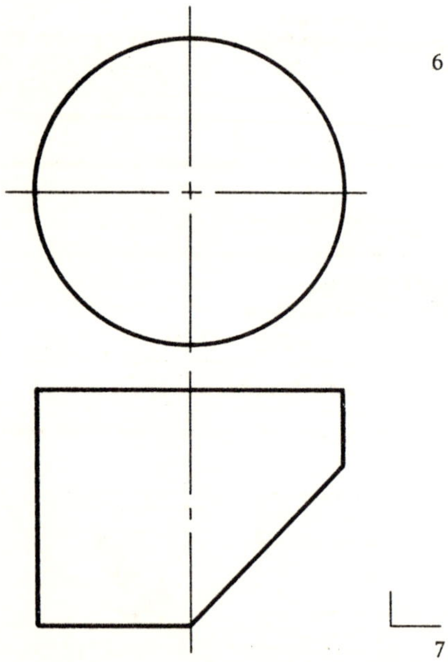

6. Letter the points in both views and construct an inside development of the cylinder beginning with the shortest element. Letter the points on your development. (18 pts)

7. Letter the points in both views of the cone (the top view is a half view) and construct a development of the whole cone beginning with the shortest element. Letter the points of the inside development. (18 pts)

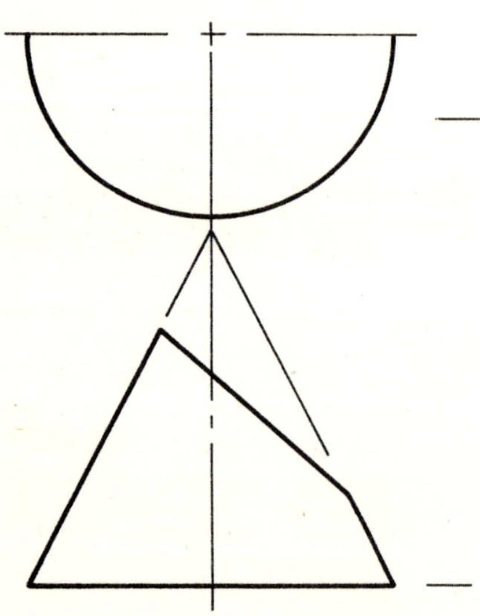